UPSAND

THE INSIDE STORIES FROM LEEDS UNITED'S BIGGEST MATCHES

JAMES WILLOUGHBY

CREATIVE
GROUP

Published in 2019 by Grid Creative Group, Melbourne, Australia
Email: info@gridcreativegroup.com
www.gridcreativegroup.com

NATIONAL LIBRARY OF AUSTRALIA

A catalogue record for this book is available from the National Library of Australia

ISBN: 978-0-6487283-0-6

Designed by Dave McCabe

Distributed worldwide by York Publishing Services, York, England
64 Hallfield Road, York, YO31 7ZQ

Photographs taken by Andrew Varley Picture Agency, Alex Knight Photography, Steve Riding, Dubravko Lenert

Printed and bound by CLOC Ltd, London, England
Unit 10, Milmead Industrial Centre, Mill Mead Road, Tottenham, London, N17 9QU

CONTENTS

FOREWORD BY NORMAN HUNTER

Leeds United is a very special football club that gets under your skin. I am just one example.

I arrived from Gateshead at the age of 15 and more than 60 years on, I still live in Leeds.

Making more than 700 appearances for Leeds United was an honour, a thrill and a pleasure. I was lucky enough to play with some great players who turned out to be great friends and we were winning things and competing for European trophies on a regular basis.

Don Revie deserves so much credit for his role in transforming Leeds United. He made training so enjoyable that every morning I was excited to get there, meet the lads, train and have a laugh.

I was just a boy when I signed for Leeds and, unfortunately, I didn't know my father because he died when I was very young. The closest I had to a father figure was Don Revie and he had a massive influence on me.

Terry Cooper was my long-time roommate, even before I signed professional terms at Elland Road. Terry, Mick Jones, Paul Madeley and myself were all very close and that whole Leeds United team has a special bond that will never break. They were wonderful times.

My involvement with Leeds United did not stop after my playing days. I would have hated that to be the case.

I watched the lads for years doing co-commentary on BBC Radio Leeds and, more recently, I do corporate work for Leeds United.

It is a major honour to have the 'Norman Hunter Suite' at Elland Road and it is a beautiful room with a great atmosphere. I am absolutely delighted with it.

I go up in the press gantry to watch the home games and I still get a major buzz in the two or three minutes before kick-off when I look out at Elland Road and the team comes out. It is a great feeling.

Sometimes, I struggle to enjoy the matches but that is because I am so tense about the outcome!

People will occasionally say to me that Elland Road can be a difficult place to play at for the Leeds players but I do not agree. I do not think that there is a better place to play your football, particularly when it is full.

If you give it your all, the Leeds United fans will never stop backing you and that is something I found out very quickly.

There were better footballers than me in the team I played in but I gave it everything I had, every single time. I think the fans saw that and appreciated that.

The Leeds United fans are very knowledgeable but they will read plenty of new stories in this book, which provides rare insight into the club's most famous matches.

Every player has a story to tell, no matter how big or small their contribution to Leeds United was, and I particularly enjoyed going down memory lane with James Willoughby and reliving so many happy memories.

We discussed the lows, too, but that is all part of the story of Leeds United.

Older fans will be taken on a nostalgia trip as the book starts in the Revie era, with younger supporters set to gain a great understanding of Leeds United's glory days through the voices of those who were directly involved.

Readers are taken behind the scenes at Elland Road across many other eras, too, including our title-winning side of 1992 and the team that shook up Europe in the UEFA Champions League.

I am one of many voices that feature throughout the book, with the likes of Johnny Giles, Eddie Gray, Allan Clarke, Howard Wilkinson, Gary McAllister, Mark Viduka, Lucas Radebe, Lee Bowyer and Jermaine Beckford just some of the others included.

This book is essential reading for any Leeds United fan. I hope you enjoy reading our stories from the football club's biggest matches.

Finally, I want to send a message to the amazing Leeds United supporters all over the world. Stick with the lads and support them like you have always done. We will rise again.

It would be a dream for me to see Leeds United back in the Premier League in my lifetime.

Norman Hunter

October 2019

INTRODUCTION

For supporters caught up in the relentless world of football, most matches are forgotten fairly quickly.

A scrappy 1-0 win that meant the world to a fan six months ago quickly becomes a distant memory, replaced by what is on the horizon, be it the next match, the next away trip or the next transfer window.

Some matches are utterly memorable, though.

It could be because of the magnitude of the fixture and what was on the line.

There are also the comeback victories, late winners, shock triumphs and outstanding team performances that live long in the memory.

Other matches are unforgettable for all the wrong reasons, seared into our minds due to the agony of defeat or the crushing sense of hurt that comes with a season-ending loss.

For good or bad, these are the matches we will talk about for years, in pubs, stadiums, cafes or on that next away day.

You are probably thinking about some of them right now.

These are the days we can remember like it was yesterday, from what we did before the game and our mid-match feelings to how we celebrated or commiserated.

These unforgettable fixtures are the subject of this book, as Leeds United's biggest names take readers behind the scenes for the matches that mattered.

More than 70 former Leeds United players and coaches have been exclusively interviewed for this book, talking with great insight about the highs and lows of one of England's biggest football clubs.

Every quote in this book, unless attributed, comes from these interviews.

What were the manager's final words? What really went on in the changing room at half time? How did the players celebrate?

These questions - and so many more on transfer decisions, confrontations and trips away - are all answered.

Many of the match selections were guided by the interviewees, be it the matches they remembered most vividly or who was available to talk about them.

It was a difficult decision to leave some games out but I hope you will agree the list is comprehensive and covers your favourite fixture.

The book begins in 1965 and it is important to acknowledge that Leeds United played in many significant fixtures before this year.

The names of Ernie Hart, Willis Edwards, Tom Jennings, Wilf Copping and, of course, John Charles, are integral figures in Leeds United's history.

But this book is dependent on those directly involved telling their stories and, for obvious reasons, it was not possible to go back to the club's inception in 1919.

It has been a great thrill to write this book and I hope you enjoy the trip down memory lane. Happy reading.

James Willoughby

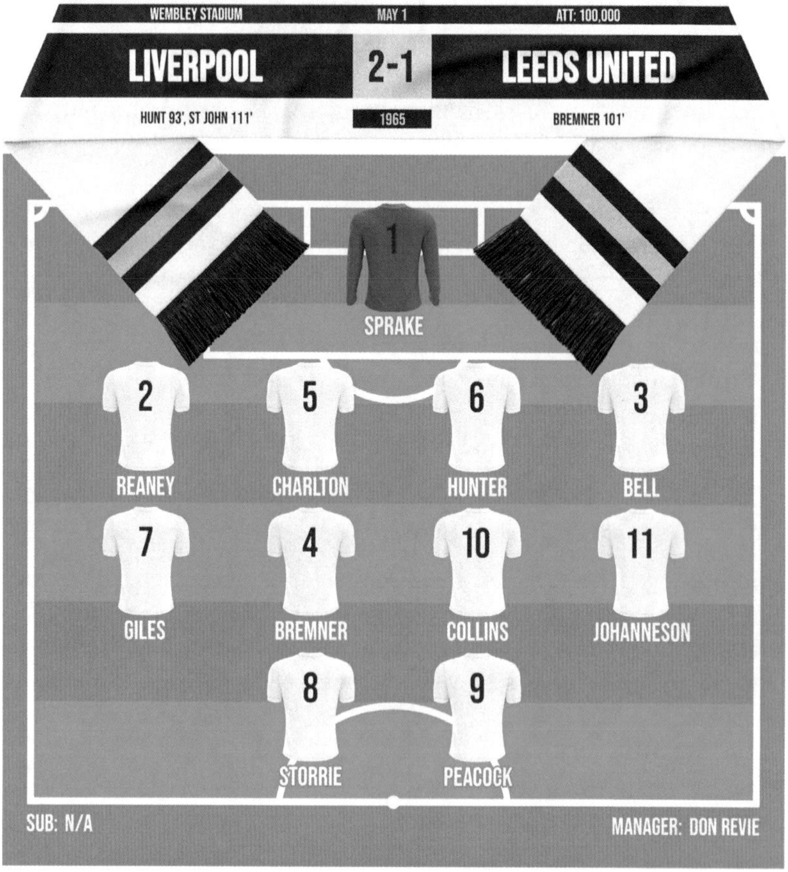

LIVERPOOL

LAWRENCE, LAWLER, BYRNE, STRONG, YEATS, STEVENSON, CALLAGHAN, HUNT, ST JOHN, SMITH, THOMPSON

SUB: N/A

MANAGER: BILL SHANKLY

OUR FORM HEADING IN

BIRMINGHAM	3-3	LEEDS UTD
SHEFF UTD	0-3	LEEDS UTD
LEEDS UTD	2-0	SHEFF WED

"The saying at Old Trafford in those days [was], 'Nobody leaves Old Trafford and does well'. That was the word ... I said to my wife, 'I will haunt them'."
- Johnny Giles

Leeds United's newest signing had a point to prove. Johnny Giles cost just £33,000 from Manchester United in 1963 but would prove to be one of Don Revie's greatest acquisitions as he continued to build a team that could get out of the Second Division. "I started at Manchester United and I played in the [FA] Cup semi-final in '62 against Spurs. [I] didn't play very well at all ... [manager] Matt Busby lost confidence in me," Giles said. "It went on for a year ... I knew I didn't have a future there and I decided to ask for a transfer. I went on to the transfer list on Tuesday and I was at Leeds United on the Thursday." Giles acknowledged that wanting to "haunt" Manchester United was "probably an immature approach" to the situation, but that it suited him. "That's the way I felt at the time. It wasn't a bad way to be. I mean, when you've got something to prove ... it helps." It was the arrival of players like Giles and Bobby Collins, who both dropped a division to join Leeds, that elevated standards. "One of the reasons I went to Leeds United ... was because Bobby Collins was there," Giles added. "Bobby Collins was one of the great players in my time. He was 10 years older than me but he was a schoolboy idol of mine because when I lived in Dublin, the League of Ireland used to play the Scottish league and Bobby Collins was a great Celtic player for 10 years ... I thought he was brilliant. I played against him when he moved down to Everton and I felt that if Bobby Collins is there [at Leeds], then something is going right. That was my feeling."

Collins arrived at Leeds in 1962 when Revie's team were seemingly destined for the Third Division. Revie, a centre-forward who ended his playing career at Leeds United, replaced Jack Taylor as manager in March 1961, taking charge of a club that had bounced between the top flight and the Second Division on a regular basis. Leeds had never played in the Third Division, though, and it was on the cards until Collins joined from Everton and inspired a nine-match unbeaten streak to end the 1961-62 season. Leeds still needed a point on the final day at Newcastle United to stay up, but won 3-0 to remain in the second tier. "When he [Revie] came in, he went and got a player who, in my opinion, started the Leeds United as I knew it. That was Bobby Collins. He went and brought Bobby from Everton," Norman Hunter, who was just months away from making his debut, said. "Bobby's influence - I don't think you can underestimate what this man did for Leeds United, playing wise and everything."

That a 19-year-old midfielder called Billy Bremner was Leeds' top scorer in the league in that relegation-threatened season, with 11 goals, said it all about Revie's squad. Jack Charlton was next best, with nine, but Revie needed out-and-out forwards. He brought club legend John Charles back from Juventus in a big-money move, while Jim Storrie arrived from Airdrie. Charles' move did not work out as hoped and he soon returned to Italy but Storrie scored 25 goals in 38 Second Division appearances as a much-improved Leeds finished fifth in 1962-63. A key moment in that season was a trip to Swansea Town [now Swansea City], as the United manager threw a bunch of youngsters in and was duly rewarded. "The gaffer took Rodney Johnson, Paul Reaney, myself and Gary [Sprake] … he took us to Swansea," Hunter said. Sprake, a goalkeeper, had played once for Leeds but the other three were yet to feature. "What he [Revie] used to do then, he used to take young players along with the first team to give them experience," Hunter added. "[I] can remember, Saturday morning, we were in the dressing room and he said to the four of us, 'Come and walk with me'. We just thought he was going to talk to us and we just walked and he said, 'You're going to play', … we went to Swansea and we won. Then he just kept us [in] … there's not many people [who] would turn around and do that, stick four young players [in], because I was only 19." Hunter, a centre-back, right-back Reaney and Sprake became first-team regulars and had experienced defender Charlton nearby to guide them through. Revie's jigsaw was coming together.

The manager was also trying to bring in players. "I was playing for the Glasgow schoolboys and there were a lot of clubs chasing me," Eddie Gray said. "A chap called John Barr, a scout for Leeds, he went up to my dad at the game … he said, 'I'm from a club called Leeds United. I would like your son to go down and have a look. I know he's been to other clubs and we're a Second Division club, I'd just like … for him to have a look'. My dad came up to me after the game … he said to me, 'There's a scout for Leeds United - [he] would like you to go down'. I looked at my dad and said, 'Who?' I swear to God, I'd never heard of them because they were in the Second Division. I'm a Celtic supporter, Scottish football's still great in those days … so I thought I'd go down, no intentions whatsoever of signing for them. I just thought I'd go down for a weekend." Gray, just 14 at the time, took the train from Glasgow to Leeds and Revie later told him he was there to train "for the first team". "My first experience of playing with the first team was picking the ball up in Fullerton Park [Leeds' training base] and going up to a big centre-half called Charlton," Gray added. "I knocked the ball through his legs and I was running around the other side of him and he booted me up in the air! He did! He booted me up in the air and I was lying in the snow and he looked down at me and he said, 'Don't do that to me again, you little bastard'. Then he turned to Don and he said to Don, 'Don, I would sign this boy. He's going to be a player'. That's what happened." Gray soon returned to Scotland and said "because of Don", he told his father: "I'm going to Leeds United."

Revie was not done there. "Leeds United - I'd never really heard of them," Mick Bates said. "He [Revie] came round and knocked on the front door which is highly unusual in a village, because they always use the back door. He knocked on the door, my mum and dad were there, we weren't expecting him at all and he came in, we chatted … he was absolutely brilliant. He spoke to you like a father spoke to you and there and then, I looked at Mum and Dad … and said, 'Yeah, I want to sign'. I didn't even know … what division they were in! It didn't really matter." While Gray and Bates were signings for the future and would initially help out with tasks around the club, like sweeping the stands, one man who would make more of an immediate impression was Giles. "The day they bought Johnny Giles, we [Eddie and I] were in the stand looking out at the players' entrance, the East Stand it was," Bates said. "Johnny came out and he had no socks on. He had a shirt on and his shorts but he had no socks and Eddie and I looked at each other and said, 'Wow! What's this?' I mean, we've never seen that before. And he came out and he was playing in a little bit of a five-a-side with the first team on the main pitch and he was absolutely fantastic. He never wasted a ball - quality."

With a midfield consisting of Collins, Giles and a continually improving Bremner, Leeds now had the basis of a side capable of promotion in the 1963-64 season. United lost just one league match before Christmas in what would be a three-way fight between Leeds, Sunderland and Preston North End for the two promotion spots. "It was different for me - I'd never played in the Second Division before," Giles said. "I played on the right-hand side and it was different to Manchester United. It was more direct and it took me a while to settle down … it was hard graft, but the Leeds team were prepared to graft and graft very hard as well." A key signing arrived during the season, too, England international Alan Peacock making his debut in February and weighing in with eight crucial goals. "He was a very good player, so he was a great signing for us at that particular time when we were on the run-in," Giles said. "Alan scored a lot of important goals. Alan was a top-class player, a good leader of the attack, good header of the ball, could hold the ball up, so he was a big signing for Leeds." Peacock scored twice in the 3-0 win at Swansea that secured promotion, Giles getting the other goal, while Peacock also got a double in a 2-0 last-day win at Charlton Athletic that saw Leeds go up as champions.

Revie barely changed his team for the 1964-65 season, confident in what he had. Keeping Bremner was important, too, given the Scot had previously put in a transfer request. "I was in digs with Billy with a lady in Beeston," Hunter said. "He was homesick. He wanted to see her [his wife] and then he put in a transfer request but, naturally, the gaffer just said, 'No'. There was no such thing as agents and things like that. He just said, 'No, you're staying'. Then he [Billy] became one of the best midfield players that I played with." Hunter remembered Leeds being tipped to struggle back in the big time. "Everybody in the country, all the so-called media and all the TV [pundits said] … 'Leeds will get relegated. They won't have enough for the First Division'. We finished second!"

Giles said Leeds' absence from the top flight worked in their favour. "Nobody knew what to expect when we got promotion. I mean, a lot of lads had never played in the First Division before, so there wasn't a great deal of expectancy from a team that had just been promoted. But actually, what we did in the first season was, in my opinion, sensational.

I mean, teams that were usually promoted in those days struggled a bit to stay [up], as they do today in what is now the Premiership. But we were the first team to get 60 points or more and not win the First Division and this is with a very inexperienced team. Gary Sprake, Paul Reaney, Terry Cooper coming into the team, Paul Madeley coming into the team - all young players - Billy Bremner was very young. So to do what we did was remarkable. We chased Manchester United all the way ... a Manchester United team with [Denis] Law, [George] Best and [Bobby] Charlton." Leeds were outstanding at home, scoring 53 goals in 21 matches, form that saw them surge up the table. Leeds came from 3-0 down to draw 3-3 at Birmingham City in their last match of the season, leaving them level on points with Manchester United, who still had a game in hand. The Old Trafford outfit lost that fixture but still won the title on goal average, the system used before goal difference was introduced. A remarkable season was not over yet, though. Leeds United still had the FA Cup Final to play.

Revie's men conceded just twice in a run to the final that started with a 3-0 success over Southport. A replay was needed to see off Everton in the fourth round, Charlton and Don Weston scoring in a 2-1 success, before Leeds accounted for Shrewsbury Town. Peacock was back in the goals, getting two in a 3-0 quarter-final win over Crystal Palace that set up a semi-final clash between the two best sides in England. Leeds played out a goalless draw at Hillsborough against Manchester United, forcing a replay at The City Ground. It took 89 minutes of that game for a goal, Bremner nodding in a Giles free-kick to book Leeds' first FA Cup Final appearance. "Billy was larger than life. Billy was funny. Billy was a real character. A great player, inspirational," Gray said. "People talk about Billy being a great captain, from the point of view of leading the club but Billy led the club more by his attitude and his performances on the park as opposed to words. Giles was the astute one. He was a man that would dictate how we would play. Billy was the type of character - if we were playing in a semi-final of a cup and we'd go a goal down, Billy would be off. He'd forget his midfield duties. [He would think], 'I'm going to get the equaliser, I'm going to get the winning goal'. Nine times out of ten, Billy would do it. That was that. He would do it. That was the amazing thing about Billy."

"With me being a Geordie and supporting Newcastle, the FA Cup was everything up there," Hunter said. "The FA Cup, at the time, meant more to me than winning the league, because that's what I was brought up on. FA Cup glory." A planned warm-up the day before the Wembley final did not go to plan, as Hunter explained. "Little Bobby [Collins] was very feisty … we were playing a five-a-side in London, day before the final. Little five-a-side and Bobby got the ball and I went and I won it. Never thought anything about it and I passed it and then two minutes later, Bobby got the ball and he overran it. Well, Bobby Collins never, never overran the ball. So I went for it and he jumped two foot right over the ball and luckily he missed me, because he would've really hurt me! And the gaffer said, 'Stop!' I said to him [Bobby], 'What did you do that for?' He said, 'Look here, you kicked me'. I said, 'Bobby, I never did, I wouldn't do that to you'. So the gaffer called the five-a-side [off] … no more!" The remonstrations were not physical but it did prove one thing. Revie's Leeds were right up for the challenge.

Wembley was hit by rain during the final and it affected the spectacle, the first 90 minutes a relatively tame affair even if Sprake was the busier of the two goalkeepers. Leeds might not have been at their best in the final third, but Giles was still proud at how they had stopped their opponents. "Liverpool were a terrific team," he said. "Really, really top-class team … they won the league the year before, they won the [FA] Cup that year and the league afterwards, so it was the first great Liverpool team under [Bill] Shankly … Roger Hunt, Ian St John, Tommy Smith, Ron Yeats, Ian Callaghan, Peter Thompson - this was a terrific team and we took them to extra time."

The match exploded into life in extra time, Hunt giving Liverpool the lead with a close-range header after good work down the left from Gerry Byrne. Leeds had an answer, though, and it was no surprise who provided it. "We were hanging on and we were 1-0 down … I had it on my left and the big man [Charlton] was up on the edge of the box," Hunter said. "I just knocked it up to him. If you put it anywhere within [his] radius in the air, big Jack was going to get it. The big man got up and he knocked it down and little Billy hit it … it flew in!" Bremner's volley was a great strike and Giles was not surprised. "Billy scored spectacular goals at really important matches and he had a great temperament. Billy was full of confidence. [He] really, really was full of confidence and the confidence was justified, because he could do it. I think Billy, every match he played in, before we went out, Billy felt he was going to be the star of the game. And he was in many of the games."

Back on level terms, Leeds were in with a chance of winning the FA Cup, a reward that would have been fitting given their excellent season. "I can remember the Liverpool players actually going like that [looking deflated]. If we'd have had a little bit more experience at that time, we'd have beaten them ... we were going [for it] ... they just weathered the storm and then they came back into it," Hunter said. Liverpool were able to find another gear when it counted and it was another header that finished the job, St John scoring the winner. "I can remember being so, so disappointed but then I looked at it and I thought, 'Well, we've played nearly the top team in the country,'" Hunter added.

Giles was also buoyed by the performance, even if it ended in defeat. "I found that a really, really remarkable season from a newly promoted team ... to finish runners-up in the Cup and finish up [second] in the league, when you've just been promoted, I thought that was an outstanding season ... they [Liverpool] were a terrific team and I think they were a better team than us in those days. And I think what we did ... having been a goal down - it was a really, really terrific performance. Mostly people remember winning as a terrific performance but I thought this was a terrific performance for the team that we had at that particular time."

That Leeds United team would only get better, too. Revie was just getting started.

ARSENAL

FURNELL, STOREY, McNAB, McLINTOCK, URE, SIMPSON, RADFORD, JENKINS, GRAHAM, SAMMELS, ARMSTRONG

SUB: NEILL

MANAGER: BERTIE MEE

OUR FORM HEADING IN

LEEDS UTD 2-1 NOTT FOREST

LEEDS UTD 2-1 WEST HAM

LEEDS UTD 3-2 DERBY

"That was the most important game ... the club had never won a major honour."
- Eddie Gray

Leeds United had developed an unwanted reputation, one of a good side that could not win trophies. After bursting into the First Division and pushing Manchester United all the way in the 1964-65 season, Leeds lost the FA Cup Final. In the following season, they were again runners-up in the league before being eliminated in the semi-finals of the Inter-Cities Fairs Cup. Leeds then made a poor start to their 1966-67 quest for silverware, stuck in mid-table as injuries piled up. United suffered some heavy defeats, too, thrashed 7-0 at West Ham United in a League Cup tie before a trip to Anfield less than a fortnight later ended in a 5-0 loss. Questions were being asked about Don Revie's men, who were also struggling for goals. Had Leeds been figured out? Were they on a downward spiral? How would they cope without Bobby Collins?

Collins, Leeds United's key man in midfield, would turn 36 in February 1967 and his body was starting to let him down. "Bobby was probably the most influential player, I feel," Eddie Gray said. "I think a lot of my teammates would agree with me. There's been a lot of great players at the club over the years, especially going back to John Charles [and] then Don [Revie] took over. But I don't think there's ever been a more important player walk through the gates than Bobby Collins because he taught everybody how to win. He was a great Celtic player, a great Everton player and he came to Leeds, supposedly in the twilight of his career, and helped Leeds get promotion. [He] obviously played in the Cup final of 1965. He was [1964-65 Football Writers' Association] Footballer of the Year, Bobby, when he was thirty-odd. He was some player. He set the standard and I think he taught all the players about how to have a winning mentality."

Collins could not play forever but Leeds had a replacement waiting in the wings. Johnny Giles played on the right-hand side of midfield when he joined Leeds, with Collins and Billy Bremner combining in the middle of the park. But Giles' preferred position was through the centre and, even though he was injured through some of the 1966-67 campaign, he showed his class with a host of eye-catching performances and many important goals. Revie's faith in the young players at the club was rewarded as well, as the likes of Gray, Paul Madeley, Terry Cooper and Jimmy Greenhoff broke through to feature regularly and suggest they were stars of the future. Peter Lorimer's rapid development continued, too, while Jack Charlton was outstanding as Leeds went from a side stuck in the wrong half of the table to, all of a sudden, challenging for 1966-67 honours. "There were a lot of great players that played, got the team out of the old Second Division into the big league [but] Don started to evolve the team," Gray said. "He started to make a few changes, bring a few young players in like Peter Lorimer ... myself, Jimmy Greenhoff." Collins left for Bury but his departure did not rob United of momentum as Leeds reached the FA Cup semi-finals before losing to Chelsea. Leeds finished fourth in the league, five points behind winners Manchester United, with Charlton named the 1966-67 Football Writers' Association Footballer of the Year for his terrific performances. Supporters then had the final stages of the Inter-Cities Fairs Cup to get excited about, as Leeds chased that elusive first major honour. But although Leeds beat Kilmarnock over two legs to reach the final, Dinamo Zagreb were too good in the decider.

More near-misses had only strengthened Leeds' resolve ahead of the 1967-68 campaign. It was time to win a trophy. "When we played Liverpool [in the FA Cup Final], it was 1965," Giles said. "It was obviously three years later, where the players were getting a bit older ... three years in football is a long time for a team maturing and it was a different team in that respect. We still had the same work ethic, we had all the things that we had then but the team was coming on." Leeds were winless in their first three matches in the 1967-68 season but a 10-match unbeaten streak in all competitions got things heading in the right direction, as United were in the running for the title and already in the semi-finals of the League Cup by the time Christmas arrived. Lorimer was in an outstanding vein of form, scoring 22 goals in just over three months to ease United's goalscoring woes in emphatic fashion. Gray remembered feeling like all Revie's early scouting work was coming together. "I think it all goes back to when Don first took over the club, realising that it couldn't compete with sides like Arsenal, Manchester United, even Liverpool from a financial point of view. The chairman then was a chap called Harry Reynolds. Harry doesn't get as much credit, I don't think, as he should do for building the club. He was the chairman, he was a local man and I think Don put a plan to him [saying] that, 'Okay, we can't compete but let's have a three or four-year plan and we'll put all our efforts into trying to sign the best young schoolboys in the country', ... he went out and he did that. He got Peter Lorimer, [the] record goal scorer in Scottish schoolboy football, beating other clubs."

"I'll never forget, I was in Glasgow in 1962," Gray continued. "I was playing with the Glasgow schoolboys and the Scottish schoolboys were playing against England at Ibrox. It looked as if I was going to play for the Scottish schoolboys the next year - I get invited to go to the game as a Glasgow schoolboy player. I'd never heard of Lorimer, I'd never seen him. He was playing that night for Scotland against England schoolboys. I was watching the game and I thought, 'Geez, who's that? Who's this guy?' I looked in the program and it goes, 'Peter Lorimer', ... I watched him that night and I thought, 'Bloody hell'. He was whacking balls from all over the shop. He scored two that night, but he could have scored six. The little English goalkeeper - balls were flying at him! He could still hit the ball as hard then as he did when he grew up. Then, obviously, he came to Leeds and I followed him. We were roommates for 10 years, playing all the games together. He's still my mate."

With Lorimer and Gray dazzling, Greenhoff chipping in with goals and Giles and Bremner running the show in midfield, Leeds fans were hopeful that the wait for a major trophy would soon be over. The League Cup would be United's first chance to end the hoodoo and they reached the last four after conceding just once in four straight-forward victories. Lorimer's hat-trick kickstarted their run in a 3-1 home success against Luton Town in the second round and Leeds also scored three at Elland Road when defeating Bury. Greenhoff then got both goals in a 2-0 triumph at Sunderland before Lorimer and Bremner were on target in a 2-0 fifth-round win over Stoke City that booked a semi-final with Derby County. Leeds would play Derby three times in three weeks, with a third-round FA Cup tie sandwiched in the middle of their two-legged semi-final, but United won all three fixtures, Giles starting the run of triumphs with the only goal of the game at The Baseball Ground. Lorimer and Charlton then scored in a 2-0 FA Cup win before Rod Belfitt's double helped Leeds to a 3-2 success at Elland Road and a 4-2 aggregate victory.

Waiting for Leeds in the League Cup Final would be Arsenal, who beat Huddersfield Town 6-3 over two legs in their semi-final. In Arsenal's side was George Graham, who would manage both the North London outfit and Leeds before the turn of the century. Graham said Arsenal were expecting a tough final. "Everybody knew they were one of the best teams in the country playing very, very good football, even although they had a reputation … of being a bit physical, being a bit tough. I always respected them for the good football they played, especially in the midfield with Bremner and Johnny Giles. I thought they were fantastic," he said. "They had excellent players throughout the team … the [League] Cup Final - we knew it was going to be tough." Arsenal had reason to be confident, though. "They [Leeds] dominated the majority of the games they played … they didn't get the end product which … was trophies," Graham continued. "I can't understand why that was because they played good football, they could tough it up if they wanted to but they still didn't win the number of trophies that they should have won, I think."

While many of Leeds' players travelled to London in a confident frame of mind, Mick Bates remembered nerves getting the better of United's goalscoring hero on the eve of the final. "Terry Cooper scored and Terry didn't get a wink of sleep that night. He was so nervous … we all got up and he was walking around the gardens [of the hotel] and he said, 'I just haven't had a wink's sleep … I don't know how I feel.'" Cooper was feeling great just 20 minutes into the match, though. "I took the corner kick," Gray said. "When we took corner kicks, if we were taking them from the right-hand side of the pitch, I would usually take them and big Jack Charlton would probably stand on the goalkeeper's toes. It was always a threat." Gray's corner was a good one and the versatile Paul Madeley, playing up front because Mick Jones was cup-tied, challenged Arsenal goalkeeper Jim Furnell for the ball. Neither of them touched it and Graham headed off the line, only for Cooper to thump a volley into the back of the net. "'TC' was my roommate. I remember it dropping to TC and he smacked it and [it] flew in!" Norman Hunter said.

"They were excellent at set-pieces, especially corner kicks, with big Jackie coming up on the near post and [he] always was intimidating ... that was always a problem [for] anybody who played Leeds. Their set-pieces were excellent using Jackie Charlton," Graham recalled. Arsenal had plenty of time to respond but found it difficult to break through against a stubborn Leeds team. Having watched Madeley clatter into Furnell earlier, Arsenal's Frank McLintock tried the same at the other end but his challenge on Gary Sprake was ineffective, with the goalkeeper catching the ball before a skirmish broke out. "We always expected, not only some good football, but some really tough physical battles on the pitch," Graham added. "Bremner and Giles were probably two of the smallest midfield players in England at the time, the ability they had ... they could look after themselves, by the way. They were not just excellent footballers, they could dish it out and take it as well."

Chances were few and far between for Arsenal, although John Radford did force a good save from Sprake in the latter stages. Leeds deserved to win, though, and the sound of the final whistle sparked outpourings of relief among players and supporters. Leeds United had finally won a major trophy. "I think to win the first trophy was brilliant," Giles said. "It was the first trophy Leeds had ever won and it was the first trophy that most of the lads had won. It was very, very good. Very good ... it was a bit rough and ready, the game, but the main thing for us on the day was winning it. You couldn't say that we won it in style but we won it." Gray concurred. "That game was, looking back and being honest about it, it wasn't a great game of football. It was a bit of a dour battle ... not a great game of football but a winning mentality will see you through the game. I think that's what got the team through the game that day." Gray added that victory fuelled United with belief. "The 67-68 League Cup Final - that was the catalyst for the club to go in there and think, 'Yeah, we can compete against anybody', ... I think it gave everybody the belief that we could compete with the top sides, regardless of who it were, whether it be Liverpool, Arsenal, Manchester United."

Bates, who travelled down to London but was not part of the squad, said a trophy was more than overdue for his teammates. "It was going to happen. It had to happen ... it was the start. We knew we were a good side, though. Even if we hadn't won that, it was only a matter of time before they did win something … a great side can't go without winning something. So, yeah, we were all absolutely delighted. [It] got us on the road to 10 years of total success." Hunter said the day was full of happy memories. "That was exciting because that was our first one. It was the League Cup … it was a start … it just started from there."

Billy Bremner proudly shows off Leeds United's first major trophy. Photo: Andrew Varley Picture Agency

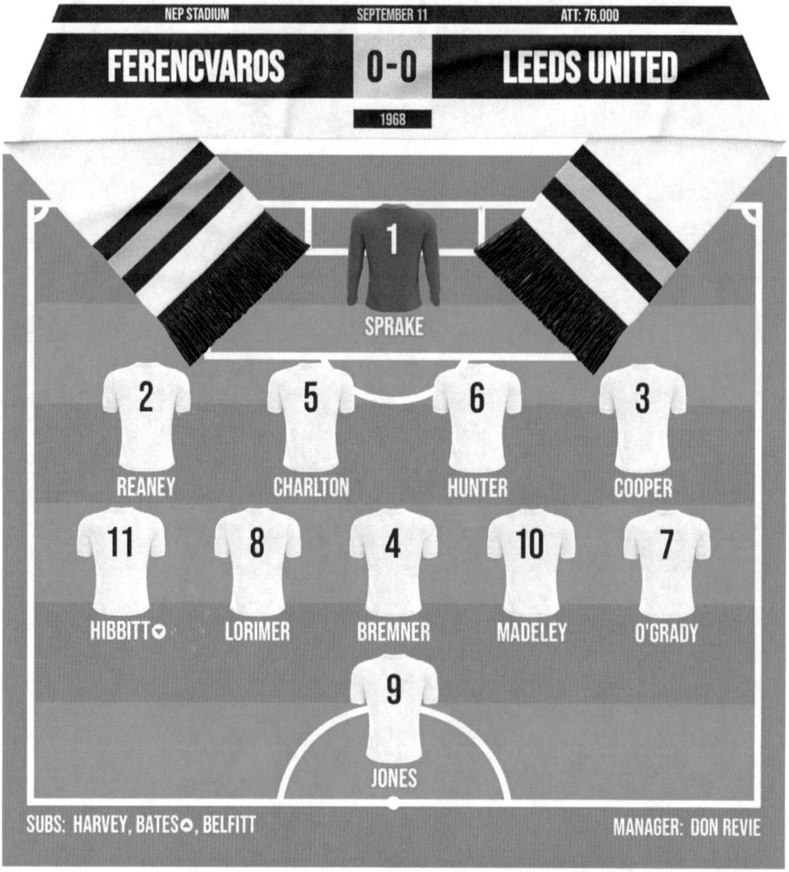

FERENCVAROS

GECZI, NOVAK, PANCSICS, HAVASI, JUHASZ, SZUCS, SZOKE, VARGA, ALBERT, RAKOSI, KATONA

SUBS: KARABA, OTHERS UNKNOWN

MANAGER: KAROLY LAKAT

OUR FORM HEADING IN

LEEDS UTD	2-1	WOLVES
LEEDS UTD	1-0	CHARLTON
LEEDS UTD	1-0	LIVERPOOL

"I said, 'Hello, Mr Revie. What are you doing here? Pleased to meet you'. And he said, 'I've come to sign you'."
- Mick Jones

Driving back from the supermarket, Mick Jones was not expecting visitors. But Don Revie was after a striker and was waiting patiently on the Sheffield United forward's doorstep. "We went to the supermarket and came back and it was a lovely day," Jones recalled. "I saw all these cars and these cameras and scaffolding and I said to my wife, 'Look, that's Don Revie there', ... I said, 'What's he doing here?' About ten to one, Friday afternoon it was, and he [had] come with his chairman. I got out [of] the car and I've got groceries in my hands." Jones was just 22 but was an in-demand talent for his regular goals and impressive work-rate.

"He [Revie] said, 'Well, I've been after you [for] two years'," the striker continued. "They wouldn't let you know anything, Sheffield United never [said]. It's different now to what it was then, you didn't have agents or anything and I didn't know a thing. I said, 'Come in, sit down'. And he came in with his chairman and he said [again], 'I've come to sign you'. I said, 'Well, let me sit down!'" Revie's next comment would convince Jones that Leeds United was the right club for him. "He said, 'Are you ambitious?' I said, 'Yes, very much so, very much so'. He said, 'Well, if you're ambitious, then you're the guy I want and I want you to sign for us'." Revie then asked Jones how much he was getting paid at Bramall Lane. "I said, '£35 a week and £4 for a win and £2 for a draw'. He said, 'I'll double it'. I said, 'Give me the pen'. And within meeting him, it must have been 10 minutes and I'd signed for Leeds United ... all the clubs and players in the country, at the time, knew that Leeds were going upwards. I'd played against them three or four times and they beat us at Bramall Lane, 4-1 and 3-0 ... they had a good side then, but he just wanted to get the final pieces, [to complete] the jigsaw." Leeds spent a club-record £100,000 fee on Jones in 1967, with news of his departure leading to unhappiness from Sheffield United fans and manager John Harris. Jones was impressed by Revie's ambition and it would not take long before he was playing a major role in Leeds winning silverware.

Leeds United entered the 1967-68 Inter-Cities Fairs Cup hoping that it might be third time lucky. The club's first ever involvement in European football came in the 1965-66 edition of the tournament, Billy Bremner fittingly opening United's account in a 2-1 win over Torino. That triumph helped fuel a run to the semi-finals as Leeds also beat Lokomotive Leipzig, saw off Valencia in a fiery encounter and then toppled Ujpest Dozsa. Leeds would be eliminated by Real Zaragoza over three tense semi-final fixtures, with a replay required to separate the two teams. United went one step further in 1966-67, reaching the final in a campaign memorable for the fact a coloured disc, red on one side and white on the other, was tossed to determine who progressed from a quarter-final against Bologna. The two sides were locked at 1-1 after two legs and the disc landed on the white side, helping Leeds progress in the days before penalty shootouts. United also beat DWS Amsterdam, Valencia, again, and Kilmarnock to set up a final against Dinamo Zagreb, but Leeds lost 2-0 in Croatia before a goalless draw in West Yorkshire. "Zagreb were a good side," Norman Hunter said. "Alright, you're disappointed when you lose, but I think if you lose to a better side, then you have no real complaints. They were a good side."

Jones notched his first Leeds goal in a 9-0 win at Spora Luxembourg in the first round of the 1967-68 Inter-Cities Fairs Cup, with United then winning 7-0 at Elland Road. Peter Lorimer scored five goals across the two matches, while Jimmy Greenhoff added four and Albert Johanneson chipped in with a second-leg hat-trick. With only champions of each nation playing in the European Cup, the Inter-Cities Fairs Cup was a very difficult competition to win, and the Spora tie was an anomaly. Lorimer scored in both legs of a 3-2 triumph against Partizan Belgrade in the second round and Leeds then needed a late goal from Jack Charlton to get past Hibernian and book a quarter-final meeting with Rangers. There would be more than two months until that tie, though, a period that saw Leeds win their first trophy, Terry Cooper's goal settling a League Cup Final against Arsenal. Buoyed by that triumph, Leeds held Rangers to a goalless draw in Scotland before Revie's men won 2-0 at Elland Road. Leeds would again face Scottish opposition in the last four, in the form of Dundee, Eddie Gray's 80th-minute goal in the second leg sealing a 2-1 aggregate win.

It set up a final against 1964-65 Inter-Cities Fairs Cup winners, Ferencvaros, the first leg played more than 10 months after the first round started due to international commitments and the summer break. A surge in ticket prices was blamed for a crowd of less than 26,000 at Elland Road for the first leg and it was a dour struggle as the Hungarian side tried to keep the damage to a limit. But in Jones, Leeds United had a man capable of converting a half-chance and his desperation to win was only enhanced by the fact he missed the League Cup success due to being cup-tied. Leeds, who wore blue shirts in their home fixture, could have taken the lead when Lorimer forced a save from Istvan Geczi, but Revie's men were in front before the break and it was all thanks to Jones. "I just happened to be in the six-yard box in the right place … two defenders were around me, the ball was bouncing around and I got my foot just in between them. It wasn't a great goal, but a goal's a goal. An important goal, it was." The striker pounced after Charlton won a header from Lorimer's corner and his goal would prove to be the only one of both legs. "The game at home, that was a dour [one]," Hunter said. "We battled, but we could do that. That's why we were quite good in Europe … we were disciplined enough to stop them from scoring but we also had people up front ... 'Jonah' [Jones], Peter Lorimer, Eddie, Billy, Johnny [Giles] who could sneak a goal. And big Jack [Charlton] from corners."

Leeds headed to Hungary for the second leg, played more than a month after the first, without two of their stars. "I got injured for the second leg … I had a bit of knee trouble," said Giles, who stayed in Leeds. "I was getting treatment at the time and I didn't want to go, to be quite honest. When you're not part of it … I think in football, you're either in it or you're out of it, and if you're injured … no, I didn't want to go." Gray would miss out, too, with Mike O'Grady and Terry Hibbitt drafted into Revie's side as they hunted the club's first European trophy. Buoyed by a 76,000-strong crowd in Budapest, Ferencvaros came out firing and Florian Albert, the 1967 European Footballer of the Year, was only denied the opener by a Cooper block. Cooper made an important clearance, too, while Leeds goalkeeper Gary Sprake was in outstanding form. At the other end, Jones could have scored, but nodded against the crossbar.

The second half was one-way traffic, though, as Ferencvaros piled on the pressure. "Gary Sprake was absolutely awesome that day," Hunter said. "I think, above all, Gary won us the Fairs Cup over there. His performance over there was unbelievable, because they were a good side and they put us under a lot of pressure, but Gary made some absolutely spectacular saves … I can remember some saves in my head and, at the time, you think about it, you think, 'Wow'. You stand there and think, 'Well, he's [having] one of those days. They're not going to score'." Hunter and Charlton were fantastic at the back, too. "It was a combination. We were good at that," Hunter added. "We were known as a team that if we got our noses in front, we'd very rarely give many goals away. That ends up [happening] just by playing with the same people and training with the same people, week in and week out, day after day. You get to know - I instinctively knew where Jack was going to be."

Mick Bates came on with 28 minutes to go in place of Hibbitt and said despite the circumstances, the likes of Hunter, Charlton and Bremner made him feel at ease. "It [atmosphere] is very hostile but it doesn't really matter to you … you're just a young lad. You go out there, you're nervous, you go out there and if you've got natural ability, you'll be okay. You've got a team around you that every time you pick the ball up, there's people to pass it to. It's not easy but it's easy if you've got talent … I only realised how hard football could be when I left Leeds, really, honestly! I used to pick the ball up [at other clubs], there's nobody to pass it to. They just weren't there." Sprake denied Albert and with the clock winding down, he then made a stunning save to keep out Dezso Novak's free-kick as Leeds held on for a goalless draw that would go down in history. "He was absolutely magnificent," Jones said of Sprake. "He made some real saves. The Leeds fans didn't see him because obviously it's in Hungary … he had a great night that night. Gary Sprake was a big player of us winning that competition."

United's players were delighted, hit with feelings of pride and elation. "Absolutely proud," Bates said. "It was great but I didn't realise until I'd be 50 years old … how important it is to the fans. We were going out there to play for ourselves, the team and Don Revie. We went out there and played and we won. We didn't think, 'Wow, that's great for the fans'. It didn't enter our heads like that. We were playing to earn a living and be successful and wanting Leeds United to do well. But when I'd finished playing, I realised that grown men cry, things like that. I was shocked. I thought, 'Wow, how important is this to these guys?' And it is, so it must have been very important to the Leeds United fans when we were winning [trophies] ... we wanted to win, [of] course we did. But the fans, I mean, I've spoken to fans at our golf club now who ... used to hitchhike it all over Europe and sleep under the hedges and then pay their money to come and watch us. And I used to say, 'You did that?' They say, 'Yeah, yeah, absolutely brilliant'. But it didn't strike home to me until I had finished football and then realised how important [it was]. I became a fan then, of Leeds."

Giles said winning the tournament was a big deal. "It was great for the lads to do it ... it was a very, very prestigious cup to win and a difficult cup to win so that was a great win for the Leeds team at that time." For Jones, triumph in Budapest was complete vindication. "It was my first trophy ... when I signed on, I knew they were going places. I knew we were going to win things. You've got pressure on because you're paid a lot of money but it never bothered me, that. When I got on that pitch, it never bothered me one little bit. I just wanted to play and get out and do my best. I never felt the pressure because I was playing with great players ... you live on what you've achieved in life. I'm a believer that you can have all the money in the world but it's what you achieve in life. I look back and people still come up to me now and I'm 74 years old now. They still remember [these victories], they still want to chat with you and you can't beat that, can you? It's part of your life ... that never leaves you, the success that you have."

LIVERPOOL

LAWRENCE, LAWLER, STRONG, SMITH, YEATS, HUGHES, CALLAGHAN, GRAHAM, EVANS, ST JOHN, THOMPSON

SUB: UNKNOWN

MANAGER: BILL SHANKLY

OUR FORM HEADING IN

EVERTON	0-0	LEEDS UTD
LEEDS UTD	2-0	LEICESTER
ARSENAL	1-2	LEEDS UTD

"I used to get nervous [before games]. Very, very [nervous] ... sometimes being sick and things like that."
- Norman Hunter

He was one of the hardest men in British football but even Norman Hunter was hit with pre-match jitters. Leeds United's players had six days to stew over a crucial April 1969 trip to Liverpool and the equation was simple: win or draw at Anfield and they would be crowned champions of England for the very first time. Don Revie's Leeds had proven themselves as one of the best sides in the country over a sustained period but had no title to show for it. They were runners-up in the 1964-65 and 1965-66 seasons, followed by a pair of fourth-placed finishes in the next two campaigns. Triumphs in the League Cup and the Inter-Cities Fairs Cup in 1968 had finally broken United's major trophy drought, though, and that allowed Leeds to focus on their goal of becoming league champions. "It's the hardest thing to win ... the league," Mick Jones said. "The FA Cup is great but it's not the best ... win the league, you are the best team. It does take some winning over a nine-month period."

Jones made a fast start to the 1968-69 season, scoring in the first three games, which all ended in Leeds victories. In just his second season at Elland Road, Jones continued to prove his worth with the only goal in a victory over a Liverpool side who would push Leeds all the way in the latter stages of the campaign. It was the season before Allan Clarke would arrive, meaning Jones shouldered a heavy workload as Revie's main man up top, but the striker said his manager never put pressure on him to perform. "I just went out to try and do my best," he said. "If goals came, goals came. If they didn't ... Don Revie always used to say to me, 'What a fantastic job you're doing for me'. That gives you that [confidence]. He was just a great man. He never criticised ...I was playing with Jimmy Greenhoff a little bit and Peter [Lorimer]. Peter used to play alongside me."

Greenhoff left early in the season for Birmingham City, but Mike O'Grady, Johnny Giles and Billy Bremner were also valuable sources of goals in a thrilling campaign. It took 10 matches for Leeds to lose in the league, defending champions Manchester City beating them

3-1 at Maine Road, but three straight wins seemed like the perfect response. That was until United travelled to Turf Moor and were thumped 5-1 by Burnley on October 19, a result that forced a defensive rethink. Amazingly, it would be the last time Revie's men lost in the league that season. A trio of goalless First Division draws followed as Leeds tightened up at the back but United soon returned to winning ways before Revie released the shackles when Burnley visited Elland Road just four days before Christmas. The result was emphatic, Leeds trouncing the Clarets 6-1 as Lorimer netted twice, with Bremner, Jones, Giles and Eddie Gray joining him on the scoresheet.

A third-round FA Cup exit at the hands of Sheffield Wednesday eased fixture congestion, at least, and United were simply outstanding in front of their home fans, winning 18 of 21 First Division fixtures at Elland Road through the season. Leeds conceded just nine goals at home, Hunter and Jack Charlton combining in a formidable defensive partnership. Hunter said Revie knew how to get the best out of him. "The gaffer used to say to me, 'You win the ball and give it to those who could play', … it used to annoy me but then I'd go out and I'd win it," he said. "Then I only had Giles [or] Bremner … if I got stuck, on my left I had Terry Cooper and Eddie Gray. Or if I wanted to go over that [right] side, I only had Paul Reaney and Pete Lorimer and then if I wanted to go up front, I only had Mick Jones! For me, as a defender, I just used to win it and get rid of it. He [Revie] used to say that to me now and again. I remember one day … I was really angry with him, because he said, 'Give it to those who could play', … I was winning it and I was giving it … after the game, he came in … he kneeled down and he took my boots off. I remember [being] sat there, he took my boots off and he just tapped me on the back of the leg and said, 'Well played, son'. And you go strutting [off] … that's what he could do."

A seven-match winning streak in the league saw Queens Park Rangers, Coventry City, Ipswich Town, Chelsea, Nottingham Forest, Southampton and Stoke City all beaten, and when United were knocked out of the Inter-Cities Fairs Cup by Ujpest Dozsa in the fourth round, they had just one focus: winning the league title. Leeds had a tricky run of fixtures to finish, though, with trips to Liverpool, Everton and Arsenal - who ultimately finished second, third and fourth respectively

- in their last five matches. There was also a chance for revenge against Manchester City at Elland Road in April and Giles got the only goal in an important victory.

"We had a tough run on paper. The run-in and those particular matches - we had Manchester City at home, who had won it the previous year," Giles said. "Then we had Arsenal away ... then we had Liverpool away ... so we had quite a difficult run-in." After a 1-1 draw at West Bromwich Albion, Leeds travelled to Highbury and goals from Jones and Giles helped them to a vital 2-1 success. Jones, who finished top scorer for Leeds with 17 goals in all competitions in 1968-69, added another in a 2-0 win over Leicester City before a 0-0 draw at Everton set up an intriguing clash at Anfield. It was the penultimate fixture of the season for Leeds, who were five points clear of a Liverpool side who had one game in hand, meaning one point would be enough for United. "It was a tough place to go," Gray said. "At that particular time, they still had hopes of winning the league championship ... they still had hopes if they could beat us that night." Hunter was nervous - but was Giles? "Everybody handles it a different way," he said. "I don't remember being too nervous because it was a very, very tight race leading up to that particular game and it was typical Leeds - we never won anything easily ... we only had one match to play after that and we still hadn't clinched the title."

Liverpool found it tough to make any inroads in the first half and it was United who came closest to scoring through Bremner. Leeds got to the break unscathed and Gray remembered a distinct feeling of control throughout the match. "We felt [we were] good players ... [we thought], 'It's going to be hard for them to break us down. We've still got the opportunity against them to score goals', ... we basically controlled the game from the point of view [that] we never gave them many chances in the game ... a memory that night is feeling in control of the game." With players like Ian Callaghan and Ian St John in Liverpool's ranks, Leeds were still wary at the break. "It was still the great Liverpool team," said Giles, while Jones added Liverpool "always have had a good side".

The hosts were improved in the second half, too, but Alun Evans was wasteful in front of goal while Gary Sprake kept out a Callaghan effort. Leeds were never under siege, though, as Giles remembered. "They didn't have many chances. We tied up the game pretty well. We didn't have many chances ourselves ... we knew we needed a draw - that's for sure. We knew we needed a draw and we got it." That they did, the sound of the final whistle wildly celebrated by the players. Leeds United were finally the champions of England. "We were up, jumping around and hugging each other," Hunter recalled, before Revie had an idea. "When the whistle blew, Don Revie came on the pitch towards us and hugged us all," Jones said. "And he said, 'Right, go and walk up to the Kop'. It holds 20,000, that Kop at Liverpool. And we're going, 'No, thanks, no'. Billy said, 'Come on, lads, let's creep up'. And it was deadly quiet and I thought there's going to be bottles and all sorts coming at us. We walked to the 18-yard box all in a line and, all of a sudden, this guy - just one Liverpool fan with a big scarf. I can see him now ... halfway up in the Kop, [he] got on somebody's shoulders and he got his scarf up ... he's chanting, 'Champions! Champions!' to us and all the Kop went, 'Champions!' ... Amazing. It brought tears to your eyes, honestly."

"We're all thinking Don had lost his marbles, sending us down to the Kop [laughs]," Gray said. "We're thinking, 'What's going to happen here?' As we started to walk down to the Kop ... you've got to remember that the tunnel at Anfield is at the far end from the Kop. It's right up at the other end of the pitch. So when you're walking, you're walking a good 50, 60 yards to get there because we're all milling around the tunnel area. Liverpool players are going off. We're thinking, 'Well, it's great. We're going to have a nice celebration in the dressing room'. That's when Don says, 'Hey, listen, walk down to the Kop, they'll give you a good reception'. I'm thinking, 'Ah, yeah, right. It's okay, you're not coming with us! It's us on our own', expecting maybe 20,000 people jumping over a wall. When we started walking, it was a slow ripple of applause ... they all started chanting, 'Champions!' ... which was a great feeling. Then we all eventually get back in the dressing room and Don looks at all the faces and said, 'I told you'. You think, 'Alright, okay. He told us'. But it wasn't like that at the beginning! That was a great moment."

"That's the type of moment that you'll never forget," Gray continued. "You'll always remember a moment like that ... there was mutual admiration between the two clubs. I think it stemmed from the two managers, Don and Bill Shankly. In those days, the [top] managers were [Matt] Busby, Shankly and Revie and even going back a little bit further, Bill Nicholson at Tottenham ... the highlight of that game for me was I think it showed how far our club had come." For Hunter, the appreciation the Anfield crowd showed him and his teammates was "unbelievable". "The hairs on the back of your neck stood up," he added. Giles said the moment showed why Liverpool had a "great football crowd". "I think we were all a little bit worried," the Irishman said. "Should we go to the Kop end? Because we'd just pipped them for the league ... Don insisted [for us] to go down and I must say, they did give us a great reception."

Just one match was left for Leeds, Giles scoring the only goal in a 1-0 home triumph over Nottingham Forest. "We won it with a record number of points, which was 67 points," Giles said, Leeds having won 27 of a possible 42 fixtures. "I was delighted to win the championship ... it was a great achievement and it is what you play for," he added. Hunter remembered another act of Revie generosity. "You win the league ... he [Revie] used to say to the wives, 'I've had them away all season, now you come down to London ... we'll have a dinner and you can have it exactly as you want. You can have what you want. You can do what you want.'" What about his message for the players? "He just used to say, 'Go on. Off you go. Have a good holiday with your family but don't get overweight. Then we'll come back and we'll start again'. It was the same every season ... he was brilliant. I know he doesn't get the credit that he deserves outside Yorkshire but within Yorkshire and Leeds and that, he was a God, wasn't he?"

It might have been a goalless draw but the magnitude of that night was put into context by Gray. "That was a great night. To win the first league championship ... when I look back at my career ... you win a [FA] Cup Final against Arsenal ... and the League Cup Final before that, you've [also] won the Inter-Cities Fairs Cup. To win the league championship - I think that is the pinnacle."

OLD TRAFFORD | APRIL 29 | ATT: 62,078

CHELSEA 2-1 LEEDS UNITED

OSGOOD 78', WEBB 104' | 1970 | JONES 36'

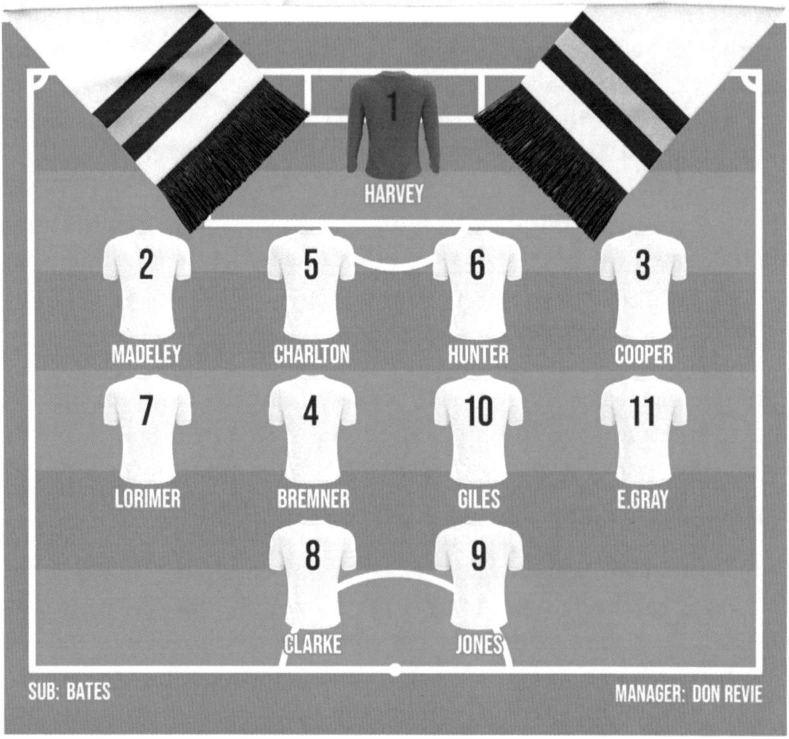

CHELSEA

BONETTI, HARRIS, McCREADIE, HOLLINS, DEMPSEY, WEBB, BALDWIN, COOKE, OSGOOD ▼, HUTCHINSON, HOUSEMAN

SUB: HINTON ▲

MANAGER: DAVE SEXTON

OUR FORM HEADING IN

IPSWICH	3-2	LEEDS UTD
LEEDS UTD	1-3	MAN CITY
CELTIC	2-1	LEEDS UTD

"I never, ever, in my career, considered myself to be a winger ... I was a midfield player that was asked to play out wide."
- Eddie Gray

He made his name as an outstanding winger but it was not a position Eddie Gray envisaged playing in when he arrived at Elland Road. Transformed into a left-sided midfielder, Gray was classy and creative, possessing a wand of a left foot that made him a constant threat. The Scotsman was capable of scoring outrageous goals, too, his pair of unforgettable strikes against Burnley in 1970 a perfect example. Just one week later in the FA Cup Final, Gray simply destroyed Chelsea in a man of the match performance that deserved to end in victory. The Londoners managed to get a draw, though, and then went out and relentlessly targeted Gray in a tense Old Trafford replay. It was the only way to stop him. "When I made my debut for Leeds, I was a centre-midfield player," said Gray, who added he had "never played left-wing in my life" before arriving in England. "I scored against Sheffield Wednesday [on my debut] ... I'll never forget the day Don [Revie] called me into his office. He said to me, 'Eddie, I would like you to have a go at playing outside left', ... no disrespect to anybody else, he said to me, 'I think we need somebody out wide that can run at people and open defences up. It would be easy for you'. So I said, 'Oh, I'll have a go'. Because when I was 17 and made my debut here ... all the early games I played were in midfield. Even played centre-forward a few times but I'd never played wide [at that time]. I ended up playing left-back - I played most positions. I remember one night in Villa Park, I played [as] a sweeper, a centre-back. We beat them [scoring] four!"

"I could play anywhere, but I always considered myself a midfield player," Gray continued. "But I understood what Don was on about because at that particular time, when I was making a breakthrough, Bobby Collins was still in the side as well. He was a midfield player. When John Giles first came, he was playing outside right. Midfield was Bobby and Billy [Bremner]. Then when Bobby finished, Johnny slotted in. When I first got in and Bobby was injured, my debut, I was at midfield. Central midfield. Playing outside left, you expected defenders to have a go at you and have a kick at you ... it didn't bother me. Didn't care." Leeds United started the 1969-70 campaign as champions and beat Manchester City 2-1 in the Charity Shield, Gray and Jack Charlton on the scoresheet. They had a new striker, too, Allan Clarke having joined from Leicester City for a British record transfer fee of £165,000, breaking the previous record set when the Foxes signed Clarke from Fulham just one year earlier. "Les Cocker was our trainer and coach [at Leeds] and also for England," Clarke said. "Les was the instigator [to] getting me in. He wanted me to come to Leeds, because when I was playing for the [England] Under-23's he said, 'Do you fancy coming to Leeds?' I said, 'Yeah, I do', ... the gaffer came with the chairman to my house in Leicester ... he [Revie] said, 'How much do you earn at Leicester?' I said, 'Well, I'm on £100 a week'. I could have asked to double my wages because they're paying a [big] transfer, but I didn't. What I did ask for ... he said, 'Well, how much do you want to come to Leeds?' I asked for £10 more, so that'd be £110. You know what he said to me? 'Can't give you that, son, all my players are on the same wage'. Who was I to disbelieve the gaffer? I said, 'Give me a contract, I'll sign it here'. I signed for the same wage. Do you think they'd do it today? I don't think so ... I wanted to play for Leeds United ... they were the upcoming team."

Clarke scored on his league debut for Leeds, a 3-1 success against Tottenham, but United made a poor start to their title defence, winning just one of their next seven fixtures. Five of those matches ended in draws but the start of the European Cup seemed to sharpen their focus, Leeds going on a 15-match unbeaten run - including 10 victories - in the First Division until Christmas. Fixture congestion started to rear its head in the final months of the season, though, as Revie's men continued to fight for trophies on three fronts. "We're playing, sometimes, three games a week," Mick Jones remembered. "We hardly did any training through the week ... we were so fit [because of the matches]." Clarke said that while it was taxing, it was also enjoyable. "We went for the championship that year. Went for the FA Cup. And we were involved in the European Cup ... we went for the three ... in them days, we were playing Saturday, Tuesday, Saturday, Wednesday, every week. We very rarely had a mid-week off but we wanted to play. We've played when we shouldn't have been out there, because you want to play. I love my training - but I'd rather play a match."

The fixture pile-up was never more evident than in late March and early April, when Leeds played 10 matches in 22 days. Only five of those 10 were First Division clashes, with Leeds unable to initially defeat Manchester United in an FA Cup semi-final, forcing not one but two replays before a Bremner goal settled matters. Two European Cup fixtures came in that chaotic three-week period, too, the second leg of a successful quarter-final against Standard Liege before Scottish giants Celtic came to town in a much-anticipated semi-final. "Celtic probably had peaked before us. We hadn't peaked at that time but they were a great side then. Couple of years later, I think we'd have done them," Clarke said. Of the first leg, Jones said: "We didn't play well. They kept us out and we had to go to Hampden [Park] with a deficit of 1-0."

Leeds had to play at West Ham United only 24 hours after hosting Celtic, with Burnley to visit Elland Road just two days later. The fixtures were coming thick and fast. A week without a match between Gray's Burnley masterclass and the FA Cup Final was a luxury for the Leeds players but the Wembley pitch was ruined by the Horse of the Year show. "You went on the pitch before the game and you sank ... your boots, you could hardly see them," Jones said. "What we did before the game, Les Cocker, the trainer, came round and said, 'Right lads, take one of these apiece', and we said, 'What do you mean, one of these? What are they?' 'Tablets', he said, 'take one of these'. [They were] salt tablets - they're horrible ... they make you feel sick ... he said, 'That's for cramp, because you will get cramp on that pitch', ... honestly, they wouldn't have played the game today." Norman Hunter said "that pitch was an absolute disgrace" while Giles said it detracted from the occasion. "The pitch was a disaster because it had the Horse of the Year show on it a few days before. We were playing on a mud heap at Wembley. All players used to look forward to playing in the [FA] Cup Final because the pitch was in such good condition but that year it was [in] dreadful condition." Substitute Mick Bates remembered being amazed at how bad the pitch was during the warm-ups. "I'm thinking, 'Here I am at Wembley, kicking the ball around. All my life, this is just something I've wanted to do'. And it was like a ploughed field! Just my luck."

Despite the conditions, Leeds made a great start, Peter Lorimer only denied by a terrific save from Peter Bonetti. Charlton soon gave United the lead, nodding in Gray's corner, with Eddie McCreadie missing a goal-line clearance because the ball barely bounced off the surface. Gray then danced around David Webb twice before shooting over in a sign of what was to come. But Chelsea, who saw Charlton clear an effort off the line, were level by the break after Gary Sprake fumbled a tame long-range effort from Peter Houseman into his own net. "Gary Sprake made a bad mistake … we were well on top in the first half and we lost a goal," Giles said. Bates added: "He [Houseman] must have been 25 yards out and he hit it … the lads turned round as if Gary was going to pick it up."

Gray almost produced a swift response, going from inside his own half and forcing a great save from Bonetti, and when play resumed after the break, he was at it again, testing the goalkeeper. "Eddie Gray was awesome that day. He absolutely destroyed David Webb. He turned him inside out," Hunter said. Clarke shared a similar view. "He absolutely tormented him and I felt sorry for 'Webby', really." Sprake went some way to making up for his mistake when he came off his line to deny Ian Hutchinson, but Leeds still needed Hunter to make a goal-line clearance to keep Chelsea out in the same move. United then ramped up the pressure in the hunt for an elusive second goal, Jones and Clarke having efforts before Gray struck the crossbar with a fierce shot from 20 yards.

Leeds kept pressing and got their reward seven minutes from time despite Clarke hitting the post with a diving header from Giles' cross. Jones read the rebound well and did not have to break stride, scoring on his left foot with a delightful first-time effort. "It came out to me, I was about 15 yards out and as it was rolling towards me on my left foot, it bobbled up on the bad pitch," Jones said. "I just caught it nicely, even though it had bobbled, and it just went in the left-hand corner. [I] couldn't believe it, actually … I thought it was the winner, obviously." The Leeds fans went crazy, convinced their team was about to win the FA Cup for the first time.

Chelsea had other ideas, though, Hutchinson nodding in a late free-kick. "It was a good goal to be fair," Jones said. Both sides still had one major chance left, Sprake making a good save to keep out John Dempsey before Clarke thumped an effort onto the crossbar at the other end, forcing extra time. With the pitch in an incredibly poor state, Jones remembered how heavy his legs felt. "By this time, people were going down … Eddie McCreadie, I went down, Norman Hunter went down. There was about seven or eight going down with cramp." Giles went close for Leeds in extra time before Sprake made another important late save but there was to be no winner at Wembley, much to United's disappointment. A replay was required.

"Peter Bonetti for Chelsea was awesome that day," Hunter said. "He saved everything that we shot at them that day … to not win that after the situation and the way we had played - it was a disappointment." Gray was annoyed with the result. "I won the man of the match trophy … but we never won the game. Because we should have won that game by five or six. We dominated the game. That was a disappointing thing from my point of view. It's nice to look back [on] after you eventually win an FA Cup Final but that game wouldn't have meant anything, and the trophy wouldn't have meant anything, if we wouldn't have eventually won the FA Cup … you think, 'Yeah, it was a good day [for me]'. We should have won the game. That was the disappointing thing."

Just four days later, Leeds were in Scotland for the second leg of their European Cup semi-final against Celtic. "They really were a great side. It's the best side I've ever played against," Jones said. "They've never bothered me, [away] crowds, and I walked out … I heard this roar and the crowd - I'm going, 'Christ'. 136,000 … I was thinking, 'Jesus, what an atmosphere', … Billy scored, so we were 1-1. Anyway, there was a 50-50 ball with a player called Bertie Auld, who'd had a reputation for being a very, very nasty boy … I couldn't get out of his way and he went over the top … he split my [shin] pads down the middle … if I hadn't got the pads on, my leg would have just shattered … Les Cocker said, 'Boy, you're a lucky boy'." Celtic scored twice in the second half to win the tie 3-1, with the 136,505-strong crowd the biggest in UEFA competition history. Leeds were out of the European Cup but Jones had at least survived to tell the tale.

With Everton guaranteed to be First Division champions, Revie rotated his squad for the final two matches of the league campaign and Leeds lost to both Manchester City and Ipswich Town. Something bigger was on the horizon, though, as Leeds prepared to face Chelsea again. Leeds made just one change from the team that played in the Wembley fixture, David Harvey replacing Sprake in goal, something he only found out "a couple of days before". "Obviously, I was excited. It's what you start … playing the game for, is to play in games such as that," Harvey said. The replay would prove to be another entertaining encounter full of end-to-end action but the match was also notable for the brutal physicality on show. Leeds made a fast start, Gray crossing for Jones who nearly scored with a near-post flick. McCreadie then had to clear a Lorimer effort off the line before Jones headed wide. A Leeds goal was coming and it was Jones who put Leeds in front again, the striker storming inside the penalty area and scoring a terrific goal after superb build-up work by strike partner Clarke. "I'm thinking, 'Ah, we're going to do it this time,'" Jones said. "But they hung in there. They were a good team, Chelsea."

Chelsea's tactics on how to stop Gray were obvious. Ron 'Chopper' Harris was positioned at right-back to blunt his opponent's influence with force. One particular challenge caught Gray on the knee and Bates was getting angry on the bench. "He really was vicious and he injured Eddie in the replay," he said. "They talk about hard men now but he was vicious. He would try and really hurt you and he did. He got into Eddie and Eddie wasn't the same in the second leg but it wouldn't happen nowadays. It couldn't happen nowadays … he [Eddie] played on but he wasn't right." The physical battles were not limited to Harris and Gray, with Tommy Baldwin and Terry Cooper involved in a running battle, while McCreadie clashed with Bremner, and Charlton and Peter Osgood were at each other. It was tough, uncompromising football. "There were some tackles flying around on that day," Hunter said. "I think there was only one person booked ... how?!"

Leeds continued to have the better of the chances, Giles going close before Cooper tested Bonetti but United's inability to find a second goal would prove costly, Osgood scoring a diving header from Charlie Cooke's cross with just 12 minutes left. "Paul Reaney ran and he said, 'Go with Ozzy'. I didn't go with him and he knocked it in," Hunter said.

For the third time in the FA Cup Final, Chelsea had come from behind to level proceedings. That meant extra time was required again and all the momentum was now with Chelsea. A long throw from Hutchinson would prove decisive in the 104th minute, Harvey coming for the ball but not getting there. Charlton got his head on it but could only direct it backwards, with Webb, of all people, getting the final touch and bundling the ball over the line. "The second one was down to me," Harvey said. "That was my fault. I was late coming for it and if I'd have had my time over again, I would either have stayed back or gone that little bit earlier. I knew straight away. I knew I'd got it wrong." Asked how that made him feel, the goalkeeper simply said: "Almost physically sick."

Leeds still had a chance to get level but were unable to produce an equaliser, leaving Chelsea to celebrate victory in one of the most-discussed FA Cup Finals of all time. "The first game, we deserved that," Hunter said. "We were absolutely brilliant that day on the surface we played on, but anyway, we lost it again. We did lose one or two finals." Amplifying the sense of disappointment was that, after a marathon season of 62 competitive matches, Leeds United were left empty-handed. "It was very disappointing. I mean, nobody remembers the losers … it took a bit of getting over," Clarke said. "Runners-up in the league, we lost the FA Cup … and we lost to Glasgow Celtic in the semi-final of the European Cup … we ended up winning nothing." Jones added: "We deserved to win that [Chelsea game]. We were so disappointed when it [Webb's goal] went in because we were going for three [trophies]."

Giles felt that Chelsea were deserved winners, though. "We didn't throw it away," he said. "We didn't make any terrible mistakes. Chelsea were a very, very good team. That's the way it happened on the day. We didn't throw it away. They won it and they deserved to win it." And what about Gray? What did the man so obviously targeted make of it all? "They put Chopper Harris to play against me … we should have won the game. The ironic thing about that game is David Webb scored the winner. That's the nature of football." A chance run-in between Harris and Gray decades later gave the pair the opportunity to discuss the match. "Not that long ago, maybe about five or six years ago, I was playing in a celebrity golf thing … down in Cornwall. I didn't know Chopper was playing in that … I get into the bar and it was busy … I get a tap on the shoulder and I turned around and it was Chopper. He just looked at me and said to me, 'Eddie, could I please have my studs back?' I just burst out laughing."

Norman Hunter made 726 appearances for Leeds United from 1962 to 1976 and was voted PFA Player of the Year in 1974. Photo: Steve Riding

Eddie Gray made his debut for Leeds United in 1966 and retired in 1984. He has also managed Leeds twice and worked in a variety of other roles at the club. Photo: Alex Knight Photography

LAYER ROAD | FEBRUARY 13 | ATT: 16,000

COLCHESTER UNITED 3-2 LEEDS UNITED

CRAWFORD 18', 25', SIMMONS 55' | 1971 | HUNTER 60', GILES 73'

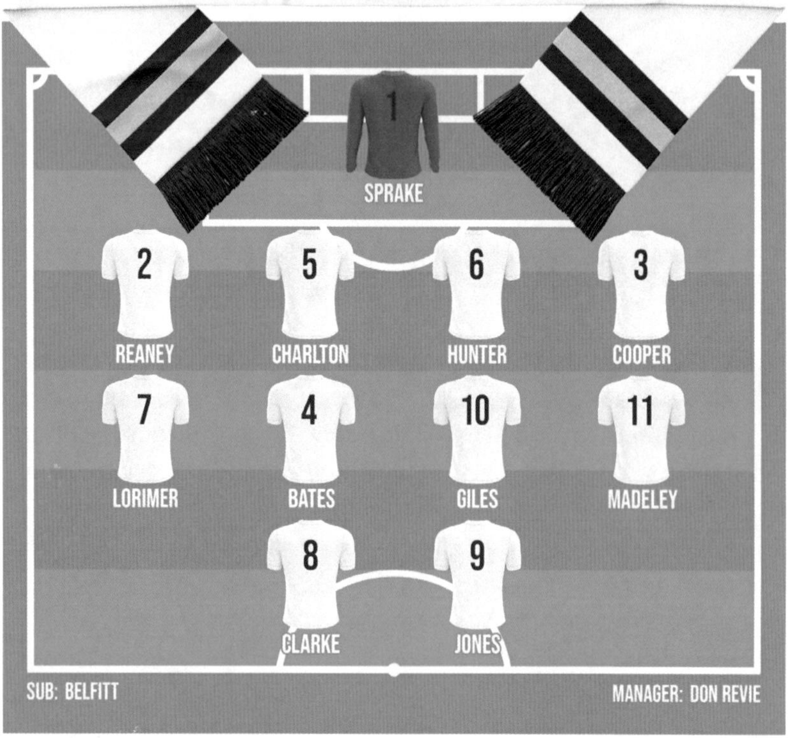

COLCHESTER UNITED

SMITH, CRAM, HALL, GILCHRIST, GARVEY, KURILA, LEWIS, SIMMONS, MAHON, CRAWFORD, GIBBS

SUB: COOK

MANAGER: DICK GRAHAM

OUR FORM HEADING IN

LEEDS UTD	0-1	LIVERPOOL
MAN CITY	0-2	LEEDS UTD
LEEDS UTD	4-0	SWINDON

"Mick Bates said, 'What's wrong?' I said, 'I don't feel very well', ... about 10 minutes later, there's a knock on my door and it's the gaffer [Don Revie] and Les Cocker, our trainer."
- Allan Clarke

Leeds United's star striker was feeling off-colour and it was not because Don Revie's players travelled to a fifth-round FA Cup tie at Colchester United by plane. Leeds were desperate to win the FA Cup in the 1970-71 season, after losing the final to Chelsea in agonising circumstances in the previous campaign. Leeds also lost the 1965 FA Cup Final to Liverpool and they were sparing no expense in their bid to win the famous trophy, flying down to Colchester. It seemed a little excessive but few could argue with just two defeats in more than three months as Leeds pushed for the First Division title, the Inter-Cities Fairs Cup and FA Cup glory. Leeds led the league when they travelled to Colchester and, on paper at least, were on the receiving end of a favourable draw in the oldest national football competition in the world. A third-round tie against Third Division outfit Rotherham United was first up for Leeds and Revie's men needed a replay, winning 3-2 at Elland Road after a goalless draw on the road.

A fourth-round victory against Swindon Town was far more convincing, Mick Jones getting a hat-trick in a 4-0 win over the second-tier side, and the draw then sent Leeds to Fourth Division side Colchester United for what looked to be a one-sided affair. Billy Bremner, the 1969-70 Football Writers' Association Footballer of the Year, was missing for Leeds, and Eddie Gray was also sidelined, while Allan Clarke was feeling poorly. "We actually flew down from Leeds ... on the Friday to a place near where we [were staying]. It was a propeller job," Clarke remembered. "On the Friday travelling down, I didn't feel very well. We got to the hotel and normally when you get to the hotel, you're normally checked in your room and then you go downstairs and you go in the restaurant and you have a meal with your teammates and with the gaffer and his staff. But when I got to my room on the Friday night, I just took my clothes off, got my pyjamas on and I went to bed."

Bates was Clarke's roommate and the former told Revie something was amiss with his star forward. It was not long before Revie and Les

Cocker were at Clarke's door. "The gaffer said, 'What's up, son?' I said, 'I don't feel very well, boss'. When you play a league match or a cup match in England, you don't take your club doctor with you. But when we went abroad in Europe, the club doctor always travelled with us. So, Les and the gaffer went out [of] the room. About half an hour later, there's a knock on my door and it's the gaffer and Les again with ... he's got a doctor. This doctor is examining me and asking me questions. He's giving me an injection in the backside and doesn't say ... he just said, 'I'm giving you an injection', ... I must have dropped off and when I woke up ... we always had to be down for about 11am and we had to be clean shaven, collar and tie on, suit on ... his [Revie's] philosophy was - and I'm a great believer in that - his philosophy was, 'If you look smart, you'll play smart at football. If you look scruffy, you'll be scruffy' ... we always had to have a collar and tie on."

"When I woke up Saturday morning, the day of this game, I did feel a lot better, but when I breathed in it was really, really sore," Clarke continued. "I come down and the gaffer comes up to me and he said, 'How are you this morning, son?' I said, 'Well, to be fair, gaffer, I feel a lot better, but when I breathe in it's really sore'. He said, 'Well, go and breathe some sea air in your lungs'. So I went out [of] the hotel and I'm breathing this sea air in my lungs and come back. Rod Belfitt ... if Mick Jones and I were suspended or injured, he would fill in for Mick and I. He hadn't travelled down with us on the Friday but when I got down [on the Saturday], he was there ... I went for this walk and when I came back in he [Revie] said, 'How do you feel now?' I said, 'Well, just the same'. He said, 'Well, I'd rather have a half with you'. Anyway, I played. Now, how I got through that game - only he knows." Everything would make sense to Clarke after the match.

Less than ideal conditions greeted the Leeds players when they inspected Colchester's Layer Road surface. "The pitch was awful. It was very difficult," Jones said. "They let the pitch dry out [to] make it bumpy and it was windy and bumpy so it brought the level down ... it brought the level down to their level, which they wanted, really." Norman Hunter admitted that he got an uneasy feeling when he walked out, too. "I can remember going out on that day ... the pitch was bumpy," he said. "I remember saying to Jack [Charlton] ... 'This pitch and this situation could be a bit tricky'." Colchester might have been in the Fourth Division but they did have Ray Crawford up front, an England international who would give the hosts a surprise lead with a bullet header when Brian Lewis whipped a free-kick across the box and caught Gary Sprake in two minds. "It was a misunderstanding between Gary and myself," Hunter said. "Gary went for it, he shouted, 'Mine, mine, Norm'. Then he said, 'Yours, Norm'. Then he said, 'Sorry, Norm' [laughs]. Crawford headed it in."

The crowd sensed an upset could be on the cards and urged the Colchester players on, with the hosts keen to waste no time in setting up attacks. "We had a bit of a nightmare," Bates said. "These long balls were being pumped through and Gary was coming and stopping, coming and stopping. Jack [Charlton] didn't know what to do and they scored a couple of goals." Colchester's second goal came from a cross into the box, Crawford heading an effort into Paul Reaney and then reacting quickest to the rebound, shooting past the onrushing Sprake before watching his effort hit the post and cross the line. The shock was on. The fourth-tier side were two goals up against the best team in England.

Even the chance to regroup at the half-time break did not help Leeds, who conceded a third goal when Terry Cooper lost the ball inside Colchester's half. Crawford started a quick counter-attack by releasing Lewis and his punt up the field isolated Reaney and Colchester's Dave Simmons. Sprake was indecisive, again, and when Reaney lost his footing, Simmons had just enough time to head over the goalkeeper and in to spark wild celebrations among the home faithful. "We had a bad day. To be honest, Gary Sprake had a particularly bad day and they took advantage of it," Johnny Giles said.

Leeds mustered a response, though, as Colchester goalkeeper Graham Smith, perhaps taking cues from Sprake, came for a corner and did not get there. Hunter took advantage, scoring a towering header to give Revie's men hope and 13 minutes later, Leeds were within a goal of the hosts. Giles played a lovely one-two with Jones on the edge of the penalty area, the latter drawing three defenders before releasing the Irishman who, despite being off balance, scored an excellent first-time strike on his left foot. "We made it to 3-2 [in] the second half and their goalkeeper was saving them all over the place … he played really well," Bates said. "We're coming back [but] their keeper was saving shots that were going in. It just wasn't going to happen. Hunter also remembered one-way traffic in the dying stages. "We battered them. We battered them - but we couldn't score."

Leeds' best chance to get an equaliser came when Peter Lorimer got to the byline and cut the ball back for Jones but the striker, inside the six-yard box, saw Smith pull off an outstanding point-blank save to keep Colchester in front. And that was how it stayed in what is one of the most famous upsets in FA Cup history. "My wife had to pull up. She was in the car at the time, back in Yorkshire," Bates said. "She had to pull up because she thought, 'I've heard that wrong. I must have heard that wrong, we've lost'. She just was shell-shocked … nobody could believe it. We couldn't believe it." Hunter said the defeat "was embarrassing" but paid credit to Colchester for their triumph. "To their credit, they didn't half play well, early doors. To be fair to them, they deserved to be in front." Jones was not as damning in his assessment of Leeds' performance. "It's one of those things that happens in the FA Cup." Clarke agreed. "We've got beaten by … a Fourth Division club. The great side … a shock, but it happened. That's the Cup. It's not so much embarrassing but you're so disappointed."

Clarke got through 90 minutes but was not as effective as normal. He soon found out why. "I'm coming back to fly back to Leeds … the gaffer comes up to me. He said to me … 'How are you, son?' I said, 'Well, gaffer, apart from losing', … I said, 'Apart from losing … very poorly', … he said, 'Well, you've done alright, son'. He said, 'When Les and I went out [of] the room last night when the doctor came out, he told Les and I, 'That lad's got pleurisy', ... I said, 'Pardon?' He said, 'Oh, aye', … I said, 'Gaffer, you knew I'd got pleurisy and you let me play? I could have dropped down dead'. I said, 'I did alright. You said I did alright'. I said, 'Well, I'll tell you what. If I played with pleurisy, I don't know about 'do alright'. I think I did brilliant'. You know what he said to me? 'Ah, but you didn't score'," Clarke said with a huge laugh.

Hunter felt like the national media enjoyed the result, with Leeds' shock defeat making headlines. "The press had a field day … we weren't that well-liked by the press and this was exactly what they wanted … it was probably how we were. We were a physical side but we could play … unfortunately that [physical] image and that tag has stayed with Leeds, even to this day. They still get this 'dirty Leeds' bit and all that, even now. We didn't mind. The gaffer used to pin things on the board [and say], 'Look at what they're saying about us'. We used to look at it." Hunter also felt that the north-south divide had something to do with it. "It was a bit like that - but Liverpool were a great side but they never got branded anything like we did. Don't worry about it, that Liverpool side, they could be quite physical when they wanted to be … we used to like to go down to the capital. We used to like to go down to London and he [Revie] used to say, 'Look what they're saying about us, lads'. We used to go and try our best to upset them."

Giles said he was sick of seeing the Colchester highlights on the television each year and that the magnitude of the upset and Sunderland's shock win over Leeds in the 1973 FA Cup Final overshadowed the team's achievement in winning the tournament in 1972. "It happens to all teams … Colchester was a bad day. These things happen … when people are talking about Leeds United, they usually leave '72 out [laughs]. But if you look at the record, we lost to Colchester but we didn't lose another [FA] Cup tie until we were beaten by Sunderland."

Success in the FA Cup was just around the corner for Leeds United. Finally.

JUVENTUS

TANCREDI, SPINOSI, SALVADORE, MARCHETTI, FURINO, MORINI, HALLER, CAPELLO, CAUSIO, ANASTASI, BETTEGA

SUBS: NOVELLINI, OTHERS UNKNOWN

MANAGER: CESTMIR VYCPALEK

OUR FORM HEADING IN

JUVENTUS	2-2	LEEDS UTD
LEEDS UTD	2-0	NOTT FOREST
LEEDS UTD	0-0	LIVERPOOL

"I really couldn't believe [it]. I've just scored against Juventus in Turin in a European final ... I was a lad from a pit village in Armthorpe and I just couldn't believe it."
- Mick Bates

He still struggles to comprehend what he achieved on a famous night in Italy but Mick Bates' key role in Leeds United's 1971 Inter-Cities Fairs Cup triumph makes it a very happy memory for all involved. The midfielder epitomised the 'side before self, every time' attitude of Don Revie's Leeds United team, content to play an occasional role and turning down chances to leave for more first-team football. Bates simply loved being part of things at Elland Road, continually learning from his teammates and enjoying the camaraderie of a tight-knit squad. He enjoyed his best moment in a Leeds United shirt in Turin, scoring a vital away goal in the club's ultimately successful quest for a second European trophy. Leeds United fans were, by now, used to watching their team go on lengthy European runs, and Revie's men entered the 1970-71 edition of the Inter-Cities Fairs Cup - which would soon become the UEFA Cup - with a strong record. Leeds, of course, won the tournament in 1967-68, while they had also reached the final, semi-final and fourth round in three other attempts. Leeds also went all the way to the European Cup semi-final in the 1969-70 campaign, only beaten by an excellent Celtic side, and that meant optimism was high as Leeds entered what would be the last edition of the Inter-Cities Fairs Cup.

A 6-0 aggregate win over Norwegian side Sarpsborg saw Billy Bremner, Peter Lorimer and Jack Charlton score twice each but United needed the away-goals rule to get past Dynamo Dresden in the second round. The second leg in Germany was a heated affair, with Bates sent off as both sides ended with 10 men, but Leeds were back to their fluent best in a 6-0 demolition of Sparta Prague at Elland Road in the third round. Eddie Gray scored twice on that night as Leeds led 5-0 by half time and they also had a big lead at the break in the return leg, ahead 3-0 at the interval before Sparta pulled back two second-half goals. As part of another marathon season, Leeds then edged Portugal's Vitoria Setubal 3-2 over two legs, Lorimer scoring in both matches as part of a streak of form that saw him net in seven matches in a row. That result set up a much-anticipated semi-final against Liverpool and Revie rolled the dice on selecting Bremner, who was rushing back from a leg injury. Bremner stepped up for the big occasion, scoring a second-half header that decided a tense Anfield fixture. When asked about some of his favourite matches in a Leeds shirt, Johnny Giles quickly said: "Going to Liverpool and beating them 1-0 in the Fairs Cup match, the semi-final."

"It was great because anybody who plays Liverpool at Anfield are up against it, basically. The crowd are fantastic, the players are motivated," Bates said. "It's nip and tuck. It's unlike some of the games where we know we are better. It's just a matter of producing what we can do. Liverpool at Anfield is, 'We know we can compete and it's all on the night', … it can go either way but it went for us … we did well to beat Liverpool." The second leg at Elland Road finished goalless, Leeds hanging on despite both Allan Clarke and Mick Jones being forced off with injury. That left just one opponent, Juventus, standing in the way of Leeds and another European trophy. Juventus beat Cologne to reach the decider and in Helmut Haller, Fabio Capello and Pietro Anastasi, had a star-studded team.

Leeds United's motivation was only enhanced by the chance another season could end without a trophy. Leeds were bundled out of the League Cup in the second round by Sheffield United, while a fifth-round FA Cup exit to Colchester United stunned the nation. Most frustrating, though, was the fact that Arsenal had pipped Leeds to the First Division title by just one point. A 2-1 defeat to West Bromwich Albion at Elland Road in April was the turning point, a match marred by controversial decisions and fan angst, and the mere mention of the fixture draws a frustrated response from Jones. "Don't want to talk about it," he simply offered. Leeds returned to the top with a win over Arsenal later in April but Bertie Mee's side had a match in hand and won it at rivals Tottenham Hotspur to claim top-flight glory.

There were almost four weeks between Leeds' last league match, at home to Nottingham Forest, and the first leg in Turin and the players were determined to take something from the season. "We arrived in Turin on the Monday, obviously the game is Wednesday night," Clarke said. "We arrived in Turin and it was absolutely bucketing down. We went to the ground on the Tuesday morning … there was thousands of Juventus [fans] watching us train. It was raining [again]. Anyway, Wednesday comes, another session. So in the afternoon we're in our rooms just resting … the gaffer [was] with Les Cocker and Bob English, he was the physio, they'd been down to the ground in the afternoon to put all the kit out and that. The gaffer, in his team meeting, he said, 'This game shouldn't be on'. He said, 'It's waterlogged … I don't know why they haven't called it off but it's on so we have to prepare. It's on'. We kick off and there's so much surface water, once the ball drops, it's a joke. Absolute joke."

Leeds would suffer an injury in the first half, Eddie Gray needing to be replaced by Terry Yorath. "I had got injured playing for Scotland," Gray said. "Funnily enough, it was against Northern Ireland. It was George Best I went up to … and George brought me down. I put my arm out and I did my shoulder. The shoulder injury bothered me for a while. We went to Juventus and I knew. I thought, 'This isn't going to go well for me today', because the pitch was flooded. There was no way you could keep your feet. They started the game. Automatic reaction when you go down … I put my hand down, my shoulder went again. That was me [finished]." Giles managed to hit the bar for Leeds, while Juventus were also denied by the woodwork, but the match was abandoned after 51 minutes due to the weather conditions. "I think if we played the 45 minutes, then they didn't have to refund the money [to the fans]," Norman Hunter said with a laugh, a theory backed up by Clarke and Bates. The two teams would attempt to play the first leg again on the Friday, as Leeds remained in Italy. "The wives loved it because they could stay another couple of days," said Jones, while Gray remembered being told to join them by Revie. "Don sent me up to the mountains with the players' wives. They were all at a different hotel to us. My wife was there, so he said, 'You might as well, Eddie, go and have a few days [off]'."

Gray's injury robbed Leeds of creative skill but the abandoned fixture did give United an insight into what to expect from Juventus. And although Roberto Bettega gave Juventus a first-half lead, Paul Madeley's long-range effort levelled proceedings just after half time.

Parity did not last long, Capello restoring Juventus' advantage before Jones went off injured, replaced by Bates. "I came on again to do a job," Bates remembered. "It was a torrid atmosphere, obviously, in Turin. It had to be. We were doing okay, we were doing alright but when Mick came off … it would have been, 'Well, we better sit tight and hope we just get there, back to Elland Road, 2-1, then we'll have a chance.'" Bates was determined to make an impact, though, and just four minutes after being introduced he was in unfamiliar territory as Giles had the ball. "[I] found myself on the far post which is very, very rare. I do remember taking it down on my right thigh and volleying it in with my left foot … it was a good goal and as I was going back to the kick-off, running back, I just couldn't believe [it] … I used to play in the streets under lamp posts in between the gates … it was crazy … I'm running back, thinking, 'How lucky am I? What have I done here?' It was fantastic. I'll never forget that, I know that."

Leeds held on from there, taking back not one but two crucial away goals to West Yorkshire. "We had a great night afterwards. It was two each but we had every chance at Elland Road … I was ecstatic," Bates said. The goalscorer's teammates were absolutely delighted, insisting his moment in the sun was the least he deserved. "Mick Bates was so happy to be at Leeds, to be involved with it," Jones said. "He always said that. He could have gone on [elsewhere]. He was a good player, Mick, but he wanted to be involved in the achievements … he was always capable of doing that, Mick. He was on the bench with Don Revie for about seven years, I think! So he got to know him quite well." Gray's selfless nature is shown in the way he described Bates' goal, too. The Scotsman was injured and could have been annoyed but was over the moon for someone he describes as "one of my best mates in life". "Mick played a lot of games here … people never considered him a regular but he was always stepping in for people. That will probably be the highlight of Mick's career, will be scoring against Juventus, Inter-Cities Fairs Cup Final. What's bad for one person is good for another. 'Batesy' will never forget that."

"I never kidded myself. I knew how good I was. I knew how good Billy was and Johnny … they dictated games. I would never dictate a game," Bates said when asked if he was ever frustrated at regularly being left on the bench. "I would never let anybody down ... I would play a good game ... Johnny, Billy, Eddie and Pete, they were top class. Billy and Johnny thought they were the best in the world - they actually thought that and they weren't kidding themselves ... I'd be a fool to say I should be playing ... it's just common sense. [You have to] be honest with yourself. I think all the lads were alike, really, they are honest and, I mean, Paul Madeley was the same. If Paul came into midfield, he would come in if there was an injury. He knew ... is he better than Norman [Hunter]? Is he better than Jack [Charlton]? No. So Paul would accept it but Paul played a lot of games and he played for England ... I was the only [one] who didn't represent their country out of the squad there. They were all full internationals except for me. So, what does that say about me? I obviously can play because I play with full internationals. But I do know my place and I was quite happy. We were successful, I knew my place, I loved every second of it, the lads were great, Don Revie kept me involved all the time ... I was always happy .... [Gary] Sprake, [Paul] Reaney, [Terry] Cooper, Bremner, Charlton, Hunter, Lorimer, Clarke, Jones, Giles, Gray. That is the great side ... if they were all fit, they would play, whether they were having a bad time or [in bad] form or anything like that. Don would always still play them and that's the way it should be."

There was, of course, still one leg to go and more than 42,000 fans attended Elland Road for a June 3 fixture against Juventus that would determine who the last winners of the Inter-Cities Fairs Cup would be. Leeds took an early lead, Clarke scoring in the 12th minute. "I hit it from just outside the box or edge of the box. I remember Billy jumping on me," he said. Juventus found a quick response, though, Anastasi making it 3-3 on aggregate. Jones had a couple of chances to put Leeds back in front, but the hosts were not chasing the game like Juventus, given the away-goals rule, and with Hunter and Charlton in control at the back, Leeds held on.

"We did the lap of honour. I've got plenty of photographs for it with the Fairs Cup in my hand, along with Billy and Johnny, I remember that," Bates said. "We went round, it was great but you take it for granted in a way. Looking back, it's not like it is now ... we just went round, thanking the fans, showing the Cup and that was basically [it]. Obviously, when we went in, we were ecstatic, delighted, we'd beaten a very good side. A very good side." Jones remembered "going round with Paul Reaney with a Juventus shirt on" in the aftermath, while Gray, watching from the stands, hailed it as a landmark moment. "It was a great occasion for the football club. To win a European trophy, it was tremendous ... it meant a lot. You're playing against one of the huge names in football ... for me, even though I was injured, I still say I played in the final!"

For Clarke, "it was great, just to win it in front of [the fans] at Elland Road", while Giles said Leeds were the better side. "We deserved to beat them. They were a top team, we played well, we got the two goals away [at] Juventus, which was crucial to us. We deserved to win it and that was a big win ... it's nice to have the home crowd there ... they [fans] were good. They built it up over the years. My first match for Leeds, when I went there, there was only about 14 or 15,000 at the game. Don's ambition was to build it up to 40,000, which he did, and more. By the time we played in those particular matches, [there was] a very, very enthusiastic crowd going to the games."

After the previous season ended without a trophy, Jones was delighted to give something back to the passionate Leeds fans. "Football's all about players and supporters. Nobody else. That's all it is. And if you keep the supporters happy, they will back you ... I know the Leeds supporters. They are fanatical." Leeds would then play Barcelona in September 1971 for the right to keep the Inter-Cities Fairs Cup trophy, given the Catalan giants were the inaugural winners. United lost 2-1 at the Camp Nou but Bates' special moment could not be taken from him. "I always tell the lads, 'It's always the second goal away from home'," he said with a laugh. "You've had a couple of drinks and say, 'If it wasn't for me, we wouldn't have won', and all this ... I'm only messing about with them ... they [lads] knew I didn't score a lot of goals so they made me feel really good about it. I'm in the history books, it's there, I've done it. I look back on it, it's wonderful. I can't believe it at times but football does that for you."

A delighted Elland Road crowd watched Leeds United claim more European glory. Photo: Andrew Varley Picture Agency

ELLAND ROAD | MARCH 4 | ATT: 34,275

LEEDS UNITED 7-0 SOUTHAMPTON

CLARKE 37', 60', LORIMER 42', 64', 68', CHARLTON 73', JONES 78'

1972

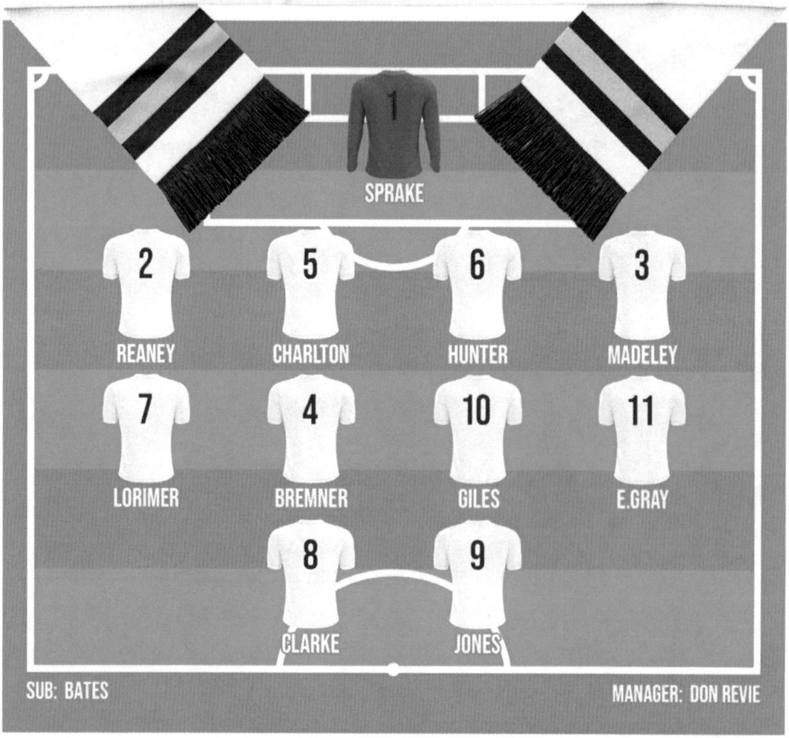

SOUTHAMPTON

MARTIN, McCARTHY, FRY, STOKES, GABRIEL, STEELE, PAINE, CHANNON, DAVIES, O'NEILL, JENKINS

SUB: BYRNE

MANAGER: TED BATES

OUR FORM HEADING IN

CARDIFF 0-2 LEEDS UTD	LEEDS UTD 5-1 MAN UTD	EVERTON 0-0 LEEDS UTD

"We played our best football from Christmas of '71 to the end of the season [in] '72. Absolutely brilliant."
- Johnny Giles

A pair of 1972 performances in successive home games against Manchester United and Southampton are the stuff of legend and Johnny Giles believes both came in the finest spell Don Revie's Leeds United team ever had. "I think that was Leeds at our peak," he said. "Manchester United were still a very, very good team. [We] beat them playing exhibition stuff, Southampton the same." Leeds scored 12 goals in those two fixtures at Elland Road that saw hat-tricks, clinical team goals and outrageous passing sequences delight the home fans and captivate the nation.

The 1971-72 season did not start so well for Leeds, though, losing 3-0 at Sheffield United in the second game of the campaign. Forced to play their first four matches away from Elland Road due to the West Bromwich Albion pitch invasion in the previous season, Leeds played twice in Huddersfield and once at Hull City's Boothferry Park and Sheffield Wednesday's Hillsborough. They only won one of those fixtures, a 5-1 triumph over Newcastle United in Sheffield, and had just won five of 12 league matches by mid-October. It was far from title-winning form. Leeds had been dumped out of the UEFA Cup by that point, too, and had lost a match to Barcelona that decided who kept the last Inter-Cities Fairs Cup trophy. October also saw Leeds knocked out of the League Cup but, crucially, Revie's men started to find some league form. They won seven of eight league fixtures, a run only broken by a 2-1 loss at Southampton, with Peter Lorimer's incredible form shown by the fact he scored in all seven triumphs. Leeds would really click after Christmas, according to Giles, with wins over Derby County and Liverpool helping United put themselves back in the title race.

Leeds were now playing with more freedom, perfectly shown on a February afternoon at Elland Road when they scored five times in 27 second-half minutes in a 5-1 win over Manchester United. Mick Jones was on the spot to score a hat-trick, all of his goals coming from inside the six-yard box. "They weren't the greatest of goals but goals are goals," he said. "They weren't anything from 18, 20 yards - but you've got to be in there to score them. I always scored against Man United, funnily enough. At Old Trafford, I scored a few goals … I wish I had have got the match ball [from Elland Road] now when I think about it. At that time, I think that's when we peaked as a team." Eddie Gray agreed and said the confidence flowing through the team at that point was contagious. "There was a feeling running within the football club then," he said. "People say to you, 'Your best moment in football?' … The highlight for me was sitting in the dressing room before every game and just looking at the players I was playing with and thinking, 'There's no way we can get beat today'. That's a great feeling to have, that. That's not being big-headed … we were going to play against Manchester United, Bobby [Charlton] and George [Best] and all the rest of the Man U players. We thought we were going to run over the top of them … we just played them off the park that day."

Gray was outstanding against Manchester United, while Giles' range of flicks and passing were on show as Leeds registered more than 20 successive passes in the latter stages to the delight of the Elland Road crowd. Jones has happily retold the story of his hat-trick on countless occasions. "It's a memory that I'm still getting stopped for it, now … I still get talked about, [people saying], 'Oh, Man United, Mick, you got three'. Because they hate Man United and Man United hate Leeds and to put one over on them - they just love it … it is nice. It makes me proud and if it makes them happy, I'm pleased about it … we played so well." That rivalry has grown over time and Norman Hunter said he does not recall it being anywhere near as fierce as it would become. "I can't remember there being a rivalry then … it happened later on … it became very [bad], quite bad at one time, Leeds and Man U, but not then. Not in our day." Hunter was full of praise for Jones, who fully deserved his moment. "I think Mick Jones would've been one of the first names that Don Revie would put on a team sheet," he added. "I thought Mick Jones was a great centre-forward … Mick was great in the air for his size. He could hang there … and I'll tell you what he had - not many people realise. He had pace. Mick Jones could run."

Jones' strike partner, Allan Clarke, also scored in the Man U victory, while it was no surprise to see Lorimer on the scoresheet. Clarke said his partnership with the hat-trick hero worked from day dot. "We just hit it off straight away because we were two different types of strikers. Mick was what I call the target man ... Mick would hold the line where I would drop into midfield, so you've got a balance there." Clarke said Jones' heading made him the ideal player to line up alongside. "Mick could direct it into my path ... it was a special partnership, that." The performance left Leeds full of confidence and Mick Bates felt like it was a pivotal moment in the national recognition of Leeds United. "I think that's when people all over England were thinking, 'Wow. These [Leeds players] are not only [a] hard team, this team can play'. Because we murdered Manchester United."

Leeds kept up their winning run in between, Giles getting both goals in a fifth-round FA Cup tie at Cardiff City, but United needed 37 minutes to open their account against Southampton in front of the Match of the Day cameras. "Funnily enough, as daft as it may seem [given] we beat them [by] seven - for 20, 25 minutes the game was quite close. And then 'Clarkey' scored," Hunter said. Clarke's goal opened the floodgates, Lorimer getting in on the act before the break with a smart finish, too. The half-time interval barely disrupted Leeds, Clarke getting his second on the hour mark before Lorimer produced a sensational piece of skill and fired in his second. Just four minutes later, Lorimer had his hat-trick and Leeds were 5-0 up. "I was sitting there to start with and thought, 'I hope nobody goes down because this is fantastic'," substitute Bates said. "This is my attitude again, my confidence ... [thinking] 'If anybody gets injured here, I've got to get on here and play like these lads are playing' [laughs]." On the pitch, Hunter and Jack Charlton were in conversation. "I think we were five up ... I'm stood at the back with big Jack and the big man said, 'I'm bored, Norm'. I said, 'So am I. So am I, Jack'. He said, 'Come on, me and you, go up there. Let's see if we can score'. I'll never forget, Paul Madeley got the ball and I ran around his outside and Paul played it down the line and I just got it before the dead ball line and I clipped it. I clipped it right to the far post. Who is stood there? The big man! He knocked it in!" Hunter cannot tell the famous story without laughing and it was an indictment on Southampton, Leeds United's two centre-halves combining for a sixth goal.

Jones capped the rout with a seventh in the 78th minute before Leeds, again, passed the ball around to the delight of the home fans. Giles was at the centre of it, his trickery and range of passing prompting BBC commentator Barry Davies to cry: "To say that Leeds are playing with Southampton would be understatement of the season ... poor Southampton just don't know what day it is!" Clarke said the famous passing sequence was a result of Revie's instructions. "I'm about 10 yards from the touchline and the ball ... I think Billy [Bremner] plays the ball to me and I hear the gaffer shout [to me], 'Sniffer!' [Clarke's nickname]. The game's over. Now just pass the ball and keep out of trouble', ... the last thing he wanted was injuries ... we just kept possession of the ball." As the pass count grew, Jones did not want the ball. "I'm stood up front with this young lad who's making his debut for Southampton and talking to him while the lads are just knocking it about. And I said to him, 'I hope they don't give it to me. I don't want to lose it because the one who loses [it] will get so much stick!'" While Clarke rejected the suggestion that Leeds were showing off, Hunter said regardless of the circumstances, if the shoe was on the other foot he would not have been able to accept it. "I wouldn't have liked to have been a Southampton player on the end of that ... I wouldn't have been able to stand that. There was only one person trying to run around and get the ball back. That was a lad called Mick Channon up front. Good player, Mick. I must be honest - if somebody would have done that to us, we'd have got into them."

Hunter was still able to enjoy what was unfolding, though. "The ball came to me. I thought, 'Well, I'm not giving it away', so I got it and knocked it [away]. Then it came back to me ... it went to Paul Madeley. Paul lost it and then what did he do? He went back and won it again. That's when Billy and Johnny started ... that was quite awesome, really, when you think about it." Bates remembered a crowd who could not contain their excitement. "We had to work hard to get to a place where we could knock the ball around ... it's the easiest thing in the world, honestly, to keep the ball, you can go back, square, back again, knock it forward, come back, easy. It's absolutely easy but the fans absolutely loved it ... once you're four or five up [at] Elland Road, they [opposition] half give up and you just knock the ball around but the crowd loved it ... they were just fascinated by it." The final whistle soon put Southampton out of their misery and Clarke said he was quickly able to appreciate the magnitude of the performance. "From a manager's point of view, you're always looking to get the perfect 90 minutes," he said. "I would say that game against Southampton - it was probably as perfect [as] you're going to get. All the great things we love and admire about football … everything was involved in there. Passing, goals, touch, control, everything that's good about the game we love and admire was in that 90 minutes … that's the perfect match."

Giles preferred playing in closer matches but acknowledged just how good Leeds were on those two occasions. "It was great skill, it was great stuff … the Southampton match would be probably one of the most talked about games in my time at Leeds United, but it wouldn't be up there with one of my memorable games. It was an exhibition rather than a contest … they were great exhibition games for the skill of the Leeds United team." Giles did add that only Leeds were able to produce that sort of performance, though. "The Southampton match and Manchester United match in particular - there were no teams at that time and our time [that] could do to Manchester United and Southampton what we did. These were skilful players. I mean you've got Eddie Gray, Peter Lorimer, Allan Clarke, Mick Jones, Norman Hunter, Billy." Bates was again pleased with the way the country was forced to appreciate United's style. "Everybody, begrudgingly down south, would say, 'Yeah, okay, they obviously can play. You don't beat Manchester United [scoring] five and Southampton [by] seven'. It was brilliant. We had a good run at that time."

But was it the best performance Revie's Leeds side produced? "I've got to agree," Gray said. "You look at the possession of the ball … the goals we scored, the manner of the goals. The goals were clinical but the football was great. It'd be like watching the Man City team of today playing against somebody and the way they played the football … the disappointing thing against Manchester United [was] that [it] wasn't seven and we conceded … those highlights of the Southampton game … people always remember that. The Southampton players always remember it. They talk with no great affection on the game but how it was to play against the Leeds United side then … people will look at that game and think it was one of the best performances ever."

WEMBLEY STADIUM | MAY 6 | ATT: 100,000

LEEDS UNITED 1-0 ARSENAL

CLARKE 53' | 1972

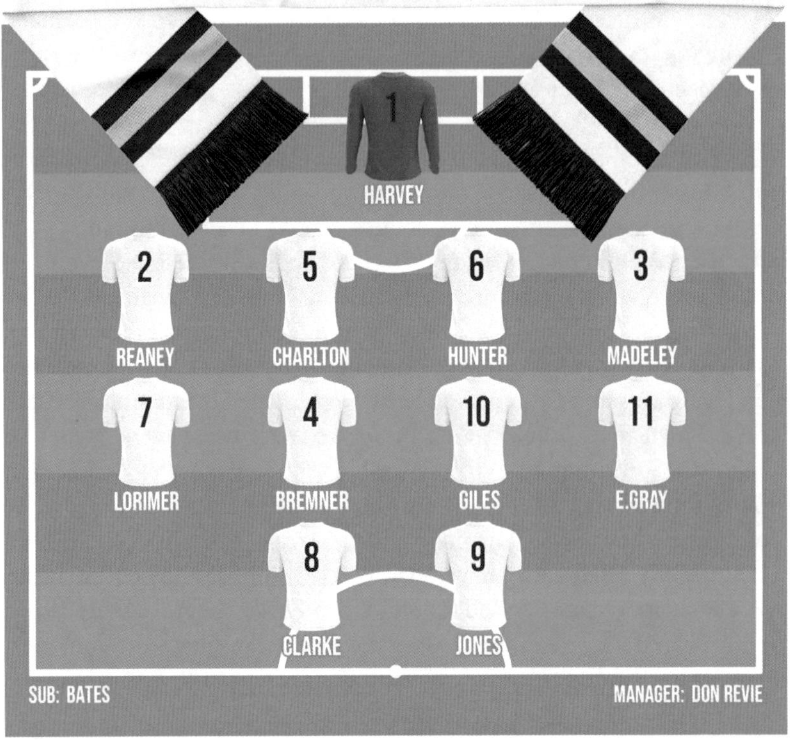

ARSENAL

BARNETT, RICE, SIMPSON, McCLINTOCK, McNAB, ARMSTRONG, STOREY, BALL, GRAHAM, GEORGE, RADFORD

SUB: KENNEDY

MANAGER: BERTIE MEE

OUR FORM HEADING IN

LEEDS UTD	2-0	CHELSEA
WEST BROM	0-1	LEEDS UTD
NEWCASTLE	1-0	LEEDS UTD

"I think because we'd beaten Arsenal before in the League Cup [Final], I think we fancied our chances ... I know our [FA Cup] track record wasn't very good, but I thought we were going to win that."
- Norman Hunter

Leeds United's run of near-misses in the FA Cup could have filled players with doubt ahead of the 1972 final against Arsenal. Leeds' two previous trips to Wembley for the biggest match in British football had been spoiled by heartbreak. Ian St John's late winner helped Liverpool to victory in the 1965 showpiece and Leeds then dominated the 1970 final, but were forced to a replay by Chelsea, who would come from behind in both matches to ultimately lift the trophy. There was something the Leeds players could use for confidence, though. Revie's men had already beaten Arsenal in a Wembley final, Terry Cooper's goal settling the 1968 League Cup decider. Norman Hunter said that helped give him confidence as the match approached, while Mick Jones said Don Revie's morning message was about making up for the past. "Right, lads. I want to make up for 1970," is what the manager told his players at London's Royal Garden Hotel, according to Jones, who added that Revie's words struck a chord with the players. "All the lads - we were all quiet and I knew they were all ready for it ... we were getting really prepared ... we were determined to win it."

Leeds played some outstanding football in the 1971-72 season, dishing out hidings to the likes of Manchester United, Southampton and Nottingham Forest after Christmas as they surged up the league table. Leeds impressed in the FA Cup, too, conceding just twice on a run to the final that started with a 4-1 success against Bristol Rovers. A replay was needed to get past Liverpool, Allan Clarke scoring twice, before Johnny Giles netted a double of his own at Cardiff City. Leeds then beat Tottenham Hotspur in an Elland Road quarter-final before thrashing Birmingham City 3-0 to book a trip to Wembley. Leeds United were eye-catching in more ways than one, though. Inspired by sports artist and entrepreneur Paul Trevillion, Leeds players were now doing pre-game warm-ups with their names on their backs, waving to fans before they played and giving away iconic 'sock tags' to fans, all part of softening the team's image and adding a touch of glamour to a side playing seriously glamorous football. It was new, daring and the fans loved it, so Birmingham tried it, too. “Birmingham tried to out-psych us,” Mick Bates said. “They did exactly the same thing … we used to wave to the crowd in the middle, get into two lines, warm up, [trainer] Les Cocker used to go through the routines and they were doing the same on the other side. We were looking over, thinking, ‘What are they doing? They didn’t do this’. Anyway, as it turned out, we murdered them 3-0 and so we went on to the final.”

“Before the game, there was a great deal of confidence within the ranks,” Eddie Gray said. “You knew you were playing against a top side, obviously. A top Arsenal side. But I think there was a feeling [of] third time lucky in the FA Cup Final. We knew if we play, we’ll win the game. If we were on song, we thought we’d win the game because we thought we could beat most sides in England.” Arsenal, who pipped Leeds to the 1970-71 title, were fully aware of just how good United could be on their day. “They had got a lot of class players and physical players as well, so they had the right combination,” Arsenal star George Graham said. “So whatever final it was, whether it was the League Cup Final or whether it was the FA Cup Final, it didn’t make any difference. We knew we were going to be in for a hard game.” Was revenge for 1968 on the agenda? “I don’t think revenge is probably the right word,” Graham added. “We just thought that Leeds were just a bit vulnerable when it came to picking up trophies - but they did well against us.”

The Arsenal match would be Leeds’ third FA Cup Final appearance in eight years but it was Clarke’s third in four. “My first Cup Final [was] for Leicester City, the year before I joined Leeds, against Man City.” Leicester lost the 1969 decider but Clarke was still named man of the match for his excellent performance. Another agonising defeat followed for the forward in 1970 but he had a third chance to live out a childhood dream. “I can remember growing up in the ’50s, in the West Midlands, [I was] brought up in a council house. My mum could look out the window and there’s a council football pitch - I lived and breathed on there. And all I ever wanted to be when I grew up was a professional football player,” he said. “Dad bought our first television [in] 1954 and I was a West Bromwich Albion supporter, although I didn’t see them very much. I remember Ronnie Allen, who was the striker and he scored and that was my first [FA] Cup Final I ever watched … Len Millard was the captain of West Brom, he went up and received the trophy … I'm thinking, 'I'd love to play in the Cup Final when I grow up'." For a prolific striker like Clarke, failing to score in two FA Cup Finals and a replay also left him with a point to prove.

Revie had a decision to make about his goalkeeper with Gary Sprake fit again, but he opted for David Harvey, who spent the majority of 1971 on the transfer list. "I asked to go on the transfer list. At the time, I was playing so few games in the first team and Gary was really at the peak of his career," he said. "He was probably one of the most naturally gifted goalkeepers that I've ever seen. My chances were going to be very limited and I thought to make any progress, I was going to have to get another club, but luckily for me, it never came about. I was on the transfer list for about 10 months and I'd had two or three whispers from people within the game that clubs wanted me but the boss obviously wanted to keep two goalkeepers of that standard at the club at the same time. He wasn't going to let me go, that was pretty obvious, really." Harvey describes the situation as "very lucky" and Revie showed his faith in him with his team selection. "I wasn't sure that I was going to be playing … Gary had become fit again, so the odds were that he was going to play but as it turned out, the boss stuck with me." Harvey was excited but admitted that the morning of the game was agonising. "John Giles and I had a bit of training to do in the morning, so we try and make that [last] as long as you possibly [can] - whatever you're doing, you try and make it just fill the time in."

"We'd been [given] made to measure suits for the match. Arsenal came on with all open neck shirts and jeans and we absolutely looked the bee's knees besides them. They were casual," said Jones, while Clarke remembered chatting to Arsenal's Alan Ball before spotting another opponent. "I saw Charlie George. I went, 'Charlie', and he looked at me. I said, 'Should have got your hair cut, son', and he's looked at me, thinking, 'What's he on about?'" Jones could sense a different mood as kick-off approached. "It was so quiet in the dressing room … nobody laughing and joking or anything." But that quietness was down to determination and desire, he felt, and midfield genius Giles also picked up on "a mood of confidence". "We knew the size of the occasion but we had great belief in our own ability as a team," Harvey added.

Harvey's opposite number, Geoff Barnett, was not a first-team regular and Clarke was trying to get inside his head in the early stages. "'You're nervous, son, aren't you?'" Clarke asked. "He said, 'I am, Allan'. I just put something in his mind." Gray was fouled early but said he was not getting déjà vu after being targeted in the 1970 FA Cup Final replay. "I never thought about that when I played football. The game was a bit different then. People in those days weren't going to let you just go on the ball and run at them. The old saying … 'The first one [challenge] was always free'. They can boot you up in the air and they never get booked and sent off and our players used that to their advantage as well … it didn't make any difference how late the challenge was. It'd be easy to play today, with the pitches and no challenging from the back! If somebody hits you right away, they'll be off first challenge if it's bad enough. So, yeah, you expected to get knocks in a game. It didn't bother me."

Arsenal could have been in front when Ball rifled an effort towards goal, only for the well-placed Paul Reaney to clear it off the line. It was a sign that maybe, just maybe, this might be Leeds United's day. Leeds responded well, Jones shooting just wide before Peter Lorimer forced a save out of Barnett, and only the woodwork denied United the opener, Clarke heading a thumping Lorimer effort into the crossbar. "He had a shot there … I just took the sting out of it, just placed it. [I thought] 'Oh, crikey'. I thought it was in," Clarke said. "Peter could hit the ball but I just took the sting out of it and just cushioned it and it hit into the bar."

Clarke was not to be denied, though, scoring the only goal of the game after outstanding work down the right from his strike partner Jones. "I'm near the halfway line, 15 yards from the touchline and Frank [McClintock] is behind me and I actually slip," Clarke said. "I'm by the halfway line and he actually treads on my hands. Six studs on it, it's a bit sore … I've been trodden [on] - it does give you a bit of pain. Paul [Madeley] intercepts it and then gives it to Peter Lorimer, who was in the centre circle and Mick [Jones] is out on the right wing. So he passes the ball to Mick and I saw Billy go past me and I'm thinking, 'Christ, I've got to get in the box here'." Jones said Lorimer's pass triggered a thought. "Something went through my brain straight away, 'Take him on'. [Facing me] was Bob McNab, left-back. I take him on, knocked it past him. I wasn't the quickest but I wasn't slow and I'm just getting past him and he's got his legs round the ball … he thought he'd got it but it bobbled out and he said, 'You lucky bastard', as it happens, because it rolls out from under his legs … I can see the ball now … I'm looking at it and I got my foot round it and whipped it in."

"As Mick crosses it, I tell you what, I'm thinking the right-foot volley," Clarke said. "I'm not far off the penalty spot. I'm thinking a right-foot volley and I fancy my chances but as it's coming towards me, I think. You have only got a split second to think about it but I'm thinking, 'It ain't going to get to me'. So, then I dive. And, I tell you what, as soon as I dive and head it, I knew it was in the back of the net. The rest is history." Wembley erupted as Clarke's superbly placed diving header gave Leeds the lead. "I ran across to Mick and we just hugged each other," Clarke added. "And all the lads came, big Jack [Charlton], everybody just hugged each other." Gray was always confident Clarke would take the chance. "Mick did extremely well to get the cross across the box. When it got across the box, I was right behind Allan. When I saw him running in, I thought, 'Goal', because 'Sniffer' [Clarke] was a great finisher, as good as any of them. [He is] up there with the best finishers that have played the game and it was a great header."

"Great header, great goal," is how Hunter described it, Harvey said the moment was "sheer relief", while Giles said it was a "a brilliant header" designed and scored by an outstanding strike partnership. "[Allan was a] great finisher - he was nicknamed 'Sniffer' because he was sniffing out the goals," Giles added. "Allan was very good. He was a good header of the ball, he was good on both feet, he was a good finisher, he was cool, great confidence in himself. Allan was up there with the best finishers in what was then the First Division. Mick was a good lad, grafter, he scored his fair share of goals as well. He wouldn't have been as clinical as Allan but he scored his fair share. He was the one that could do the running and get in behind people and that. Mick was a terrific lad, great lad. Top player."

Clarke's goal came in the 53rd minute, leaving Arsenal with plenty of time to mount a comeback. Harvey said the remaining minutes "felt like two or three years". "Dave made one or two crucial saves," Hunter said. "They look quite simple but they were hit in with a bit of pace and he got down and he caught them and then he held onto them and that." Arsenal would hit the crossbar, too. "I remember Charlie George, because I wasn't far off him," Hunter added. "He went bang and he dropped his shoulder and he hit it on the volley. Bang!" George's effort bounced off the bar and into the path of Peter Simpson, who skewed high and wide. "Obviously, you're glad to get away from it ... it was a break we got but overall, in the game, we deserved to win," Gray said.

Clarke and George would cross paths again before the match was done. "They have a free-kick about 25-30 yards out. Alan Ball and Peter Storey ... they're on the ball. So Mick Jones and I, we're in a defensive wall ... 'Jonah' [Jones] is here and Charlie George is next to Jonah. Long, black hair. And I put my arm around Jonah ... [waiting] for Peter Storey to have his shot and as he's touched it, I've got hold of Charlie George's hair and you see his head go [back] like that! And he looked at me - I said, 'I told you to get your hair cut'. He's never forgiven me!" With time running out, Jones went on another run down the right. "Unfortunately it couldn't just happen for us that we win," Hunter said, referring to a problem-free triumph. There was a problem, as Jones collided with Barnett and fell on his left elbow, badly dislocating it less than 30 seconds before the final whistle. "I fell over him ... I went down to stop the fall," he said. "Well, the Wembley pitch is not like any other pitch that I've ever played on. It's like carpet but about 10 times thicker ... it's very spongy and when my arm went down [and dislocated] ... the pain was incredible. I'm laid there and the goalkeeper, he says, 'Get up you effing softie'. He didn't realise ... he thought I was trying to play a bit of time [wasting]. But I wasn't ... honestly, I was in agony."

On the bench and unaware how much time was remaining, Bates was getting ready to come on. "I thought, 'I'm going to get on here', ... I was getting my tracksuit off and everything because Mick [Jones] wasn't coming back. In those days, there was only one sub and time was ticking by and I hadn't even got my tracksuit off and he [referee] blew [his whistle]." The whistle sparked celebrations among the Leeds players, who quickly embraced each other. "Just so proud," Harvey said when quizzed about his emotions. "To be part of such an achievement as winning the Cup for the first time … it can never be taken away." Like Clarke, Hunter had lived out a childhood dream. "That was a great thing to win the FA Cup. That was my thing as a kid," the defender said. Attention soon turned to Jones as it became clear he was in absolute agony. Asked to describe the pain out of 10, Jones initially opted for "nine and a half" before going with "11". "I can remember Les Cocker coming and he said, 'We've got to carry you off, got to carry you off. Come on, the ambulance. I'm going to get the ambulance', … I said to Les, 'Nah, I'm not going off, Les, I'm going up there'." Jones wanted his medal. "[I said], 'I'm not here every day', and he [Les] said, 'No, you can't, you're in a bad way, in a bad way!' And the doctor came and said, 'No, you've got to go off, Mick, let's get you off into the dressing room'. I said, 'No, I will not go. Get me up on my feet and I'm going to walk up those steps'. Well, they got me up and they strapped my arm to me … I'm walking across and I'm losing vision … Dr. Adams, what a man he was. He took me, walked me across towards the Royal Box."

Jones wanted to personally collect his medal but it had already been taken by Bates. "I'm the only player who had two medals off the Queen! It's like a quiz [question]," Bates said with a laugh. "I went up and the Queen said, 'Would you give this to Mick, Mick Jones?' I said, 'Yeah, that's fine'. So I took them down … gave it to Mick. He said, 'I'm going up'. I said, 'Mick, no. I've got your medal', and he was all strapped up and he said, 'No, I'm going up, I [want to] see the Queen', and he did." Jones took the story from there. "I'm starting to feel sick because that's when shock sets in with an injury, it's like bad injuries, shock sets in your body. So I get to the bottom of the steps and the doc says to Norman Hunter, 'Take him up the steps, Norman', … I walked up and, all of a sudden, my wife put her arms around me as I'm halfway up the steps … I said, 'I'm alright, love, I'll see you later'." The Wembley crowd was captivated by this point as Jones gingerly climbed the steps. "She [Queen] said, 'Are you alright?' I said, 'Yes, thank you, I'll manage', … she said 'I haven't [got] anything to give you' … Mick Bates had picked the medal up but I wouldn't have altered it because it's just part of the [story] … you're not there every week!"

Jones was then taken away on a stretcher, but he still had time to wave to fans before doctors got to work. "The joint had to go back in … I wanted to be sick because of the shock." Despite their victory, there was no time for Leeds to celebrate as just two days later, they would play at Molineux, chasing a league and Cup double. The journey to the Midlands gave the players time to reflect on what they had achieved. "It was the first time Leeds had ever won the FA Cup, which was history for Leeds United and great," Giles said. "The FA Cup was a really, really major competition to win, glamour competition compared to today when a lot of teams are resting players … in those days, winning the FA Cup was huge and it was great to win it that day."

Gray said the previous final heartbreak made the win even sweeter. "To win the FA Cup Final and the centenary Cup Final [1972 was the 100th year of the FA Cup], it was just a tremendous occasion. A wonderful occasion. It was something I think that the players all wanted to do, especially after the disappointments of '65. Because a few of the players were still around that played in '65. They'd played in that game, they'd played in the '70 game, then won it in '72. We should probably have won three or four FA Cup Finals. We never [did] … but that one, you have won it. It's the centenary Cup Final and it goes down in history. It was a great occasion for everybody at the club." Graham was disappointed but said there was no shame in losing to a great Leeds United team. "They were fantastic … Eddie Gray was unbelievable on the wing and Peter Lorimer with the rocket shot, Allan Clarke, the goal snatcher, the little goal snatcher. He always finished up, got goals … and big Jack at the back, two good full-backs, they were an excellent, excellent team and I think the majority, not just myself, the majority of football realised that Leeds were an outstanding team."

The last word, fittingly, belongs to Clarke. "I played in four FA Cup Finals but I only won one … I won the big one. The centenary Cup Final, 100 years of the FA Cup, when the Queen was there to present the trophy to Billy. It is special."

Third time lucky! Leeds United finally had the FA Cup in their hands. Photo: Andrew Varley Picture Agency

WOLVERHAMPTON

PARKES, SHAW, TAYLOR, HEGAN, MUNRO, McALLE, McCALLIOG, HIBBITT, RICHARDS, DOUGAN, WAGSTAFFE

SUB: BAILEY

MANAGER: BILL McGARRY

OUR FORM HEADING IN

LEEDS UTD	1-0	ARSENAL
LEEDS UTD	2-0	CHELSEA
WEST BROM	0-1	LEEDS UTD

"If there was an obstacle to be put in our way, it would be put there."
- David Harvey

Leeds United's players were perplexed. Just two days after they won the 1972 FA Cup, Leeds had to play their final First Division fixture of the season at Wolverhampton Wanderers' Molineux. This was no ordinary match, either. It was Leeds United's chance to do the double. "We just needed a point to do the double and we deserved the double that year," Allan Clarke said. After back-to-back finishes of second in England's top flight, a draw in the Midlands would be enough for United to be crowned champions, unless Liverpool beat Arsenal at Highbury by a ridiculous scoreline on the same night. Don Revie had tried to push back the Molineux fixture to give his players more time to recover from Wembley but upcoming international matches caused a problem. The manager's relationship with Football League secretary, Alan Hardaker, did not help, according to Eddie Gray. "I don't think the game should have been played on a Monday night. I think we should have played the game on the Wednesday or Thursday, but the powers that be [decided]. Don wasn't the most popular with Mr. Hardaker, I don't think … I think it [timing of the game] was stupid. It wouldn't happen now. Not for such an important game like that."

The short turnaround had a major impact on FA Cup Final day, too, with players unable to properly celebrate. "There was nothing. Absolutely nothing," David Harvey said. "Every other team that wins the [FA] Cup Final gets the chance to celebrate and the powers that be had decided that the one remaining game had to be played on the Monday night." Gray said the frustration was made worse by the fact that FA Cup glory had proved so elusive. "The players had waited so long … to win an FA Cup Final. And not to have the celebration with the players and the wives and the families, like a traditional banquet in London after the game was disappointing … it was straight from Wembley to Wolverhampton. On the bus in the tunnel, straight up. You've not seen your wives or families or anything." Gray had briefly seen his father in the aftermath of the Arsenal win, though, and the encounter left his head swirling with emotions. "Right after the game, Don came to me and said, 'Your dad's not very well. He's in the tunnel'. So I went to see my dad in the tunnel. He looked as if he'd had a heart attack or something like that. My mum was with him - but we had to go." Gray knew something was up and vowed to return to London after the Wolverhampton match was over. "I had to go and meet my mum and go to the hospital in London. They told me that my dad had - it wasn't a heart attack at all. He had cancer in his body, they couldn't do anything for him. He died in September … finding out about my dad and how he was in London [on FA Cup Final day] and my mum … she was down there on her own with him. It was all a bit hectic, that [Wolves] game."

"I know hindsight is a great thing but what he [Don] should've done - he should've let us go, have a few bevvies with our wives [on] Saturday night … he took us [to Wolverhampton] straight away," Norman Hunter said. "Why not just say, 'Go on, lads, have a few bevvies, we'll travel up tomorrow'. But that wasn't his nature … we just got on the bus and came up." Clarke remembered the journey well. "When you get to a [FA] Cup Final … you have a banquet and everybody involved with the club is invited, obviously in a hotel in London. But obviously we've got this important game on the Monday … instead of going to the banquet, which the directors [attended] … we got on the coach … I know where I'm going [in] Wolverhampton … I was born around there. So we drove from Wembley to a place called Tettenhall, which is near Wolverhampton. Lovely hotel." A low-key Saturday night followed, before photographers snapped a now-iconic photo of Billy Bremner and Jack Charlton on Sunday morning in their hotel room. The pair were great friends and roommates and newspapers are strewn across the room as Bremner, lying in bed smoking a cigarette, is surrounded by the remnants of his breakfast and a cup of tea. Charlton, in a separate bed, is simply yawning.

But while Bremner and Charlton relaxed, others were doing everything possible to play. "Sunday morning, Johnny Giles, Eddie Gray and myself - we went to West Bromwich Albion's ground to have some treatment," FA Cup hero Clarke said. "Because if that game on the Monday, if it was not important, there's nothing at stake - Eddie, Giles and myself wouldn't have played. But because of the stakes, we had to play." Giles said his groin was causing him problems. "In those days, we didn't have a big squad of players. The same players played all the time.

So by the time we got to Wolverhampton … we weren't in the best physical condition, definitely not. Definitely not. It was very unfair to have to play such an important game on that particular Monday … I was having a bit of a problem in my groin and the matches catch up on you. We didn't get a break at all." Giles needed painkilling injections to play and when asked if he was anywhere near 100 per cent fitness, he said: "I don't think I was more than 60 per cent." Mick Bates also remembered talk about the game's integrity being raised. "We stayed in a hotel [on] Sunday, just relaxed, talking away … rumours were around that we were bribing Wolves," he said. "It was big news that somehow we had tried to bribe Wolves, which was a lot of rubbish."

On Monday morning, the matches at Molineux and Highbury were the talk of England. A draw would have almost certainly secured the title for Leeds, but if they lost, Liverpool could have won the First Division with victory at Arsenal. If Leeds and Wolves finished goalless, Liverpool would have had to win 11-0 or more, while a 2-2 draw at Molineux - which nearly transpired - would have required the Anfield outfit to win 8-0 or more in order to sufficiently boost their goal average. Any goals Liverpool potentially conceded would make their incredibly difficult task even tougher. If Leeds were beaten and Liverpool drew or lost, Brian Clough's Derby County, who were not playing, would be champions. It created a fascinating set of permutations and Leeds hoped that mid-table Wolves would have one eye on their UEFA Cup Final against Tottenham Hotspur. Five days before the crucial league clash at Molineux, Wolves lost 2-1 at home to Spurs in the first leg of the decider. "Wolves were a good team. They were never going to be a walkover, by any means," Giles said. With Mick Jones injured after dislocating his elbow in the FA Cup Final, Revie went for a makeshift strike partnership. "The gaffer played Billy up front with me," said Clarke, who was feeling the pinch. "The one ground that did take it out of your legs was Wembley … Wembley was the one."

Jones, back in Leeds, travelled down to Wolverhampton with club doctor Ian Adams. "I met him at Elland Road and I got in his car and we got on the M1," he said. "It was bumper to bumper with Leeds supporters all the way down to Wolverhampton … all it was was Leeds fans with scarves out … what a sight. We got there, I got out of the car

- I couldn't get a ticket! I couldn't get a seat. So I went to the dressing room, met the lads and wished them all the best." Jones remembered thousands of Leeds supporters at the ground without a ticket but he managed to find a spot to watch the game. "I was in the stadium. I happened to get in where they do the commentary on the radio and all that. I had to just stand in there."

An early incident indicated it would not be United's night, with penalty appeals for a handball by Wolves' Bernard Shaw being turned down. "There was controversy … the ball was knocked into their box," Hunter said. "He went with his hands - everybody in the ground shouted, 'Penalty!' The linesman was there and the linesman froze. He just played on. That was early on … if we'd have gone in front then …" Bates, who deputised for Bremner in midfield, was positive it was a penalty. "This ball bounced up to Bernard Shaw and it hit his hand. It was a penalty." Clarke said the non-penalty call was symptomatic of a night where other penalty appeals were turned down, too. "We had some bad decisions by the referee."

Wolves took the lead just before half time, Frank Munro scoring the opener at the far post. "I still thought we had enough," said Hunter, recalling his thoughts at the break, but the hosts doubled their lead when Derek Dougan fired past Harvey. "When they got the second, I think we went a little bit deflated and that, thinking, 'Here we go again,'" Hunter added. "I'm watching and I'm thinking, 'This is so unfair. We play all season to get to this position for the double and they do to this to you,'" Jones said. Leeds could have been down and out but Bremner, as he so often did, scored an important goal. The Leeds captain fired into the roof of the net from Paul Madeley's cross, setting up what would be a grandstand finish. "Billy scored and we only needed another goal and we were pushing … we had every chance of getting this goal. We were pushing. They were backs to the wall," said Bates, while Giles said: "We were back in with a chance of doing it."

Wolves could have had a third goal, too, but a John Richards effort was ruled out for offside, while goalkeeper Phil Parkes was in good form for the hosts as Leeds searched for an equaliser. Wolves were desperate, though, Bates recalling an incident with Munro that still bemuses him. "Quite late on ... I was standing next to him on the half way line and he was virtually praying, saying, 'Please, please, please'. He was desperate to beat us, totally desperate ... he was a big beast and yet he was virtually praying, honestly. I couldn't believe what I was hearing ... I couldn't believe it, how much it meant to them, they were in the middle of the table. It meant nothing to them, really ... he was virtually, 'Please, please, please don't let them [win]'. And I'm thinking, 'What does it matter to you, really?'" Clarke acknowledged that Leeds United were not well-liked by the nation, though - something that pleased him. "That team that I was a part of - and it's a fact, even to this day - unless you're a Leeds fan, the rest of the nation, they hate us. We caused that. I don't care though. That's what we wanted ... the reason it could be ... we beat most. We didn't lose many. And I think the Chelsea players at the time like Peter Osgood ... that [1970 FA] Cup Final, they're saying, 'Oh, dirty Leeds'. And you say that word enough, people will start to believe it." Whatever Wolves' motivation was, they held on, surviving a late scare when Terry Yorath's effort was cleared by Gerry Taylor. "It was obviously one of those nights where it wasn't going to go our way ... that's part and parcel of the game, I'm afraid," Harvey said. The final whistle soon followed. Leeds United were beaten. The double dreams were over, as Derby won the title after Liverpool and Arsenal played out a goalless draw.

"It was sickening," said Clarke, while Bates said being so close to getting an equaliser just made things worse. "Little bit of luck, toe poke here or whatever [and we would have scored]. But it didn't happen. I think that's probably why we were all so upset after. We were pushing for this goal, it could have come, it could have happened quite easy and it didn't and we walked off just knowing what could have been. It was bad." Bates remembered emotions running very high in the Leeds changing room. "We were all crying, virtually. I'd never cried after a game but I was crying that night. It really, really got to us, [missing] that double and I saw all the lads, these hardened pros who played for England 50, 60, 70 times, they were all in tears. That's the worst we've ever felt ... the shock does that ... there were grown men, grown professionals, hardened professionals crying. It meant so much. It meant so much that day and we were so upset. So upset ... it was awful, really. I went out to my mum and dad and I was crying outside, with my mum and dad and Jill, my wife … I couldn't help it … we'd had a big weekend, a big weekend, the FA Cup … such an important match, to do the double, we didn't do it. It could have gone either way again but it all came out. I've never seen our dressing room like that."

"It takes some of the shine off winning the cup," said Harvey, something Giles was in strong agreement on. "It finishes up as a disappointment. If we'd played that match the week before and then won the FA Cup, you're finishing on a high, whereas we were finishing on a low." Approaching 50 years on, anger over the timing of the match still lingers. "We were physically and mentally tired after Saturday," said Hunter, while Clarke was more forthright. "Why did the FA [Football Association] make us play on the Monday night? Because it's Leeds United. They don't like us."

Allan Clarke scored 151 goals in 366 appearances for Leeds United. He also managed the club in the 1980s. Photo: Alex Knight Photography

Mick Jones finished as Leeds United's top scorer in both First Division title-winning seasons under Don Revie. Photo: Alex Knight Photography

SUNDERLAND

MONTGOMERY, MALONE, GUTHRIE, HORSWILL, WATSON, PITT, KERR, PORTERFIELD, HALOM, HUGHES, TUEART

SUB: YOUNG

MANAGER: BOB STOKOE

OUR FORM HEADING IN

BIRMINGHAM	2-1	LEEDS UTD	SOUTHAMPTON	3-1	LEEDS UTD	HAJDUK	0-0	LEEDS UTD

"It's the only game I've played in where every player on this team didn't perform. You always get two or three off. You know you can pull them through but when you get all the team not performing, which was that day, that's the worst match I've played in ... everybody didn't perform."
- Mick Jones

Mention the name 'Sunderland' and the heroes of Leeds United's greatest era wince. The memory of the 1973 FA Cup Final is a painful one, Leeds stunned in front of the nation by a Second Division side who outfought and outworked them at Wembley. It was to be a season defined by disappointment in finals, one that nearly ended in the departure of legendary manager Don Revie. United were full of determination after the bitter end to the 1971-72 league campaign at Molineux and Revie made a move for Huddersfield Town defender Trevor Cherry, who had just suffered relegation with his hometown club. "I wanted to play in the First Division, as it was then," he said. "When Leeds came in, it was a no-brainer for me, really. I couldn't, in all honesty, understand why they'd bought me because you could name their team as household names." Jack Charlton's fantastic career was coming to an end, though, and Revie also thought he could convert Cherry into a left-back. "Mr. Revie bought me to play left-back to fill in for Terry Cooper because he'd broke his leg and then he thought, longer term, I could replace Norman [Hunter] as centre-back, which was my best position ... [I had] never played left-back and he just thought I could do a job ... one thing was moving to Leeds but moving to a position I'd never played in before ... fortunately it worked out for me!"

Entering such a settled team could have been daunting but Cherry was immediately made to feel welcome by Billy Bremner. "Billy was the main man, Billy and Johnny Giles," he said. "They were the lads who ran the team as well. Billy took me under his wing ... my style of play was to win the ball [and] tackle, which probably suited Leeds. Johnny Giles was the real brains. Johnny was a great player ... pre-season, I'd always go back a week early and Johnny was always there and we'd run for hours together, just to get ourselves [right] for the pre-season. But Billy was the heart and soul of the team. Great lad off it, great lad on it." Gordon McQueen arrived from Scotland, too, while David Harvey became first-choice goalkeeper. Harvey was injured in a 4-0 opening-day drubbing at Chelsea, though, replaced in goal by Peter Lorimer in a result that set the tone for a frustrating start to the campaign. Mick Jones was struggling to recover from his horrific elbow injury sustained in the 1972 FA Cup Final, too, and made just two appearances in the first month of the season. "I had to go to hospital for three months before the start of the season to get that back straight," he said. "My confidence had gone … I didn't start the season very well at all … 1973, I had a bad season. I think so, anyway." Jones is a harsh critic and did score in four successive games in late September, but Leeds won just five of their first 11 league games. A 5-0 hammering of champions Derby County at Elland Road lifted spirits, though, and came as part of a 12-match unbeaten run in all competitions.

United were back on track and Revie was leaving no stone unturned in his bid to keep his players happy. "I'd been there about six months," Cherry said. "I used to go in early [for] training … Les Cocker was always about [and I would say], 'Morning, Les!' I like to think I'm quite bright and bubbly and I must have just been one degree under … just, 'Morning, Les', and Les said, 'What's up with you?' I'd agreed to buy a new house and there was no gas in this house and there was a national gas strike on. [I was] married and I'd got a little baby then and in those days, you agreed to move out [of] your other house, so I was moving out [of] the house, without having one to move into which wasn't the end of the world. We could've gone in a hotel or something but [they are] problems that you could do without. Les said, 'Go down and see the gaffer', and I said, 'There's nothing he can do, there's a national gas strike on' … I didn't go to see the boss because I'd only been there six months … went in the morning after, I was bright as a button [and said], 'Morning, Les!' [He said] 'Morning, gaffer wants you now'. And when you're told to see the gaffer, you go. And basically I just said, 'There's a national gas strike out, there's nothing you can do. It's a new estate with a house and all this'. And he just said, 'Bring me this guy's number you're dealing with'. So I took him the number and this guy rung my wife up and he said, this was Thursday, I think, and he said, 'Can't get there this weekend but we'll put a gas pipe in on Monday'." Cherry later asked Revie how he worked his magic and it transpired that the manager had offered a host of tickets to watch Leeds, including tickets to the FA Cup Final "if we get there". "He said, 'All I want is a gas pipe', and so he got the gas pipe … he got that bothered about the players. He didn't want me going home worrying and not sleeping, perhaps. The gaffer was brilliant."

After going more than two months without a league defeat, Leeds then stuttered, winning just four of 14 league fixtures through February, March and April, form that saw Liverpool and Arsenal fight it out for the title. It left Leeds to focus on the cups and although United's FA Cup defence started in patchy fashion, needing three matches to get past Norwich City, wins over Plymouth Argyle and West Bromwich Albion followed before Lorimer's goal settled a quarter-final with Derby. Another 1-0 victory was on the cards in the semi-final, Bremner's effort helping Leeds defeat Wolves at Maine Road and setting up a clash against Second Division opponents Sunderland. Allan Clarke was in excellent form in the Cup, scoring six times as he prepared to play in his fourth final of the competition in just five years.

Hunter approached the final in a confident frame of mind. "You're a professional but without getting carried away with yourself, they're in a lower division than you so you automatically think, 'Oh, we're going to win this.'" Hunter's mood was reflected by the nation, with Leeds huge favourites to make it back-to-back FA Cup successes. United had the stars and the experience and, as a result, Sunderland had widespread support as the underdogs. The Black Cats wasted no time in trying to disrupt Leeds. "Straight from the kick-off, they had a player [Richie Pitt] who was marking me. He fouled me straight away, straight from the kick-off, so you could see their intentions. But that didn't bother me," Clarke said.

Giles remembered Leeds being profligate in the early stages. "It was one of those days. The goalkeeper [Sunderland's Jim Montgomery] played exceptionally well. We had good chances early on in the game that we didn't take." Sunderland had chances, too, and took a 32nd-minute lead when, after a corner was not properly cleared, Ian Porterfield had enough time to take a touch and fire past Harvey. "It was knocked in and we challenged for it but we didn't clear the header," Hunter said. "I think Paul Madeley and myself were at centre-half … we didn't clear the header between us and it dropped to Porterfield and he just hit it on the volley and it went in." Harvey recalled the shot taking a minor deflection. "It just got a slight deflection off Allan Clarke's shoulder, which was a bit ironic, as in he had scored the winner the year previously, but it was just enough to deflect it in." The goal gave Sunderland the belief they could pull off one of the biggest upsets in FA Cup Final history, while Eddie Gray was struggling with his persistent thigh injury. "I shouldn't have played in that game," he said. "It was the thigh again. I wasn't really fit. I hadn't played a lot of games. I wanted to play in the game, I wasn't sure about playing in the game because of my thigh and I think that my performance reflected that. I was useless that day. I was."

There was still plenty of time for Leeds, though, and they should have been level in the second half. Paul Reaney's cross was met by Cherry and his diving header was well saved by Montgomery, but the goalkeeper could only push the ball into the path of Lorimer, with the Scotsman just six yards from goal. "I headed that quite well, really. I was happy with it but [Jim] Montgomery made a great save," Cherry said. "It came out to Pete Lorimer … 100 times out of 100, he'd have tapped that in, but it just wasn't to be." Montgomery had just enough time to get back to his feet before diving in the direction of Lorimer's shot, somehow tipping the ball onto the bar. "Of all the people in the world to drop to, on his right foot, Peter Lorimer," Hunter said. "I thought, 'Pick this one out'. Then, Jim, when you think about it … such brilliant reflexes. He was here saving Trevor Cherry's shot and then the next thing, he's over there … and he gets a hand to it. Amazing, amazing save … if he bobbles it, it goes under his body and everything."

"The double save was just … I don't think he [Montgomery] even knows to this day how he did it," said Eddie Gray, while Harvey simply dubbed the goalkeeping as "out of this world". There was still a further chance for Leeds to score just after the double save, as the ball bounced back off the bar and towards Cherry, who was flat on his stomach. He swung a boot at it, hoping to turn it in, but contact was minimal. "Flicked my heel … it could've gone in," he said. The feeling amongst the Leeds players was that one goal would open the floodgates. "If we'd have got level with them, we would have beat them … I remember [thinking],

'If we don't score from that, it's going to be very, very difficult, which it was,'" said Giles, while a frustrated Clarke said "if we'd have got one that day, we'd have got ten".

Leeds kept pushing for an equaliser but Sunderland continued to scrap and almost scored a second, Harvey forced into a great save. "They worked their socks off. They got a lot of breaks in the game and it was their year and all credit to them," Eddie Gray said. "That's the nature of football. We should have won the game, regardless of the situation." Sunderland were victorious, though, Bob Stokoe's men rewarded for a gritty, fighting display. "All credit to Sunderland, they set their stall out to frustrate us … I could not say that Sunderland were lucky but we were certainly unlucky," Harvey said. Cherry felt it was one of the rare occasions in his career Leeds were outfought. "Sunderland, on the day, they absolutely fought and battled as if their life did depend on it … they were better than us on the day, so far as competing. I wouldn't have anything but praise for Sunderland. They were wound [up] to [the] top of the tree. They got stuck in more than us, which was never heard of, to be honest. Leeds competed with anybody … but on the day, they perhaps competed a bit better than us."

Frank Gray, Eddie's younger brother who also played for Leeds, sat alongside Revie throughout the match but said he kept calm despite the unfolding disaster. "I was sat next to him on the bench at Wembley that day and that was a big disappointment for the whole club. They were overwhelming favourites and everyone fully expected them to win … it was a massive disappointment for everybody at the club … I very rarely heard him raise his voice that much but he let you know when he was disappointed … if you ask any of the Leeds players involved in that game, they'd say it's probably the biggest disappointment of all their careers."

While Jones felt the defeat was embarrassing, Clarke hit the nail on the head when he said "it's one of them you have to live with". Leeds' players have had to live with the defeat ever since, as the match is constantly raised as one of the great FA Cup upsets. "Everybody remembers Sunderland," Giles said. "When I see it on the television on the BBC, when they're showing the [FA] Cup Final going back over the years, they always show us losing against Colchester. They always show the game against Sunderland." Eddie Gray's reminders are more than annual BBC clips, too. "I've watched that game over and over because I've got a great friend that's a huge Sunderland man … he keeps reminding me, keeps sending me videos of it … still see Jim [Montgomery] occasionally. I go up to Sunderland because I have a few friends up there and I've seen him on occasions. I think he shut his eyes and just threw himself across the goal and the ball hit him," he said with a big laugh.

"The player that played right-back that day is a guy called Dick Malone," Eddie Gray continued. "I'm not being funny when I say this but every time I played against Dick, I gave him a chasing. I did. In that [FA] Cup Final that day, he never gave me a kick of the ball. I was useless. That's what I say, 'He'll never forget that Cup Final, Dick'. He's a Scottish guy. He's a good lad and we laugh about it to this day. That's football."

Don Revie and Billy Bremner were left with plenty to ponder after the shock defeat. Photo: Andrew Varley Picture Agency

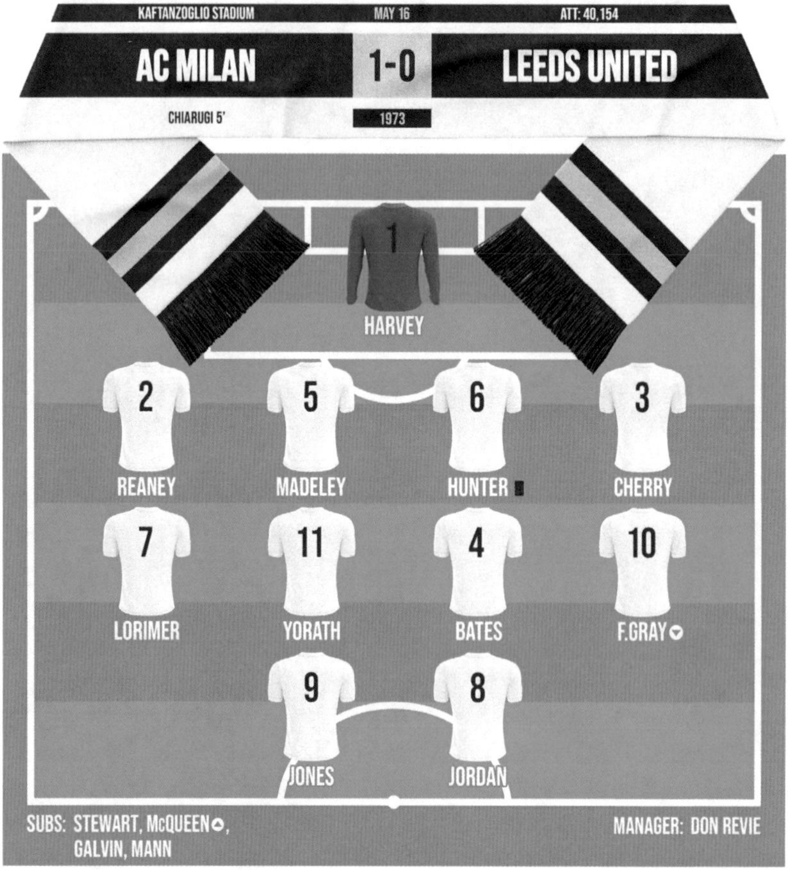

AC MILAN

VECCHI, SABADINI, ZIGNOLI, ANQUILLETTI, TURONE, ROSATO, SOGLIANO, BENETTI, BIGON, RIVERA, CHIARUGI

SUBS: DOLCI, BELLI, CASONE, MAGHERINI, GOLIN

MANAGER: NEREO ROCCO

OUR FORM HEADING IN

LEEDS UTD	6-1	ARSENAL
SUNDERLAND	1-0	LEEDS UTD
BIRMINGHAM	2-1	LEEDS UTD

"[We were] really cheesed off ... but we did have another problem that cropped up. The boss, Don Revie, was going to go to Everton. It hit the papers on the Monday."
- Trevor Cherry

Already distraught after a shock FA Cup Final loss to Sunderland, Leeds United's players were now contemplating life without Don Revie. "We were very upset, obviously, because we were a team ... I was very close to the gaffer," Trevor Cherry said. "He treated everybody like his son. He knew exactly what he wanted, he was very thorough, he looked after the lads ... he was great, he was good fun to be around. You knew he was the boss and you knew what was expected of you. He'd do anything for you, yourself or your family, all he wanted you to do was play football."

Cherry had only played under Revie for one year at that point but others, like Mick Bates, had been in the first-team mix for almost a decade. "We'd do anything for him," Bates said. "When you want to go out and play well, not only for yourself and the team, you want to play well for him as well - now that was the magic. We wanted to play well for him." Talk of Revie's Merseyside move dominated headlines but Leeds United still had a European final to play, a Cup Winners' Cup decider against AC Milan in Greece. "That [talk] obviously distracted the players," Cherry added. "We knew he was going, really, and he told us." Revie was more than a manager to many of the players, as David Harvey said, too. "It was a huge shock ... he was basically a second father to me ... [he was] one of the all-time greats, without question. He was a very, very loyal man. If you did the best you could, he would certainly do the best he could for you."

If the talk about Revie was not distracting enough, Leeds would enter the final missing four of the finest players to ever wear the famous all-white strip. Billy Bremner and Allan Clarke were both suspended in a tense semi-final against Hajduk Split while Johnny Giles and Eddie Gray were injured, making United big underdogs. While Bremner was booked in the goalless draw in Croatia that sealed Leeds' place in the final, Clarke, who scored the only goal of the two-legged tie, was given a straight red card for lashing out in the Elland Road fixture. "There was this centre-half marking me, fouling me all night," Clarke said. "I'm saying to the referee, 'Come on ref'. [He responds], 'Keep playing Allan, keep playing'. So it's 0-0 [at] half time but he's fouling me all the time, this fella. I score, we're 1-0 up and there's about 20 minutes to go and I've dropped deep a bit. And, all of a sudden, he comes in at me and we both go to the ground. Well, I'm getting on my feet before him. Well, I must have had a rush of blood, because I'm up on my feet and as he's getting up, I just go whack. I'm walking, aren't I? I've lost it. First time ever. I don't normally lose it, but I lost it then … from the kick-off I've been saying, 'Come on, ref, give us some protection here.'"

With just a one-goal lead, United produced a resolute display in Split, continuing their impressive defensive record in the competition. Playing in the Cup Winners' Cup for the first time after their 1972 FA Cup Final success, Mick Jones' Elland Road goal gave Leeds a 2-1 aggregate win over Turkey's Ankaragucu in the first round. Goals from Cherry and Jones saw United beat Carl Zeiss Jena of Germany 2-0 in the second round before Revie's men turned on the style in an 8-1 quarter-final drubbing of Rapid Bucharest, six different players scoring over the two legs. AC Milan, meanwhile, booked their spot in the decider with a pair of 1-0 victories against Sparta Prague, Luciano Chiarugi scoring both goals.

United's high-profile absentees meant Frank Gray, just 18, would start in a European final. "I didn't think I'd be playing. I thought I might have had a chance [of] being on the bench because there was a few injuries and suspensions going into the game. I knew I had a chance of being on the bench at least. Then, on the morning before the game, we trained and the boss just walked around and said, 'Listen, you're playing tomorrow night', and that's the first time I had any inclination so, obviously, [I was] very excited and I was looking forward to it immensely."

The suspensions of Bremner and Clarke led to a bizarre scenario, the latter recalled. "In those days, we used to have the home internationals," he said. "The night before [the Milan final], I'm playing for England against Wales in a home international at Wembley." Bremner played for Scotland 24 hours later, against Northern Ireland, and national duty in the build-up to the Greece final saw Giles ruled out. "I had been away with the Irish team in Russia at that time. I got injured ... I couldn't play in it, either, so we had a few players out, definitely," Giles said. It looked like it could be a long night for Leeds as early as the fifth minute, as Chiarugi's free-kick took a deflection and went in. "I can remember the deflection and the goal," Cherry said. "It [conceding early] is the last thing you want in a final or the last thing you want in any game because it gives them the edge ... it gives them the confidence and then we've got to dig in and get a goal back to get on equal terms."

Norman Hunter, getting more and more frustrated with referee Christos Michas, then had a good chance to level proceedings. "I should have scored with a header ... [but] they were just kicking people up in the air inside the box." United's players were positive they should have won a spot-kick when Jones was clattered in the penalty area. "I got chopped to bits in the box, [an AC Milan player] just swiped my legs from underneath me ... Revie was going barmy," Jones said. Bates also remembered the incident. "Mick Jones was brought down, it was a penalty. It was a stone-cold penalty, he [referee] was waving play on."

Harvey said the Leeds players were giving Michas plenty of feedback throughout the match. "Usually when players give abuse to referees, they don't let you away with very much, they'll be down on you like a ton of bricks. But this fella - we were giving him absolute dog's abuse and he was just taking it. He was just taking it." Leeds had to stay positive during the half-time break, though. "You're still thinking that you can win it. We're dominating the game," Hunter said. "You're thinking, 'Oh well, we'll still play. We'll still get out there and we'll still try and get something and that', ... the team we were, we were going to try our best."

But Leeds' best was not good enough to produce an equaliser, with Michas turning down further penalty appeals, one for handball before Peter Lorimer was brought down. "You're thinking, 'What have we got to do here to actually get a penalty or score?'" Bates recalled. The Greek crowd made their displeasure with the officiating known and in the latter stages of the game, the sense of anger grew among the Leeds players.

Hunter had had enough and lost his cool. "I got sent off then. I got frustrated and everything ... I was just thinking, 'What's all this about? We're playing in a top European competition', ... I can remember just feeling so drained ... you look at the lads and they're all down and desperate. I felt it [anger]. I felt it as much as anybody." Hunter and Riccardo Sogliano were red carded for clashing but it made no difference to the outcome as Michas blew for full time with AC Milan in front, ending a frustrating season without silverware for United.

What followed was incredible, the majority of the crowd booing the AC Milan players as United's team were showered with praise. "We were the better team, we felt," Frank Gray said. "We felt we should have won the game." Hunter said being hailed by the crowd was a bizarre experience. "We went on like a lap of honour. You'd have thought we'd won it."

Back in United's changing room, the mood was one of anger and frustration. Frank Gray could not help but think about the game's big moments. "There was some major decisions [that] went against us in the game, two or three very controversial decisions went against us ... the referee who refereed the game, the referee was actually banned for life [Michas was later banned for life by UEFA for match-fixing]. But that didn't do us any good on the night."

"The trouble with any game, once it's over, it's over and you can't go back and say, 'Can we play another 10 minutes?' The more you dwell on it ... you feel more angry," Cherry said. "Obviously, you're disappointed but what can you do? There's nothing you can [do]. You couldn't change anything or relive it in any form," Harvey said. Bates felt like his team did almost as much as they could have. "We performed well. We were the best side. They scored early doors ... but we performed well. Nothing to be ashamed of type of thing - we went out there and performed."

A petition to investigate the result surfaced in later years, gaining more than 10,000 signatures, but nothing came of it. "I'd heard of it ... but it's been and gone. You can't go back and play the game again ... I don't really know. It's happened and it's gone," a resigned Cherry said.

The defender's days at Leeds could have been done after the AC Milan fixture, too, as he revealed a conversation he had with Revie once he was back in England. "Mr. Revie sent for me, I think on the Thursday after we got back from the Cup Winners' Cup Final and he said, 'I'm going to Everton and I'm going to take you with me'. I was only young and green behind the ears and you just say, 'Yeah, fine'. I'd only been at Leeds [for] 12 months. But then Mr. Cussins, the chairman, sorted Don Revie's contract out."

Revie was staying at Leeds. It would prove to be an inspired piece of business.

LOFTUS ROAD | APRIL 27 | ATT: 35,353

QUEENS PARK RANGERS 0-1 LEEDS UNITED

1974

CLARKE 57'

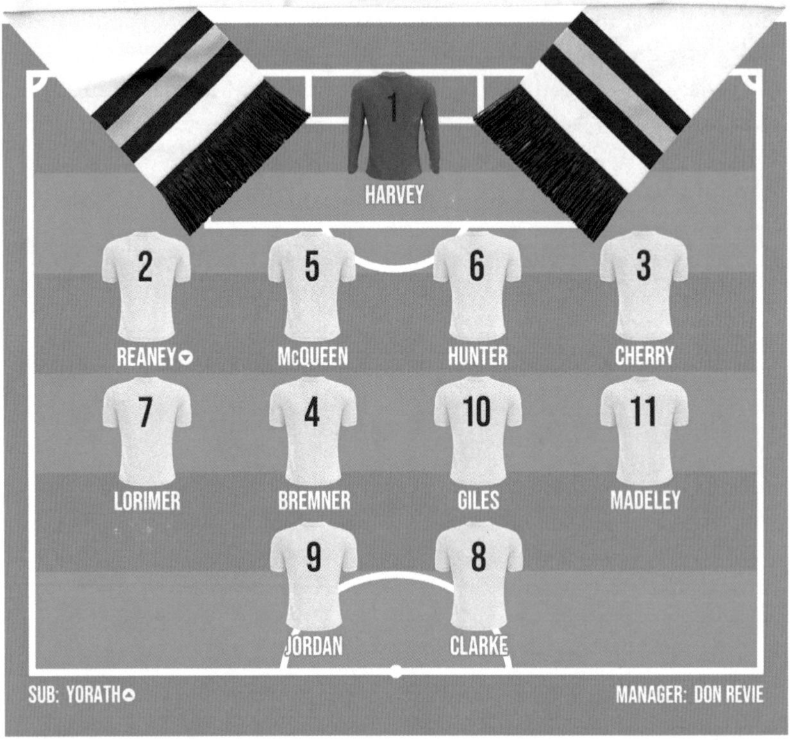

QUEENS PARK RANGERS

PARKES, BUSBY, GILLARD, VENABLES, MANCINI, HAZELL, THOMAS, FRANCIS, LEACH, BOWLES, GIVENS

SUB: UNKNOWN

MANAGER: GORDON JAGO

OUR FORM HEADING IN

LEEDS UTD	3-2	IPSWICH
SHEFF UTD	0-2	LEEDS UTD
LEEDS UTD	0-0	SHEFF UTD

"We couldn't wait for the season to start again because we got dreadful press ... Billy [Bremner] and I got terrible, terrible stick in the paper."
- Johnny Giles

Leeds United were not lacking motivation when the 1973-74 season begun. Sections of the media criticised Johnny Giles and midfield partner Billy Bremner, the former recalling comments about how they "were finished, were done" after the shock FA Cup Final loss to Sunderland. That only fuelled the Irishman throughout an arduous pre-season, though. "We set out next season as a team to prove everybody wrong," Giles said. "It [Sunderland] was really, really hard to take and what most teams would do at that time, they would start blaming each other, a lot of criticism. We stuck together and Don [Revie] stuck together." Allan Clarke had another source of motivation. "I think it goes back [to] when we lost the [FA] Cup Final to Sunderland," he said. "I can remember going up to the banquet in some hotel in London [after the match] and Billy and I were sat together. And I will never forget it, because you don't forget things like this ... [I] looked out the window, I said to Billy, 'Look at that'. A Leeds fan, got their scarf on ... there's about two or three, they weren't kids, they were grown up men. Crying. I said, 'We've let them down'. It hurt me ... it killed me and Bill." Clarke also remembered that at the same function Don Revie was already talking about pre-season. "Our gaffer said, 'You've had a half decent season but when I get you back for pre-season training, rather than four weeks we'll have five weeks and we'll sweat blood'. And Christ, we did." Clarke's strike partner, Mick Jones, also remembered being annoyed by media coverage. "We wanted to prove to people that we weren't finished because we were being written off. John Giles, the best player I ever played with ... John was getting on a bit, he would have been 33 ... we wanted to do another season to prove that we still are a great side."

With pre-season finished, United's players congregated at Elland Road on August 25, 1973, for one of Revie's most famous speeches. "We are playing Everton, first match of the season, 1pm we have a team talk in the players lounge," Clarke said. "Although we were the best for a decade in that First Division, in my day there was probably 10 or 12 teams before you kick a ball [that think], 'We can win this First

Division Championship', so it was much stronger opposition [than it is now] or a more level playing field. We sat there. The gaffer, he said, 'Right, lads, I've had a little thought here in the close season. I'd like you to go through the whole season unbeaten.'" Trevor Cherry said Revie had his sights set on just one trophy. "He had only one focus. We were going to win the league. He set his stall out for that. He told the lads it was purely to win the league. It was his total focus." Jones was quickly able to recite Revie's words. "'Right, lads, everybody's writing us off. We are not done yet. We have not finished. Let's make sure that we're not written off. We're going to go into this season and go through the season without losing a game … I mean that. We are not going to lose a game'. We set off, we were all determined."

Determined they were, Bremner, Giles and Jones scoring in a 3-1 win over Everton that kickstarted a run of seven league wins in a row. Leeds United's record goalscorer, Peter Lorimer, scored six times in that run, while Clarke and Bremner chipped in with four each. Hunter found a 3-0 triumph at Tottenham, secured by three goals in the first 28 minutes, particularly encouraging in that streak. "I can remember going down to London … we beat them 3-0, it was a great performance because Tottenham had a great side." The winning run ended in a 0-0 home draw with Manchester United in late September, a match that would be Eddie Gray's last until April, his only other appearance of the season. A troublesome thigh problem that significantly hampered the Scotsman over the next five years was to blame. "I played in the first eight games of the season [in all competitions] - we never lost a game. I never played on a losing team that year!"

Leeds' focus on the league was helped by the fact they did not make major runs in any of the cup competitions, bowing out in the second round of the League Cup, the third round of the UEFA Cup and the fifth round of the FA Cup. United thrived in the league, though, Jones getting the only goal in a 1-0 home win over title rivals Liverpool. "Bill Shankly and our gaffer, they're not only rival managers, they were great friends," Clarke said. "And they used to ring each other every Sunday … I remember 'Shanks' had a half decent side at Liverpool. And I remember Shanks … he was quoted in one of the papers which I read. He said, 'If somebody doesn't hurry up and beat Leeds United, they'll have it won by Christmas." Leeds had won nine and drawn three going into a late October match at Manchester City and Cherry remembered Revie's team talk like it was yesterday. "I can see his team talk now. He basically said, 'I'm going to win the league. If you lads aren't going to do it for me, I'm going to go out and buy players who are'. Looking back, it was just a wind-up to make sure we went out and won." Leeds triumphed 1-0 thanks to a goal from Mick Bates and Cherry said it was an example of Revie's great "man-management".

A 4-1 win over West Ham United at Elland Road followed, Jones scoring twice, and when Leeds went to Ipswich Town, who would ultimately finish fourth, and won 3-0 in early December, Revie's Leeds were the talk of the nation. Fascination over the club's unbeaten league record continued to build, as Jones remembered. "We went 10 matches without losing, 15, 20 and everybody's sitting up now, all the press." Eddie Gray's injury gave him a new perspective on his club, too. "Sometimes when you play on a side, you don't actually realise how good they are until you watch them play." What particularly struck him was how the side worked for each other. "Discipline, defensively - I'm not just talking about the defenders. I'm talking about players working hard, high up the pitch to win the ball back ... if a team made breaks at us, we could have three defenders back and they may have four or five but our defenders were good enough to cope with it. [We had great] creative ability, scoring goals. You just looked back and thought, 'What a team. A great team'. It was great to watch at times."

Even when Leeds were not at their best, they found a way to get a point, Joe Jordan scoring late in a 1-1 draw at Birmingham City in late December, while David Harvey made a string of saves in a goalless draw at Everton. And Cherry fondly remembered a second-half goal he scored against Chelsea that helped the unbeaten run continue. "I scored a diving header ... I tended not to go in the other half when we're winning three and four nil. In the Leeds team, you could get a cigar out and sit back and watch, let Johnny Giles do his thing and that. When we were losing, it was a bit different ... you would battle a bit more. But I scored a diving header and that made it one each for us and that kept our roll going."

Jones and Jordan got the goals in a 2-0 win at Old Trafford but as the run continued, Harvey admitted he found all the talk about an undefeated league campaign an unnecessary distraction. "You don't feel as though you're invincible … the media and people in general, the chat was, 'Can they possibly do it?' Well, you've enough worries and enough problems and enough things that can go wrong without even thinking along those lines and as people really started to talk about going the whole season [unbeaten], sure enough we finished up getting beat." February 23, 1974, was the day, Leeds United's 29-match unbeaten run to start a league season ending at Stoke City. "We were two up. Two up! They kept coming, they came back at us and they ended up beating us," Hunter said. Stoke's 3-2 win came against a Leeds side missing Jones, Eddie Gray, Gordon McQueen and Paul Reaney and the striker said if everyone stayed fit, things could have been very different. "I think if we'd have all been fit, we might have gone through the season without losing a game and that takes some doing."

Leeds wobbled after that first defeat and although they followed successive draws with a 1-0 home success against Manchester City, Revie's men lost their next three to Liverpool, Burnley and West Ham United respectively. A response was desperately needed at home to Derby County and Lorimer and Bremner netted in a 2-0 victory. Lorimer would prove a key figure in the run-in, netting a double in Leeds' next win, a 2-0 triumph over Sheffield United, and he was on target again in a 3-2 success over Ipswich Town just five days later. "Peter's goal scoring record for the football club … unbelievable. Great finisher. Ice running through his veins, Peter," Eddie Gray said. "He wouldn't worry about walking on to take a penalty kick in the last minute of a European Cup Final or [an FA] Cup Final. He'd just think the ball's going in the back of the net … his goalscoring record will never be beaten at this football club."

On the same day as that Ipswich win, Liverpool were held to a goalless draw at home to Everton. That meant that Leeds would be assured of the title with one match to play if Arsenal went to Anfield in a mid-week fixture and won and they did just that, starting celebrations in West Yorkshire. Leeds United were the champions of England. "To win the league, that's the ultimate. It is the ultimate because it's the best league in the world. It was then and it is now, the Premier League," said Jones, while the sense of achievement hit Harvey quickly. "We'd won the league without actually playing which was unusual … [I felt] just sheer pride of having done something. It's monumental. There's great players who play for 20 years and never get anywhere near winning something like that. So you just feel privileged and so proud of the fact that you've been able to pull it off. And, as a side, we'd been together for quite some time so it wasn't a case of it was a new team that had been built or a team that had been rebuilt. It was a team that had been coming together for so long and we'd achieved something quite remarkable."

"I probably got more satisfaction from winning that particular league than any other trophy," Giles said. "That was a great year for Leeds. A brilliant way to fight back [from Sunderland] and win the championship. It was brilliant." For Hunter, the way Leeds won the league was just as good as lifting the trophy. "The manner in which we won it, I think it was very good, because the way we played, we played with no fear. We were way and above the best team. People had matured. They were at probably the height [of their careers] … you can't put it into words, how you feel. You just love the club and you look at these players and the bond - the bond is still there now."

One last assignment was in store for Leeds, as the champions travelled to London to play Queens Park Rangers. "We were champions as we ran out and to be fair to QPR, they applauded that," Clarke said of the pre-match guard of honour given to Revie's men. A huge crowd attended, boosted by the thousands of Leeds fans that travelled to see a slice of history. Harvey made a string of important saves in the second half but it was Clarke who got the only goal in a match that had a bit of a party-like atmosphere. "I remember 'Sniffer's goal … we were always comfortable in that game," Cherry said. "It was a bit of a carnival-type [atmosphere]. Leeds could ping it around. There probably wasn't the physical presence there might have been if we needed three points … winning the league with Leeds United, it doesn't get any better than that, really." Cherry also recalled Revie letting "us have a drink on the train" on the way back to Leeds. "The atmosphere was great. The whole trip was because we knew we'd won the title."

Leeds were so good in that 1973-74 campaign for many reasons, with the Bremner-Giles partnership one of them. "He [Giles] had total and utter belief in himself. Not in any sort of big-headedness or anything like that, [he] just totally and utterly believed that he was a good player," Hunter said. "I used to get the ball. There was an Irishman [Giles] and a Scotsman [Bremner]. If I gave the ball to the Irishman, I got a bollocking off the Scotsman [laughs], and if I would give it to the Scotsman, I would get a bollocking off the Irishman. But 'Gilesy', he was always there. How he did it, I don't know. I used to win the ball [and hear], 'Yes, Norm', and I'd look and he'd be there. Then I'd move somewhere else, win the ball [and hear], 'Yes, Norm', and he'd be there again." Giles said Bremner was the perfect midfield partner. "We got on very well. We complemented each other. We played together. We would talk on the pitch. 'I move there, you move there'. We just had a good understanding of each other and we complemented each other."

The goals of Jones, Clarke and Lorimer were very important, too, with Jones finishing as the club's top scorer in both title-winning seasons under Revie. But it was Hunter who would win the inaugural Professional Footballers' Association Player of the Year award, the defender rightly recognised for a tremendous 1973-74 campaign. "That's something that is very, very special with it being the first one," he said. "I can remember the run-in. They were talking about myself [and Liverpool's] Ian Callaghan. Well, 'Cally' was a great player but squeaky clean. A brilliant professional and everything. The gaffer said to me, 'Don't worry. You'll win it. You'll win it'. I said, 'Nah', … I can remember going there … that was a great moment for me because when you think about it, there's only been six defenders in the whole time that [have won it]. I think there was myself, Colin Todd, John Terry, Gary Pallister, [Virgil] van Dijk and Paul McGrath. I'm in good company … I can't explain to people what it was like to just be part of Leeds United and football. It's something I always wanted to do all my life and you get the chance. I thought, 'Well, if it's down to hard work, I'm not blowing this one'. Then you get to play with these players and you get to train and you go all over the world and all you do is play football. Unbelievable! It's not a real life!"

Harvey said consistency was crucial in Leeds' success. "[We had] just so many good players who were performing just about every week at a very, very high level. Normally, a side will have two or three players each game who are not on top of it and the rest will pull them [through] or carry them through and then the following week, it would be another two or three different players who maybe weren't performing at their highest level but in that particular season, just about everybody in every game was really at it … the whole team was at such a high level so consistently." Hunter echoed the goalkeeper's thoughts, too. "I think if you look at it and analyse it, everybody in their position was exceptional. And then you put that together as a team. There's certain people that will get the applause and the credit and everything else … like the gaffer used to say, 'We defend together, we attack together'. It was the overall team that was brilliant."

Frank Gray felt that Revie's decision to give his players more freedom was extremely beneficial. "They were all very, very talented players and they just hit form at the right time, all came together at the right time … the 73-74 team, it probably was the most consistent season they had as a group. They were fantastic to watch, they played some great football … I think the shackles came off a little bit, I think they were allowed to play with a little more freedom than they had previously. I think the manager realised the talent that the players had … the manager was a little bit more cautious in seasons before that."

And the QPR win was Revie's last match in charge of Leeds, as he moved on to take the England job. The level of respect his players still have for him is immediately evident and Giles, when asked about the manager's greatest strength, had multiple answers. "I think attention to detail and never getting carried away with success, always starting from scratch and [being] demanding of the players, creating a good atmosphere and obviously getting great players into the club and making great players like Norman Hunter and Paul Madeley and Paul Reaney and Eddie Gray and Peter Lorimer, who were brought up in the club as young players, coaching them with Syd Owen and Les Cocker and never getting carried away. Always the next game … I had great respect for him [Don] and a great admiration for him as one of the top managers."

CAMP NOU | APRIL 23 | ATT: 110,000

BARCELONA 1-1 LEEDS UNITED

CLARES 69' | 1975 | LORIMER 7'

SUBS: LETHEREN, E.GRAY, HAMPTON, HARRIS, REANEY

MANAGER: JIMMY ARMFIELD

BARCELONA

SADURNI, MURINHO, GALLEGO, BIANQUETI, DE LA CRUZ, NEESKENS, REXACH, HEREDIA, CRUYFF, ASENSI, CLARES

SUBS: RIFE, OTHERS UNKNOWN

MANAGER: RINUS MICHELS

OUR FORM HEADING IN

LEEDS UTD	2-1	IPSWICH
ARSENAL	1-2	LEEDS UTD
LEEDS UTD	2-1	BARCELONA

"The board turned down the recommendation so I was left in a situation of being turned down for a job that I hadn't applied for. Then, of course, they made the decision to hire Brian Clough."
- Johnny Giles

In Germany watching the 1974 FIFA World Cup, Johnny Giles picked up a newspaper. "I read in an English paper over there that Don [Revie] was leaving. I didn't know that and I thought, 'I'd better go back', because my contract was up, to fix up my contract before he left." Revie's glorious stint in charge of Leeds United was over, the legendary manager taking on the England job, and he had a shock for Giles when he returned to Yorkshire. "When I went back, he [Revie] said, 'I'm recommending you', recommending me for the job, which was a total surprise. I had no intentions [of managing]. I just wanted to get back playing and that took me by surprise ... it came very unexpectedly to me when Don was recommending me for the job. The board turned it down, they appointed Brian Clough and, as far as I was concerned, that was the end of it." It was not the end of it for Giles, though, as one of the most tumultuous periods in the club's history unfolded as they attempted to defend their league title. "It was an unusual appointment, to be quite honest," the Irishman added. "Brian Clough had been very, very critical of the Leeds team for years. We were just league champions and he did have a meeting with the players ... he said, 'Right, all the medals, you can get them and throw them in that effing bin over there.'"

There was more to the infamous meeting where Clough questioned the merits of United's success, too, with Eddie Gray singled out. The 26-year-old was unsure about the future of his career, with a lingering thigh injury causing him major problems. "I was going through this injury period and he [Clough] said to me, 'If you'd have been a horse, I'd have shot you', ... a few of the boys took offence at that, nearly them all." Gray said he "laughed" at the comment and knew it was intended as "an off-the-cuff remark", but his teammates were not pleased. "They all knew I was disappointed with how things were going at that time. I was just waiting to hear from the Football League insurers about packing the game in, basically." The Scotsman suffered "a bad thigh injury when I was about 15, 16" and estimates it "cost me about three or four hundred games". "The thigh injury was always a problem ... I learned how to play with it." He picked his moment before responding to Clough's jibe. "I went to see him after it, because I wasn't frightened of him. I said to him, 'A strange comment coming from somebody like you, that'. He said to me, 'What do you mean?' I said, 'You had to finish the game through injury'. He didn't know what to say to me. He looked at me and went, 'Oh, right'. I said, 'Don't forget it'. That was it. I think that was his way, though. He thought he was being funny." Clough's ill-fated 44-day stint in charge of Leeds United was off to a terrible start.

Replacing Revie was an impossible job and the next man in was always up against it, according to Frank Gray. "He [Don] was a massive influence on my career as he was [for] all the players at that time. It was a big disappointment when he went but I think it was on the cards for a season or two that something like that might happen. It wasn't altogether a massive shock but a big disappointment … it was almost impossible to follow him. The way he [Clough] reacted when he came into the club, that was his biggest problem, what he said to the players, experienced internationals who'd just won the league championship, that they could throw all their medals in the bin and stuff like that. It's not the ideal way to get off on the right footing with a group of players like that and I think from that moment, his days could have been numbered." Clough signed Frank Gray later in his career, the pair winning the European Cup with Nottingham Forest in 1980. "I spoke to him later in life and he [Clough] realised at that time that he'd made a bit of a mistake. He should have just let things calm down and, okay, do things his way, but over a longer period of time."

More trouble was around the corner for Clough, who watched captain Billy Bremner sent off for fighting with Liverpool's Kevin Keegan in the 1974 Charity Shield, an incident that saw the midfielder hit with an 11-game ban. "Billy getting sent off with Keegan, the big ban … it did not go down well with him [Clough], because he always wanted the players to be disciplined," Eddie Gray said. Liverpool won that match on penalties and without Revie and Bremner, Leeds made a terrible start to their title defence, winning just one of their first six league matches, scoring only four goals in the process. Results were poor and the morale was shocking. "The way he [Clough] treated the Leeds lads was very, very bad. Really poor," Mick Bates said. "He would do everything to aggravate the team. He'd be late. He'd tell us to, 'Put your suits on', [and] he'd turn up in his tracksuit … at Elland Road, the lads despised him." And a League Cup tie at Huddersfield Town would be Clough's last match in charge, the manager sacked after a 1-1 draw. A board meeting saw Giles emerge as the preferred candidate. "There was a board meeting, who voted for me three to two to have the job," he said. "I turned that down because I thought, 'If there's two against me before I start'. I wasn't keen on the job anyway … I was only 33 at that time. I would have probably had to finish playing. I didn't want to finish playing, to be quite honest, so it wasn't a disappointment to me … the vote was three [to] two for me after Brian Clough left and I said, 'No, I don't want it'."

Caretaker Maurice Lindley stepped up to guide Leeds through their first European Cup assignment, a 5-3 aggregate win over FC Zurich. Allan Clarke scored three goals in the tie and Jimmy Armfield took over from Lindley ahead of a second-round meeting with Ujpest Dozsa of Hungary. Duncan McKenzie, one of three Clough signings, was sent off in the 15th minute, but goals from Peter Lorimer and Gordon McQueen gave Leeds a terrific 2-1 away win. Bremner returned to European football in the second leg and scored, Leeds progressing with a 3-0 success. League form picked up under Armfield, too, but the former Bolton boss saw his side at their best in Europe. "We weren't the same after Don left but I think we got together as a group when we came to the European Cup matches," Giles said. "We didn't do all that well in the league. I think the Brian Clough situation and everything else broke up a bit of morale in the team, to be quite honest, but we got together for the European Cup matches." Giles was also told by Armfield he struggled "in heavy going" ahead of one fixture, according to Bates, an incident that saw many of the squad lose faith in their manager. "The manager didn't think Johnny could play in the mud … ridiculous!" Bates said. "Players are thinking, 'How can our manager think that?' … The whole credibility [took a hit]."

A quarter-final against Anderlecht was next up for Leeds and a 3-0 win at Elland Road in the first leg followed, Joe Jordan, McQueen and Lorimer on the scoresheet, with Bremner scoring a delightful chip in a 1-0 triumph in Belgium that booked a last-four meeting with Spanish giants Barcelona. "It was massive, it was a huge game," Frank Gray recalled. "We felt we could go and beat them, although, at that time, they had a top side, Johan Cruyff and [Johan] Neeskens and all the top, top players in their side. I think they were favourites in most people's books … certainly everybody outside Leeds thought they'd beat us but we were confident, we knew we were a decent side." Form was not on Leeds' side heading into the first leg in Yorkshire, United on a seven-match winless run and Armfield changed things up. "Jimmy Armfield left me out. I didn't play … I wasn't very happy," said Norman Hunter, while Lorimer and Trevor Cherry were also on the sidelines.

More than 50,000 fans crammed into Elland Road and witnessed a United masterclass as Bremner fired Leeds in front in the ninth minute. The chances kept coming but Leeds were unable to add to their lead before Juan Manuel Asensi drew Barcelona level. Leeds deserved to lead by at least one goal going into the second leg and Clarke stepped up in their time of need. "It was late on, I volleyed one in from about 12 yards and that turned out to be the winner," he said. Eddie Gray also impressed on the big stage and insisted his side "should have beaten them [by] three or four … we were in a different class to them". Frank Gray said Barcelona's goal left him with a nagging sense of doubt. "We were a bit disappointed at Elland Road to only win the match 2-1. It's not the biggest lead to take somewhere like Barcelona, where they only need to score one goal to go through. The away goal killed us a little bit. We felt we were dominant enough to win by another couple of goals, [but] we didn't … they would have been happy with the result, I think. They would have been delighted with only losing 2-1." Still, Leeds were one match away from being just the second English side to reach the European Cup Final and they held the lead.

Crucial to any chances of United's progression would be nullifying the impact of the outstanding Cruyff, who was a threat during the first leg and was one of the finest footballers on the planet. A man-marking job was required and Armfield decided on Cherry. "Man-marking - [the job] was basically just to keep him quiet … he [Armfield] told us the day before, I think. You just gear yourself up for it," Cherry said. "If you're a good professional, you're never afraid of playing against anybody. You're always wary of how good they are and obviously

Cruyff was up there in the top drawer." Cherry was one of three Leeds inclusions, Lorimer and Hunter also recalled as Reaney, Eddie Gray and an injured Giles made way. "I broke a rib on the Saturday, so I couldn't play in the second match at Barcelona," Giles said.

A huge crowd could have unsettled Leeds as they ran out, but Frank Gray said that by now, United were used to these sort of fixtures. "110,000 ... fantastic atmosphere ... at that time, it was the biggest crowd I'd played in front of. But most of the lads had experienced Wembley and 100,000 so it wasn't anything that new to them. Okay, it was away from home in a foreign country, but we had a lot of experienced players in the side, Bremner, Norman Hunter, Paul Madeley, they'd been and seen it and done it all. So they were a big help ... [for] the younger players in the side like myself, Joe Jordan, Gordon McQueen, who'd only been in the side a few years. We felt confident we could go there and get a goal and we felt if we did get a goal, there's every chance we could go through." Clarke was not as convinced. "The second leg at the Nou Camp, we knew we had to score first to stand a chance." Lorimer did just that, though, netting in the seventh minute. "I remember it vividly," Frank Gray said. "Dave Stewart was in goal because David Harvey was injured. He's knocked a long ball, a long goal kick, up top, Joe Jordan's got up fantastically well, flicked it on and Peter's got in behind the defence, right side of the box and smashed one into the top corner. That was a fantastic start for us ... it was massive for us. The confidence that we did have obviously grew a lot stronger from that point ... it must have been a bitter blow for them to concede at that stage."

If Barcelona, now two goals behind on aggregate, were to qualify, Cruyff needed to take control, but Cherry did not let him. "I just had one of those games - everything suited me against Barcelona. I don't think he was up for it," Cherry said. "He didn't like the physical presence of Leeds. I did [go through him early], to be honest, yeah. He's a great player but he just had one of those games that you hope he does ... he never really got going, which obviously suited us ... that was my job, to win the ball. In those days, you could tackle a lot stronger than you can in the modern game and you could tackle from behind and things." The hosts threw everything at Leeds in the second half, though. "David

Stewart in goal had made some really good saves that night and we felt comfortable," Frank Gray said. But that was all about to change, Manuel Clares nodding in a 69th-minute free-kick to level proceedings before McQueen was sent off for losing his cool and lashing out at the goalscorer in a separate incident. With the home crowd roaring, Leeds were, all of a sudden, up against it. "Big Gordon McQueen lost it ... [it was] backs to the wall. We battled and battled," said Clarke, while Cherry recalled a "lively last 20 minutes". "Leeds, if you look at the side, we had a team that could battle and fight and we'd got the goal," Cherry added. "Leeds United were good, we've got another gear, you've got to do a bit more defending, you've got to cover a bit more, you've got to be a bit more aware than perhaps you were before. You're not coasting against Barcelona. With 10 men [it] isn't easy, obviously." Hunter, full of praise for Lorimer's strike, said even when Leeds were defending deep, he still thought they might score. "You don't mind battling away and defending when you know you've got somebody in your team that can bang a goal in like Peter did."

Giles, watching on from the sidelines, remembered a "nerve wracking" finale, as Stewart made a string of late saves to ensure things remained level. But the final whistle was not far away as United's players were hit with feelings of relief and elation. "We got there ... we're thinking, 'We're in the European Cup [Final] ... it's unbelievable,'" said Clarke, while Cherry could reflect on a job well done. "Absolutely delighted, [we had] done the job in Barcelona ... not being big-headed about it [but] I had one of those games you dream about. Everything went well for me and Cruyff had the opposite, he didn't get out of second gear. I think he got in a bit of a mood with himself." Frank Gray remembered the "little pocket" of Leeds fans making "themselves heard" and said he was just so proud of his teammates. "Immensely proud. It was a great achievement to [make] the European Cup Final and I was lucky enough to do it with a great bunch of lads like that." His feelings of pride were shared by his brother, Eddie. "They were obviously a team with a big reputation, with the likes of Johan Cruyff and Neeskens and all the other players they had but our players coped very well."

Frank Gray remembered McQueen being "distraught at the end of the game" because he knew he would miss the final but for the rest of

United's squad, it was time to celebrate. "They fly back after matches now but in those days, we used to fly back the day after so we'd fly back on the Thursday," Clarke said. "Before the match … Billy said, 'Win, lose or draw, we aren't going to bed tonight'. I said, 'Fine'. And I've got my brother-in-law, one of my wife's brothers, he was on business not far from Barcelona … I did say to him, 'Look, after the match, come back to the hotel and you know, you can have a drink with us'. Because he was going to fly back on business, somewhere in Spain … we get back to the hotel, my brother-in-law is there … Mick Jones didn't play that game, he's come [over]. Billy could have a drink but after two or three, he's drunk, but he won't get any worse … we had to get up about 9am to have breakfast and then we get into the airport. So we're having a drink and that, anyway, it gets to about four in the morning and I look around and I'm just having a drink with Mick and my brother-in-law and I see Billy. He's gone up the stairs! He's gone … then as we arrived back at Leeds-Bradford Airport, our wives met us and we were in a right state … been up all night drinking … but we're in a European Cup Final!"

BAYERN MUNICH

MAIER, DURNBERGER, ANDERSSON, SCHWARZENBECK, BECKENBAUER, ROTH, TORSTENSSON, ZOBEL, MULLER, HOENESS, KAPELLMANN

SUBS: S.WEISS, WUNDER, RUMMENIGGE, G.WEISS, ROBL

MANAGER: DETTMAR CRAMER

OUR FORM HEADING IN

TOTTENHAM	4-2	LEEDS UTD
WOLVES	1-1	LEEDS UTD
BARCELONA	1-1	LEEDS UTD

"He [Don Revie] wanted to be champions of Europe, win the European Cup ... he wanted to build a team on a par with Real Madrid."
- Allan Clarke

Don Revie's desire to see Leeds United win the European Cup was a major source of motivation for everyone at the club, even after the manager had left Elland Road. Revie was in charge of England as Leeds went on an exciting European run in the 1974-75 season, but he had not been forgotten. Playing on Norman Hunter's mind in the build-up to a European Cup Final against Bayern Munich, the biggest match in Leeds United's history, was a message Revie once gave his players. "[Revie said], 'We're going to wear the white shirt and we're going to be the next Real Madrid and we're going to win that European Cup.'" Revie's Leeds played just once in Europe's premier club competition, with the tournament exclusively for title-winning sides in those days. That 1969-70 campaign ended in a semi-final defeat to Celtic but this Leeds team were older, wiser and raring to go. It would not be an easy task against Bayern Munich but Frank Gray recalled a major buzz around Leeds in the preparation. "We knew we were going to have a massive following in Paris," he said. "We knew the buzz in the city. Leeds is only a one-club city, so it's not as if they're splitting in two, like Liverpool or Manchester, blue and red or whatever. Leeds is one city with one football club and the whole city was buzzing and looking forward to the final. We knew Bayern Munich had just won it ... we knew how tough a game it was going to be with the players they had in their side, the [Franz] Beckenbauers, the [Gerd] Mullers ... we knew it was going to be a tough game but we felt we had enough players in the side who were good enough to win it."

The exact make-up of the United side would be the source of much consternation as Jimmy Armfield pondered how to include the fit-again Johnny Giles and replace the suspended Gordon McQueen. He eventually settled on his side, bringing in Giles and Paul Reaney in place of Trevor Cherry and the banned Scot, announcing his team the day before kick-off. "Personally, it's probably the biggest disappointment of my career," Cherry said. "I still think to this day Jimmy didn't pick the team that had got the best chance of winning the game but I would do because I wasn't playing. I took that very badly,

I must be honest. I don't like sitting on a bench anyway, it wasn't my thing ... I automatically thought I'd play in the final. I never thought of not playing. It's easy for me to say it now and it's a long time gone, but I'd earned the right to play in the final ... Jimmy Armfield told us [the team] in front of everybody in the dressing room. He did say before that, 'I don't want any retribution or anything until after we've played', which I understood ... I didn't say anything." Cherry believed that Syd Owen, a member of United's support staff, had a lot to do with the decision and felt the fact he was bought from Huddersfield Town in 1972 did not work in his favour. "Syd was the old school. Even before the final, Syd didn't like Don Revie buying players ... he felt just the lads had been together for 10 years and I was an incomer, if you like ... Jimmy Armfield went for the old team, if you like, just on a sentimental thing because they'd been together for 10 years and all that." Eddie Gray was also left out of Armfield's starting line-up, though. "I was disappointed. I thought he should have played me that night. I think after the game, I think he thought he should have," Gray said.

While Bayern were trying to defend their title, there was a nagging feeling it might have been the last chance for an iconic Leeds team to win more European silverware to add to their two Inter-Cities Fairs Cups. "The team was breaking up," Mick Jones said. "I was finished ... John [Giles] was virtually finished, the team was breaking up." Giles said that knowing he was about to play his last game for Leeds gave him a strange feeling. "It was a peculiar match for me in many ways, to be quite honest. It was my last match for Leeds United and I think I knew I was on my way. I knew I was on my way before I played the match." Allan Clarke recalled a "confident" feeling amongst his teammates on matchday, but "not overconfident", while Frank Gray said he felt nerves but nothing unusual. "I think everybody who goes into a game of that magnitude and says they're not feeling nervous is telling lies because you've got to have a little bit of nerves in a game that size. But nerves is all part of the game and it's how you handle them. It's like anybody who plays any top sport ... yeah, you are nervous before the game but once you get out there and you know what you're doing, the nerves seem to go away." Like Jones, Mick Bates travelled to Paris but was not among the matchday squad and he said he could feel the nerves from Bayern's players. "I was with the lads ... but obviously you've got a suit on … they were lining up as they do, before they come out in the tunnel and they were frightened," Bates said. "Bayern Munich, I saw on their faces, they were frightened. They had fear in their eyes, really. I thought, 'Well, there you go.'"

"I remember being in the final, stood there with the national anthem being played and who's in the stand? The gaffer [Revie]. [He has] come to watch. All of us were looking straight at him … I wanted to win that desperately because he said this, 'We'll win it one day,'" Hunter said of the final minutes before kick-off. Both sides did not hold back in the early stages, Bayern's Bjorn Andersson forced off after a challenge from Terry Yorath. "I think it was the norm for that era," Frank Gray said. "Both teams were trying to, not intimidate the other, but try and prove they were the strongest and that was important in those games, the first 15, 20 minutes of any game in that time - physicality played a big part in that." Bayern sat back and it played into United's hands, with Armfield's men having good claims for a penalty after Beckenbauer appeared to handle the ball. Referee Michel Kitabdjian turned down their appeals, though, and he again declined to point to the spot in a flashpoint that still angers the Leeds players.

"I've got it, I'm coming in … inside left position, into the box. And Beckenbauer's with me but then I was going to just clip it round and I fancied my chances to score," Clarke said. "But he just took me [out] … it was a certain pen … I'm thinking, 'That's a joke'. I mean, it was a certain penalty." Hunter could not believe his eyes. "Allan Clarke was kicked up in the air off Beckenbauer. The most blatant penalty you've ever seen in your life … we all shouted, 'Penalty!' … If we get a penalty, little 'Gilesy' - he would've scored standing on his head … that would've changed the complex of the game." Eddie Gray dubbed it as "a definite penalty kick", while Cherry said he was getting flashbacks. "You start thinking about AC Milan [in 1973] again," he said. "There were some decisions that could've gone for us and they didn't do … they always seem to happen in finals, which is not exactly great."

Uli Hoeness went off injured before the first half ended, too, as Leeds were forced to settle for being goalless at the break. "In those days, you came out together at the start of the match and you also did after half time," Clarke said. "Now, we go into the dressing room 0-0. The bell goes from the referee's room - the bell goes in each dressing room. So we're out, it seems an eternity we're waiting in the tunnel for Beckenbauer to bring his lot out. It seemed ages. But they eventually come and I tell you what, I looked at Beckenbauer's face, I looked at Muller's face, their striker, Sepp Maier [goalkeeper] and you can read expressions. They could not believe it was 0-0. They could not believe they were drawing with us."

When play resumed, Maier was called into action to keep out a Billy Bremner effort before Leeds, finally, got the goal they deserved, Peter Lorimer lashing in a volley. "I just remember jumping up and thinking, 'Yes!' … the ball dropped to Peter, bang!" said Hunter, while Eddie Gray, Cherry and Bates all remembered celebrating on the bench. "The referee turned away and was off to the centre circle," Hunter added. Thousands of Leeds fans in the French capital roared in delight but Kitabdjian then made his way towards the linesman and Eddie Gray was hit with a sinking feeling, admitting he thought the decision was going to be "reversed". Giles was trying to think what might have been wrong with the goal. "I was a player on the pitch, I couldn't see anything wrong with it." There was the suggestion Bremner was coming back from an offside position when Lorimer struck the ball, but was he interfering with play? "There was no way he was interfering with play," Eddie Gray said, while Bates was equally adamant. "Billy might have been fractionally offside but was he interfering with play? No. That ball went into the top left-hand corner. Goal."

Anxiety among United's players and fans grew with every second of suspense before Kitabdjian, after consulting with his linesman, ruled the goal out for offside. "It was a perfect goal … I'm sick as a parrot and I couldn't believe it," said Clarke, while Cherry felt it was a bad sign. "You think, 'It's not going to be our night again', … when things go against you like that." Yet for many of United's players, they could not think like that, given it was still goalless in a European Cup Final they were dominating. "You can't think about that [decision] at the time because you're playing football and you're trying to win the game … you're just in the game," said Hunter, while Giles tried to stay positive. "We were playing well at that particular stage, really well."

But Bayern would soon take the lead, Franz Roth shooting through Paul Madeley's legs with a goal that came against the run of play. "It went through Paul's legs, now he didn't mean to go through Paul's legs ... you need a bit of luck," Bates said. Eddie Gray was thrown on in response but Muller soon wrapped up the German side's victory after turning Hans-Josef Kappellmann's cross in. "I remember me trying to get out and close the winger down and I tried to slide and get a touch to it. He just beat me to it and crossed it ... that was finished then," Hunter said. Frank Gray agreed. "You go one down and then you do your best to try and get back in the game but the second killed us. To go 2-0 down was too much to ask for us but we did feel we should never have been in that position. For three quarters of the game, we were the better side."

Incensed at what was unfolding, Leeds fans began showing their displeasure and started rioting as what should have been the club's greatest night turned into a nightmare, confirmed by the final whistle. "I got the football [at the] final whistle. I picked the football up and I thought, 'That's mine, I'm having that,'" Hunter said. "Then I thought, 'Well, I'll get the lads to sign it', ... and Terry Yorath came over and 'Taff's tears [were] streaming down his face. I looked at this football and then I got angry. I got the red mist. I looked at this football and I kicked it. I kicked it right in the stand ... I bashed it up in the stand because Taff was crying, tears streaming down his face." Frank Gray remembered a "very, very, very quiet changing room" after the final whistle as the sense of missed opportunity lingered. "We were the better team. I felt that some of the decisions were a bit dubious, to say the least," Eddie Gray said.

Adding to the ill-feeling was the fact Leeds had not been able to win the trophy Revie wanted so badly, Hunter insistent it made the loss "more disappointing". "Also the way we had played - and then you come back and the press are there [saying], 'Oh, they were taught a lesson', and things like that ... you're thinking, 'Well, if we'd have got our noses in front, I don't think that they might have scored.'" Frank Gray felt that Leeds deserved to win, too. "We felt on the balance of the game we should have won. We felt we had the better side on the night and if Peter's goal was allowed, I think we'd have gone on and won the game comfortably, to be honest, because at that stage we were on top."

While Leeds returned home empty-handed, United fans still sing 'We are the champions, champions of Europe' at matches, in homage to that great 1975 side. Asked if that meant anything to him, Clarke had a simple response. "When they sing that, it makes me proud."

Peter Lorimer celebrates the goal that wasn't. Photo: Andrew Varley Picture Agency

THE HAWTHORNS | MAY 18 | ATT: 23,118

WEST BROM 2-0 LEEDS UNITED

REGIS 51', MACKENZIE 87'

1982

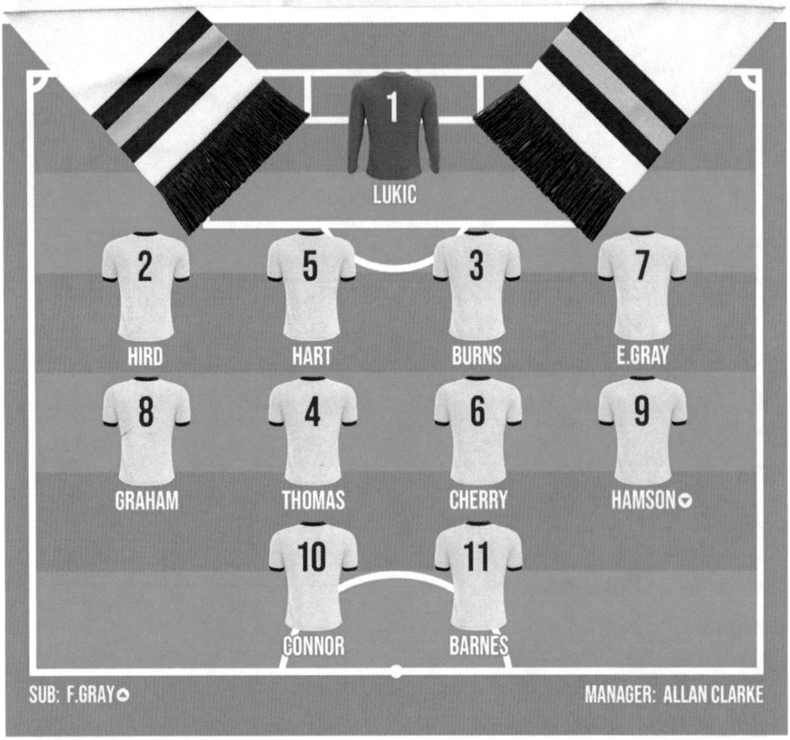

WEST BROM

GODDEN, BATSON, STATHAM, BENNETT, WILE, WEBB, COWDRILL, BROWN, REGIS, OWEN, MACKENZIE

SUB: UNKNOWN

MANAGER: RONNIE ALLEN

OUR FORM HEADING IN

LEEDS UTD	2-1	BRIGHTON
LEEDS UTD	3-3	BIRMINGHAM
TOTTENHAM	2-1	LEEDS UTD

"We probably got to the stage where some of the players didn't realise what it should mean to play for Leeds United ... that's my opinion."
- Trevor Cherry

Standards were slipping at Leeds United and the players could feel it. The end result was an unfamiliar relegation dogfight in the 1981-82 season, one that went down to the wire. Just Trevor Cherry and brothers Eddie and Frank Gray remained from the famous Don Revie side as legendary striker Allan Clarke, now in charge, tried to steer Leeds to safety. He would be the first of three United heroes in the 1980s to try his hand as manager and Clarke had an immediate impact, lifting Leeds from second bottom to ninth in the 1980-81 season after being lured across from Barnsley in September. Goals were at a premium, though, Leeds scoring a league-low 39 with a team that had been subject to constant sales in previous years. Johnny Giles left for West Bromwich Albion after the European Cup Final disappointment, while Mick Jones retired, as Jimmy Armfield led Leeds to fifth in 1975-76. Billy Bremner, Norman Hunter, Terry Yorath and Mick Bates were the next to go, Hunter summing up the mood for change. "That was really the [beginning of the] end of my time at Leeds when Jimmy and Don Howe came to the club. For some reason they didn't want me, so I said, 'Fair enough, I'll go'. I ended up going to Bristol City ... I was desperate to stay here but they didn't want me." Duncan McKenzie was sold to Anderlecht, too, and although Leeds brought in Tony Currie and Ray Hankin, a new-look side could only finish 10th in 1976-77, with a run to the FA Cup semi-finals that ended in defeat against Manchester United the most memorable aspect of the campaign.

Armfield's Leeds continued the theme of mid-table mediocrity in the following season, finishing ninth, as a Cup run was again the highlight, United reaching the semi-finals of the League Cup. Gordon McQueen and Joe Jordan then both left for Old Trafford, while Clarke and Paul Reaney departed as well. Clarke headed for Oakwell to begin his managerial career but Leeds finished fifth in 1978-79 and qualified for the UEFA Cup. Another semi-final defeat in the League Cup ensured Leeds' wait for a trophy continued but the achievements were highly commendable given the distraction that term. Ex-Celtic boss Jock Stein was appointed as Armfield's replacement in August 1978 but lasted only 44 days before leaving to take on the job as Scotland manager. Jimmy Adamson then came in from Sunderland to replace Stein, and the early signs were encouraging. Adamson made a host of changes to his squad in his time at Leeds, as Peter Lorimer, Ray Hankin and David Harvey all left for Canada, while Frank Gray and Tony Currie were sold, too. Replacing them were the likes of Kevin Hird, Alan Curtis and Brian Greenhoff, with transfer activity becoming more and more common. "The freedom of transfers came in a bit more and there wasn't the loyalty to the clubs," Cherry remembered. Despite all his work in the transfer market, Adamson did not last at Leeds, the club finishing 11th in a difficult 1979-80 campaign, before he was moved on after a slow start to the following season, replaced by Clarke.

"The season before that [Adamson departure], we lost Tony Currie, we lost Frank Gray, John Hawley left [to Sunderland] and Ray Hankin," Paul Hart said. "My feeling, for me, is we seemed to be losing a lot of players and not bringing in what maybe we should have been … I thought Allan Clarke did a great job. We rallied that season when Jimmy Adamson went, we rallied and finished reasonably strong. There was nothing there then that suggested we would find it difficult the following season." Clarke got to work in the transfer market ahead of the 1981-82 campaign and targeted a familiar face from Nottingham Forest. "Allan and I were good friends, actually, at the time," Frank Gray said. "He'd not long taken over the job at Leeds and he was looking to change things around … after winning the European Cup with Forest … [there was] going to be some changes at Forest and a few players left the club at that time. Martin O'Neill was leaving just after me, Trevor Francis was leaving, so that team was breaking up a little bit and the opportunity came to me to go back to Leeds. There was no other club I wanted to go back to at that time, other than to go back to Elland Road." There was also the chance for a reunion with his older brother, Eddie, and Leeds then splashed out a club-record fee to sign Peter Barnes from West Bromwich Albion.

Hopes were high but Leeds were thumped 5-1 at Swansea City on the opening day of what would be a frustrating campaign. "We were well beaten on the day, so it was worrying," said Hart, who was soon re-assured by the quality in the changing room. "I don't think we thought, 'This is going to be tough [to stay up]'. We'd look around and we had a lot of experienced players around there. The quality of the professionals that were there, I always looked at them, people like Eddie Gray, Arthur Graham … I had unwavering faith in them … the way that they carried themselves. Those players that had been at Leeds for a while always lifted me. From the minute I came into the football club, I looked at those players … I took an awful lot of confidence from playing alongside them." Graham responded to that Swansea loss with a goal in a 1-1 home draw with Everton before bagging a hat-trick in the next match at Elland Road, a 3-0 win over Wolverhampton Wanderers. It took Leeds another nine games to win again, Graham on the scoresheet once more in a 3-1 home triumph over West Brom, Cherry and Terry Connor getting the other goals.

Eddie Gray, often now playing in a left-back role, got the winner against Sunderland in the next fixture, the only time Leeds would win back-to-back league games all season. A five-match unbeaten run in all competitions raised spirits but Leeds' form nosedived from late January. "There was a belief in the camp at that time that I didn't agree with, that we had too many good players to go down. We never [did]. Results proved that," Eddie Gray said. "I just thought there was a misguided belief that we were too good to go down." Cherry said he remembered things "drifting". "We were on a bad run and we didn't have a lot of confidence and football is a lot about confidence. You're winning games, you flow. [When you're losing] - that's when you've got to dig down a little bit deeper and not just accept you're going to lose. We didn't have that backbone of a team … we obviously didn't have the commitment that the old [Revie] team had - they didn't like losing anything … we just drifted and really, we couldn't put a stop to it. I think a lot of teams do that - it's easy when you're losing … we couldn't put a halt to it and just turn things around."

The battle for survival continued but occasionally, Leeds would put in the sort of performance that suggested they would stay up. A 4-1 win at Aston Villa was one such victory, Frank Worthington scoring twice and Graham and Connor also netting in an effort Hart was quick to acknowledge. "We just didn't have any consistency," Frank Gray said. "I think that's the problem with any team that gets relegated. I think every team can win games against top teams or any team in the league, basically, at any one given time. But I think consistency is a big thing and that was one thing we lacked throughout that season. There was a lot of changes made that season, a lot of personnel came in … when we played well, we played really well, but we just didn't play well often enough."

A goalless draw against Stoke City, also fighting for their lives, followed the Villa game before Leeds lost to Everton and Tottenham Hotspur and drew 3-3 against Birmingham City. It set up a vital fixture against Brighton and Hove Albion at Elland Road in the final home match of the season and Leeds would come from behind to win 2-1, Gary Hamson and Hird scoring the goals. "We'd heard some stories and whispers during the game, towards the end of the game, that the win might have been enough with the scores from other grounds, which was false," Frank Gray said, while Cherry had a similar memory. "I remember we thought we'd done enough to stay up and then obviously things went differently."

Leeds had one game left, at West Brom on a Tuesday night, and were both one point ahead of the Baggies and Stoke City. One of those three clubs would be relegated and in a quirk of the fixtures, West Brom and Stoke played each other two nights after Leeds' last game of the season. It set up a series of possibilities but United knew that even a draw would keep them safe and Frank Gray remembered travelling to The Hawthorns in a good frame of mind. "We had to go to West Brom and get a result on a Tuesday night and we'd prepared for that. We felt after the game, the win against Brighton, that we could go to West Brom and get a result, especially after beating Brighton, which was a big win. Obviously, we'd have preferred not to have to go to West Brom to get a result but that was the case."

Leeds got through the first half unscathed but conceded six minutes into the second half, Cyrille Regis scoring for the hosts. "We didn't have that firepower to turn things around like the old team … we didn't have enough players who could address things," Cherry said. "It's easy when you're winning three and four nil, it's when you're losing 1-0 away to West Brom, you need lads to stand up. If you have to kick, you have to kick. You have to win the game, to be honest with you, at any costs, if it gets down to that. And we didn't have the players that had the heart [to] do that, if I'm honest … the worst thing was, on the night of West Brom, we didn't really perform as if we wanted to stay up."

West Brom capped off a one-sided match when Steve MacKenzie scored the second in the 87th minute, a goal that saw the Leeds fans start a riot. "What I remember about that night is our supporters being very angry at the end and rightfully so," Hart said. "We let everybody down and it was very painful. I don't think we performed very well on the night … it was a massive disappointment." The final whistle did not actually condemn Leeds to relegation, with survival still possible if West Brom, just two days later, beat Stoke City. But United's players all felt as if relegation was a formality. "I remember the circumstances but I think we felt deep down we were relegated," said Cherry, recalling the "horrendous" vibe in the changing room. "It's very quiet. You know things have not gone right … I felt, as a club, we let the fans down which is the main thing. And getting relegated is just not a nice thing at all. You don't want that on your CV, certainly for Leeds United or anybody else that you're playing for. It's your club. It was a bad time … but I think, if I'm honest, we knew it was coming."

Eddie Gray took defeat and potential relegation hard. "We got well beaten again. There's no doubt about that sat in the dressing room after the game. When I first came to the club … playing [in] European Cup Finals, we lost FA Cup Finals, getting beat by Celtic in the semi-final of the European Cup, [but] that was the most disappointing night I've had, getting relegated. You come [to Leeds] as a young lad, when you're 15. They're in the old Second Division, as it was. You get promotion and you're playing at the top flight from 1966, when I made my debut, right through. To realise that the club were going back into the lower leagues was disappointing." Eddie's brother, Frank, was in no doubt that Leeds deserved to go down. "It was huge for the club to get relegated … if you get relegated, then you deserve to get relegated. At that time it was a 42-game season so over 42 games, you're not good enough to stay in the league - you can't make any excuses about it."

With survival secured after the Leeds win, West Brom were beaten at

Stoke, future Leeds striker Lee Chapman scoring in a 3-0 win that kept the Potters up and confirmed United's relegation. "For a club like ours to be relegated was a huge [thing]. It was a big thing for everybody, especially for us. It's terrible," Hart said. "[I] never envisaged that in the four years I'd been there then. I never thought that we would be playing in the Championship, or Second Division then. It was a huge blow ... I can only blame us as players, as a collective, for just not doing well enough ... as a group, as a team, we underperformed, simple as that." In the aftermath, Eddie Gray felt for his old teammate. "I felt that we [as players] were disappointing ... I thought Allan was a good manager."

As the dust settled, Frank Gray's thoughts turned to Paris in 1975. "It's easy to say it but when you look back, I think that European Cup loss against Bayern affected Leeds a lot more than people think it did because if we'd been European champions then, things would have been a lot different, I'm sure. I think the club would have changed. It would have been an attractive proposition for players to sign for the club. The club would have gone from strength to strength, I feel. But that one game ... I just felt at that time when you had Giles coming towards the end and Billy coming towards the end, people like that ... I'm sure they'd have been replaced, if Leeds had been European champions, with top-class players, because Leeds would have been a big attraction for players to sign for. But it didn't happen and then the start of a downward spiral a couple of years later [followed]."

That downward spiral would see Leeds back in the Second Division for the first time since the 1963-64 season and Hart's mood was shared by the supporters. "It was just a fog of dismay," he said. "I remember the summer being just miserable ... it was a horrible time."

The big-money signing of Peter Barnes did not work out. Photo: Andrew Varley Picture Agency

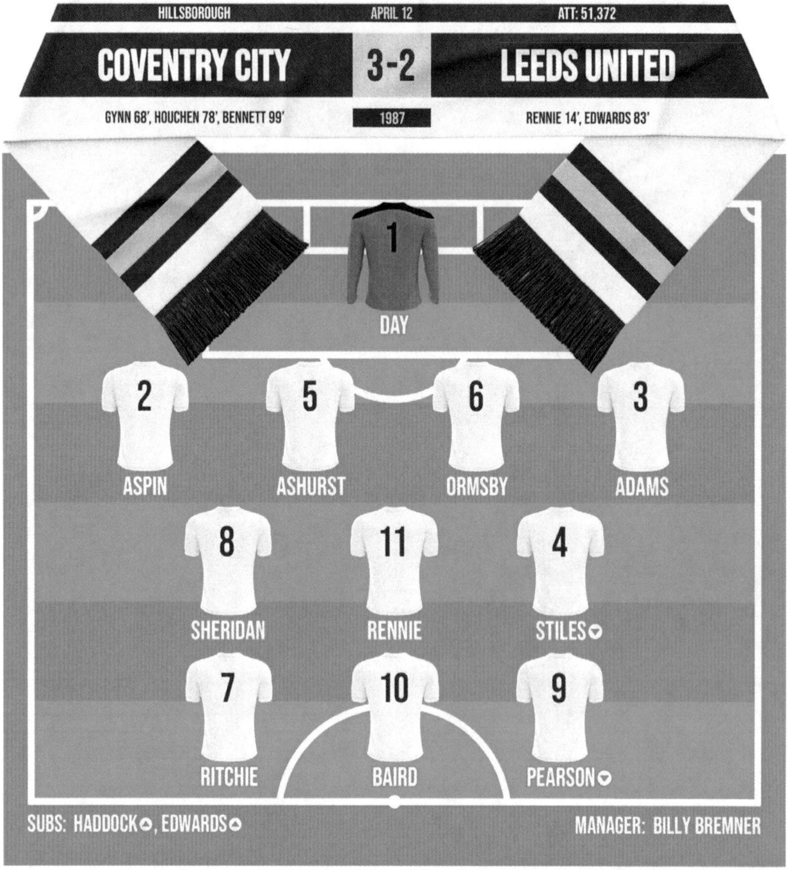

COVENTRY CITY

OGRIZOVIC, BORROWS, DOWNS, McGRATH, KILCLINE, PEAKE, BENNETT, PHILLIPS, REGIS, HOUCHEN, PICKERING

SUBS: SEDGELEY, GYNN

MANAGERS: JOHN SILLETT, GEORGE CURTIS

OUR FORM HEADING IN

HULL CITY	0-0	LEEDS UTD
LEEDS UTD	2-0	MILLWALL
LEEDS UTD	4-0	PLYMOUTH

"I was in the dugout with Billy [Bremner], with [assistant manager] Dave Bentley, and he [Billy] said, 'Right, tell Everton they can have him. I've lost it with him now'."
- Alan Sutton

Both Everton and Liverpool would not relent in their pursuit of Leeds United captain Ian Snodin and, during a 2-0 defeat at Ipswich Town on New Year's Day of 1987, star player-turned-manager Billy Bremner decided he had had enough. Snodin was to be sold. "It all changed. New Year's Day at Ipswich and that's when 'Shez' [John Sheridan] got sent off," Leeds physio Alan Sutton said. "We were struggling and were so-so. Shez got sent off and 'Snods', Ian, he went off on one ... obviously Billy was into him about something." Bremner and Snodin having words did not mean they disliked each other, though, in fact it could not have been more different. Bremner helped Snodin rise to prominence at Doncaster Rovers and made him club captain when he arrived at Leeds. The pair were close but Leeds were struggling, the Ipswich defeat their sixth in 10 Second Division matches, a run that involved a 7-2 defeat at Stoke City. The sale of the in-demand Snodin would give Bremner the funds he needed to make much-needed improvements to his squad.

Snodin would play one more match for Leeds before leaving for Everton in a reported £840,000 deal, the highest fee United had ever received for a player. "That was a big changing point because with that money we brought in four players, John Pearson, Mark Aizlewood, Bobby McDonald and Micky Adams, and that seemed to change the season then," Sutton said. Pearson and Aizlewood both arrived from top-flight Charlton Athletic, the former wooed by the prospect of playing for Bremner. "I'd just got promotion the year before with Charlton and we actually beat Leeds at home 4-0 and I scored with a volley from outside the box which I never, ever did," Pearson said. "And at the end of the game, I just remember Billy Bremner came up to me. I was a Charlton player and he went, 'Oh, well played', and I thought, 'That's really strange coming from the opposition manager'. And I remembered that when obviously Leeds came in for me ... then my mate Mark Aizlewood joined us from Charlton as well, and Micky Adams was there and I think it was Bobby McDonald. And so they signed the four of us ... it just felt really good and you could see we'd got a good team and the bond in the side grew stronger. We grew into that season." United's results picked up remarkably, the club going more than two-and-a-half months without defeat as they surged up the league table and into the FA Cup semi-finals. Leeds United were, finally, in promotion-winning form.

The years since relegation had been frustrating, club legend Eddie Gray, who replaced Allan Clarke, unable to restore Leeds' top-flight status in three full campaigns before Bremner took over during the 1985-86 season. The Gray years, which ended in finishes of eighth, 10th and seventh, were marred by regular player sales and instances of crowd violence, but Bremner would be the beneficiary of his predecessor's faith in John Sheridan. Sheridan emerged as a genuine cult hero with Bremner at the helm, playing alongside Snodin in the heart of midfield. "What Eddie did was he gave the young players an opportunity, which was massive for the likes of myself," Sheridan said. "He just wasn't frightened of putting young players in and he was probably the biggest influence on my career. He gave you that belief that no matter how old you were, you were good enough to get in the team."

Sheridan remembered the club's first few years back in the Second Division as "tough" for a fanbase so used to success. "With the years before it, obviously the likes of Billy and Eddie Gray and all them played under [Don] Revie. They were a massive club ... they were used to success, they weren't used to [Second Division]. But, I mean, the support was still there, but it was a downward slope, everybody knows it was a downward slope during the '80s ... I lived in digs for five years with Denis Irwin, Scott Sellars and Tommy Wright. We were best mates ... and we were all in the first team at the same time and we were all getting opportunities to play in the first team because of Eddie." The midfield dynamo remembered Bremner coming in and how he "got players in with a bit more experience". The shift in focus saw Irwin, Sellars and Wright sold while Terry Phelan and Andy Linighan also moved on, with the likes of Brendan Ormsby, David Rennie and Keith Edwards coming in.

And while Leeds finished 14th in the 1985-86 campaign, better times were around the corner, Bremner continuing his renovation of the squad with the Snodin sale that sparked a dramatic mid-season turnaround. An FA Cup run inspired the Leeds fans, too, Ian Baird scoring a double in a 2-1 win over Telford United in the third round before the same man got the winner against Swindon Town to set up a fifth-round tie against First Division outfit Queens Park Rangers. More than 31,000 fans crammed into Elland Road and created a special atmosphere, Adams said. "They made it really intimidating for Queens Park Rangers, the home fans." And those fans were delirious five minutes from time when Ormsby popped up with the goal that would seal a 2-1 victory. "One of the best atmospheres I've probably played in at Elland Road," Sheridan said. "QPR, who were in the top flight at the time, [were] probably our toughest test leading up to the semi-final and we deservedly beat them on the day. The atmosphere was unbelievable ... you just felt we might have a little chance." Pearson's memory was similar. "It was a really good game, a fantastic atmosphere and a real Cup tie. There's over 30 thousand in the crowd and, all of a sudden, the season was becoming special ... at that time, we thought we could do anything."

With Tottenham and Arsenal still in the draw, Leeds were drawn to play at third-tier Wigan Athletic in their quarter-final. "We got the fortunate draw of getting Wigan," Keith Edwards said. "No disrespect to Wigan, but they were [the] ones everybody wanted." Sheridan added United "got the luck of the draw" but the match would prove difficult. "They did fantastically well to get where they were and they'd had a good Cup run and they had some very good players," Andy Ritchie said. "It was obviously at their place as well, which is the old ground [Springfield Park], which was going to be tough ... it was very bobbly, the pitch ... it was a tough game, really tough game. I remember playing against Andy Holden ... he was one of these big old traditional centre-halves that as soon as you looked at him, he'd kick you, if you know what I mean [laughs]." Goals from Adams and John Stiles would prove enough for Leeds, though, in a 2-0 win. "We didn't play particularly well at Wigan. I think we got away with it, really. They missed a few chances," Adams said. "But I remember the goal because it was obviously right-footed - it just took a nice little bobble as I struck it. Top corner ... great feeling."

That set up a semi-final clash with Coventry City of the First Division, Adams' former club, but top-flight opposition held no fears for United. "We were a confident team, confident set of lads," Edwards said. "We felt that we could give everybody a game. I can't ever recall going into a game like that, being nervous, and thinking that we're overshadowed by somebody else, for example, Coventry. Leeds is Leeds, isn't it? It tends to give you that bit of confidence anyway. We were in the Second Division but I don't ever recall having any doubts whatsoever, thinking, 'We're Second Division, they're in the First Division. We've got it all to do here'. We just didn't go out with that attitude. That was most probably down to Billy Bremner's positivity, in many respects."

For Edwards and Pearson, on opposite sides of the Sheffield divide, the fact the match was played at Hillsborough added extra significance. "My first team is always Sheffield United because they gave me my start in football. You can never forget that," Edwards added. "My wife was nine months pregnant at Hillsborough. My little boy was born later on. Thank God he wasn't born at Hillsborough! Not that day, but he wasn't far off. My wife being at the game with all my daughters and [I am] thinking, 'Christ, I hope she doesn't give birth in Hillsborough of all places. I'll get strung up by Sheffield United supporters.'" Pearson, who was preferred to Edwards up front, was "born 200 yards away from Hillsborough" and had not played at the venue since leaving Sheffield Wednesday. "The perfect way for me to go back to Hillsborough was in a semi-final and not against Sheffield Wednesday … Hillsborough's always been a special place for me. I was a season ticket holder."

Sutton recalled "the bus breaking down" on the way to the game but substitute Peter Haddock said Bremner always kept things calm. "The build-up to the game was very relaxing. Billy was that type of person, anyway. We just used to laugh and joke all the time … we were all very confident and in a good mood." Leeds came out firing, too. "I had a fantastic chance in the first minute," Pearson said. "I got a diving header in and [Coventry goalkeeper Steve] Ogrizovic has dived to his left … I was absolutely gutted … but then you just felt, I just thought, 'We're going to win this'. I was looking at the Coventry players and I'm thinking, 'They're a little bit frightened here.'" Baird was denied in his attempt to convert the follow-up from Pearson's early chance but

Rennie soon headed Leeds into the lead. And if it was not for Ogrizovic, Ormsby would have doubled Leeds' account. "Steve Ogrizovic kept them in the game in the first 15 minutes, I think he made a couple of great saves," said Adams. Ritchie, who was causing several problems, recalled "a glorious day" and "just unbelievable" Leeds support. Cyrille Regis spurned a host of chances at the other end but Leeds were in control at the break. "In the first half, I thought we were the better team. When you go in the break at 1-0 and, like I say, we're the better team, we're quite confident and comfortable," Sheridan said.

The match was to swing, though, in a decisive 68th-minute moment that still haunts Leeds fans, as Ormsby tried to shepherd the ball out, only to see Dave Bennett steal in and keep the ball alive. Bennett then kept his cool, setting up substitute Micky Gynn for a game-turning equaliser. "It's a particular pet hate of mine," Adams said. "If defenders are trying to shepherd it out of play, I always want them to smash [it] into the stand and it's because of that one occasion ... it was heartbreaking, really." Sheridan said he immediately felt things change. "Once they scored, yeah, I think the momentum shifted and I think they got on the front foot a bit more than us ... there's never any blame attached to it because Brendan was brilliant all season, he was our captain, so it was just one of them things ... once they got that equaliser, they were probably the team who probably believed they'd go [and win it]." Coventry quickly got a second, a goal Sheridan said was "probably my fault" after he lost a battle with Gynn that led to Keith Houchen's strike. In the space of 10 minutes, Leeds United's FA Cup dreams looked dashed.

Bremner went to his bench, bringing on Edwards and Haddock. "Billy kept it pretty simple," Edwards said of his manager's instructions. It worked a treat, though, with the striker on the pitch for less than two minutes before he nodded in a dramatic equaliser following great build-up work from Ritchie. "I was playing on the right-hand side there, that afternoon," Ritchie said. "I remember the build-up for the goal for Keith. I think I beat maybe two players, got a little bit lucky with a bit of a ricochet but then managed to put ... a nice little dink ball across the six-yard box." Edwards hailed Ritchie's work for the goal. "Andy Ritchie was man of the match that day for us and he played ever so well. I latched onto his cross. I basically did what I did best and got myself between the two big centre-halves, because I'm not the biggest lad in the world, but by getting myself in the right position and getting the right service, I've knocked it in." The Leeds end absolutely erupted in joy and Edwards could not contain himself. "When I see footballers today, I cringe. I always pride myself on celebrating in a nice way. You salute the supporters and then you turn round and go back to the halfway line. Unfortunately, I was that excited that day, I screamed that hard … I screamed that much I hurt my vocal chords. My throat was killing me afterwards. It was a great thrill to come on and score and take that game a bit further and we were that bit closer … every time I played at Hillsborough I scored. I felt I couldn't get on quick enough!"

That led to extra time, Bennett tapping in from a goalmouth scramble for what would be the winner, before Edwards was denied another dramatic leveller by Ogrizovic's brilliance. "I've blocked it from my mind," Pearson said of the match-winning goal, while Ritchie remembered the sucker-punch it provided. "It was the elation of getting back in the game and it was deflation of letting them get that goal again." And that mood of deflation was to linger throughout the evening, as United agonisingly fell one match short of a Wembley final. "When the final whistle went, I did my usual thing. It's all routine, in many respects. I waved to the fans and I was ready to walk off," Edwards said. "I turned around and looked at my teammates and a lot of them were sat down on the pitch actually crying. I thought to myself, 'Well, it looks a bit rude if I just walk off now'. So I had to go back and sit with them … when some people say footballers don't care, well you only had to look at that dressing room, because by the time we got back to the dressing room, I think there was only me and Ian Baird who weren't crying. 'Bairdy' wouldn't have cried."

"There were a lot of tears in the dressing room," said Pearson, while Ritchie recalled the uncomfortable sight of a disconsolate skipper. "He [Ormsby] was inconsolable, really. He was crying … I think it took … a long time for him to recover from that." Haddock felt the emotions were much higher than usual because of the sense of missed opportunity. "It was a big game for the club at the time," he said. "We were in the Second Division, playing in the semi-final of the FA Cup, one step from Wembley and I think the players realised that we could've got there." Ritchie agreed. "We weren't expected to win, we were the underdogs and what have you ... they were in the First Division at the time and they had some really good players, some fantastic players. I think everybody thought that we were going to get beat there and obviously it did end up that way but it was a very, very close game ... [we] probably deserved to win the game but it just didn't pan out that way. I think that that was why we were so emotional after the game, because we just felt that we'd battled so hard and we probably deserved a bit more than we actually got in the end." For Sheridan, he was one result away from achieving a childhood dream. "It was the FA Cup. I think it's every player's dream ... the FA Cup Final, it was a massive day all around the country in those days. It was the biggest game of the season."

The players travelled back to Elland Road for a function but the mood had not improved. "Everybody was heartbroken, absolutely gutted," said Pearson, while Adams "couldn't wait to get out of there, really, because it wasn't a happy place". It was that bad, Adams said, he preferred to be in Coventry. "I was still living in Coventry at the time as well ... you can imagine going back to Coventry after they just got into the [FA] Cup Final. All the pubs are packed - but I still went in and had a couple of pints anyway."

After a couple of days, it was time to move on. Bremner's Leeds had another fight on their hands. Promotion. "The team spirit and the bonding that the team had got, we'd sort of grouped together, got back, Billy sat us all down," Pearson said. "[He said], 'Look, we're out of that, but we're still in this. We've still got everything to go for.'"

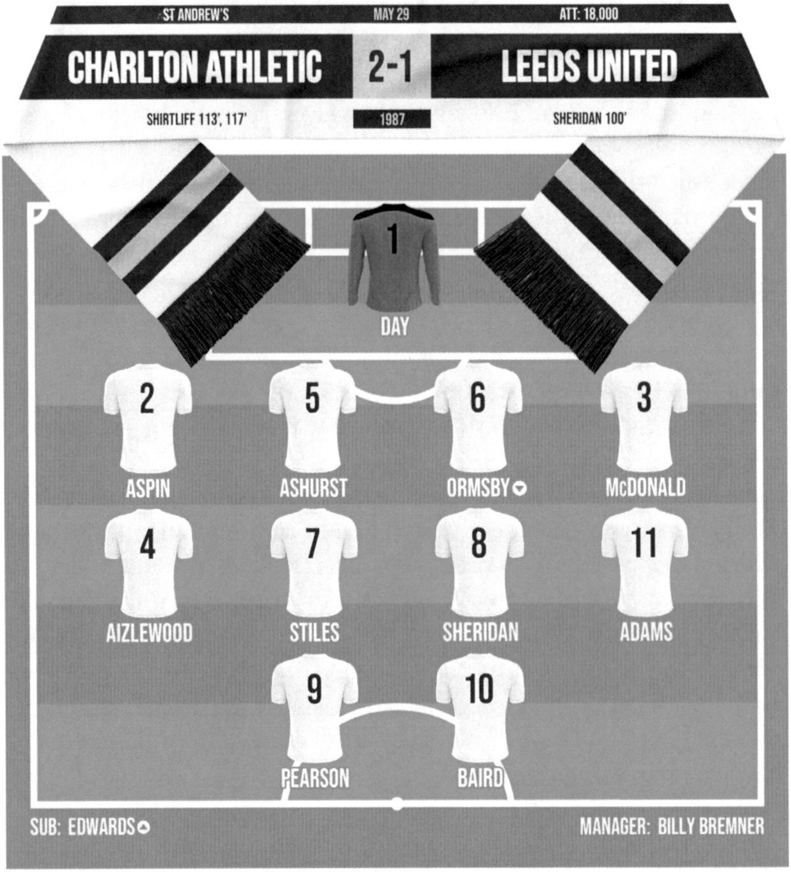

CHARLTON ATHLETIC

BOLDER, HUMPHREY, SHIRTLIFF, MILLER, REID, GRITT, PEAKE, WALSH, LEE, MELROSE, CROOKS

SUB: STUART

MANAGER: LENNIE LAWRENCE

OUR FORM HEADING IN

LEEDS UTD	1-0	CHARLTON
CHARLTON	1-0	LEEDS UTD
OLDHAM	2-1	LEEDS UTD

"We were never going to moan but if you look back now, you think, 'It's a bit ridiculous'."
- John Sheridan

May was nearly over but Leeds United's season was still going. A marathon 1986-87 campaign that had already seen Leeds play 42 league fixtures, eight cup matches and four play-off clashes came down to one last game - Charlton Athletic on the neutral territory of Birmingham's St Andrew's with a spot in the First Division up for grabs. Billy Bremner's side responded well after their FA Cup heartbreak, winning five of their last eight matches to book a spot in the play-offs, being held across the Second Division, Third Division and Fourth Division for the first time. John Sheridan's outstanding campaign showed no sign of slowing, the midfield genius adding four more goals in that end-of-season run to take his tally to 15. The first stage of the play-offs presented an intriguing proposition for Sheridan, who faced off against his two housemates, Tommy Wright and Denis Irwin, who were still living with the midfielder in Barwick-in-Elmet despite swapping Leeds for Oldham Athletic. The two sides would do battle in a see-sawing two-legged semi-final that was defined by late goals.

"We were leaving for the game and those two were leaving to go meet the bus for Oldham and I was going straight to Elland Road," Sheridan said. "I'm playing against my two best mates and they both had a really good season, Oldham were a really good team." A tense first leg in West Yorkshire remained goalless until the 90th minute, when Sheridan walked over to a free-kick, something that always filled Leeds fans with hope. Earlier in the season, he scored an outrageous effort against Derby County at Elland Road, flicking the ball up to himself before lashing in a 20-yard strike that will live long in the memory. The story behind the goal gave an insight into Sheridan's confidence, too. "I actually went away with [the Republic of] Ireland and I practiced it. It was Kevin Sheedy who I first saw do it while I was with Ireland ... I came back and I said to Ian Snodin, I said, 'There's a free-kick, if we get an opportunity on Saturday, I'm going to try it. Kevin Sheedy was doing it and he was putting them in the top [corner]'. I said, 'I'm going to try it'. Luckily enough, we just got in the position where I thought, 'There's a chance of doing it'. I couldn't have done it any better or hit it any better and, yeah, probably the best goal I scored."

Sheridan decided on something more simple against Oldham, though, whipping a ball across the box that was just asking to be headed in. "'Shez' [Sheridan] was such a beautiful, natural player," Keith Edwards said. "When he got the free-kick, it was [at] the Kop end. I looked at him and he can see me ... I thought, 'If I make the run early enough and get across the defenders, this kid will pick us out'. I was absolutely spot on. He picked us out, I got a header to it ... to score in [front of] the Kop end was special. To score in the last few minutes and to beat Oldham 1-0 and take that lead once again, that was quite [special]. I got a bit of a hug from Billy when that game finished, that was a great memory as well. It was down to Shez's free kick more than anything."

That Edwards - a player initially left on the bench by his manager - said getting a hug from Bremner was almost as good as his late winner said it all. The players loved Bremner and the atmosphere he created, with the Scotsman bringing Don Revie's carpet bowls sessions back to Leeds United. "He was a good manager, he used to like to keep us happy, in terms of on and off the pitch," Andy Ritchie said. "Away games, we always used to take carpet bowls and he'd always make sure that he got a big conference room at the hotel and make sure that we could go in and have a game of carpet bowls on a Friday night. We'd all stick in two quid and we'd play each other and what have you. That was team bonding, which was great. He was a very, very enthusiastic manager ... he played in every five-a-side and he used to kick everybody just like he did when he was playing! But I think he kicked every single ball on that pitch while we were playing ... he had such a passion and a fervour for the game." Micky Adams said Bremner's passion and love for Leeds United rubbed off on the players. "To get back into the big league ... would have been a fitting tribute to Bill ... he was one of the best football men I ever met. Just to play for him was massive and I think we all felt that. He was a fun guy, Billy. He used to make us laugh every day."

With Edwards' late header giving Leeds a one-goal advantage, Bremner's men headed to Oldham for what would be a nerve-jangling second leg on the infamous plastic pitch at Boundary Park. "Everybody hated the plastic pitches," said John Pearson, while Ritchie, who would move from Leeds to Oldham at season's end, said the surface gave the hosts a big advantage. "It was always difficult to play Oldham on their plastic pitch as well, because they were phenomenal on that. I came the year after obviously - I found that out." Sheridan, who would also end up at Oldham later in his career, echoed his teammate's thoughts. "They were very dominant on that [pitch]. They were very good and very rarely got beat ... [they] scored first and then, again, they're on the front foot ... probably puts them in the driving seat." Garry Williams headed Oldham level on aggregate in the 18th minute and Adams remembered another cagey match. "I don't think they were two good games at all. I think there was a lot of nerves, a lot of tension."

That tension lingered until the 89th minute, when Irwin's cross from the right was nodded in by Oldham substitute Mike Cecere to send the home fans wild. "They get the second one and you think it's all over," Sheridan said as supporters were hit with that sinking feeling. With nothing to lose, Leeds went for broke from the kick-off and Neil Aspin's hopeful punt forward eventually broke for Edwards. "If I'm being perfectly honest, I scuffed it a little bit, but I scuffed it into the corner ... that was a real thrill," Edwards said. "It was just a bit of a hopeful ball ... we got it forward and it worked for us. If you're 2-1 down on the basis of two games, you've just got to chance your luck and try and get [it] up there. I had an obsession with hitting the target ... I didn't hit it cleanly but I got it on target and that's the reason why it went in." Leeds United's super sub had delivered. Again. "I didn't like the 'super sub' crap, if I'm being honest with you. That used to frustrate me but you have to live with it ... I wasn't a sulker. I just got on with it."

"You concede, you're down and you're looking at where we've conceded and probably look at each other and what you could have done better and then, God, 30 seconds later, you're up the other end celebrating," Sheridan said. "I've run 80 yards down the other end of the pitch, all the way to our supporters thinking, 'We're through'. It was right at the end of the game and I'm thinking, 'It's game over and we're through', but me being stupid, it's still extra time so I've got to get myself together - we've got to get ourselves together. And at the same time, we know then we're in the driving seat." Ritchie, on the sidelines through injury, said it was a rollercoaster of emotions. "It was just so surreal because we thought, 'That was it, that was it, it was done and gone'. Obviously, the players didn't think that way because you just keep going on the pitch. But at the side, I resigned myself, [I thought], 'Oh, that's it', and then all of a sudden, from the blue, [we scored]."

For Pearson, Edwards' goal was the source of frustration. "We'd tried to play a lot of football and a lot of the time I thought, 'Well, I'm running across this 18-yard box, I'm going from one side waiting for a cross to come in'. And in the end, we put a cross in and I managed to knock it down for Keith and Keith popped it in and I just went a little bit mad because I'm going, 'I've been running and when we want a goal, you put a cross in and we get a goal'. I said, 'Best thing to do is put crosses in, first minute, let's get 3-0 up. I'll come off, you play your football!' A rare route one attempt had provided Leeds with the goal they needed and after a nervy and goalless period of extra time, United qualified for the play-off final on away goals, causing an odd night in Sheridan's house. "We went home after the game on the night, obviously those two [Wright and Irwin] were very upset after the game ... I went out and had a few pints."

United's next opponents would be Charlton Athletic, with a quirk of the new post-season system seeing a side still in the First Division playing a second-tier side to keep their spot in the league. "They were in the top division ... that's a little bit harsh on Leeds, isn't it? You wouldn't do that now," Edwards said. For Pearson and Mark Aizlewood, this meant they would face the club they had only left earlier in the season. "It was unchartered territory for everybody because it was the first play-off final," Pearson said. "I wish it had have been at Wembley but it wasn't, it was home and away. I did enjoy Charlton, I liked Charlton and I liked the people there." Charlton's home leg was held at Selhurst Park and Pearson was left wounded almost immediately. "The ball's in the air and I'm going up with [Charlton's] Steve Thompson and 'Bairdy's [Ian Baird] come across like he does and he's tried to elbow Steve Thompson and he's completely missed him, he's done me and broke my rib! I've gone, 'Ahhhh'. The first minute, he's broke my rib ... I struggled on for about 60 minutes and I had to come off." It was Leeds' turn to be hit by a late goal, too, Jim Melrose scoring as Charlton won the first leg 1-0.

That set up an intriguing second leg at Elland Road just two days later, with Pearson ruled out through injury and replaced by Ritchie, who was battling a hamstring issue. "When we came back to Elland Road, if we were going to do it, we should have done it," Sheridan said. "Very tight game, obviously we get the breakthrough with the goal. Brendan [Ormsby] and Bob Taylor are involved in the goal." Ormsby's tap-in gave Leeds the lead on the night but there was to be no late drama on this occasion. "The second leg, we played quite well," Charlton's Peter Shirtliff said. "We did okay, obviously we were under a bit of pressure due to the atmosphere and what have you, but we played okay. I hit the post from a corner with a header. It was pretty even, the game." It would not be the last time that Shirtliff, a central defender, caused Leeds problems in their own penalty area.

The stage was set for a replay on neutral territory, a fixture Sheridan wishes never went ahead. "I wish it wouldn't have gone to St Andrew's. I think it should have just got decided on penalties." United's build-up to the play-off final replay was marred by the injury issues surrounding Ritchie and Pearson. "I wasn't fit enough to play. Hamstring injuries are very difficult to shake off with those games being so close to each other," Ritchie said. "It'd been niggling from before the Oldham games and I think I just felt it again in training and I went in to see [physio] Alan Sutton and I said, 'Listen, I just know that if I really go full out [into a sprint] with this, it's not going to last', … I'd have loved to play in the game and I was desperate to but I knew that it was such an important game and a massive game for the football club." Pearson said missing out on the second leg made him even more determined to feature in Birmingham. "We beat them 1-0 at Elland Road and you're thinking, 'Ah, I've got to play in this game, I've got to play in this game', … it [atmosphere] is electric. That's what made me want to play in the final, in the replay … we were desperate to do something that season." Pearson struggled to turn over in bed, but he still wanted to play with the help of injections that "took the pain away" but "probably lasted about an hour or so". "I so wanted to play that I played at Birmingham and when I look back now I'm thinking, 'Perhaps I shouldn't have played,'" he said.

Despite the location of the match, Leeds fans made up the majority of the crowd, so much so that Sheridan said it felt like playing in West Yorkshire. "I expected it anyway with our supporters. It was unbelievable," he said. "You walk out and you're probably playing at home, aren't you?" Most of the Leeds players recalled a typically cagey play-off affair, but Shirtliff felt like his team were the better side. "We had actually played very well. We probably had the best chances and [had] not taken them. Mervyn Day made some good saves." The two sides could not be separated after 90 nervy minutes, forcing extra time, but Leeds would open the scoring from a free-kick. "I wanted to take the free-kick but Sheridan, being there a little bit longer than me, he demanded he took it," Edwards said. It was then that the striker was hit by a feeling. A feeling that Leeds were about to score. "I just knew John Sheridan was actually going to score there. We've seen it millions of times in training … I fancied him to curl it around the wall." Sheridan, who said he "didn't play well" in any of the Charlton fixtures, was desperate to make a meaningful contribution. "I wasn't in the game at all. I think it [the replay] was a very drab game. Both teams were very, I wouldn't say negative, but just not wanting to concede and just trying to get through … it wasn't a great game to watch. It was just [about] that breakthrough."

"You want to try and hit the target. All I'm thinking is, 'Hit the target, make the keeper work,'" Sheridan remembered thinking as he prepared himself to shoot. "I didn't have a big run-up. I pretended to tell the wall that they weren't 10 yards back … as I'm walking up, a quick few steps, and luckily for me I hit it and it ends up in the back of the net. You can see from my reaction … the adrenaline in me is unbelievable … [I am] thinking, 'It [my goal] is going to take us back to where we want to be.'" As the Leeds fans went wild, Sheridan's teammates were all thinking the same thing, 'Thank God for Shez'. "It was a typical John Sheridan goal. He's bent it around the wall and in the top corner and you're thinking, 'God'. I'm thinking, 'God, this is my third promotion, we're up, we're going up,'" said Pearson, while Adams simply said that Sheridan "could do things with the ball that people like myself could only dream of". Leeds had 20 minutes to get through and they would be back where they belonged. Back in the top flight.

Shirtliff had other ideas, though, initially drawing Charlton level with a side-footed finish he took like a striker. "I surprised myself there," he admitted. And there was still time for Shirtliff to score again in the only match he ever netted twice in, the Sheffield-born defender nodding in a late free-kick to break United hearts. "It was in the perfect spot for what we'd rehearsed and Andy Peake managed to clip in a ball into the area that was required. I got on the end of it with a run through the middle of two other players ... it worked perfectly. It was great that we'd got in front but there was still a bit of time left so we were just wanting to make sure that we didn't make any mistakes at the back and allow Leeds back into the game ... that last few minutes was a bit agonising, I must say."

Charlton held on, though, as Leeds' marathon season finished in soul-destroying fashion. "We were broken. Just broken. To lose two such vital and key games ... it was an absolute travesty and it was just a nightmare," Pearson said. Adams, meanwhile, was devastated - as much for Bremner as himself. "Billy tried his best to remind us that we'd had a fantastic season but to come away with nothing was devastating to everybody. But Billy was Billy. I mean, I think that we were all more devastated for him because we knew what it meant to him ... we all felt for him more than ourselves."

Again, the tears flowed and more than 30 years on, Sheridan said the nature of the defeat was still "so hard to take". "If I've got a regret in my career, it's that I never played in the top flight with Leeds ... [at Leeds] I am playing with some of the best supporters in the country. Unbelievable support, going through tough times as well ... the club weren't getting anywhere near promotion and this was a chance for us to get out of the league ... I loved it that much at the club ... I was absolutely gutted that we didn't [get promoted] because it just gives you that opportunity. You get in the top flight, hopefully you attract a better quality of player, you go after a better quality of player and it just gives you that bit of belief that the club is back where it belongs."

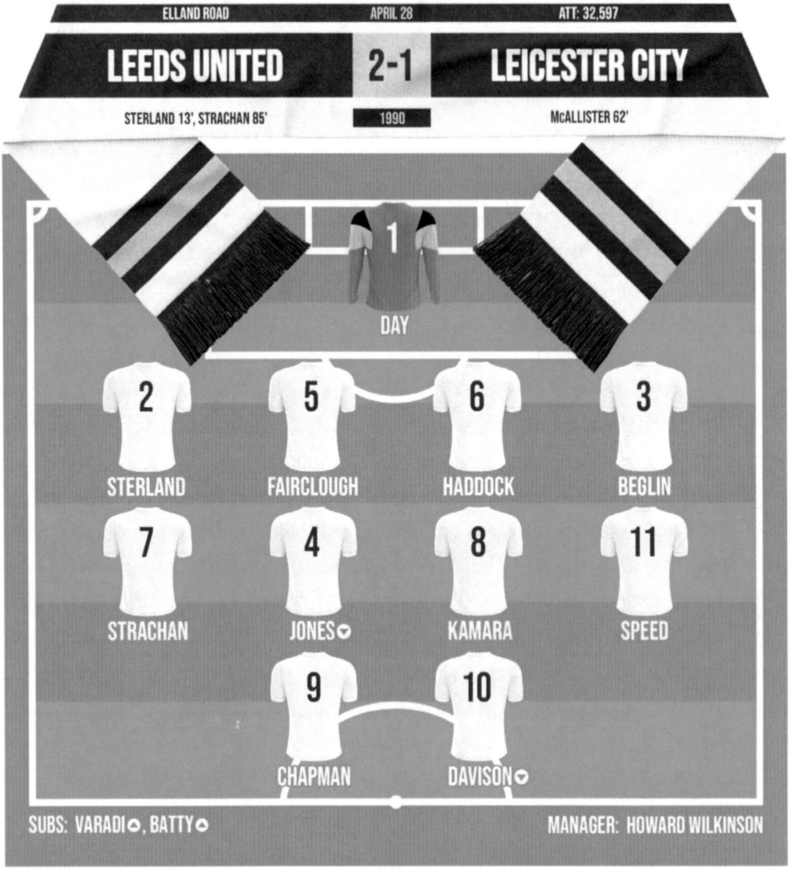

LEICESTER CITY

HODGE, MAUCHLEN, PARIS, RAMSEY, WALSH, JAMES, REID, NORTH ▼, KELLY, McALLISTER, WRIGHT ▼

SUBS: OLDFIELD ▲, MILLS ▲

MANAGER: DAVID PLEAT

OUR FORM HEADING IN

LEEDS UTD	1-2	BARNSLEY
BRIGHTON	2-2	LEEDS UTD
LEEDS UTD	4-0	SHEFF UTD

"Leeds came along ... they were second bottom, I think, in the Second Division and the first time they contacted me I said, 'You've got to be joking, haven't you?' But they persisted."
- Howard Wilkinson

In charge of First Division outfit Sheffield Wednesday, the club he also played for, Howard Wilkinson was not initially interested in dropping into the second tier. In one of the most defining months in Leeds United history, chairman Leslie Silver and managing director Bill Fotherby refused to take no for an answer. "They kept knocking ... the chairman had rung Bobby Robson and said, 'We need a new manager but we've had so many managers - we want a manager who can start with a blank sheet of paper'. So, Bobby recommended me and that's how I got the call," Wilkinson said.

Leeds were looking for a new manager after Billy Bremner's side, who cruelly missed out on promotion in a play-off final replay in 1987, failed to kick on. United scored just three goals in their first nine matches of the 1987-88 campaign, winning only two, and never really recovered. A run of five wins over the festive period was encouraging but Leeds struggled on the road and ended with just one player, midfielder John Sheridan, with double figures in league goals. Sheridan scored 12 as Ian Baird was sold to Portsmouth but was bought back before the season ended, while Bobby Davison was brought in from Derby County. David Batty announced himself as a future prospect, too, but the campaign was ultimately fruitless as Leeds finished seventh. History repeated in the 1988-89 season as Bremner's men started slowly, beginning with a 4-0 defeat at Portsmouth and winning just one of their first six league matches. It was with a heavy heart that United decided to replace Bremner and a manager from the top flight was a left-field replacement but Sheffield Wednesday's stagnation was starting to get to Wilkinson and the idea of leading a complete re-build appealed to the manager.

"We [Wednesday] had got promoted [to the First Division] in our first season and we'd done alright. We had a finish of eighth and a finish of fifth so we were coasting along but we needed to invest to get better, to really have a serious impact on winning the championship. The directors felt they couldn't put the club at risk because they'd rescued it from near doom when it had been put at risk by overspending or spending more than they'd got," said Wilkinson, who agreed to meet Leeds. "I had quite a few meetings with Leslie on his own in secret and during the course of those meetings, first of all, worked out what it was he saw the future looking like, and then me giving him my idea of how that future might be achieved and what sort of time span it would take. And we finished up with [that] if I joined them in October, which I did, promotion the year after and then within four years, so by the time we'd have five full seasons, winning the [First Division] championship. Also included in that was, then a further five years, because also included in that was the development of a proper youth development centre along with a new training ground. And the youth development centre was quite cutting edge for this country because it included accommodation and then we actually did finish up with that. We finished up with a new training ground [Thorp Arch], new development centre, accommodation on it and those kids then were in there and they were partnered with the local school. So we had a football boarding school, where they could train before school, they could train after school. So it was a very strong working relationship that we eventually finished up with." The plans were ambitious but by the turn of the century, Leeds United's first team would be packed with youngsters who had come through the system Wilkinson wanted.

Wilkinson's contract negotiations were almost complete. "On the last meeting before I said, 'Yes', I said, 'So, in summary there, you've got it. There's a quick way and there's a slower way and you know it's your choice'. Because he [Leslie] fully understood that he would have to be the insurer, that he would have to use some of his money, if necessary … he said, 'What's the difference?' And I said, 'To you, probably about £4 million and a saving of time. I'm not saying we'll spend the £4 million but I think that's about the amount that would be needed as insurance. If we wanted to take shortcuts at any point, were there shortcuts available and were they of the right standard?' And so I said, 'Yes'." Wilkinson left Wednesday in "very amicable" fashion, shocking Yorkshire when the move was announced, but the size of the challenge was something he could not turn down. "I think I said it at the time … 'It's like a battered, rusted Rolls Royce with a Mini engine', something like that," he added. "Because it was an old Rolls Royce with quality but it was old and it was battered and it had a history but that was all. It had no real heart, no engine, so it needed change and it needed change quickly."

John Pearson, a Sheffield-born striker who had played under Wilkinson at Wednesday earlier in his career, was convinced that things were about to turn. "I met one of the directors in the corridor … he went, 'Oh, we've got your old manager'. And I went, 'Yeah, you've got yourself promotion now'," he said. "Howard Wilkinson was brilliant … I just knew that Howard Wilkinson would get Leeds United a promotion." Things were about to change at Elland Road, though. "There was a lot [of] Sheffield Wednesday players there at the time who had worked under him," Peter Haddock recalled. "They were all saying, 'This is going to be a rough ride, this', because he was well into fitness and making players run and the players knew that he was going to work them hard … we knew what to expect when he came in and they were right."

Sheridan had been at Leeds for more than six years when Wilkinson arrived and got the feeling that his time might be up. "First impression was, probably, I'd find it difficult to play because I'd played against his teams at Sheffield Wednesday. I think they had a way and Howard had a way of how he wanted his teams to play - very hardworking," he said. "I just think it was the time, probably for me, for a change, not because Howard had come. Howard had his own ideas. I had no disagreement. He had a way he wanted to play. I don't think I was the kind of player he really wanted or thought that would get us out of that league and that's just the way I looked at things."

Wilkinson did not waste any time changing things around, changing the "dining room diet on day two". "I said, 'It's terrific that we're providing meals for them but we're providing them with the wrong [food] and we need to change that'." Widely regarded as being ahead of his time on sports science and diet, Wilkinson also needed to address other issues. "The first thing was the drinking culture and how did I choose to deal with that? How did I choose to deal with the dietary thing? Explain. Education. Just the fundamentals," he said, before elaborating on what he told his players. "'Do you want to be the best player you can be?

Yeah? One thing is for certain, you want to be the best player you can, you've got to be the fittest player you can be. And do you know how to get fit? Because I do. So if you genuinely want to be the best player you can be, I can tell you now I can physically get you as well prepared as anybody, better than most, for you to maximise the talents you've got. But I need to know, do you want to be the best player you can be?' … So you're introducing your new things, you're educating … I believe 100 per cent that whatever happened, Leslie would stick to the plan, so that's a big comfort. And then it's a question of putting it simply [to the players, saying], 'It's up to you whether you want to be on the jet or not and it will take off. We are going places.'"

Progress under Wilkinson was almost immediately evident, Leeds losing just two of his first 22 league matches in charge as they got out of trouble and consolidated on the way to a 10th-placed finish. There was plenty of transfer business, too, with Carl Shutt arriving from Bristol City before the manager made two of his best signings late in the season, Gordon Strachan and Chris Fairclough joining from Manchester United and Tottenham Hotspur respectively. Fairclough's deal was only a loan, but it was made permanent in a busy summer that also saw the likes of Vinnie Jones, Mel Sterland and John Hendrie arrive. Players had to go, Sheridan leaving for Nottingham Forest, while Mark Aizlewood, Neil Aspin and David Rennie were among the departures. "I went to London and talked with Trevor Francis and when I was on the way, the phone rang," Sterland said. "It was Howard and he said, 'I know you're going down to QPR but don't do anything silly'. I went to a hotel in Nottingham on the way back and Howard and Bill Fotherby sold the club to me. Howard said, 'We're signing some good players and we're going to win the league'. He was true to his word."

The signing of Jones from Wimbledon raised some eyebrows given his disciplinary record, but Wilkinson was convinced of his quality. "I told Vinnie why I'd got him there and what I thought he could do and this and that … I said to him, 'If you get booked more than three times a season - because you can get three accidents - you will not be here', … pre-season, he was brilliant. He led the training. He was up front. Anything you wanted doing, he set the standard. Vinnie was everything that I'd been told he was." An incident in a pre-season friendly against Standard Liege soon followed and Wilkinson was angry. "He's given the Belgian player 'that' with his elbow, not quite made contact … the referee asked to have a word with him and so on and so forth. So, at half time I've got in my mind, 'Right, here's my chance. I can really nail my colours to the mast with him. I can say to him, 'You heard what I damn well told you when you signed.''" But before Wilkinson even got the chance, Jones was hearing some home truths. "I got into the dressing room just in time to hear Gordon saying to him … something like, 'At this club, if we're going to be better than the other team, we show it by scoring fucking goals, more goals than them'. Something like that … 'So, fucking pack it in.''" Wilkinson was impressed. He had a natural captain who commanded respect. "I say in a dressing room, you get leaders. They create energy. You get the neutrals, who feed off energy," he said. "And you get the terrorists, who drain the energy. If you spot a terrorist, he's got to go. They're draining energy away. But if you see a leader, then you've got to make sure you use him. So I shared a lot of stuff with Gordon that maybe I wouldn't share with other people about what I was going to do and why. And, by the same token, he happened to mirror a lot of the thinking that I thought was appropriate to being a proper athlete." Jones quickly settled in, Haddock remembering him having a major impact. "He got everybody fired up in the dressing room. I think the opposition feared him … and I think that's what he played on. But him and Batty were really good on the field. There wasn't many teams that got the better of them two."

Pre-season was tough, physio Alan Sutton recalling how difficult Fairclough found it. "That first pre-season he did absolutely killed him. He said the next year he'd been out all summer running to make sure, to get ready for it, because he didn't expect anything like that." Anticipation was high ahead of the new season but Leeds, who were 2-1 up at Newcastle United, would lose 5-2 on the opening day. Slow starts had been a theme of recent campaigns but Leeds hit back in style, going on a 15-match unbeaten run in the league that lasted until November. Davison was a regular scorer, netting eight times in that streak while Strachan weighed in with six from midfield. The Scot's presence on the field was obvious but his impact off the pitch was just as vital. "Strachan and Mel Sterland - he [Howard] bought well. He spent a lot of money but he bought players who were experienced players and he had a bit of youth in the team as well with Batty and Gary Speed," Haddock said. "It just clicked. We had a good team spirit, we all liked each other on and off the pitch. We had a lot of nights out organised by Gordon Strachan, who was the captain at the time. It got you all together and got the team spirit going. That was with the wives as well ... it was a good blend ... he [Gordon] was a captain on the pitch but off the pitch he helped a lot of people ... he was a tremendous captain and a great person." Glynn Snodin had similar things to say about the skipper. "He had a great respect as soon as he walked in that changing room. He was another one, like the gaffer, that as soon as you walked in, you could feel the presence, that he was there. He was great for everybody. If you wanted to have a chat with him, he was there for you ... speak to you about anything you needed to speak to him about. Off the field, he'd try and keep the team together and do team bonding. It was always him and his wife, Lesley, that helped run things like that."

Shutt and Fairclough scored in a 2-0 win at Middlesbrough that put Leeds top of the Second Division on December 9 and Wilkinson's confidence was growing. "By the time we'd played 10, 12, 15 games, I thought we had one of the two best teams in the league and I thought we had the best players in the league at that point." Haddock, enjoying a productive partnership with Fairclough at the back, said the key to the team's success was all about pairings. "He [Fairclough] came to Leeds and it just seemed to click. He was very good in the air and I read the game well and swept up behind him ... and [was] a good tackler and quick ... you've got to have partnerships all over the pitch and that's what happened that year." Wilkinson did want a new striker, though, and signed Lee Chapman from Nottingham Forest in January, an inspired signing given he netted 12 goals in 21 appearances after making the move. Popular striker Ian Baird had to make way for Chapman but the latter scored on his Leeds debut, a 2-1 win at Blackburn Rovers in a sign of things to come. Chris Kamara and Imre Varadi joined Leeds, too, from Stoke City and Sheffield Wednesday respectively as Wilkinson geared up for a promotion fight.

United stuttered in February and early March, though, winning just one of six league games thanks to Strachan's 90th-minute winner against

Hull City. And even though Leeds ended that run by scoring the last four goals in a 4-2 win at Oxford United, Wilkinson was unhappy with his new striker. "Gordon Strachan takes the penalties," Sutton said. "Lee Chapman grabbed the ball, put it on the spot, took the penalty ... when we got in that dressing room, the manager went absolutely mad. He said to 'Chappy', 'You, *you*. You see that miss today, trying to be greedy, get your hat-trick? That might cost us the title because this could go down to goal difference', ... it did go down to goal difference! And that was a couple of months before the end of the season. That's how tight, how hard it was that season." Chapman scored three goals in his next three games, though, as Leeds made it four wins in a row.

Leeds lost form just as quickly as they found it, going winless in their next four, and even a big 4-0 home win over promotion rivals Sheffield United was tarnished by the concession of a late goal in a 2-2 draw at Brighton and Hove Albion in the following fixture. Still, Leeds had two of their last three games at home, facing Barnsley on Wednesday before hosting Leicester City on the Saturday. Fairclough's first-half goal gave Leeds the lead against their Yorkshire rivals but Barnsley won 2-1 to become the only away side to win a league match at Elland Road in the 1989-90 season. "We battered Barnsley ... we played really, really well," Kamara said. "The Barnsley goalkeeper that night had an absolute stormer ... I always remember going in the dressing room after that game and Howard just saying, 'You didn't do anything wrong. We just got a couple of sucker punches', ... he's just said, 'Look, that's football, unfortunately. Sometimes they don't go in. But if we play like that against Leicester on Saturday, then we'll still be fine.'"

Leeds could have sealed promotion with victory against Leicester City if results went their way but Haddock said there were no pre-match nerves. "We weren't nervous at all. I think we knew what we had to do then ... the Barnsley result was a bit of a fluke ... the players were full of confidence going into the Leicester game." In front of a noisy home crowd, United came out firing, Sterland giving them the early lead. "I remember it as if it was yesterday. Bobby Davison put me in with a great ball. I had a great first touch and hit it and it has gone through my brother-in-law's legs [Tony James] and in! It was a great day," the goalscorer said. Leeds pushed hard for a second but again ran into a goalkeeper in inspired form. "We absolutely pummelled Leicester that day, chance after chance after chance," Kamara said. "[Goalkeeper Martin] Hodge … he had a worldie … when you're on the pitch back in that season, '89-90, you could not hear what somebody five yards away was saying to you. That was the deafening noise. That was the buzz. It was just amazing. To play in that atmosphere every single week was just great … the noise back in that time was something special."

Leeds' inability to get a second would come back to bite them when Gary McAllister, impressing in Leicester's midfield, levelled proceedings with a fierce strike that hit the post and went in. "I had always a good goalscoring record against Leeds United," said McAllister, who had scored against Wilkinson's men earlier that season, too. "There's no better place to go and show your worth than Elland Road, especially when it was a packed house and the pressure was certainly on Leeds United … I knew there was interest from Leeds United [in me]." Asked if that made him more determined to play well, McAllister said: "Absolutely." McAllister, who would move to Leeds in the summer, remembered a "pretty hostile" atmosphere and said there was one major difference between the two sides. "He [Strachan] was 34, 35 at the time and he was just simply head and shoulders above everybody in that division … he was a class apart. It was a masterful piece of recruitment by Howard Wilkinson. Vinnie Jones had been brought in prior, similar impact, and then Gordon came and I think he was the final part, allied to a young Gary Speed and a young Batty. They had the makings there to get out of that division."

Yet as Leeds threw bodies forward in the latter stages, it seemed that McAllister's goal would see both sides share the spoils. That was until a United long throw was headed towards McAllister, who tried to boot the ball clear. It hit Strachan, though, before Speed set up his captain on the edge of the penalty area. What happened next is etched into Leeds United folklore as Strachan fired a fizzing left-foot volley in from the edge of the penalty area to send Elland Road wild. "It was just a flash of brilliance, it probably wouldn't happen again in 50 attempts, the way the ball just landed at his foot and it went like a flash into the corner of the net, hence, I think, the words that I used: 'Have you ever seen a better goal?'" John Helm said of his now-iconic Yorkshire

Television commentary. "I was lifted on a crescendo by the very sight of that ball flashing from his boot in the space of that one second into the roof of the net ... of course I followed that line by saying, 'Have you ever seen one better timed?' which just ran straight through my head because I know I'd just said, 'Five minutes to go', ... it's not that great a line, 'Have you ever seen a better goal?' But I still feel at this moment that I haven't seen a better one, really, because it was just the way it was struck. It was struck with absolute venom."

"The relief on everybody was unbelievable ... it was fitting for him [Strachan] to score because he had really put so much into that season," said Haddock, while Kamara added: "The 'skip' could always come up with a bit of magic when he was in that Leeds shirt and you always expected him to." Wilkinson felt "huge relief" and the final whistle was not far away, with fans flooding the pitch in celebration. Leeds United had not been promoted, though, despite what Jones was telling teammates. "Vinnie comes in, says, 'Lads, lads, we're up! Newcastle have drawn. Newcastle have drawn! We're up!'" Sutton remembered. "So I walked out, I saw John Helm ... I said, 'John, see we've done it'. He said, 'No, Alan.'" The information was wrong. Newcastle United had beaten West Ham United and Leeds United's promotion push would go to the final day. It would go to Bournemouth.

DEAN COURT | MAY 5 | ATT: 9,918

BOURNEMOUTH 0-1 LEEDS UNITED

1990 | CHAPMAN 49'

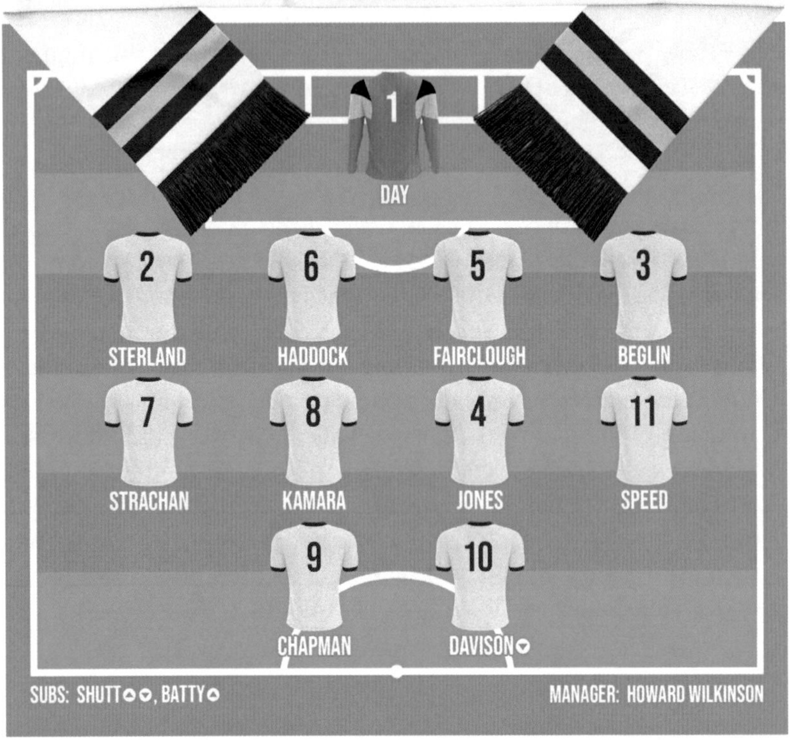

BOURNEMOUTH

PEYTON, BOND, COLEMAN, SHEARER, MILLER, PEACOCK▼, O'DRISCOLL, BROOKS, AYLOTT, LAWRENCE, BLISSETT

SUBS: CADETTE▲

MANAGER: HARRY REDKNAPP

OUR FORM HEADING IN

LEEDS UTD 2-1 LEICESTER

LEEDS UTD 1-2 BARNSLEY

BRIGHTON 2-2 LEEDS UTD

"The Bournemouth game - if anything could go wrong, it went badly wrong."
- Howard Wilkinson

Leeds United's preparation for a crucial trip to Bournemouth was far from ideal. Just one match remained in the season, with Leeds on top of the Second Division table, ahead of Sheffield United on goal difference. Newcastle United were two points adrift of Leeds and the Blades and, potentially crucially, had a better goal difference than both of their promotion rivals. The permutations were vast, given Leeds' opponents needed to win to guarantee survival, while Newcastle went to a Middlesbrough side also fighting to stay up. Howard Wilkinson's equation was simple, though. If Leeds United won, they would return to England's top flight after an eight-year absence. A draw or defeat could see Leeds pipped to not only the title but promotion, too, and for those reasons, Wilkinson was hoping for a smooth week. It did not happen.

Physio Alan Sutton was tasked with finding baseball bats and balls for a light warm-down that would end Leeds' final training session before heading south. "Went to see my mate, Shaun, [I said], 'Right, they want me to set out a baseball thing', … at the end of the training session, just something light," Sutton recalled. Wilkinson called it "Danish softball", what he dubbed as "a soft man's baseball" that used a soft ball but a proper baseball bat. "Vinnie [Jones] goes in. Vinnie thought he'd seen all this on the movies," Sutton said. "Ball comes up, missed a couple, then he smacked one, then, of course, Vinnie being Vinnie, he just threw the bat back. What does it do? It hits Andy Williams in the cheekbone, smashes his cheekbone. So, next thing is I'm taking Andy to hospital. I had to take him to hospital, get him sorted out, get the doctor sorted out to operate … Andy was expecting to be on the bench on Saturday."

There was another problem. Bobby Davison, who had been battling a knee injury in the promotion run-in, had told medical staff that he could not play. "I said, 'Well, look, I need to speak to Bobby then. Don't let him talk to anybody. Just bring him now, straight away and I'll have a chat to him'," Wilkinson told a physio. The manager had a plan. "Basically, I said, 'Look, Bob, don't tell anybody about this', ... my striking options were then Carl, Carl Shutt. So I said to Bob, 'Bob, look, this is what I'm going to do. But you must not tell him. You start the game, three minutes, four minutes, whatever, come off. Even if you just walk 10, 15 yards or whatever, so that we get the start of the game out of the way. Then you come off and I'll bring Carl Shutt on', ... Carl would score goals ... Carl had about a two-and-a-half games of nervous energy in him - because of his make-up and how he got worked up and he was using energy the night before, mental energy. So I said, 'So, Bob, he must think and hope that he's going to be on the bench. Otherwise he starts the biggest game of his life having sat there knowing it's the biggest game of his life.'" Shutt, a much-loved member of the United squad, could be "a bit nervous" before games, according to Chris Kamara, who roomed with Davison on the trip and was the only player to have knowledge of Wilkinson's cunning plan. "Bobby wasn't fit. He wasn't fit at all," he said.

Leeds headed south two days before the game and Wilkinson had another surprise up his sleeve. "It was just one of those things, right off the cuff. He [Wilkinson] just said at the hotel, 'Right, we're going out, going for a meal and a couple of glasses of wine, bit of relaxing,'" Peter Haddock said. "So we ended up in an Italian having a meal and a couple of bottles of wine and it was just so relaxed ... you were so relaxed, it was unbelievable ... we were back in the hotel for 11pm or before 11pm, back in our rooms and that. It wasn't a case of staying out and that but it was like ... he never had done that sort of thing before. I think it helped." A Friday training session followed and Wilkinson, a keen student of sports history, took his players to Oxford University, where Roger Bannister became the first person to run a mile in under four minutes. "Howard had known all about that and he was full of the nostalgia of it and all, why we were training there and all that sort of stuff," Kamara said. Wilkinson went to Bournemouth's ground, too, flanked by assistant Mick Hennigan and Sutton. "We got on the pitch and it's 80 degrees [fahrenheit], rock hard, so I thought, 'They're going to water it', and they had one little sprinkler in the penalty area," Sutton said. "So we got the groundsman [and asked], 'Are you watering it before tomorrow?' 'Yeah, yeah, I'll water it'. He was lying - they were never going to water it."

Back around the team hotel, the Leeds players were well and truly aware of the thousands of United fans who had travelled down to support their team, as they filled Bournemouth, beaches and surrounding towns in preparation for a Bank Holiday weekend. "There was a load of Leeds fans [who] came to the hotel trying to see [us] … they were on the beach. I think they came down two days before the game as well," Haddock said. Glynn Snodin, not playing due to glandular fever, had similar memories. "The day before … we thought, 'We'll just go for a nice walk out'. It was a lovely, lovely day … there were Leeds fans everywhere! On the beaches, they'd got tents up. We went, 'Wow! This is different'." The stifling temperatures stuck with Mel Sterland. "There were thousands of fans on the beach and it was red hot. Boiling hot. I couldn't believe how hot it was." The temperatures did not deter Kamara from a matchday morning run, though. "On the Saturday mornings, I always used to go for a run. I know it's crazy. In this day and age, these fitness coaches and all that would tell you not to do that but I felt so much better by going for a run and a loosener on the morning of a game. So I did that in Bournemouth. I ran all along the beach and through the town and all that sort of stuff, so I saw the Leeds fans out in complete mass. I always remember them looking and thinking, 'No. It can't be, can it? It can't be Chris Kamara running around Bournemouth on the day of the most important game in recent history', … I realised that they'd taken over the whole place."

There were reports of pre-game crowd trouble and the thousands of Leeds United fans trying to get to Dean Court would cause Wilkinson another issue, too. "On the day of the game, having gone to great lengths for the preparation to be right, we've now got Andy Williams back in hospital with a fractured cheekbone. Bobby's got a bad knee. And then about quarter to 12, the chief inspector or whoever's in charge comes to me and said, 'I'm sorry, Mr Wilkinson. We're going to have to bring the leave time from here forward'. And I said, 'What?' He said, 'Well, there's 10,000 in the ground … but there's 10,000 outside the ground and by the way … if they can't get near that one gate they're stacked up behind it and we can't get the coach through that lot quickly. It's going to take a long time'. So I said, 'Just give me 10 minutes'. When he said it, I knew what we were going to do but I said, 'Just give me 10 minutes', so I disappeared, went up to my room, went to the toilet, took my time, came down and I said, 'I've thought about it and we're going to leave at quarter past one, as is planned'. I think it was 20 past, actually. And he went, 'I definitely wouldn't advise that and I cannot guarantee that we can get you [there in] time for kick-off, et cetera'. So I said, 'Look, it's my decision. If we have to, we'll stop the bus and we'll walk'. And he said, 'No, I can't allow that'. I said, 'Well, what's your problem?' He said, 'Well, I've just told you 10,000 [fans will be there]', so I said, 'Yeah, but that's it. They're Leeds fans and it's the biggest game of their life for about the last 20 years. So if we have to, we walk'." The team bus could not get to where it needed to be, but the walk was not far. "They [fans] just parted because it's the lads and they're going to try and get us in the First Division," Wilkinson added. "The lads walked through, they parted ... so we get in the dressing room and all the tension that was on the bus, maybe at the moment we stopped the bus, had dissipated because of the distraction, it was like the parting of the waves ... then all we've got is the problem of, 'I just hope Bob can walk to the centre circle and stand there and when we start the game, at least stay on that pitch for three or four minutes'."

"To see thousands and thousands and thousands of fans who didn't have tickets, to be down there, it was just amazing. You realise ... you knew what a big club Leeds was but you realised on that day that it was a massive club because you might get one or two hundred turn up without tickets, but not thousands and thousands and thousands," said Kamara, before reflecting on the final team talk. "Before the match, he [Wilkinson] said, 'Look, we're going to have to be patient today, more than anything else', because Bournemouth needed to win to stay in the division. They had a good team, the likes of Luther Blissett and Kevin Bond and players like them. They had a decent team. So he said, 'You're going to have to be patient today. Very, very patient. We don't go willy-nilly. You sit and you hold and the goal will come'." It did not come in a frustrating first half for Leeds, though, even though Shutt, who replaced Davison in the sixth minute, made an immediate impact in the hot conditions. "'Shutty' came on and had a blinder. Should have scored, actually, a couple of times, but didn't. [He] came on, worked his socks off ... that taught me loads about man-management and how to deal with situations and everything. It was a masterstroke," Kamara said. Bournemouth goalkeeper Gerry Peyton made a good save to deny the forward but Shutt's running and work-rate was causing the hosts problems and Leeds were clearly the better side in the first half. "We were on top. We were bossing the game and that but it was nils each. You're always a bit wary when it's nils each, in case you concede a goal," Haddock said. Leeds also had other results to worry about if they could not win.

Inside, Wilkinson said he was feeling "tense". "I had two people in the stand getting the results of the other games because Sheffield United and us could have both been beaten by Newcastle, but Newcastle had to win and we had to lose. If we lose and Sheffield United win or draw and Newcastle win, we don't go up. So there were about three ways we couldn't go up and it was probably their biggest game for years so it was tense. It was tense but we had some very strong characters who were good ... people like Chrissy Fairclough was a silent rock. He didn't say a lot but when he did say something it was usually very accurate. He had really high standards. Mel was just Mel, he just played ... Chris Kamara had been there before. Gordon [Strachan] was a huge influence."

Sheffield United were 4-2 up at Leicester City at half time, too, while Newcastle's clash at Middlesbrough was goalless. When play resumed in the second half, Leeds were inches away from taking the lead with an own goal, only for Bond's attempted clearance to hit the post and bounce away to safety. But the opener was coming, Kamara setting up the promotion-sealing goal. "Two or three times throughout the first half I'd gone galloping forward and I could hear him [Howard] ... from the touchline, 'You sit in midfield and hold. Sit in midfield and hold'. I was going, 'No, no, don't worry, don't worry, don't worry', but ignoring him most of the time as well," Kamara said. "He kept shouting from the touchline. When he warmed 'Batts' [David Batty] up, I thought, 'Oh, shit. I'm in trouble here', ... obviously I crept forward, crossed the ball into the box, 'Chappy' [Lee Chapman] headed it in and I looked over to the bench and I said, 'Now I'll hold', [laughs] ... we were desperate to get a goal. We had loads of chances ... the one thing you knew about Chappy is if you put in a decent cross, he would get on the end of it. Very underrated centre-forward, but having said that, he had some great clubs throughout his career if you look at them, your Arsenals and Sheffield Wednesdays of this world. You're obviously a decent player if you go to them. I was just fortunate that Chrissy Fairclough just laid it back for me and I was able to spin it in over the two Bournemouth centre-backs, then Chappy got up and bulleted the header into the back of the net … a great moment."

"He was just like a big target man, really. He knew where to be in the box, he knew what positions to take up and if balls came in there, he would be on the end of them," Haddock said of Chapman. Wilkinson, who brought the goalscorer to Leeds in January, simply said: "Chappy had always scored goals for me." Snodin, flanking John Helm in the Yorkshire Television commentary position, said "the place erupted" and "you could feel it [ground] moving," as the Leeds fans celebrated wildly. With Sheffield United in command at Filbert Street, Leeds would need three points to win the title but promotion was all the travelling fans really cared about. Snodin, a Leeds United fan since he was a kid, remembered feeling very anxious. "You kept looking at your watch, thinking, 'Has it stopped? Hurry up, let's get this over and done with'. But goals started flying in at Ayresome Park as Middlesbrough heaped the pressure on Newcastle, with ex-Leeds striker Ian Baird getting two for Boro in what ended up being a 4-1 win. News from that game slowly filtered through and meant that Leeds were on the brink of going up and that Bournemouth would be relegated if they could not conjure up some late magic. Haddock - later named man of the match by the local press - and Fairclough kept them at bay, though, with the sound of the final whistle sparking a pitch invasion from all four corners of the ground. Leeds United had done it. Leeds United were promoted.

"We had all the Leeds fans coming on the pitch and we got off pretty quickly and back in the dressing room and we could hear them, just Leeds fans, shouting and whatever," Haddock said. "In the dressing room, we brought the champagne and that but I think it was just a case of relief that we had done it … it was a great honour to win man of the match that day." Kamara said that for him, it was a dream come true. "It was a dream for me to play for Leeds in the first place, to be part of a successful team … to go to Leeds at the position that they were in and to maintain that position right to the end with Newcastle and Sheffield United snapping at their heels, it was great." Snodin recalled scenes of utter jubilation amongst the Leeds players and coaches. "Trying to get over to the changing room to celebrate with my teammates, it must have taken me an hour. I was surf riding over everybody! I didn't mind. I didn't mind one bit. What a great day. It was like one big family then. Everyone was in that dressing room and hugging each other … that's how much it meant to them, even though they were absolutely shattered … everything just drained through you."

And how did the manager feel? "I was shattered … when the dressing room was empty and they'd all left, you're just knackered. Just knackered. I don't think you're proud at that point … it was relief." Wilkinson stayed with some friends afterwards but the party was just getting started. "They had all this champagne on the coach," Sutton said. "All of a sudden, Gordon goes to see Bill Fotherby, he said, 'Mr Chairman, Bill, do you mind if we stop and get some beers and some lagers because not all the lads are into champagne?' Which none of them were. [He said], 'Oh, yeah, yeah'. So we stopped in Winchester and we stopped at this corner shop … me and Vinnie Jones and somebody else, we walked in there and we just cleaned him out of every beer and every lager he had. He was like, 'Well, you've cleaned me out. I've got none for my regulars!'" Sterland remembered having "a hell of a lot to drink on the way back", while Snodin described the scene on the bus. "All the season had been done so everybody was just absolutely celebrating … some were singing. Music was on, singing, dancing up in the aisles." Trips to venues across Leeds were in store once the squad returned to Yorkshire, too. "It was amazing. Most of us went out in [nightspot] Mr. Craig's afterwards, in Leeds," Kamara said. "It was great. It was lots of Leeds supporters in there and they looked after us in there … Leeds were back after all those years. It was a special moment."

Asked to look back on Wilkinson's role in turning around the fortunes of Leeds United so quickly, the manager's players insisted he deserved major credit. "He was very organised off the pitch with set-pieces and things like that. He was the first manager to do it, I think," Haddock said. "He was very well organised about position, how we were going to play against them and their key player … what they were going to do and how to stop them and what we were going to do to win the game

… but set-pieces were his main tactic. He knew. Certain set-pieces which we did all the time … we scored a lot of goals off them [in] that year … he was very well organised. He's probably the best manager I played under."

Kamara credited Wilkinson for improving his major flaw. "The first thing that Howard did, just before I signed on the dotted line, he said, 'Right, we've got one thing to say to you. If you get booked for sliding in, then I'm going to fine you £100. If you get sent off for lunging in, I'm going to fine you a week's wages. I want you to be 99.9 per cent certain when you do your sliding tackles that you can win the ball'. Nobody had said this before and I thought, 'Flipping hell, it's going to cost me money'. So, all of a sudden, I'd been given a focus within the game itself. Instead of trying to win balls that were virtually impossible … you would bide your time and you would wait … don't forget, I'd gone there on a three-game ban that I'd had from Stoke City, for getting sent off at Middlesbrough. I only had one yellow card between then and the end of the season, I think Vinnie was the same. That's what it was. That's how good a manager Howard was. Not only did he improve you, he knew what your weaknesses were. Nobody told me that was my weakness, that I'm trying to win balls that I shouldn't be trying to get. They just left me to do it, because I was winning more challenges than not but obviously ending up with yellows here, there and everywhere … that was great."

There was no time for Wilkinson and Leeds United to rest on their laurels, though. The manager's goal was to win the First Division. It was now a possibility.

Leeds United's eight-year exile from the top flight was finally over. Photo: Andrew Varley Picture Agency

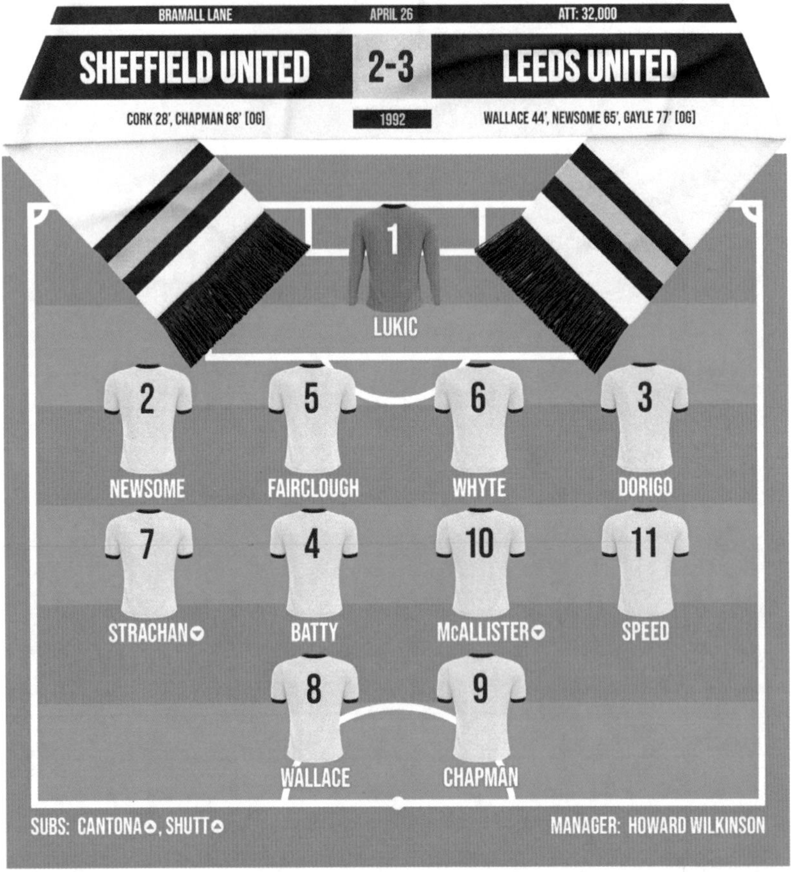

SHEFFIELD UNITED

REES, PEMBERTON, GAYLE, BEESLEY, BARNES, BRADSHAW, GANNON, ROGERS, HODGES, CORK, DEANE

SUBS: WHITEHOUSE, BRYSON

MANAGER: DAVE BASSETT

OUR FORM HEADING IN

LEEDS UTD	2-0	COVENTRY
LIVERPOOL	0-0	LEEDS UTD
LEEDS UTD	3-0	CHELSEA

"They [Manchester United] had a commanding lead and then I think the worst thing for them was that it was us that was chasing [them]."
- Gary McAllister

Judging a Wednesday night karaoke contest in the Leeds suburb of Seacroft, Gary McAllister was given some good news. Manchester United had lost. Again. McAllister's Leeds were involved in a thrilling battle with their rivals for the First Division title and, all of a sudden, it was possible that Leeds United could be crowned champions of England as soon as that Sunday. "There's loads of functions that are shared around the players - it's a rota system. I was up in Seacroft. There was a lot of celebrations that night ... that was a big turning point," McAllister said. Leeds had not won the league yet, of course, and the Scotsman said key to a strong finish was a single-minded focus. "It was a case of just trying to get results off the teams in front of us - not to look what was happening across the Pennines. That would be dangerous. We just had to get on with our own job."

It was impossible for supporters not to obsess over Manchester United's downturn in form, though, those fans thrilled to see Leeds United finally engaged in another top-flight title race. Don Revie's Leeds made an immediate impact when they first returned to the First Division in the 1964-65 season, finishing second to Manchester United on goal average, and Howard Wilkinson's men also turned heads in their first season back in the big time. That 1990-91 campaign saw Leeds finish fourth and make runs to the semi-finals of the League Cup and a northern area final of the now-defunct Full Members' Cup. In Lee Chapman, Wilkinson had a prolific scorer, the striker notching 21 league goals, while Gordon Strachan's brilliance was shown when he was named Football Writers' Association Player of the Year. New signings McAllister, John Lukic and Chris Whyte all slotted in seamlessly, too, as Leeds looked on the rise again. "I wanted to go to a big city club with a proper crowd," said McAllister, who swapped Leicester City for Leeds United. "I think we surprised ourselves a little bit in the first season and probably were a wee bit disappointed to finish fourth ... it was a case of not having any fear. We had the fans on side, the board was very supportive. We had a manager who had great experience and probably never ever received the praise that he deserves as a coach and a manager." McAllister's manager was satisfied. His initial plan, agreed on with chairman Leslie Silver prior to taking the Elland Road job, was on track. "My projection with Leslie [was] that - one year in the [Second] Division and then maybe with two or three years of that, good enough to win the championship and then beyond that, Europe."

More additions in the summer were needed to complete Wilkinson's dream and Australian-born left-back Tony Dorigo was on his radar. Dorigo, a Chelsea player at the time, recalled being driven around Yorkshire by Leeds United's charismatic managing director, Bill Fotherby. "He took me up in his Mercedes or Bentley, whatever it was, and showed me the best roads in Leeds and [said], 'This is the lovely house there', and he's trying to tell me how much they were because I was used to London prices. And I'm going, 'Wow, you can get that for that much? That's amazing'. But it really got sold to me when I talked to Howard Wilkinson ... to suddenly hear someone that had a coherent plan, who had been building his side, who had got out of the Second Division, who had come up in the first year and they got fourth and then who were looking for the gaps in the side. And he [Howard] said, 'And you're one of the gaps that I really, really need and not only you - I want to get another England international. I'm going to get Steve Hodge, I'm going to get Rod Wallace because I need lightning pace up top and we think we could really do something'. So it was a combination of all of that, of feeling wanted, of a plan and passion, I suppose." Dorigo soon joined and Wilkinson was true to his word, Hodge arriving from Nottingham Forest and Wallace - and his twin brother Ray - joining from Southampton. Jon Newsome and David Wetherall joined from Sheffield Wednesday, too, while the initial outgoings were minimal, John Pearson heading for Barnsley, while Peter Haddock and Jim Beglin retired.

Dorigo got an early taste for Wilkinson's man-management. "I've not even trained and met my teammates at all - I'd signed and gone away with England ... I had a single hernia and the other one started playing up as well, so when I got back I had to go straight [away] and have an operation ... a double hernia recovery normally takes six weeks and so now I'd turned up at Leeds' training ground, the first day and I'm waddling along because I can hardly walk because my stomach is all sewn up and everything else. I go in to see the boss and Mick Hennigan was the coach and so he's in the office [too]. I'm in there seeing the boss and so I walk in, he sits me down and he says, 'Bloody hell, I think I've signed the softest Aussie ever'. And I've gone, 'Right'. And he was serious, deadly serious face. Mick Hennigan, serious face [too] … I'm thinking, 'Hold on a sec, four or five weeks ago, you're talking to me like I'm the best thing since sliced bread, you really want me here. And now that I've signed, I've come here and I'm waddling in and you're saying, 'I'm the softest Aussie going', … at that moment, I'm thinking, 'Right, is he serious?' And I didn't respond straight away'. And he said, 'Well, you know what, the doctor said it's six weeks that you're going to be out. But I had a hell of a left-back at Sheffield Wednesday, Nigel Worthington, he was back in five weeks', … so then I go, 'Jesus Christ, if you think Nigel Worthington's good, wait until you fucking see me. And I'll be back in four', … Howard then come out into a big grin and he was just joking with me … anyway, I was back in four. I had to [be]!"

The defender was fit in time for a 1-0 season-opening win over Nottingham Forest and it took until October for Leeds to suffer their first defeat as Wilkinson's new-look side clicked immediately. That loss at Crystal Palace was met with a powerful response, too, Leeds claiming 4-3 and 4-2 league wins over Sheffield United and Notts County respectively before a 1-0 success against Oldham Athletic at Elland Road on October 26 saw Leeds replace Manchester United at the top of the table. "Our home form was fantastic and with the crowd, as games progressed, you could feel and sense the crowd getting excited," Dorigo said. "We were then excited, which made the crowd more excited … it was like this snowball effect. And I swear [in] certain games, I'd look at my opponents, whoever it was, and we would beat them in five minutes. I could see in their eyes that they weren't quite up for this because not only were the crowd going crazy, we could be physical as well, so David Batty would put a tackle into someone … we could play but we could stick our foot in as well. We could do it in all sorts of different ways and the crowd just helped us so much."

National interest in Leeds United was growing and growing, with the midfield quartet of Strachan, McAllister, Batty and Gary Speed the envy of every club in the country. "I played with a lot of good players, played against a lot of great players," McAllister said. "I'd quite simply say that the [Leeds midfield] four would … they would definitely compete today, even when there's a lot more tactics around but we were never a straight line of four … there was a lot of interchange. Obviously, Gordon Strachan didn't play wide, he played in the park. It was Gary Speed who gave us a bit of width but [he] came in the park. David Batty was, before [Claude] Makelele was even known, was a holding midfielder who preferred to just sweep across his back line and I was an attacking player, so there was resemblances of a diamond … Strachan had experience and guile … Gordon was the best player. He was very influential. He was obviously a leader but he was simply unplayable ... he had the hunger and desire but [it was] obviously allied with ability. He was technically very good. He was a fantastic player … Batty was probably one of the most underrated players I've ever played with. He had a wonderful range of passing but most importantly could intercept brilliantly. He could read people … I don't think people really respected how good he was. And Gary Speed, God bless him, he was just a young, energetic player who gave us so much on the left-hand side. Naturally left-footed, gave us width. Had good knowledge of coming in the park to allow Tony Dorigo to go on the outside … [Speed was] probably one of the best I've ever seen in the air, so any deliveries into the box from set plays or just in open play, he had a great skill at arriving and [was] powerful in the air."

A televised trip to Aston Villa in late November then saw United win in style, Chapman scoring twice in a 4-1 triumph. "We wiped the floor with them, 4-1, it was an amazing result," Dorigo said. "You're thinking, 'Wow, we can do this away from home, we're strong with home [games]. We could beat anyone, simple as that.'" A run of four successive draws saw Leeds drop to second before they impressed on their travels again, following up a 3-1 success at West Ham United with a 6-1 thrashing of Wilkinson's former club, Sheffield Wednesday, a result that gave the manager immense satisfaction. "They threw the ball out [from the back], Sheffield Wednesday, always threw the ball out," he said. "The idea was … we'd play 4-3-3, let the ball get thrown out to one of the full-backs or the other and then to have our three in midfield would mark their two [central midfielders] but Gary McAllister would mark and Gary Speed would mark but David Batty'd sit behind them and the front three would get the ball to be passed from full-back across, so, stop it going into midfield, stop it going wide or if it does go wide, stop them turning and so on … on that day, we got six, it could have been more … the discipline that they'd shown in the week and then to see it happen … when you coach, sometimes you're looking at the result and things like that but when you get to 4-1 in a game and what you've done is still working, it's one of the few times in your life you actually start to enjoy [a match]. [It is] almost like watching a show where you're the composer and every player hits every note and at the right time. You sit there worrying about nothing, enjoying the game and thinking, 'This is fantastic … even though I do say it myself'."

January also saw Wilkinson's men dumped out of the League Cup and the FA Cup by Manchester United in what ultimately could have been a blessing in disguise. There was a problem, though, with Chapman breaking his wrist in the FA Cup tie, and Leeds lost momentum in his absence, winning just one of four matches. The striker returned much quicker than expected and scored alongside new signing Eric Cantona in a 2-0 win over Luton Town but more injury trouble was around the corner, Mel Sterland suffering a bad ankle injury at Tottenham Hotspur that would lead to his eventual retirement. Sterland's replacement received an early baptism of fire. "I'd made my debut with Sheffield Wednesday as a right-back," Newsome said. "Wasn't my favourite position but when you're 20, 21 years old and you're playing for Leeds United, the gaffer asks you to play somewhere, you're happy … I was obviously quite nervous [at Tottenham] and the ball came through to me … I went to make the challenge and the guy pulled his foot out of the way and I ended up just kicking the ball long. And I remember Gordon Strachan turned around and just screamed at me and he just said, 'We're better than this!' And I thought, 'Right'." Newsome, who would play an important role in the run-in, also scored that day at White Hart Lane in a 3-1 triumph. "I remember going up for the corner and I said to Gary Speed, 'Where does Mel go on corners?' And he said, 'Oh, just stand on the penalty spot. You'll score. You're gonna score', … the ball came up, I just picked the flight of the ball straight away and thought, 'Right, I'm going to head that'. And I just thundered [it] in … it was my first goal, just didn't know how to react. And Gary

Speed was jumping on my head, laughing his head off saying, 'I can't believe that you've scored! You've scored'. So, yeah, it was a bit of a surreal moment."

Leeds lost their next game, 4-1 at Queens Park Rangers, and although they were still two points clear of Manchester United with eight matches remaining, Alex Ferguson's side had three games in hand and were title favourites. Leeds then drew successive games against Arsenal and West Ham before being hammered 4-0 at Manchester City's Maine Road, form that saw them drop to second. "We took a bad beating there … we got spanked," said McAllister, while Wilkinson remembered how everyone wrote Leeds off. Manchester United were now one point ahead of Leeds and had two matches in hand, too. "Everybody said, 'That's it - finished'," Wilkinson said. "So, on the Sunday, I thought long and hard. I spoke with my assistant Mick Hennigan … by the end of Sunday afternoon, I'd started to be absolutely certain about our best team from the players we had available." The time for chopping and changing was over. Wilkinson wanted to show faith in his players. "I got them in on Monday and I said, 'We've got five games and we're going to play the same team for every game, except one game, Liverpool away, when I will make one change'." Dorigo remembered his manager urging the squad to make the most of the opportunity. "Howard and how he dealt with us then was really good after that … he said, 'We're still not out of this … but we have to go and win everything now. What have you got? What are you about? You've done all this work to this point, how strong are you? I think you are strong', so he'd build you back up again." Wilkinson also gave his players reason to believe, eyeing Manchester United's trip to Anfield on the penultimate weekend of the season. "I said this to them, 'I'm telling you. If Liverpool think they can spoil their party, they will'."

Three days after Manchester City beat Leeds, they went to Old Trafford and got a point in a 1-1 derby draw, and Cantona scored a memorable goal in a 3-0 win over Chelsea that saw Leeds briefly go top. April 18 then proved somewhat of a turning point, as league leaders Manchester United dropped points to a Luton side who would be relegated, meaning Leeds' goalless draw at Anfield was not the worst result. And Leeds were given a massive boost when Nottingham

Forest won at Old Trafford on April 20, before Wilkinson's men beat Coventry City 2-0 at Elland Road. It set up a huge trip to West Ham for Leeds' rivals and they were stunned 1-0 by another team who would be relegated, giving Leeds the ascendancy in a thrilling title race. That swing of results meant Leeds prepared for a trip to Sheffield United on the penultimate weekend of the season leading the league by one point, while Manchester United, who had no games in hand left, had to travel to Liverpool. "Liverpool were not going to give Manchester United any favours. There was a massive air of confidence that we could take care of Sheffield United - not to disrespect Sheffield United," McAllister said. "All of a sudden it was, 'You know what? This is on. This is on', … I just remember going into it thinking, 'Right, you've got to hold your own'," Newsome said. "I'm a Sheffield lad brought up as a Sheffield Wednesday fan, so to go and play at Bramall Lane and try and beat them is like the cream on top of the cake for us."

Newsome remembered much of Wilkinson's pre-match team talk. "Howard was into golf… his words were, 'Trust your swing. [A golfer] doesn't stand on the first tee in the last round of the major and start analysing his swing, he trusts his swing. He trusts what's got him here'. And that sat with me a little bit. Just carry on doing [the normal], don't start questioning yourself, just carry on doing what's got us here and that will see us through … I thought it was a really good analogy, really. He took the pressure off us, there was no pressure on us [saying], 'We've got to win the game', none of that. It was just, 'Go out and play and what will be will be'. And I think that saw us through."

Bizarre conditions greeted United's players, Wilkinson summing up the weather of the day. "It was an awful day in the sense that it was sunny, then it pissed it down, then it'd be a gale, then it'd be sunny again. Then the wind would suddenly change direction." Sheffield United took a 28th-minute lead, Alan Cork bundling in from close range following a goalmouth scramble from a corner, but Rod Wallace levelled in odd circumstances as a clearance cannoned off Speed and into the scorer. "It was the most bizarre game of football … really bizarre goals, own goals and deflections," Dorigo said.

Leeds went into half time level and after Speed was denied by the woodwork, the visitors scored the most normal goal of the day from a free-kick. "I was just trying to whip it in towards the back post and then you've got your people going across the line of the ball. 'Newse' wanted it the most," McAllister said of his set-piece that was nodded in by Newsome at the far post. "Set-pieces were a massive part of football back then and we used to work on them a lot," Newsome said. "We spent hours on the training ground and one of the bugbears of them [Howard and his staff] was for free-kicks or corners to come in and go out past the back post unopposed. You see it all the time today. And they always used to go on about … 'Whoever's around the back door, you can't let the ball go out of play. That's your job, to be there to stop that'. And that was my run on the day, my run was to peel out and go round the back. Floaty ball from Gary 'Mac', keeper came out, made a mistake … I just couldn't believe it. As it's coming over, probably a millisecond from [when] you're heading it, you're thinking, 'This is a goal', … before you know it, it is a goal and everybody's jumping on you." McAllister said set-pieces were a great asset to that Leeds side. "We didn't lose many goals from set plays. The hours spent at the end of sessions just repeating and repeating, it just became a bit of a muscle memory. I knew where everybody was moving, I knew where I had to put the ball."

Sheffield United found a way back into the game, though, thanks to a Chapman own goal. "Corner came in, John Pemberton, who was a very good friend of mine, who ended up at Leeds, he turned, swivelled, hit it. It hit 'Chappy' on his shin and went in and we were like, 'Ugh. Here we go'," Newsome said. The Leeds United players and fans could not believe it.

But if the equaliser was a lucky goal, so was the 77th-minute winner. Cantona, inside his own half, nodded the ball forward in what initially looked like a harmless situation. "I'm thinking, 'Go on, Rod, you'll get on the end of it, chase it down type of thing'," Dorigo said. The speed of Wallace and Cantona's follow-up caused problems and Sheffield United's Brian Gayle was feeling the pinch when he used his knee to lift the ball in the air, backing himself to win the resultant header. Gayle did win the header, too, but only beat his teammate, Mel Rees, to the ball after the goalkeeper charged off his line, leaving Wallace and

Cantona to race after it and watch it bounce into the back of the net. "Good bit of skill from 'Gayley' there," McAllister said. "His first touch, I'm thinking, 'Decent'. Then he's flicked it over … it was a bizarre day. It was windy and it was messy. He lost his bearings and I think the presence of Eric was obviously worrying him. These things happen at these moments and you need a bit of luck." Dorigo remembered the moment with fondness. "It's bouncing and I'm thinking, 'Oh, crap, it's going in, it's actually going in!' And then, of course, that's it. You're going nuts … I am just deliriously happy … what he did - I have no idea why. I am forever thankful that he did!"

Leeds then had to hold on for all three points. "We had two centre-halves who were just fantastic. Chris Whyte and Chris Fairclough, the most honest players you'll meet all day long," Dorigo said. "They keep putting their head in the danger area. It was fantastic and we held out." Leeds United now knew that if Liverpool were to beat Manchester United at Anfield, they would be champions of England. The entire team and staff did not watch the match together, though, Wilkinson going home for a meal while Dorigo headed for his in-laws in preparation for national team duty. Others, like Newsome and Speed, were keen observers of the action at Anfield from Sheffield. "Ian Rush scored … that was his first ever goal against Man United," Newsome said. "Gary Speed was obviously in the Welsh squad with Ian Rush, so there was a connection. We were like, 'This is nailed on, this.'" It took some time for a second goal to come, Mark Walters eventually extending Liverpool's advantage to the delight of West Yorkshire. "We were like, 'Yes', punched the air and that kind of thing," Newsome added. "And then thoughts really went to, 'Right, how are we going to celebrate this?' It was about the time when mobile phones had just started coming in, so a couple of the guys had got mobile phones and we were on the phone to each other. We made some arrangements to meet up in Leeds, so me and Gary were just, 'Right, let's get in the car and let's get back to Leeds as fast as we can.'" McAllister, who watched the game at Chapman's house in front of television cameras, had an earpiece on and had just watched Manchester United boss Ferguson give an interview. "He was heavily mentioning that Leeds hadn't won the league and that Manchester United had lost the league. I flippantly said, 'Well, as gracious as ever in defeat', and obviously he heard it. I had an earpiece on so it had gone live into the tunnel!"

Wilkinson did not even watch the match and it was his son, Ben, who had the honours of providing the good news. "We invited Bill Fotherby and his wife and two friends to our house for lunch … Ben came down the stairs … he was about three or four, I think … just walked in the dining room and said, 'I think we've won the championship, Dad. They've just scored again.'" Wilkinson's afternoon meal soon morphed into a house party. "That was fantastic because I'd had a few drinks, got over the game, got my second wind. I've got some friends there and then it was good because people turned up spontaneously, just come round to say well done … you say, 'Hey, come in and have a drink', and before you know it's 8pm, 10pm, 11pm, it's a full house. Some of the staff had come round and it was just a nice feeling." The manager said the feeling of vindication that came with winning the First Division was incredible. "It's just an unbelievable sense of satisfaction, really, and it's an actual proper stamp in your book that you've got it right. It's as if somebody said, 'We've gone through your papers and we agree with the marks of the examiner. You deserved to be marked top of the class', sort of thing. It's that. Because it's not a one-off. It's 40-something games and all sorts of things happen."

While Wilkinson was at his Sheffield home, Sterland, who was in the stands at Bramall Lane earlier in the day, was having a drink. "I didn't watch it. I was in a pub, having a few pints … there was no Sky in the pub or anything like that. I didn't watch any football. A couple of my mates rang me and said, 'You've won the league!' I said, 'Fuck off'. But they said it again … I was celebrating with my mates in Sheffield." Dorigo was in Pant, close to the England-Wales border, where he watched the game before preparing to meet his England teammates in London the next day ahead of a friendly in Russia. "I get a phone call and it was from the boss, Howard Wilkinson," he said. "And he said, 'Tony, congratulations and everything else'. I said, 'Yeah, fantastic, it's incredible'. He said, 'I've had a word with the England boss, Bobby Robson it would have been then. And he said, 'He understands and you don't actually have to travel if you don't want to, you and 'Batts' [Batty] don't have to go'. At least that's what I think he said because he mumbled like hell! I said, 'Fantastic. No, I don't want to go, I want to stay and celebrate', ... so then I did jump in the car." Dorigo missed his teammates in Leeds on that night for the initial celebrations at the iconic Flying Pizza restaurant, but he would have plenty of time to toast the success over the next few weeks.

Wilkinson's men had one match left, a 1-0 victory against Norwich City, and the players were given a huge reception at a famous parade through the streets of Leeds. "That day was unbelievable, especially to be on that balcony and see [everyone] … every conceivable way into that place was blocked with just people … and then you really appreciate what a one-club city it is," the manager said. "Oh my God, that was amazing," Sterland said. "To see the thousands and thousands of fans - I have flashbacks about that. You just don't forget things like that … going round on that bus was amazing." Newsome remembered nearly causing an incident as the celebrations continued. "The parade was crazy. There were thousands and thousands of people. Incredible … it was just a party, carnival atmosphere on the bus. We were just laughing and joking, we're having a couple of beers and a few drinks and yeah, it was just good fun … we got introduced one by one [to the fans]. We got the trophy and we held the trophy up and I remember holding [it] up and the top of the trophy fell off. It landed on the wooden stage, otherwise if it had gone down, I have no idea what would have happened. I'd have been in some real trouble."

Leeds United's manager then called his players to Elland Road for one last meeting. "Howard was saying, 'I just want to congratulate everybody. You put a real shift in, done an immense [job]', … he was full of praise to us," Newsome said. "I remember at the end he said, 'Has anybody got anything else to say?' So Chris Fairclough has put his hand up and said, 'Oh, aren't we going away, gaffer?' Because we always used to go on an end of season trip. And he said, 'I didn't think you'd want to go away'. We were like, 'Really?' So within a couple of days they had arranged for the lads, I think it was about 10 of us went and they took us away. We had three or four days in Spain having a bit of a party and a further celebration."

ASTON VILLA

BOSNICH, CHARLES, EHIOGU, McGRATH, SOUTHGATE, WRIGHT, TAYLOR, DRAPER, TOWNSEND, MILOSEVIC, YORKE

SUBS: OAKES, STAUNTON, JOHNSON

MANAGER: BRIAN LITTLE

OUR FORM HEADING IN

LIVERPOOL	3-0	LEEDS UTD
LEEDS UTD	2-2	EVERTON
BLACKBURN	1-0	LEEDS UTD

"We kicked off at 5pm. At half past four, Tony Yeboah comes to me and says, 'Alan, my knee is not right' ... half an hour before the game!"
- Alan Sutton

Leeds United's first Wembley final in 23 years was just 30 minutes away but star striker Tony Yeboah was getting cold feet. He confided in Alan Sutton, putting the physio in a difficult position. "I thought, 'Bloody hellfire. Here we go'. We had Brian Deane on the bench and I think there were one or two other people. I think Tomas Brolin was on the bench as well. Anyway, I said, 'Tony, look, I daren't tell the manager'. I daren't just say, 'By the way, he's [out]'." Sutton, a very popular figure among United's players, was torn. Did he throw a major spanner in the works or was Yeboah just getting nervous? "Whether there was a little bit, I don't know, panicking before the game?" So he tried to talk Yeboah round. "It was all about using a bit of psychology, [saying] 'Tony, look, what you do is go out and start ... go out, play. Right? See if you can run it off. If need be, if you don't [think you can], pretend you've twisted it or you've got in trouble and you've twisted it. Then he [substitute] can go on and then they can take you off ... that solves the problem'." Yeboah got through the 90 minutes but it was a frustrating day for Leeds United.

Howard Wilkinson had already seen one of his best players ruled out in the days leading up to the League Cup Final, Tony Dorigo injuring his hamstring in a late fitness test that forced a major United re-shuffle. "I got injured in the semi-final, the League Cup semi-final against Birmingham City," Dorigo said. "I had a problem with my sacroiliac joint in my pelvis ... I then got stupid hamstring injuries quite a lot ... I had this repeated cycle which was really frustrating and, of course, got injured in the semi-final, so I'm trying to get back fit for the final. And basically the boss [Wilkinson] was telling me, 'Listen, just get fit and you're starting, obviously you're straight back in, just make sure you're fit for the final'. And so I recover, recover, recover. I start training on the Thursday for the game, leaving it really late. So, on the Friday, I kind of join in a little bit [at training] but not fully. Think I'm going to play, think I'm going to make it. And then I needed just a fitness test ... we're at Bisham Abbey in London so we're already down there, got one local training session before we play the final ... I'll never forget,

Gary Speed came up to me and 'Speedo' said, 'Please, please be fit', because he hated playing left-back, he did not want to play left-back. He says, 'You've got to be fit, I don't care, strap your leg up, just get out there and play'. I said, 'Mate, I want to play left-back, don't worry about that. I want to play - it's the final. I dream about these things, it's what you want and against Aston Villa, my old club, it's one occasion … I want it'. Desperate to play, Dorigo made it through to the dying stages of his fitness test. "I needed just to do four sprints, like 20-yard little sprints. First one, boom out [of] the blocks, fine. Second, boom, third one, boom, fourth, bang. Pulled it [hamstring]. And I just thought, 'Ahhh'. So I was devastated, in tears, so it was flipping awful. And the lads saw me and Speedo, he came up and he said, 'Jesus, sorry mate', because obviously he felt for me, but it was awful. So that was it - back to the hotel, getting treatment." Speed, who fractured his cheekbone in the build-up to the final, would have to deputise in more of a defensive role.

The injury news was a blow to Wilkinson, in his eighth season in charge at Elland Road. The Sheffield-born manager had overseen significant change at Leeds since the 1991-92 First Division success, even if the club's start to the Premier League era almost ended in disaster. Leeds finished that campaign in 17th, just two points above the relegation zone in a 22-team league, as they struggled to get to grips with the new backpass rule. Eric Cantona, who scored a hat-trick for Leeds in a 4-3 Charity Shield win over Liverpool in 1992, was sold to Manchester United later that season and his £1.2million move across the Pennines was a source of constant discussion in the years to come. Gary McAllister maintained that Cantona had to be sold, though, and that Wilkinson's decision to let him go was necessary. "The relationship [between Wilkinson and Cantona] had completely broken," McAllister said. "When you've got a player on the training ground who doesn't want to commit, the manager's got to make a stance. There's nobody bigger than the club. Cantona's a fantastic footballer. I think everybody knows that … but at that moment in time, for the benefit of the squad, Eric - it wasn't right."

Leeds' European run in the 1992-93 campaign was short-lived, too, but Wilkinson steered Leeds to fifth-placed finishes in the next two seasons as the likes of Rod Wallace, Brian Deane and then Yeboah impressed, while Gordon Strachan moved on to Coventry City in 1995. Yeboah scored famous goals against Liverpool and Wimbledon in the 1995-96 season and his hat-trick in Leeds' return to European football, in Monaco, delighted supporters. Wilkinson's side shipped eight goals over two legs to an excellent PSV Eindhoven team in the second round of the UEFA Cup, though, and indifferent league form meant the only way to return to continental action was through the cups. Leeds made good runs on two fronts, reaching the quarter-finals of the FA Cup, while their run to the League Cup decider was highlighted by a series of Speed winners, the Welshman scoring the decisive goal in second round, third round and quarter-final victories against Notts County, Derby County and Reading respectively. Leeds also saw off Blackburn Rovers in the fourth round, but the come-from-behind win over Reading set up a two-legged semi-final against Birmingham City. "We dispatched Birmingham in the semi-final, won pretty comfortably," McAllister remembered. A 2-1 away win in the first leg set up Leeds' progression, with Phil Masinga, Yeboah and Deane scoring in a 3-0 success at Elland Road.

"My own feelings going into it [the final] were excitement. Playing at Wembley in a cup final is something, as a kid, that you dream about," David Wetherall said. "To have that as a possibility going into it, in the weeks building up to it and the days building up to it, I just felt a sense of excitement. I didn't feel like we were pressured, I suppose, and [I was] just really looking forward to the day, to the match and to the occasion." Lucas Radebe might not have dreamed of playing at the home of English football as a child but now 26, the South African defender could not wait for matchday, either. "I watched teams playing at the old Wembley. It was a great honour and a privilege to be able to join all the greats, in all those matches, big matches they've played at that special stadium. I was looking forward to it."

Liverpool knocked Leeds out of the FA Cup just four days before the Wembley final, but Wilkinson remained confident. "It [Villa] wasn't even a game that I thought we might win. It was a game I thought we could and should win," he said, while McAllister hoped a good record against Aston Villa would help his side end that Wembley final drought with victory. "We were very much aware [of the drought]," McAllister said. "In my six years there, there was never really any great runs in any of the cups … [but] over the years we had a decent record against Villa, so it was probably a 50-50 game. There wasn't an outstanding favourite." Under Wilkinson, Leeds had lost just three of 14 matches to Aston Villa, but one of those defeats came less than two months before the final, Dwight Yorke scoring twice in a 3-0 success at Villa Park.

Andy Gray, then 18, was a second-half substitute in the FA Cup loss at Anfield and had made just three starts for Leeds but was given an inkling his fourth might come at Wembley from youth-team coach Paul Hart. "I remember on the Tuesday, Paul Hart saying to me, 'Make sure you're ready for the weekend', and I thought that was a bit strange," Andy, the son of Frank Gray and the nephew of Eddie Gray, said. "He didn't elaborate on it too much, just, 'Make sure you're ready'. We actually had a reserve game that night away at Stoke … I think I only played 50, 60 minutes, came off … it was in the back of my mind that I might be involved but I didn't know until the day before the game when we went down to London." The late notice meant Andy's father was stuck in the Middle East, forced to watch his son's breakout performance in Bahrain with Arabic commentary. "I didn't need the commentary - I could see what was happening … things went from bad to worse," he said. The teenager remembered Wilkinson's calming influence in the hours before the game. "With Howard, he didn't make a big deal of it at all. I remember him just saying to me, 'You're playing tomorrow, just go out and enjoy it and do what you're good at'. That was it, there was no big speech or anything like that. Very, very low key. Obviously, I was delighted and I remember speaking to my dad and people about it and they just said, 'Make sure you take everything in because it goes very quickly', … my mum was there, Eddie was there, family were there, my sisters and a lot of my friends. They're all Leeds fans … I'd grown up in Leeds so I was always a Leeds fan."

Gray would start in a support role to Yeboah in a 3-5-2 system that many of United's players did not remember playing often. "We hadn't spent a great deal of time working on a back three. It was makeshift, to say the least," said McAllister, while Wetherall felt Dorigo's injury forced the change. "That gave Howard some decisions to make and

I'm sure he could've gone a number of different ways going into the game. Aston Villa played three centre-backs which probably wasn't a system that was employed too often in the league at the time, so that presented its own challenges. They had a system that was embedded and they fully understood what they were doing so that presented more challenges, I suppose, from a tactical perspective … I don't recall playing it [3-5-2] much … you want to go into any game knowing that you've got whatever system you're playing well embedded and you're used to it and everybody's used to the positions and everybody's had time in previous games to bed the system in."

It did not really matter what formation Leeds used in a very one-sided League Cup Final, though. Despite his inexperience, it was Gray who was Leeds' best player, and he shot wide after beating Gareth Southgate on a surging run into the penalty area with the score still goalless. "Howard Wilkinson was always encouraging me to attack players and try and go past them and that's what I tried to do … try to take people on and make things happen. Unfortunately, that shot went past the post. It looked like it was [in] and then it started curling wide." Shortly after, Savo Milosevic opened Villa's account with an excellent strike from distance. "I was stood right behind it … you're almost thinking, 'Yeah, go on, hit it', because it was that far out," Gray added. "But it just went straight like an arrow, right into the top corner. It was a great strike. He was a very underrated player." Wetherall said the goal "set us back". "The last thing you want to do in any game is fall behind, particularly there when you know you're up against a strong Villa team. With the occasion, you just want to get the upper hand in the game or at least maintain the status quo."

The chances kept coming for Villa, too, but Leeds managed to get to half time trailing by just one goal. "We actually started the second half quite well. We were on top and we looked like we might [score]," Gray said. "We had a five, 10-minute period where we looked like we might score … I can remember he [Wilkinson] brought Mark Ford off at half-time and I think he brought Brian Deane on and changed it around a little bit." Leeds did enjoy a good period after the break, Gray having a pair of attempts on goal. "We were on top … I was getting quite a bit of the ball and a bit of joy down the left-hand side and [had] a couple of efforts. I got a corner and one the keeper saved - maybe I could have squared one across goal." A second goal in the game was coming but it was to be Villa's, Ian Taylor making the most of a shoddy clearance from Radebe with a tremendous volley from 12 yards. "I was on the line and, to be honest, I thought I had got it," Wetherall said. "It was quite a low one [volley] so I kind of swung myself to my right and with a diving header … I thought I was so close to getting it and clearing it so I just had that real disappointment. It was one of those things, it was so close but just not to be, that was my overriding sense of it in the immediacy of the second goal, that by an inch, an inch more towards me and I would've got it."

Villa's two-goal lead "did really knock us" according to Wetherall, while Wilkinson bemoaned his luck. "The first two [goals] were quite decent … you're like, 'Bloody hell', because normally those … normally it's about one in bloody 30 of them [that go in]." Wilkinson put Brolin on in an attempt to chase the game but it did not work, Yorke capping a famous Villa day with a third goal in the 90th minute. That produced an angry outburst from the Leeds fans, with Wilkinson the target of their frustration. "It's not enjoyable but it's part of the job," the manager said. "I can honestly say it's the only time ever, the first time ever I've experienced that up until then. Ever. That's Sheffield Wednesday, Notts County, Leeds United. Never experienced that but I mean it's part of the life. It's part of the life. What can you do about [it]? Not a lot." McAllister could hear the criticism during the match and was very unhappy with it. "I was captain … it was not good. When we lose, we lose together, so to pick an individual, that's not right. If there was going to be any angst from the crowd, it should have been aimed at everybody. To pick on the manager was poor … I didn't like it. I didn't like the fact that the manager took the brunt of the entire defeat. Obviously, we were massively part of [the defeat]. Players lose games, not managers."

The abuse continued after the final whistle, too. "We went across to applaud our fans, we could hear it," Gray said. "It was loud and, to be honest, as an 18-year-old kid having grown up and seen Leeds win the championship under Howard, I thought it was out of order. I could understand the fans' frustration to an extent but that was the first major cup final Leeds had been in for a long, long time. I know we didn't perform but we still got to a major cup final at Wembley and anything could happen on the day."

Whether it was because of the defeat or the criticism, Sutton remembered a shattered Wilkinson on the way back to Leeds. "What I remember was [being] sat on that coach going back to get the train, because we went by train. I remember he's sat on the coach … he looked like a really broken man … I was surprised." Wilkinson said he was stewing over a number of questions. "Was it my fault? Did we train too hard? Didn't we train hard enough? Did we get [to] the hotel too early? I don't know … I've never been as flat in my life going back on the train, never, not in football terms." The day still provokes strong memories from those involved, too. McAllister winced when the Villa match was raised, but Wilkinson summed it up best when asked how he remembered the fixture. "With horror."

ELLAND ROAD | SEPTEMBER 7 | ATT: 39,694

LEEDS UNITED 0-4 MANCHESTER UNITED

1996 — MARTYN 3' (OG), BUTT 49', POBORSKY 77', CANTONA 90'

SUBS: BEENEY, COUZENS, HATELEY ▲, RADEBE ▲, GRAY ▲

MANAGER: HOWARD WILKINSON

MANCHESTER UNITED

SCHMEICHEL, NEVILLE, MAY, JOHNSEN, IRWIN, POBORSKY ▼, BECKHAM ▼, BUTT, GIGGS, CANTONA, CRUYFF ▼

SUBS: VAN DER GOUW, McCLAIR ▲, COLE ▲, SCHOLES, SOLSKJAER ▲

MANAGER: ALEX FERGUSON

OUR FORM HEADING IN

BLACKBURN	0-1	LEEDS UTD
LEEDS UTD	1-0	WIMBLEDON
LEEDS UTD	0-2	SHEFF WED

"I drove to the training ground for about four weeks not really wanting to drive to the training ground."
- Howard Wilkinson

Change was in the air in the summer of 1996 and Leeds United's manager was expecting a tap on the shoulder. Leeds had new owners, The Caspian Group, a media company who initially gave the manager a significant transfer budget to freshen up his squad. Leeds limped to the finish line in the previous campaign, winning just two of their last 16 Premier League matches in a run that included the League Cup Final disaster. Howard Wilkinson's eye for young talent was shown in the signing of Lee Bowyer, who arrived from Charlton Athletic in a £2.6 million deal that broke the British transfer record for a teenager. More proven signings were made, too, as Lee Sharpe crossed from Manchester United for a joint club-record £4.5 million fee, while goalkeeper Nigel Martyn joined from Crystal Palace and veteran striker Ian Rush moved from Liverpool.

There were plenty of outgoings at Leeds as well, as United opted to cash in on club captain Gary McAllister and Gary Speed, moves the club would come to regret. While Speed went to Everton, McAllister linked up with Gordon Strachan at Coventry City. "I think he [Wilkinson] was trying to make change but at no point did I feel that I was going to be part of the change," McAllister said. "I didn't want to leave Leeds United, certainly. So, when they accepted an offer from Coventry, I was still reluctant to go. It was when the monies of Sky were starting to impact and I was 31 at the time. It probably was one of the first times I'd made a monetary decision. But I still would've probably stayed at Leeds if they had offered probably half of what Coventry offered … my six years there was probably where I played my best football. It was when I was in my prime. I was very sad to leave … I think there was a fourth, first, fourth, fifth. We had one bad season, obviously the year after we won it [First Division], but we qualified for the UEFA Cup … I think my mind was made up when the club felt they were quite willing to take £3 million on a 31-year-old, which, I can understand that, because as an asset, as you go up into your 30's, your value goes the other way. But I think I proved that I still had a few years of football left."

John Lukic, Phil Masinga and Nigel Worthington also left, with four of Wilkinson's new signings starting in a 3-3 opening-day draw at Derby County. Leeds' defending was poor in that fixture, to say the least, but Bowyer popped up with his first goal for the club in an encouraging display. A 2-0 home defeat to Sheffield Wednesday followed, a match that Wilkinson partnered Rush with fellow 34-year-old Mark Hateley up front. The manager's hands were tied, given Tony Yeboah, Brian Deane and Rod Wallace were sidelined, but Leeds returned to winning ways with 1-0 successes against both Wimbledon and Blackburn Rovers. From four matches, seven points represented a reasonable return but rumours about Wilkinson's future continued to swirl. And the man himself said he had been told "by another manager" that he was about to be sacked. "I'd been told that the company that had bought [Leeds], Caspian … had already appointed a manager and it was just 'when' and not 'if'," he said. "It wasn't only me that knew, but the players knew. They knew because in football, as someone once said to me a long time ago, 'If you fart in the dressing room at Newcastle, they smell it in Southampton's dressing room the next day.'"

The rumours created an uncomfortable environment for those at the club in Wilkinson's final months, as Tony Dorigo recalled. "He [Wilkinson] was struggling. Unfortunately, we could really feel that. It was like he would walk around with the weight of the world on his shoulders and it'd become really apparent. And then that's when, yeah, [it felt like] the beginning of the end. You could see that we're trying all sorts of different things again, like training on a Saturday morning, not training on a Saturday morning, going straight to the game, not straight to the game and all that, which - it's nothing to do with that. But we're trying to come to some weird way of everything working again. I just think at that point, suddenly the meetings become longer and longer and longer and you can see someone struggling, simple as that."

A major distraction was on the horizon, though. The visit of Manchester United. "They're big games, really big games and [the] first game that obviously Leeds fans look to in the fixture list is Man United at home. That came pretty early on in the season," attacker Andy Gray, a Leeds supporter himself, said. The Elland Road faithful had good memories of recent home clashes against their rivals, winning the last two, with David Wetherall's effort helping the Whites to a 2-1 success in September 1994. Wetherall thrived in these matches, also scoring the winner in a 1997 clash. "The Man United-Leeds games have a unique atmosphere for matches at Elland Road," Wetherall said. "It's the most intense atmosphere that I experienced, and it is incredibly intense. Leeds, I suppose, hasn't got that natural local derby if you like, being a one-club city. And that rivalry is there with Manchester United and that's the one where there is that real extra level of buzz around the place ... I can't remember which Man United game it was but we arrived very early at the ground and you sat inside the stadium and, all of a sudden, there's noises outside and you're looking around and asking people, 'What's that? What's happened?' And someone just [says], 'The Man United team bus has just arrived'. The noise [when] you run out for those games was just incredible ... to be fortunate enough to be on a side that got a couple of positive results against them at Elland Road and get on the scoresheet a couple of times was a fantastic experience for me." Leeds beat Manchester United in West Yorkshire again in 1995, McAllister, Yeboah and Deane scoring in a famous 3-1 win on Christmas Eve. "It was a cracking atmosphere ... Elland Road was bouncing as it can do," Richard Jobson said. "The crowd were really up for it - they were up for it anyway for any game - but especially Man United. They were the team to beat, they had a strength right through the team, obviously [Eric] Cantona ... and with it being Christmas Eve, there was the Christmas spirit amongst the fans and it was a fantastic occasion, probably the highlight of my short spell at the club."

There would be no way that Caspian could have dispensed with Wilkinson if he could mastermind another win over the old enemy and Manchester United had won just one of six league clashes at Elland Road since the manager helped Leeds back to the top flight. The transformation of the Leeds squad was shown by the fact just four players - Wetherall, Jobson, Gary Kelly and Carlton Palmer - who started the pre-Christmas fixture in December were involved from the beginning less than nine months later. And that much-changed team made a disastrous start, Ian Harte's attempted clearance hitting Martyn's head and crossing the line for a bizarre own goal in the third minute. "Playing against your local rivals at home in a must-win game, it was a big blow to concede so early," Gray said. The goal did little to spark Leeds, too, and the visitors had a chance to double their lead when Wetherall pulled Jordi Cruyff back inside the penalty area. Up stepped public enemy No.1 and, to the delight of the home fans, Cantona shot wide, as Leeds got to the break just one goal down. Leeds physio Alan Sutton remembered Wilkinson trying to use the moment to lift his side. "I remember him saying at half time, 'Well, obviously even they're feeling the tension about the game'. Because Eric never missed penalties."

Nothing could inspire Leeds, though, and Nicky Butt soon doubled Manchester United's lead. Wilkinson rolled the dice, as Gray, Hateley and Lucas Radebe all came on in a triple substitution after Bowyer was injured. "I went off with a detached retina. I had a shot … it got blocked and it hit me straight in the face and I went down and then I got up and I opened my eyes and I couldn't see out of one of them," Bowyer said. "The physio said, 'What's wrong?' I told him, 'I can't see out of that eye', and I had to obviously come off." Even though Leeds only trailed by two goals, Gray felt like the game "was over by then". "I don't think we created any chances or anything," he said. "I remember in the game it was pretty [much] one-way traffic all the way through."

Karel Poborsky got the third goal of the match as a feeling of utter resignation swept through Elland Road, only momentarily replaced by anger when Cantona scored in stoppage time and celebrated with his arms outstretched in front of the Don Revie Stand. "It was just a devastating day, really," Gray added. "I think everybody, more or less, [was] resigned to the fact that the manager might be going and it was almost a case of 'this is the end of the road' type of thing. It wasn't, from what I recall … I don't think it was as spiteful as it had been [previously]." Jobson said Cantona was a very difficult opponent. "For whatever reason, he transferred to Manchester United and that was the catalyst for them … he was the final piece of the jigsaw for them and it was just a superb fit for him and for Man United. So, no doubt, there's obviously a clear animosity between the two clubs and, obviously, Eric was probably [bearing] the brunt of that on that day, but he probably left the pitch with a smile on his face, no doubt. He was at the height of his game … he was a very tough player to play against."

United's players would be hit with feelings of guilt over the next 48 hours before Wilkinson was sacked on Monday. "Everyone was down and there was speculation for the rest of that weekend about Howard's position. You just felt down … there was speculation all weekend, after the game on Saturday, all day Sunday and then on the Monday morning," Jobson added. "I felt sorry for Howard … I was one of his signings and played in quite a number of the games leading up to his sacking." Wetherall said "real disappointment" summed up his mood after the match. "I knew Howard from Sheffield Wednesday. I was a young player at Sheffield Wednesday and he brought me up to Leeds so we went back further than Leeds, although obviously I was only a junior player at Sheffield Wednesday. To see what he'd achieved at the club, at Leeds and the situation that they were in … I obviously wasn't there in the first period when they were near the bottom when he first took over, near the bottom of what is now the Championship, I suppose, [to see] where he'd taken them, getting them promoted and a high finish in his first season - that's then when I joined. He won a championship … it's then obviously extremely disappointing that it finished … I think it was the first time for me that I'd been involved in a first-team environment where the manager lost his job and I felt really guilty. We're the ones who go out on the pitch and, of course, the manager has a role to play making sure people perform and [with] organisation … I felt it. I felt for him and just real disappointment. I played a part, I've been part of a team that haven't got the results that would keep him in the job."

Bowyer, stuck in hospital after an operation on his eye, also had plenty of time to contemplate. "I remember waking up after the operation and the doctor saying to me, 'You might never play again'. And I left thinking, 'Wow! So I'm 19, I've moved up north, I could be blind in one eye and the manager that brought me up here has left'. It wasn't a good day." Sutton remembered a simple parting message from Wilkinson. "On the Monday morning we'd gone in - obviously he'd been told on the Sunday that it was all over … or he knew after the game, anyway. And then he obviously called everybody to see him, to say that he'd finished … he just said, 'That's it'."

Wilkinson's departure marked the true end of an era at Elland Road, one that saw Leeds lifted from the doldrums of the Second Division to top-flight glory, Wembley trips and a European run. There could be no argument. Wilkinson left Leeds United in a much, much better place. Given the length of his tenure and his drawn out goodbye, was he sad to leave? "Very, very," he said. "The worst thing about that, possibly, was the fact that that summer you're looking at the kids who are now there or thereabouts. [I had] already given Harry Kewell a debut, given Ian Harte a debut. There was Paul Robinson there, 'Woody' [Jonathan Woodgate] was there ... 'Smithy' [Alan Smith] up front. We had then, by then, got waiting in the wings, seven, possibly eight certainties for the team and then Lee Bowyer was another one. So we were on the threshold of having the team I'd promised Leslie [Silver] which was young, fresh, vibrant, brought up here, all we need to do is add to them and we're nearly there. You're at the training ground and you go and watch a reserve game the season before that, before the end, and then that pre-season you watch them and you think, 'Wow'. I mean Woodgate was a Rolls Royce ... pace, good in the air, great temperament ... Alan Smith was - he scored goals but he was one of those strikers who - he let you know he was playing. Ian Harte, big and strong. Paul Robinson. Gary Kelly had proved [his ability] ... you know you're looking [good]. I think we finished fifth the season before [1994-95] but you're looking forward to these kids [playing] and thinking, 'There's another dawn here.'"

There was to be no new dawn under Wilkinson, though, the manager saying Leslie Silver later regretted selling the club to Caspian when he did. "Leslie afterwards on a number of occasions was full of, 'Well, why we did that, I don't know. I don't know how I was persuaded', and so on. But it was the forerunner to what we see now which is people seeing it as a business rather than as a football club which needs to be run in a businesslike way to succeed." Wilkinson's soft spot for Leeds remains obvious and he added how proud he has been to watch so many young talents progress from the youth system he asked for. "It was good to be in at the rebirth. To go in there and climb into a battered, rusty old Rolls Royce with a Mini engine and leave a proper Rolls Royce, although not quite with the right engine but nearly there ... yeah, it was good."

Howard Wilkinson is one of just two Leeds United managers to lead the club to top-flight glory. Photo: Alex Knight Photography

Gary McAllister made 295 appearances for Leeds United as a player. He also managed Leeds in 2008. Photo: Steve Riding

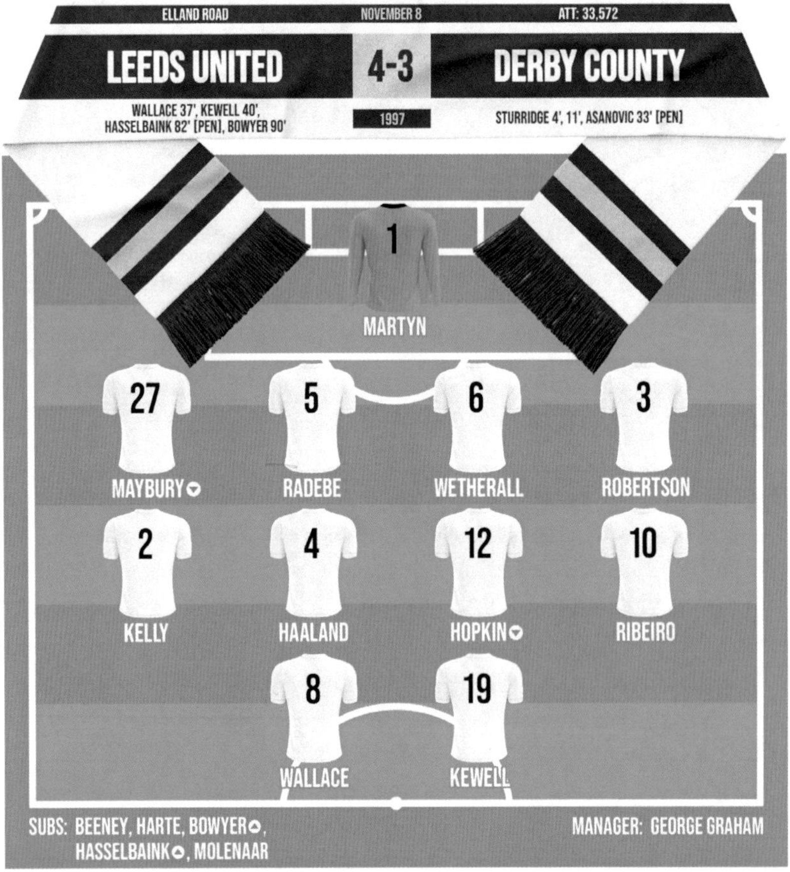

DERBY COUNTY

POOM, ROWETT, LAURSEN, CARBON, C.POWELL, DAILLY, CARSLEY, D.POWELL, ASANOVIC, BAIANO, STURRIDGE

SUBS: HOULT, WILLEMS, KOZLUK, TROLLOPE, HUNT

MANAGER: JIM SMITH

OUR FORM HEADING IN

TOTTENHAM	0-1	LEEDS UTD
WIMBLEDON	1-0	LEEDS UTD
LEEDS UTD	4-1	NEWCASTLE

"I mean, 3-0 down and you think, 'What the hell is going on here?'"
- George Graham

After turning Leeds United into one of the best defensive teams in England, George Graham watched on with horror as his side conceded three times in the first 33 minutes of a 1997 Premier League fixture against Derby County. The Elland Road crowd was restless and a rout looked on the cards, much to the frustration of a manager who had a defence-first mentality. "It was always my philosophy," he said. "When you start something, a project … I just thought, 'Right, let's get a base', so we can move onwards and upwards. But let's get the back right first … get the foundation right and then you can slowly build it into the midfield and then up front. That was always my philosophy at every club I was at." Graham took over from Howard Wilkinson in September 1996 and acknowledged it was a tough ask to follow in the footsteps of a man who enjoyed so much success at Leeds United. "They'd won the league under Howard … they were one of the top sides for quite some time, but one bad season … you didn't get much time. You don't have time in football. Everybody remembers when you do well but as soon as you get a blip, a big blip, then you're judged on that. In a way, it's unfair." Graham also said his friendship with Wilkinson made the situation more difficult. "We were both on the same LMA [League Managers' Association] committee, Howard and I, so I was quite friendly with him, actually. It was very, very sad to be taking over from Leeds with Howard getting the sack."

Leeds won just two of Graham's first nine matches in charge but his work on the defence would soon be recognised, United keeping five clean sheets in a row in the Premier League, following 2-0 wins over Southampton and Chelsea with goalless draws against Middlesbrough, Tottenham and Everton. "We did a lot of defensive work," Alan Maybury recalled. "George Graham was brilliant with us as young boys - we did a lot of work in the afternoon … often he would get the youth team over to play against the first team. My youth team included Harry Kewell, Jonathan Woodgate, Steve McPhail, Paul Robinson, players who went on to have top careers." A blip over the festive period was followed by a seven-match unbeaten run that included a fourth-round FA Cup win at Arsenal, Rod Wallace scoring the only goal at Highbury in the highlight of the season. Leeds lost to second-tier Portsmouth in the next stage of the FA Cup, though, and with goals extremely hard to come by, form waned in the last two months of the campaign. Leeds recorded a respectable 11th-placed finish but scored a league-low 28 goals. Only three sides had a better defence than Leeds but supporters, who watched United play out nine goalless draws and fail to score in 21 league fixtures, were desperate for more excitement.

United's struggles in attack were shown by the fact they endured a goal drought of more than two months on home soil before Brian Deane netted on the final day of the 1996-97 season but there were positives, like the excellent form of Lucas Radebe. "I loved his passion - that was the main thing," Graham said. "I look for that when I'm building a team, that's one of my first priorities, to see how he looks on the pitch - is he a winner? Does he come out and give his all, winning or losing? I want to see how they react ... I liked him, I just thought he was safe at the back and I thought he was excellent for me." Radebe also had the bonus of being versatile. "Playing in the midfield, he was very comfortable," Graham added. "It was ideal. In midfield, he was ideal for protecting the back four ... I could see him playing both positions but I wanted my back four to be right first then, before I moved on to midfield. That's how I usually built my teams but Lucas was very comfortable in both positions." Graham would make Radebe captain later in his Leeds United tenure but, in the summer of 1997, he turned his attention to other areas of the pitch knowing the South African was reliable.

"I thought we needed more power up front," Graham understandably said of his transfer philosophy that summer. Brian Deane, Carlton Palmer, Tony Yeboah and Tony Dorigo were among the departures, while the likes of David Hopkin, Alf-Inge Haaland, David Robertson and Bruno Ribeiro all joined Leeds. Graham's best signing was a man by the name of Jimmy-Floyd Hasselbaink, though, a striker who proved a hit with supporters after arriving from Boavista. "A great coach, a guy called Ian McNeill ... I was very friendly with Ian," the manager said. "He was out of a job at the time so I wanted him to start scouting ... we had some money to buy but not a fantastic amount so I asked Ian to go and cover Europe, to cover the different countries and to see who were the top three or six goalscorers in each country. And Ian went to Portugal … he got back to me, he said, 'George, you've got to see this guy', … he said, 'He's not a playmaker, he's a finisher, an out and out finisher with an unbelievable shot', … I watched him and one game, that was enough."

Hasselbaink scored in his first appearance, an encouraging 1-1 draw against Arsenal that saw five Graham signings make debuts. A 3-1 triumph over Sheffield Wednesday was followed by successive losses to Crystal Palace, Liverpool and Aston Villa before Leeds' blunt attack finally found form, United scoring seven goals in five days to see off Blackburn Rovers and Bristol City in the Premier League and League Cup respectively. Also in September, David Wetherall got a famous winner against Manchester United and when Leeds followed up a 3-1 League Cup success at Stoke City with a 4-1 league win over Newcastle United, confidence was high. Graham's attack was starting to click.

Leeds entered a home fixture against Derby on the back of a 1-0 win at Tottenham Hotspur, too, thanks to Wallace's eighth goal of the campaign. "We played Tottenham away and won, so you're on a high. [We] played really well against top players," said Maybury, who made his first start of the season at White Hart Lane. "My family was over [for] Derby … my home debut … we had been expected to beat Derby." But the visitors took the lead in the fourth minute, Dean Sturridge pouncing after Nigel Martyn spilled an awkward and challenging high ball. "It was one of those things, I suppose, you don't see it often at all … he was one hell of a goalkeeper," Wetherall remembered. Sturridge was quick to double his tally, shooting past Martyn after the keeper charged off his line, before Aljosa Asanovic was given the chance to put Derby 3-0 up from the penalty spot. "David Robertson had given away a penalty," Maybury said. "I felt if he let him shoot, I was blocking … the shot. It never hit me and I'm thinking, 'Where is it?'" Asanovic sent Martyn the wrong way, scoring comfortably, and Maybury acknowledged the Croatian was giving him a hard time. "I played right-back … he stayed really high and wide. I defended like I was taught to defend, so I would narrow up … but they pinged it wide, he took a touch and he delivered crosses. I couldn't get near him. We started the game on the back foot and then, suddenly, before you knew it, were 3-0 down. Bad situation to be in."

"It was so disappointing … we were conceding silly goals," Radebe said, while Wetherall feared the worst, even if he did not think Derby deserved to be so far in front. "3-0 down at home … the game is likely to go one of two ways and most of the time, it's going to continue to be huge trouble," he said. "It was a real strange one … I seem to remember the game not being one of those where if you're 3-0 down, you think, 'It's just been one-way traffic all day'. I don't seem to recall it being like that … it was just one of those games where three of theirs went in, I suppose, and, at that point, none of ours had gone in." For Maybury, this was "a new experience". "It's unravelling a little bit before me - I found it really difficult. I know my mum and my dad are over for the game and I'm stuck in a rut … a young boy, my home debut and I'm struggling here a bit, personally … to be 3-0 down, a big crowd, this was the second season under George Graham so we were expected to kick on and do a little bit better and then we're struggling. You're definitely feeling under pressure but it seems like every time they come up the pitch, they were scoring. It just deflates everyone." Asked about his mood, Graham said: "I think not happy would be the right expression."

Wallace gave Leeds some hope, though, turning in Ribeiro's long-range effort before Kewell thumped in an excellent volley to bring the crowd to life. Amazingly, Leeds would have been level by half time if Chris Powell had not cleared Haaland's effort off the line, meaning Graham had to rip up his team talk. "When you pick up two goals again before half time, then I don't have to really get into them about the goals they've conceded," he said. "They've got us back into the game again so, really, you think of what you've done in the last 10, 15 minutes … [you tell them], 'That's the way I want you to approach the next 45', … they were expecting, the boys, a bollocking at half time, instead they got the goals back, so we were on the offensive." Changes were necessary, though. "A bit of tightening up," Graham added. "This is what coaching [is]. When you're coaching a team, this is part and parcel of the game. Can you spot the problems? And can you put it right?" Radebe remembered a positive feeling in the changing room. "There was that feeling that we could beat Derby. I thought we were better than them … we know that we were capable of scoring goals."

Maybury was replaced at the break by Lee Bowyer, the defender acknowledging it was the right call. "I'm disappointed … but I'm also realistic enough and I'm sensible enough to know I was, maybe, struggling a little bit. And I learnt a lot from that game. I learnt then there's how you're taught to defend and then there's the reality of a game … I don't feel I made a big error in the game, it was just maybe [being] naive or a lack of experience. I was having a tough time in the game … it's the right call taking me off." Bowyer gave Leeds more of an attacking threat but, ironically, that was why he was finding starts hard to come by. "That was a period when George Graham said to me he's not going to play me until I do the defensive side of the game, so I was on the bench," Bowyer said.

"Once you get the fans at Elland Road behind you and you get that momentum … kicking towards the Kop [in the] second half … you feel you've got a great chance to kick on," said Wetherall, who was involved in Leeds' equaliser as Christian Dailly, trying to mark the defender at a corner, gave away a penalty for an obvious handball. Up stepped Hasselbaink, who was introduced for Hopkin as the hosts chased a result. Asked if he was confident when Hasselbaink prepared to take the spot-kick, Graham said: "Definitely, because he had one of the best shots, not only at Leeds, but the whole first division at the time. He's an unbelievable striker of the ball so when he's on a penalty, the keeper has got to do brilliant." Graham's confidence was justified, even though Hasselbaink went for placement instead of power to level proceedings.

Leeds were now throwing bodies forward, urged on by a passionate home crowd. "I missed a real good chance … a diving header," Wetherall said. "When I missed the chance it was [like], 'That could be it. That could be our last one'. You're just hoping that we get another one, another chance and someone takes it to get all the points. I thought the chance had gone." Hasselbaink took matters into his own hands, though, bursting down the right before cutting the ball back. Making a late run into the penalty area that would become his trademark was the 20-year-old Bowyer, who remembered his stoppage-time winner with fondness. "It came across my body onto my left foot and I struck it …

and it was just so true and just flew in there into the far corner and the place just erupted, just went ballistic … that was a good memory and it definitely must have been good because Jimmy passed and he never passes!"

"He [Bowyer] was always capable of scoring goals from midfield," Graham said of Elland Road's new hero. "He was a good finisher for a midfield player, very good, very calm, good technique. It never surprised me because he was always the one breaking from midfield into the opposition penalty box … when the crowd are roaring at Elland Road, which they were, I mean, it was fantastic … it was an unbelievable finish and the crowd loved it, the crowd really enjoyed it." Bowyer's teammates enjoyed it, too. "I remember Lee smacking in that left-foot strike and [I felt] just great relief and a sense of almost disbelief that the whole game had gone like it had - 3-0 down to come back and get the points was just one of those games that, I suppose, makes football such an amazing spectacle sometimes," Wetherall said. "Lee - he was just an all-action midfield player. I think probably his greatest quality - and this is not criticising his technical ability, because he could pass a ball and receive the ball and be creative - was his energy and his ability to arrive in the box at the right time. I think that was his greatest strength, just his non-stop energy and the ground that he covered during a game. He could be in the box defending one minute and the next minute he'd be up there looking to get on the end of a cross or being part of a breakaway."

"It's a great sign to come back from a huge margin. It shows the potential that the team had … it was brilliant," Radebe said, while Maybury added that comeback victories like that were the best part of playing football. "To come from a position of losing [where] you're dead and buried, to win, it's always the best," he said. "It's about momentum. If we had gone in at 3-0 [at half time], it would have been maybe impossible to win that game but to get back to 3-1, a goal out of nothing, 3-2, it just gives you belief … to win it with a late goal … it's happened a few times in my career. It's why you play. It's just raw emotion, it's hard to explain. It is everything."

Lee Bowyer scored 55 goals for Leeds United in 265 appearances. Photo: Andrew Varley Picture Agency

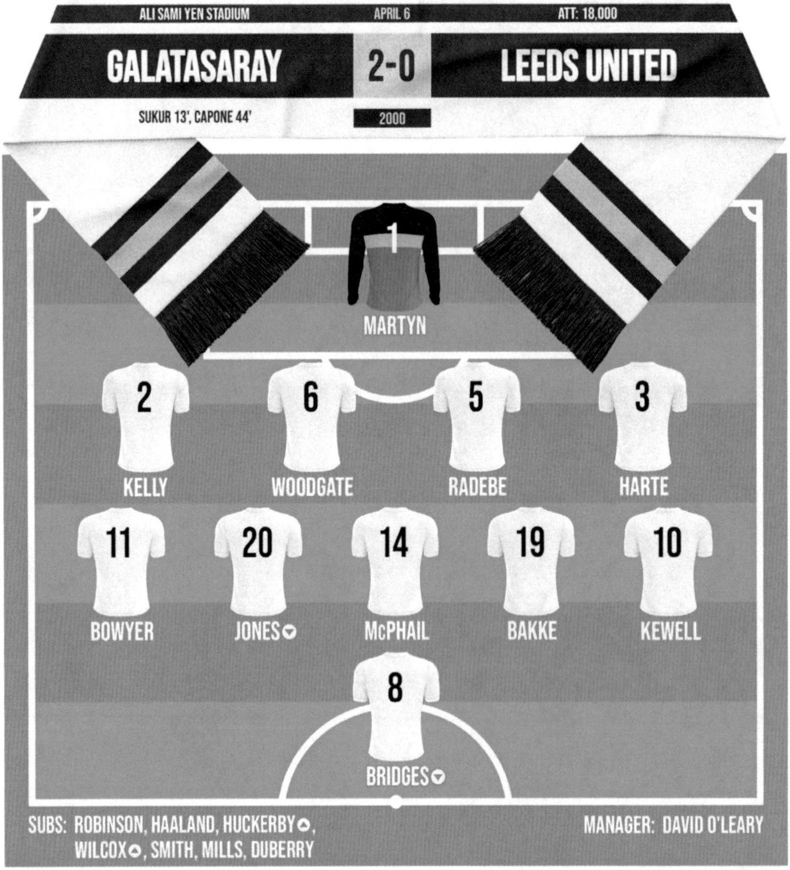

GALATASARAY

TAFFAREL, BULENT, POPESCU, CAPONE, ERGUN, OKAN▼, SUAT, EMRE, HAGI▼, ARIF▼, SUKUR

SUBS: BOLUKBASI, HASAN▲, FATIH, EMRAH, AHMET▲, HAKAN▲, MARCIO SANTOS

MANAGER: FATIH TERIM

OUR FORM HEADING IN

LEEDS UTD	0-1	CHELSEA
LEICESTER	2-1	LEEDS UTD
SLAVIA PRAGUE	2-1	LEEDS UTD

"The phone rang, then I could hear the voice on the other side saying: 'You're not going to come out alive. You're going to get killed'. It was terrible."
- Lucas Radebe

It was the night before the first leg of a UEFA Cup semi-final and Leeds United's captain was rocked. He quickly hung up his hotel room phone, something he should not have answered, remembering he had forgotten to follow team instructions. "We were warned before that when we travel that we should take the phones off the plug but we forgot about that because we were focused on the game," Lucas Radebe said. "We were only there to play football. We know the hostility in Turkey but it was a terrible feeling ... it was horrible to hear." Travelling through Europe brought its different challenges and United's players were continually targeted during their run to the last four. Most attempts at rattling them failed but this one had the desired effect. "I think it was our first trip to Russia and you get a knock on the door and it was room service at midnight," Michael Bridges said. "Then you get a phone call, then the fire alarms would go off. So there were all these tactics. Then we took our own security - Kevin and the boys from Manchester. And the big man - we nicknamed him 'Titch'. He was about six foot nine." Bridges could not remember the match but recalled boats near the Leeds hotel tooting horns throughout the night on one trip, while he also experienced "opposition trying to send women to your room". Bridges was not threatened before the Galatasaray game, though. He had remembered to disconnect his phone.

David O'Leary was now in charge of Leeds, the former assistant manager taking the top job after George Graham left to join Tottenham Hotspur. Under Graham, Leeds were on the rise again and finished fifth in the 1997-98 Premier League campaign. United's progress could easily have stalled when the manager walked out during the following season, but O'Leary stepped up and guided United to a fourth-placed finish - a position that allowed them to enter the 1999-2000 edition of the UEFA Cup. Leeds' young squad impressed in the European tournament, with many of the 1997 FA Youth Cup-winning team taking their chance to shine. Leeds reached the last four after a run that included victories over Partizan Belgrade, Lokomotiv Moscow, Spartak Moscow, Roma and Slavia Prague. Lee Bowyer and Harry Kewell scored five goals each in the competition, while new signing Bridges looked a star of the future.

The defensive partnership of Radebe and highly rated youngster Jonathan Woodgate was particularly encouraging, too, as David Wetherall was sold to Bradford City. "It was the emergence of Jon that, I suppose, hastened my exit from the club," Wetherall said. "Moving on from football clubs is part of the game and looking at the quality of player that Jonathan was, I'd have moved me on as well! If you've got a centre-back pairing of Jonathan and Lucas, I wouldn't be picking me over either one of them … he [Jonathan] had everything, he was calm on the ball, he was quick and he could head the ball as well." Wetherall was also full of praise for Radebe. "People just didn't seem to be able to get past him. I talk about his man-marking - you could put him to man-mark somebody and that would be it. You can just play 10 against 10. You could forget those two … he just had a knack, I suppose, of being in the right place at the right time and [was] just a real tough character who would put his body on the line and just get in the way … he wasn't the biggest, he had a decent spring in the air, but on the ground, particularly, he could just seem to snuff out and nullify high-quality centre-forwards who just didn't seem to get a yard of space when they played against him. He got better and better. Obviously, when he came over initially, he was quite raw with a lot to learn and to learn the English game, but my God, did he do that? He developed into such a fantastic player for the football club."

With youngsters Woodgate, Kewell, Ian Harte, Stephen McPhail, Alan Smith and Matthew Jones all in the first-team mix, Leeds had energy all over the pitch. Woodgate said the work of youth coaches Paul Hart and Eddie Gray in nurturing that batch of players was vital. "[They were] really, really important. They were tough with us and that's what you need," he said. "You realise when you get older, they were tough on you because they like you. If they didn't like us, they wouldn't be tough with us. That was the biggest thing. What always stood out to me was their mentality to want to win. Even if you're running, even if you're doing a cross-country run, you always want to be the best, the winners … [they would say], 'If you're playing a three against three game, I want you to win the game. If you're playing four against four, I always want you to win'. That was the biggest thing that you got from the coaches and obviously the standards were top drawer." Woodgate remembered the youth team playing the senior professionals at training and giving as good as they got on occasions. Many of the group were ready for consistent first-team football and Woodgate credited O'Leary for giving them the chance. "We had a good team, he [O'Leary] invested well, they got some good players in. We bought young players [Bridges, Danny Mills, Eirik Bakke and Michael Duberry] and vibrant players who wanted to succeed in the game. We didn't go for 28, 29-year-olds who sometimes were a bit settled. We tried to buy young. That was the key with that. The fans bought into it, the fans were brilliant. But it takes a manager with a big set of balls to put you [academy lads] in there and to see if you're ready. Not many coaches do that. But credit to David O'Leary, he saw the potential in the players ... he didn't have qualms about ... leaving a big-name player out and [saying], 'You're in', ... we had a coach who was willing to give us that opportunity."

Those opportunities helped Leeds reach the last four of the tournament for the first time since 1971, when United won the trophy then known as the Inter-Cities Fairs Cup. A little wiser from previous European trips, the Leeds players were aware of what they might see when they arrived in Istanbul. "The hostile reception we were going to get when we arrived - we knew all about that," Bridges said. "We'd seen footage and we'd been warned by, obviously, the staff. And being young lads we were kind of like, 'Oh yeah, we'll just go and face up to it'. But nothing could really replicate that when we got there. It was so hostile at the airport, I remember the cutthroat gestures, the fans were all there."

McPhail recalled "a lot of hate in the air" but no one could have predicted what was to come next. United's players were not together, some watching television in their rooms, others like Bridges, playing computer games when bad news started to filter through. "We're in the hotel the night before and there was a bit of stuff on telly in the local Turkish television reporting that there was violence and stuff," said McPhail, while Radebe added: "We watched TV and we were hearing news." Woodgate and Bridges recalled phone calls starting to come in, too, before tragic news was confirmed. Leeds United supporters

Christopher Loftus and Kevin Speight had been fatally stabbed on the streets of Istanbul. "The initial shock was just one that you'll never forget," McPhail said. "I remember going back to the room in the hotel and just being in total disbelief of what happened." Club captain Radebe added that receiving the news was "the most terrible feeling we've ever had".

"Straight away, you just feel for their families. They just come to support us and then they've had their life taken … it's unbelievable," Bowyer said. Feelings of shock and pain were soon joined by anger and fear. "As the captain of the club, I wouldn't have liked to play under those circumstances … I remember most of the players didn't want to go and play … it made us very sad and not want to play," Radebe said. Woodgate said the fact the match went ahead was "a disgrace". "We thought the game should have got called off but it never did and it went ahead. It was just a disgrace, really. Our heads were all over the shop with it all. There's two Leeds fans [dead], our families are out there in Istanbul. We were obviously scared for them. It was just a terrible, terrible moment for the football club." The decision was made to proceed with the match, though, and United's players were worried. "If we could win the game, what's going to happen?" Radebe remembered thinking. "We thought, 'What's the worst that can happen in the field of play?' It can only take one of their supporters [to] run on the field and cause trouble in the field. It was one of the scary things. The atmosphere was not right and it was horrible. It was the worst time."

That worry was only enhanced when Leeds had to travel to the stadium. "I remember even the day of the game and getting on the bus, going from the hotel to the match, how we had to keep the curtains closed, because [of] the abuse and, yeah, the atmosphere … the horrible hatred towards us," McPhail said. "We couldn't see, we couldn't look out the windows, we had to stay low in our seats. It was just things getting smashed off the bus … it was horrendous. Even going out for the warm-up, I remember Eddie Gray at the top of the line, in the tunnel … I remember just seeing army, sort of riot police, covering the top of the stairs, the top of the tunnel where we came out. Eddie's just shouting down to be careful coming out because there was obviously a lot of things being thrown from the stands." Bowyer recalled that moment, too. "There were riot police holding up shields as we were walking up … things [were] bouncing off the shields, they were throwing things and things were popping around you and we were thinking, 'Where are we?'" All Radebe could think about was going home. "The soldiers with the shields - they were shielding us from the crowd. The atmosphere wasn't great. I remember running on the field of play. We thought, as players, 'We just want to go home … let's just play the game and go home'. That's the feeling we had. You could see during the game, I don't think we were mentally fit to play that game."

There was no official minute of silence before the match and the home side did not wear black armbands, moves that angered the Leeds players. "I remember being disgusted in how they behaved on the night, especially after the events the night before … there was no respect shown at all towards what happened that night before. Yeah, we were devastated. We were all probably still in shock," McPhail said. "The game shouldn't have gone ahead but at least it should have been a minute's silence. Everyone should have wore armbands, at least," said Woodgate, furious at "a lack of respect". The Leeds fans in the stadium held their own tribute, momentarily turning their backs to play.

"I think I might have lost Hakan Sukur for one of the goals," Woodgate said of the 13th-minute opener. But this was not like the normal concession of a goal. "We didn't feel bad about conceding because of the situation and the hostility around the stadium," Radebe said. "We just wanted to get on with the game and get home because we didn't really feel safe in that city." The hosts netted again before half time, Carlos Capone scoring after Leeds failed to clear a free-kick, with the visitors having no answer for Gheorghe Hagi during the first 45 minutes.

"I have to say it's the most intimidating place I've ever been and I've been up and down the country [of England] and all over Europe," Bowyer said. "You accept, especially myself, I got abuse wherever I went, especially in England, but there it was just crazy … it was relentless, just the whole 90 minutes [they were] constantly throwing things at you. It was crazy, so intimidating … because of the circumstances of what happened the night before, I just don't think the game should have been played. I think us, as a group, weren't in the right frame of mind."

Woodgate remembered Galatasaray's stars being very difficult to stop. "We should have done better on the night. I remember Gheorghe Hagi and Hakan Sukur, basically they were running the show. He was hard to get grips of, Hagi, and we didn't have any players as good as him to really cope with him and Hagi was a lot more experienced." Bridges admitted he was in awe of Hagi. "He was just phenomenal. You couldn't get the ball off him. I remember at half time, O'Leary saying, 'Can somebody try and get a hold of Hagi? If we contain him and contain Hakan Sukur, we've got a chance'. The boys just looked around [at] each other … I'm looking at 'Millsy' [Danny Mills] saying, 'Any chance?' He was like, 'Can't get fucking near him - we'll try', … it was just incredible how good he was in that game. And the other thing I remember is the guy that was marking me, Capone. He was a centre-half. [I was] having a good tussle with him but he was one of the defenders - there were only two I came across in Europe that were horrible and tough. Capone was one of them where he would … kick you, punch you … when the ball was away from you, just really try and put you off your game. I look back and I think, 'Yeah, I know what he was doing', … you never really got that it in the Premier League. I don't know whether there was more tension [in Turkey] or more cameras [in England] but there wasn't that kind of gamesmanship and that's what I found in that game. He really put me off my game, Capone, by the antics that he used."

Bridges could and should have scored for Leeds, but put a second-half effort into the side netting after an initial shot was blocked by goalkeeper Claudio Taffarel. The striker was very self-critical when reflecting on the match. "For me, in front of goal, it was a shit night. I could have probably sent us through to the final had I been on form … it was a double [chance]. I remember having probably one of the shittest games I ever had for Leeds, to be fair, in front of goal." That was as close as Leeds got to a first-leg goal, with players turning their attention to leaving Turkey as soon as the final whistle went.

McPhail remembered being overcome with sadness in the build-up to the second leg, which away fans were banned for. "It was terrible, it was really sad, the whole week leading up to the game," he said. "We had the family in and around the training ground, the families that lost members. So it was just devastating … it was really difficult to try and concentrate on anything towards the football side of things, really. It was just devastating seeing the families of people who were lost. Obviously, the city in general and the club came together massively. It was a real emotional week and day leading up to the second leg."

This time both sides paid their respects with a minute of silence, while players from Leeds and Galatasaray wore black armbands. Like the first leg, football was a distinct second on the evening, and Woodgate conceded an early penalty that Hagi stepped up to score. Bakke pulled a goal back for Leeds but Sukur struck before the break to restore the visitors' three-goal lead. Both Kewell and Galatasaray's Emre were then sent off and Bakke's second goal was no more than a consolation as Leeds United's European campaign came to an end. "We know that we could have played better," Radebe said. "We could have got a better result but I think we conceded silly goals, two easy goals … we were always capable of scoring but I think, knowing what happened, for us, we were still not in a good frame of mind."

RIP

Christopher Loftus
Kevin Speight

Marching on Together.

LIVERPOOL

WESTERVELD, BABBEL, CARRAGHER, HYYPIA, ZIEGE, MURPHY ▼, McALLISTER ▼, HAMANN, SMICER, BERGER ▼, HESKEY

SUBS: ARPHEXAD, HENCHOZ, FOWLER ▲, GERRARD ▲, BARMBY ▲

MANAGER: GERARD HOULLIER

OUR FORM HEADING IN

TRANMERE	3-2	LEEDS UTD
BRADFORD	1-1	LEEDS UTD
LEEDS UTD	1-1	BARCELONA

"It was Guy Fawkes Night [and] my wife was by herself at home with the dog ... the dog kept barking all night and she was scared ... she rings me up at three o'clock ... and I go, 'She will be alright'. At five o'clock in the morning, again, she rings me up and she goes, 'Tara is barking, I'm scared'. And I go, 'You know what? If I have a shocker tomorrow!'"
- Mark Viduka

His preparation was far from ideal but Mark Viduka was about to produce one of the greatest performances in Premier League history. The Australian struggled to sleep in the hours before an important fixture against Liverpool due to his dog, even though he was staying in a team hotel far away from the family home. It was the Friday before Guy Fawkes Night, an annual November tradition in Great Britain where people light bonfires and set off fireworks, and Viduka's Rottweiler was going completely berserk. "That [game] was an early kick-off ... we were in a hotel in the city centre before the game," Viduka said. The striker was rooming with goalkeeper Danny Milosevic, who was also woken up through the night by the phone calls. Asked if he was tired as he prepared for the match, an 11.30am kick-off, Viduka said: "That morning, yeah ... early morning kick-offs ... it's not a normal thing so your body is not really used to that ... when it's like that, you usually have breakfast at eight o'clock in the morning. Everybody gets up at seven, which is early. It's an early thing. Normally, I like to sleep in and then have a certain breakfast." The early start was also creating issues in the Liverpool camp, Markus Babbel remembering "it was the earliest kick-off in my career". "It was new for me. I never had this before," he said. "It was very difficult to bring your best performance on the pitch because everything was different ... it was the first time in my professional career I had this and not only me - many players were struggling."

Leeds pipped Liverpool to third just four months earlier, a position that came with UEFA Champions League football, but the visitors made a much brighter start to the 2000-01 campaign and faced a United side so ravaged by injury they could not even field five substitutes. Liverpool made a great start to the match, too, as Sami Hyypia and Christian Ziege both headed in early free-kicks, while Jonathan Woodgate was forced off with a thigh injury for Leeds. Woodgate's replacement, New

Zealand's Danny Hay, remembered feeling like United's day was done after just 18 minutes. "[I] literally run on and they've gone and scored from [another] set-piece. You just want, a little bit, the ground to open up and swallow you. Dead silence [in] three quarters of the stadium, all you could see down the far end was a bunch of red shirts going absolutely nuts." Dominic Matteo, who had only moved to Leeds from Liverpool in August, thought the writing was on the wall. "I never thought I'd ever leave Liverpool, that's the truth. I had five years left on my contract when I signed for Leeds. It was very bizarre that I did sign for Leeds, in that way. But I don't regret it, I think it was a great club going in the right direction when I did get there … [but] I was fearing the worst at 2-0 down. They're the type of team [that] can go on and punish you and get four or five." Viduka, another new Leeds signing in the summer, was also expecting an uphill battle. "I was under pressure, obviously, to score goals. New club, new fans, new surroundings and all that … you can't afford to concede goals to teams like Liverpool, easy goals, especially in the first 20 minutes … I thought to myself [laughs], 'This is going to be a long day.'"

Leeds needed a spark from somewhere and Alan Smith provided it, charging down a Ziege clearance. "He's like a terrier when he starts getting hold of somebody's ankles. He doesn't let go," Viduka said. "So I actually made a little bit of a run towards the goal to see maybe if he gets something here, or to block the pass back to the goalkeeper so Ziege didn't have that option. And 'Smudger' [Smith] closed him down. He [Ziege] went for a clearance, [Smith] closed it down and it popped exactly to me. And then in those situations, you don't think. Your body just goes by itself." Viduka's instinct saw him take two touches before dinking an effort over Sander Westerveld. Leeds had their first. Viduka had his first.

In one of the most open games at Elland Road in years, both sides spurned chances before the break as Liverpool took their one-goal lead to the interval. "The belief, the confidence was quite extraordinary at that point in time in the changing room," Hay said. "We hadn't won in a few, so that was quite unusual. But I remember the likes of Gary Kelly, senior players like that, were really like, 'Fuck!' We felt like we really had an opportunity to get right back in the game and get something out of it." Kelly's optimism was justified and he crossed for Viduka to nod Leeds level in the 47th minute. "I thought, 'Anything's possible'," the goalscorer said. "We could beat anybody on the day. We were about energy. We had an energy. I don't think many teams had an energy like us."

There was more to come, of course, but Viduka's two goals to that stage meant he had netted doubles in three home Premier League games in a row. The £6 million signing had already proved his worth and it did not surprise Woodgate. "I remember one game where I think I just made my England debut. I was 19 years old and we went up to Celtic to play them in a pre-season friendly. And I was thinking to myself, 'I've just made my England debut, no one's going to get near me'. I played against Viduka and I was like, 'Oh my God'. I couldn't get near him! He always had the 'Cruyff turn', it was one of his famous moves. He was just that big, but he had the turn of pace as well at that time. He absolutely annihilated me ... they probably saw him play against me and thought, 'Yeah, we'll buy him'."

Vladimir Smicer restored Liverpool's lead at Elland Road but Gerard Houllier's men never felt comfortable, according to Babbel. "I never had the feeling that [we were] clear, because they put so much pressure on you. We were really struggling. We didn't play our best game and even [at] 2-0 up - it was more a surprise for us that we were 2-0 up because we were not good on this day."

A crazy game would soon be 3-3, Viduka getting his first Leeds hat-trick with an unforgettable goal. "Olivier Dacourt, for that third goal, passed me a through ball. 'Ollie' was good like that. I really liked playing with Ollie ... he was a ball-winner type of player ... he was a simple player, when he sees somebody on he plays [it to] them straight away. In that situation, he played it straight over," he said. Viduka would then twist, turn, tie Patrik Berger in knots so much he badly injured his knee and then finish on the angle past a despairing Westerveld and a diving Jamie Carragher. "Did I think I was going to turn or hit it to the left? I didn't think. It just happened by itself," he said. Instinct. Again.
"He was such a threat physically and also with his feet because he was so skilful. And I don't think a lot of players realised that with him

until they played against him," Matteo said. "We needed something to happen quickly and, obviously, the big man produced. Patrik did his knee, didn't he? ... Jamie Carragher [hit the deck] as well, he put a couple of them on to the floor ... he just kept twisting and turning and twisting and turning and you're thinking, 'He's going to get the shot away', and eventually it finds the back of the net and [there's] Liverpool players sliding in from all angles trying to get it out. It has to be that goal for me that stood out." Dacourt saw Viduka perform tricks like that at training but was still amazed he managed to do it in the heat of battle. "He was so technically [good]. You cannot expect to have a big fella like him to be [so] technical! He can keep the ball, he can pass players, he had everything. Mark was a top quality player ... they said it was an assist but it was more Mark did something crazy than my assist!"

Viduka's compatriot and friend, Jacob Burns, had the perfect view. "I was in midfield, I was behind the lead-up to it. He was renowned for that, big 'Dukes' ... I suppose he probably made that kind of move his own where he would 'Cruyff' people in and around the box. For such a big guy, his feet [were] so quick that often he'd catch midfielders or defenders going the wrong way. I just remember the momentum of Berger, the desperation in trying to stop him then and him [Viduka] almost turning on a dime to score that goal. And that's really, I think, when we knew we were going to go on to win this. After being down 2-0 and then being able to bring it back on that third for 3-3, you thought, 'Well, this is our day now.'"

Burns' premonition was right as Dacourt and Viduka linked up again, the striker taking a touch before dinking the onrushing Westerveld with aplomb. "That was ecstasy ... I don't know what to say. It was just something that rarely happens ... in this game, I had four chances to score and all four of them, they went in," Viduka said. "All four of them, I scored. I took them." As the striker ran away to celebrate, Elland Road was delirious. Fans that had seen the likes of John Charles, Allan Clarke, Lee Chapman and Tony Yeboah had a new goalscoring hero. "There was great supporters, great atmosphere in this stadium, even at 11.30 in the morning. They were pushing the team. This is still in my head - the fantastic atmosphere in the stadium," said Babbel, who was also thankful he was not marking Viduka. "He was an incredible player because he was technically good. He was strong, he was good in the air … all the skills that you need as a striker. And, to be fair, I was lucky because I was playing right-back, so not as a centre-back [laughs]."

Michael Bridges, recovering at home after suffering a serious ankle injury in a UEFA Champions League tie at Besiktas, knew he would face one hell of a battle to get back in the team when fit. "I watched that game on telly and I realised if the injuries didn't stop us playing for Leeds United, Mark Viduka would stop us playing for Leeds United," he said. "I became a fan after that [injury]. I didn't really want to hang around the football club for mental reasons because I was so badly injured and needed just to be bedridden and rested for like, literally, two months. The old comedy sketches where they'd have your leg in the air in the plaster cast - I had to do that, literally, to keep the blood draining out of my leg after the operation … but that game was incredible. I remember my father coming up the stairs going, 'Are you watching this game?' And I said, 'Yeah'. He went, 'Fuck, he's good. He's in your position as well!' … He was a marvellous player, 'Vidukes' … you would see Vidukes in training and he could do things nobody else could."

In the Elland Road director's box, Glynn Snodin could not help himself. The boyhood Leeds United fan, who also played for the club, was on official duty. "I remember scouting for Charlton Athletic … we'd got Leeds coming up for Charlton Athletic." Snodin's old boss at Leeds, Howard Wilkinson, then England's Under-21 manager, was in the room, too. "So I'm watching this game … then when Viduka got that hat-trick and then got the winner, I forgot myself. I'm in the director's box going, 'Get in! Get in!' And Howard's going, 'Oi! You're supposed to be a scout. You're neutral'. I went, 'No, no, no, no, no. I'm Leeds', … what a game!"

As for the players on the pitch, they were struggling to hear each other. "That's what I remember, getting back to 3-3 and the crowd going absolutely bananas … I looked at Dom Matteo and I was trying to yell something to him," Hay said. "We were literally five metres away from each other and he couldn't hear a thing. And I think then the fourth one, when we got the winner, I can remember feeling like it was almost like a bit of an earthquake. You felt like the ground was moving, the actual pitch was reverberating. It was pretty cool." Lee Bowyer said he was in awe of his teammate, insistent Viduka was "unplayable" and that "he had a lot of them days". "To go score four against Liverpool in the manner that he did was unreal … he was outstanding, great for me to play with. His awareness and attention to detail with his weight of pass for people like me running off of him … he was a pleasure to play with."

Late drama would not have surprised given the open nature of the match, but Leeds managed to see it out in one of the Premier League's most entertaining fixtures ever. The cameras rushed to Viduka as soon as the final whistle went, who said, 'Hi, Mum' to the viewing millions. "That day was my mum's birthday so I knew that they were going to be watching from Australia and I gave her a big wave just to say, 'Happy Birthday'."

Surprisingly, Viduka does not consider it as his best game for Leeds, saying that came in a 1-0 UEFA Champions League win at Lazio where he held the ball up, drew defenders to him and then set up Smith for the winning goal with a clever backheel. "In that [Liverpool] game, I didn't think I ticked all the boxes at all … hold-up play, bringing other people into play, possession. I played better games in those segments … I took them [chances] which in one way, as a striker, that's what you're there for. But in another way, if you're saying in a complete game, I wasn't happy with the other side of play, fully … as a striker, it's not just - it is scoring goals. But it's also the other things. It's hold-up play. It's bringing players into the game. It's creating space for others. I liked playing the little one-twos. In that game, I don't remember having to do that many things like that." Regardless, the four-goal haul is still an extremely fond memory for Viduka. "Obviously, I was rapt. It was one of the best moments of my footballing career. Definitely."

Lucas Radebe is still blown away by how good Viduka was against Liverpool, insistent his performance was "absolutely brilliant", no matter how self-critical the forward is. "Vidukes was on top form and he was absolutely amazing … to score four against Liverpool, I mean, that's a good thing! For Dukes, that day, he was the hero … to get the result was amazing." Matteo concurred. "When you talk about that game, you think, 'Thank goodness for Mark Viduka'. Because it was the 'Mark Viduka Show' really, wasn't it? Without him, we'd have probably got hammered. It was one of those performances that I think always sticks out … we all thought Mark was a good player, but I think when there's a performance like that against the level of players you're up against … I'd been at Liverpool so I knew how good they were and he made certain players look average that day and only certain players can do that in world football. Mark certainly proved to a lot of us that he could. It was just an incredible performance … personally, I felt a bit drained afterwards because we'd conceded three and I never liked conceding goals anyway. But I think I just gave Mark a big kiss and a cuddle after the game and just said, 'Thanks very much, because you pulled me out of one there definitely'."

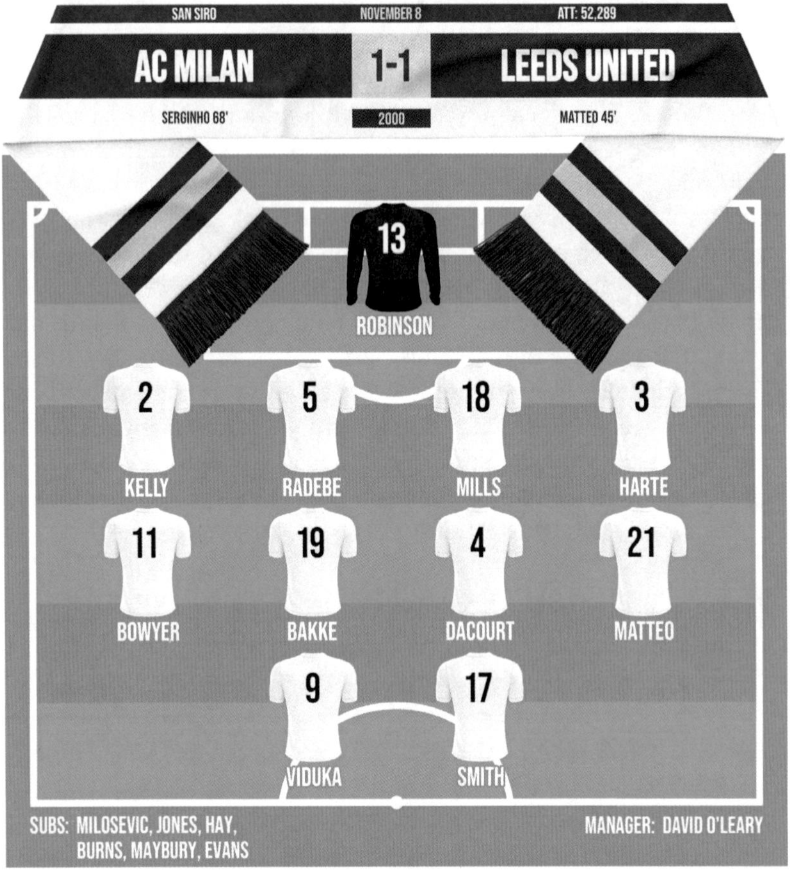

AC MILAN

DIDA, JUNIOR, CHAMOT, MALDINI, HELVEG, GATTUSO, ALBERTINI, SERGINHO, LEONARDO, SHEVCHENKO, BIERHOFF

SUBS: ABBIATI, BOBAN, JOSE MARI, AMBROSINI, GULY, SALA, COCO

MANAGER: ALBERTO ZACCHERONI

OUR FORM HEADING IN

LEEDS UTD	4-3	LIVERPOOL
TRANMERE	3-2	LEEDS UTD
BRADFORD	1-1	LEEDS UTD

"The first game we played was in Barcelona and they beat us 4-0 and it was like, 'Welcome to [the] Champions League'. We said, 'Oh, it will be very difficult', I remember."
- Olivier Dacourt

Leeds United's return to Europe's premier club competition was a disaster, Rivaldo and Patrick Kluivert running riot in a one-sided Camp Nou rout. "That game in general was probably a baptism of fire in the Champions League," Stephen McPhail said. "The year before [in the UEFA Cup], we played huge games, huge European nights, huge atmospheres but going to Barcelona was probably an eye-opener for all of us. I think we definitely got outplayed and outclassed that night."

Leeds just scraped into the qualifying rounds of the UEFA Champions League after the final day of the 1999-2000 campaign nearly went pear-shaped for David O'Leary's men. Leeds only had to win at West Ham United to finish third above Liverpool but were held to a goalless draw, meaning they needed Bradford City - playing for Premier League survival - to get at least a point against the Anfield outfit. Bradford went one better than that, though, winning 1-0 as former Leeds man David Wetherall scored the only goal. "To beat Liverpool on the last day of the season was an amazing achievement ... and then to hear that it had also played a part in Leeds qualifying for the Champions League - the day couldn't really get that much better," Wetherall said. "One of my great memories from that day was [when] Gary Kelly phoned me from the Leeds team bus as they were coming back and they were all singing, all singing my name on the bus ... it was just brilliant." Lucas Radebe remembered "absolute jubilation" on the coach back to Leeds and said involvement in the Champions League was another sign of progress. "As a footballer, you want to play at the highest level and for me to be with a club that played [at] the highest [level of] football in Europe, it's a great honour. It showed that there is quality in the team and the team was doing so well. Everyone was improving. It showed the improvement ... the club is becoming stronger."

Leeds still had to qualify for the group stages and an injury-hit United side battled past 1860 Munich 3-1 on aggregate to earn a spot in a tricky Group H that also featured Barcelona, AC Milan and Besiktas. If it looked tough on paper, that realisation was confirmed in the Catalan city, with Barca's Frank de Boer not holding back in the aftermath of the 4-0 win. Among a series of inflammatory comments reported in The Independent, De Boer said that he "wasn't impressed by any of the Leeds team" and that "they seemed intimidated". It would not be the last time the club's ability was questioned in Europe but the Barcelona horror show was, according to McPhail, "the best thing that ever happened to us a group because we realised we needed to stand up". Dominic Matteo agreed and felt the defeat was "a learning curve". "Going forward, it was like, 'Right, we need to defend better', but also, 'Let's have some belief in ourselves'. The Barcelona game for me - we were beaten before we even got there," Matteo said. "You are walking down that tunnel and it's like you're doing a tour. It's like you're a fan going to Barcelona as a player sometimes."

Both Michael Bridges and McPhail have tales of pre-match antics, the former annoying Rivaldo while he and Alan Smith went on what he described as "a stadium tour". "Going down the tunnel, there were these two wooden doors ... I just thought, 'Fuck, let's go in here'. So we burst the doors open thinking it would be like a kit room or a ball room," Bridges said. "We were just young kids, enjoying it, and as we burst in, there were these candles everywhere and there was a guy with his top off praying. I remember me and 'Smithy' going, 'Who the fuck is that and where are we?' And he turned around and it was Rivaldo and we were like, 'Oh'. It was weird. The eerie feeling that I got when Rivaldo turned round and gave us this stare ... we knew exactly who he was - he probably thought we were two fans. He didn't know who we were ... he shushed us off to get out so we shut the [door to the] room and it was almost like when we shut the room, you could feel the candles flicker a bit. It was just this horrible, eerie feeling and I said to Smithy, 'We've just been cursed - we've cursed the club here, mate'. I said, 'It's wrong'." McPhail and Kelly would also venture into the same room later on. "It's probably three or four flights of stairs down to the pitch and there's a little chapel halfway down on the left as we were coming down ... we walked by and I looked in and I thought, 'There's a chapel' and 'Gaz' said it to me as well," McPhail said. "So we went out, we did our warm-up and as we come back in, he pulls me [aside] and says, 'Come on, 'Mac', say a little prayer', ... so we went in and had a little minute inside and had a little prayer and went back up, I ran up to the dressing room and got ready, got back into the game. Just after the game, we're going by it again and Gaz ... says, 'Well, that prayer didn't work, did it Mac?' We just started laughing."

Next up came AC Milan, the Italian giants travelling to West Yorkshire on a wet evening. "Going into the game we had a lot of injuries," Michael Duberry said. "I remember the team being announced at Elland Road and it was, 'Danny Mills, Michael Duberry, your centre-half pairing', ... there was a few groans at the selection." Duberry felt like the fans were thinking, "Oh my God, we're going to get more of the same, it's going to be another 4-0 beating" but was not deterred. "I've never played with 'Millsy' at the back and now we're playing against [Oliver] Bierhoff and [Andriy] Shevchenko, who, in Europe, just score goals for fun. A potent strike force. But, Millsy, a bit like me - he's defiant, loves proving people wrong ... on top of him being a great defender as well. So it wasn't like we were buying into what they [fans] were saying or we were scared. He loves a challenge, I love a challenge ... that's what you want to do as a player. You want to play against the best in the world, the best players and put yourself against the best ... standing there and hearing that Champions League music is the best feeling in the world." Duberry also remembered the conditions being a big boost to Leeds. "It's to our advantage, it's a wet, rainy Tuesday evening at Elland Road, they don't like the conditions, we're used to it, we love it - the night games at Elland Road were the best ... the atmosphere, 35 to 38,000 Yorkshiremen, screaming, making noise." Lee Bowyer sent those fans crazy in the 88th minute, his shot fumbled into the back of the net by AC Milan goalkeeper Dida, and victory gave Leeds a sense of belonging. "We felt that we'd come of age and belonged in that competition and put everybody on notice. There was a lot of teams that went, 'Hang on a minute, they've just beat Milan,'" Bridges remembered.

A 6-0 rout of Besiktas at Elland Road followed, Bowyer scoring twice in a win that gave Leeds genuine belief. "They didn't know what they were in for when they came to Elland Road," Matteo remembered. "Those nights at Elland Road ... some teams can't cope." The reverse fixture in Turkey ended in a 0-0 draw, Bridges suffering an ankle injury that could easily have ended his career. "I went for an MRI scan to see what the damage was and I rang [Leeds physio] Dave Hancock about two days later and I said, 'Mate, you've got to come and see us at the house'. I said, 'My leg has gone black up to my knee'. I had an internal bleed and I got rushed in to get the operation done. I almost lost the bottom half of my leg because there was so much damage going on … that was when I was told I'd never play again …. he [the surgeon] said, 'You'll never play. I've only ever seen this in a motorbike accident'. So my whole world fell apart." Without Bridges, Leeds could have booked their spot in the second group stage with a home victory against Barcelona and were less than a minute away from doing so, Rivaldo scoring a stoppage-time equaliser in a 1-1 draw most notable for Paul Robinson's brilliance in goal. So a trip to already-qualified AC Milan was on the cards, Leeds needing a point to guarantee their progression at Barcelona's expense. Defeat might have been enough for United, too, but that would mean Besiktas had to get a result against the La Liga side.

The game came just four days after Mark Viduka's four-goal haul against Liverpool and Danny Hay remembered how no expense was spared on the travel on "this private jet". "[It] was a bit of a nice experience for players - I remember I was hopping off the plane and even then I found it a little unusual because normally you should clear customs and that but we literally walked off the plane, didn't touch anything, straight onto a bus and we're whisked off to a hotel in the middle of the night. No customs, nothing … I remember waking up and opening the curtains and [thinking], 'Wow, there's Lake Como'." Matteo quickly remembered the hotel's name and it was clear it left an impression. "I always like to remember the good hotels - me and big Viduka were loving the lasagne there and were going back for seconds all the time on the lasagne. It was amazing!"

Any suggestion AC Milan would take the game lightly was silenced when the teams were announced and winger Serginho caused early problems before he won a penalty when Kelly handled his cross. Up stepped Shevchenko, in front of the Leeds fans, but he could only shoot against the post, a massive relief for the visitors. "Milan was a funny game," Viduka remembered. "Shevchenko - it could have went either way and that's how it is in football. Now, that's a big moment for us." Radebe, who rushed back from injury to play, then cheaply gave the ball away before recovering to divert a Shevchenko effort over the bar as the Italian side started to pile on the pressure. "As a footballer, you want to play games like that on the big stage," Radebe said. "Having to sacrifice in terms of putting your career on the line with injuries like that - I think, for me, it was my sacrifice to the club ... we only needed a draw."

Then came Matteo's defining moment as a Leeds player, one still sung about at football grounds up and down England, as he scored with a near-post header. "I have made that run for that corner a million times and Lee Bowyer has never found me," he said. "I always used to moan at him and I'll always say, 'Why are you trying to miss me out and get somebody else?' ... For once it came and I didn't really get the cleanest of connections on it but I got enough on the header to just get it in ... for me, personally, a very proud moment to get a Champions League goal."

Leeds were in front at the break and had one foot in the second group stage. A stern examination was still to come, though, as Robinson was kept busy, forced into several good saves. And it was no surprise to see Serginho finally rewarded for what was a sensational performance with a 68th-minute equaliser. "He was having an incredible game down the left-hand side, he was a powerful player," Matteo said. "They had a lot of corners, a lot of attacks, obviously with Shevchenko you've always got that goal threat of a superstar striker. Paul Robinson was in goal, he had an incredible game, really incredible game, made a lot of stops. But you needed your goalie to play well in these stadiums." As AC Milan kept pressing for a winner, United's goalscorer was thankful for the state of the pitch. "I think the pitch, in a way, might have helped us because it was a bit of a leveller, the pitch that night. The San Siro wasn't the best of pitches back in those days ... I think that maybe helped us out a little bit because some of their more flair players didn't really have the surface to do what they do best."

Leeds would ultimately hold out for the draw, a result that would continue their European run. "We managed to hang on ... some of the players that were playing that night were world-class but we managed to do it and we managed to get through," Bowyer said. "We were pretty ecstatic in the changing room afterwards, knowing that we'd qualified," Hay said. "Somebody came in ... and said that all the Leeds fans were still in the stands, just for their own safety, they had to be locked in ... so [the] players made the decision to go out ... all of a sudden it's turned into something quite phenomenal. They [fans] would get some of the players to start a tune, or start a chant and, all of a sudden, it'd be like your own 7,000-strong orchestra, so it was pretty unbelievable." With Kelly leading the way, the Leeds players were involved in a lengthy back and forth singing session, even sitting down when a version of 'Sit down if you hate Man U' rung around the famous stadium.

Not all player attempts were successful, Bowyer's failed song providing plenty of laughter within the camp. "We'd be in that little huddle, all the players, and then they'd call you out to go and start a song and on that evening, they called me out to start a song and I thought I'd mix it up a bit and do something clever - not just a Leeds song but another song," he said. "And I started and then they started singing, 'What the hell is this?' I had to run back into the players - it was embarrassing!" All involved immediately spoke fondly of what BBC's Alan Green dubbed as "the finest example of player-fan bonding I've ever seen". "It's something strange, special ... I played so many games but I never saw that - this fusion in between fans and players," Olivier Dacourt said. For Radebe, it was "absolutely brilliant". "The atmosphere then - we felt united with the supporters. We felt that with the supporters really behind us, they were part of the team. We had to appreciate them and acknowledge that by showing them and by being part [of their songs] and showing them that we appreciate their support." Matteo said prolonged scenes of player-fan interaction like that are, sadly, not seen anymore. "I don't think it will ever happen ... that fan interaction is where memories are made isn't it?"

It was just the start of a big night for the Leeds players and Hay remembered being joined by Robbie Keane - then at Inter but soon to sign for United on loan - in the changing room. Back at the hotel, the celebrations were in full flow. "All of the directors and the chairman and all the staff were all back there," Matteo said. "And we all liked a glass of red [wine] as well so [we had] a few Peroni's to start off with and then it was the good reds. I think [chairman] Peter Ridsdale was coming down to get an early flight and I was going into the lift with a tray of bottles of red wine, probably about half a dozen. I don't know why I had that - I must have been going up to a room party or something but he said, 'Just stick them on my room bill'. And I said, 'Don't worry, I already have', [laughs] ... they actually let us stay another day in Milan ... a few sore heads the next morning but I think when you're on that kind of adrenaline and [you have won] qualification from the group that no-one thought we'd ever qualify from ... that was an amazing night."

Matteo has come to appreciate the match and his goal even more in the aftermath, too, especially given his father's Italian background. "For my family to all see that and especially my dad's side of the family, who obviously all live out in Italy, [that] was an incredible feeling for me," he said. "Because my career's been a bit hit and miss at times but that was a day where the family could get some ... [I could] give them something back, really, give my dad something back for all the times he has taken me all over the place. That felt like it was a nice moment for me."

And even though Matteo says the game was far from brilliant, he is proud of the way it is remembered. "The amount of fans I've met, at least I've met since that night ... the whole of Leeds must have been in the San Siro because every person I ever meet was definitely there! I've heard stories of broken legs, broken arms when I've scored, all those kind of stories ... the game wasn't a classic - it wasn't. It was just a hard-fought draw, really. Things like that [the interaction with the fans], I'll never forget ... I understand why the fans remember that more than the game."

DEPORTIVO LA CORUNA

MOLINA, PABLO, ROMERO, NAYBET, CESAR, SCALONI, EMERSON, DUSCHER, FRAN, DJALMINHA, MAKAAY

SUBS: SONGO'O, TRISTAN, CAPDEVILA, PANDIANI, VICTOR, VALERON, FERNANDO

MANAGER: JAVIER IRURETA

OUR FORM HEADING IN

SUNDERLAND	0-2	LEEDS UTD
CHARLTON	1-2	LEEDS UTD
LEEDS UTD	3-3	LAZIO

"Every time I got on the coach when we were playing … I always thought there was a confidence that we could do something. We could beat anyone."
- Dominic Matteo

Buoyed by their qualification for the second group stage of the 2000-01 UEFA Champions League campaign, confidence started to surge through the Leeds United squad. "We had a great bunch of lads," Dominic Matteo said. "We just thought, 'Let's go and have a go. What's the worst that can happen?' … It's like no one really knew too much about us. We were a mixed team, kind of put together, there's some lads that had been at Leeds for a while, some new players coming in." More tough tests awaited in the next phase, Leeds grouped with Spanish giants Real Madrid, then-Italian champions Lazio and an Anderlecht outfit with one of the best home records in European football. David O'Leary's side were far from disgraced in a 2-0 home defeat to Real Madrid and then made a major statement, making Rio Ferdinand the world's most expensive defender in an £18 million deal with West Ham United. "Rio, for me, was just a special player. Rio came in and straight from the off, you could just see he was like a Rolls Royce of a footballer," Stephen McPhail remembered. "He just had natural ability. Playing at centre-back, what he could do for us in that role, he was just magnificent, the way he led and the way he took the ball, the way he was so confident in his own ability. I think he just jumped us up a level or two."

Ferdinand's impact was not immediate, though, as O'Leary pondered the best way to fit the centre-back into a team containing Lucas Radebe and Jonathan Woodgate. His first move was to try three at the back but it backfired spectacularly, Leeds conceding three times in the first 29 minutes at Leicester City in a match that saw Woodgate hooked before half time and Radebe eventually sent off. Woodgate's confidence could have been ruined ahead of a crucial Champions League fixture against Lazio that was just three days later but the defender produced a simply outstanding performance in the Italian capital. "That's one of my best ever Leeds games, Lazio away," he said. "A fond memory. I cleared one off the line. I was just there at every point. When the ball would come in the box, I was clearing it. The ball seemed to be a magnet to me. I think I was playing against [Hernan] Crespo and [Marcelo] Salas. They had a really good team, [Alessandro] Nesta, Pavel Nedved, Fernando Couto - they had a proper team. But we went over there as a bunch of kids and beat them 1-0. We had no fear. We played with a style that we didn't have fear. We pressed teams, we wouldn't sit off teams, we'd press them. We played like a four, three and Harry Kewell out wide on his own at times and [Mark] Viduka and [Alan] Smith. We just pressed teams and we had energy inside. We had young, hungry players with a bit of a mix of experience [with] the Chief [Radebe], David Batty, [Olivier] Dacourt and Nigel Martyn. Those players really, really spur you on and they set standards. We didn't care who we were playing, to be honest. We just went out there and played. We didn't care who they were, we didn't care what reputation they had. I think that's the way young players should be now. They shouldn't be scared, it's only a game of football. You [have] just got to go out there and give it your all."

The Lazio game is a fond memory for all involved as United again produced a statement performance on their travels. Smith scored the only goal of the match, linking up with Viduka in a brilliant one-two. "For me, the Lazio game [is] the best game I've ever played. That's my opinion. But I didn't score in that," Viduka said. "That was a be all, end all game … that was such a tight game and Lazio were one of the best teams … they were on fire." Dacourt felt the win against Lazio - managed by future England manager Sven-Goran Eriksson - was United's finest Champions League performance. "For me, the best game we played was in Rome when we played against Lazio," he said. "They had Simeone … six months before, they won the league and we killed them … Lazio was the best for me. You had some big, big players on the pitch and we killed them." In Viduka and Smith, Dacourt felt his side had two excellent strikers. "When you play midfield and you see your striker [Smith] defend like that, like a dog, he wants to kill everybody because he was so [passionate] … usually strikers, they just think about scoring goals. But he has this mentality … he had the fighting spirit to help all his teammates. For me, Viduka and Smith was great because Mark was powerful but Alan was working a lot for the team. It was easy because usually strikers say, 'Oh, I do my job, I score goals. You are in midfield, you just try to steal some balls and after you give me the ball. Enough'. After, when I play, when I went to Rome and to Inter Milan, [it] was like that ... Alan for me was top, top, top. I loved playing with Alan because I run less. When I was playing with Alan, I used to run less than when I played after."

Watching on in Rome was Paul Hart, the former Leeds United player who then oversaw the development of the likes of Smith, Woodgate, Kewell and McPhail through the club's youth system. Hart had left Leeds by that point but said he was "massively" proud to see the academy products on the big stage. "I went to see them play Lazio in the Champions League - Alan Smith scored ... I watched them play, they were all playing ... I took great [satisfaction], enjoying watching them play absolutely brilliantly and very maturely." Leeds found themselves 1-0 down to Anderlecht at Elland Road in their next Champions League fixture and with just 13 minutes remaining, at least from the outside, it did not look good. "It was very strange because when I was in Leeds I had this feeling, even when we were not winning, even when the result was bad, I knew we could come back," Dacourt said. "Anderlecht was winning 1-0 against us at home and I knew we will come back because the team was strong. The mentality was crazy. The quality of the players was good and the mentality was excellent." The Frenchman was spot on, Ian Harte first firing United level with a free-kick from distance before Lee Bowyer, involved in an ongoing court case regarding an incident in Leeds that also involved Woodgate, scored a dramatic 86th-minute winner. Bowyer's goal was his fifth of the competition and Leeds then went to Belgium for the return clash with a point to prove after Anderlecht coach Aime Antheunis said: "I did not see Leeds as a strong side."

O'Leary's team talk was done for him and United turned on the style, Smith scoring twice in a memorable and dominant 4-1 win in Brussels that secured the club's berth in the quarter-finals. "Probably the best performance, I think, of [the] whole tournament ... they were unbeaten at home for so many games, Anderlecht," said Matteo, while Viduka instantly labelled it as Leeds' best Champions League showing. "Anderlecht was no pushover, either ... we weren't sure what was waiting for us. Everything just fell into place, everybody worked hard ... we just outclassed them." Fired up afterwards, Dacourt had a message for Anderlecht. "When we kill them, I went to the press and I said, 'Yeah, just to the coach, for the worst team, we were the worst team and we kill you. For the worst team, we are not too bad.'" With a spot in the last eight secured with two more matches in the second group stage to play, Leeds headed to Madrid's famous Santiago Bernabeu with nothing to lose and put in an excellent showing, losing 3-2 in an entertaining clash marred by a goal from Raul that clearly came off his hand. Real Madrid were guaranteed to top Group D after that victory, meaning nothing was on the line when Leeds met Lazio at Elland Road, the hosts denied victory by Sinisa Mihajlovic's stoppage-time free-kick in a thrilling 3-3 draw.

The quarter-final draw saw Leeds paired with Deportivo La Coruna, the then-Spanish champions, and once again United were written off in the press, Deportivo midfielder Victor describing them as "the weakest team in the competition". "O'Leary had a way, as any manager, [to] use that to fuel the fire and to motivate us even more," Jacob Burns remembered. "We liked being the underdogs," Viduka said. "I think the good thing about those games, we went into those games free. Obviously, there's a certain amount of pressure you put on yourself as a player, personally, and as a team also. But we went into those games and we just enjoyed them. We wanted to enjoy them." Playing the first leg at Elland Road was a major boost, according to Matteo. "Sometimes the Elland Road crowd and the atmosphere can be a bit daunting for some teams … I think we used [that], we worked off that and we used that to our advantage."

That home crowd was roaring when Harte thumped in a brilliant 25th-minute free-kick as Leeds claimed the early ascendancy against Deportivo. "Some of his [Harte's] goals he scored were amazing," Matteo said. "Certainly the best dead-ball specialist I've ever played with … I think he never used to get the credit because if you think about that season, I think David Beckham was obviously at Manchester United scoring very similar goals to what Ian was scoring. I think Ian's ratio was probably better at the time than what David Beckham's was … he [Harte] worked on them day in, day out." Burns also said Harte's free-kicks were no flukes. "He could make the ball do anything, be it from anywhere outside the box. You just knew in games, whether it was the league or the Champions League, that if a team were prepared to lunge in, in and around the box, and he had two free-kicks, he was definitely scoring one of them. So it was a nice feeling to be in a team with someone as deadly as 'Hartey' … and it wasn't by luck. He was very, very dedicated to his craft, he would stay after training and hit a number of balls and he'd be putting them in the top bin every time."

Smith nodded in a second after the break and there was time for Ferdinand to get his first Leeds goal, too. '3-0, to the weakest team,' United's fans bellowed after a magnificent performance. "They were a top, top, top side but we battered them and just the way we pressed them and the way we just smothered them, we just ran over the top of them and they just couldn't handle it," Bowyer said. "Our intensity and togetherness was unreal as a team and that's what got us so far. We just overpowered them and they couldn't handle everything that we threw at them that night. And, again, the fans played a massive part in these evenings. Those Champions League evenings … it was frightening, the atmosphere and we won by three and it probably could have been more." Dacourt headed out to celebrate and remembered Leeds being the talk of Yorkshire. "[I was] with Rio Ferdinand after the game, we went out with his wife and my wife. After, the police stop us [laughs]. The police stop us, stop Rio, because he was driving a little bit fast. Rio scored the third goal with his head and the police say, 'Yeah, it's okay, massive result, well done guys, well done'. And they let us go!"

Matteo would partner Ferdinand in the heart of defence for the second leg and had an uneasy feeling before kick-off. "As usual, I think I was struggling to play in that game with an injury and I remember speaking to one of the staff before the game," he said. "So I went out to the warm-up but I couldn't do much running because I think it was my knee again. I had a problem. So I just watched them warm-up before the game and I remember thinking to myself, 'Woah, these [players] look a bit sharp tonight'. They had some good players. I remember just thinking to myself, 'We're going to have to defend for the whole game', and we did. We didn't really get out, I think … they had some good players, a lot of Brazilian lads who keep the ball very well and [could] make it difficult for us, great stadium, great atmosphere."

In an utterly one-sided second leg, Deportivo took just nine minutes to open the scoring, Djalminha converting from the penalty spot. "The atmosphere there was unbelievable. We went there and it was like their extra man. It's like their 12th man," Viduka said. "And when we came out, they just hammered us with everything … I just remember getting constantly … bombarded." Nigel Martyn had to make a string of saves to keep the deficit to one at the break but Deportivo gambled, throwing more bodies forward in what Bowyer called "the most one-sided game I've ever played in" and Diego Tristan scored for the hosts with 17 minutes left. "We used to watch the time, we used to watch even the bench to know how long it will be until the end of the game," Dacourt said. The visitors would hold on, though, the final whistle sending the travelling fans wild. Leeds were in the semi-finals.

"I felt like I defended for the whole game," Matteo said. "I felt drained after that game. I remember thinking, 'We've just qualified for the semi-finals and [it] feels like a defeat'. I remember Rio going, 'We're through, we're through aren't we?' … I think we got away with it a little bit. But we did our work in the first game - enough to get us through."

Mark Viduka scored 72 goals for Leeds United in 166 appearances between 2000 and 2004. Photo: Dubravko Lenert

Dominic Matteo made 146 appearances for Leeds United and captained the club. Photo: Steve Riding

MESTALLA | MAY 8 | ATT: 53,200

VALENCIA 3-0 LEEDS UNITED

SANCHEZ 16', 47', MENDIETA 52'

2001

SUBS: ROBINSON, KELLY, WOODGATE, McPHAIL, WILCOX, BURNS, MAYBURY

MANAGER: DAVID O'LEARY

VALENCIA

CANIZARES, ANGLOMA, AYALA, PELLEGRINO, AURELIO, ALBELDA, MENDIETA, AIMAR, GONZALEZ, CAREW, SANCHEZ

SUBS: PALOP, DESCHAMPS, DJUKIC, ZAHOVIC, ALONSO, ANGULO, VICENTE

MANAGER: HECTOR CUPER

OUR FORM HEADING IN

ARSENAL	2-1	LEEDS UTD
LEEDS UTD	0-0	VALENCIA
LEEDS UTD	2-0	CHELSEA

"Football - it's a funny thing. It can change people's moods and atmospheres, not just in a football stadium, but the whole city. And in a city like Leeds, everybody was just talking about that and it gives everybody a lift."
- Mark Viduka

UEFA Champions League fever hit semi-final bound Leeds United as fans started to dream. Next up for United was a clash against Valencia, finalists in the tournament one year earlier. Valencia had beaten Arsenal on away goals in their quarter-final but much of the pre-match attention was on their next opponents. Like they were in the Don Revie era, Leeds United were again being talked about across Europe, and for good reason, Mark Viduka thought. "All over the park, we had good players. 'Smithy' [Alan Smith] and I complemented each other, definitely ... 'H' on the left, Harry Kewell was definitely one of the best players that I've ever seen, definitely. On his day, he could have destroyed anybody ... H was very dangerous running at players, he was unbelievable. You had 'Bow' [Lee Bowyer]. Bow, at that time, was just on fire. I loved playing with Bow because the first thing he did, he looked forward. If he could play it in to me and run past me, [it was] very difficult to defend against. And he used to get in chances doing that all over, not just in the Champions League, but the whole time that we were playing there. We used to make, create chances in that way. It's simple but it worked. Ian Harte with his free kicks, his left foot, top player. He was a top player. Then you had 'Ollie' [Olivier Dacourt]. Ollie had an unbelievable ability as a ball-winner, he had really good timing. He could win the ball, he'd stop that ball and then he could create with that. Once he's won it, he creates situations where it's dangerous for the other team. Rio [Ferdinand] was there but even before Rio, we had 'Woody' [Jonathan Woodgate]. Woody's a top class defender, quick. I mean, I saw Woody one time, Thierry Henry was already past him, already showing him his arse and he's come back and defended that - I don't even know how. He was deceptively fast ... Lucas Radebe as well, 'The Chief'. The Chief was unbelievable as well, great timing, great defender, everything. Gary Kelly as well, quick ... Dom's [Matteo] a good player ... the main thing was that was a good bunch of guys. The spirit was the best. Good bunch of guys, everybody worked hard for each other, everybody wanted to win. It's very easy to start pointing fingers when it's going wrong but I think everybody worked their hardest and was in it together."

The togetherness is something Olivier Dacourt is quick to mention, too. The Frenchman said that that Leeds team had a unity he never saw again at other clubs. "The energy, the atmosphere we had in this team … even [though] I won things and everything … I never saw a team spirit like that. Never in my career … when we used to travel, everybody was singing on the coach. It's crazy." Viduka said Kelly was always the ringleader. "There were a lot of the young players, there were a few older players and that but everybody got on well. After those games and that, we would be singing all night, all together, on buses, going to airports, going to whatever. Wherever we were, we'd be singing. Gary Kelly used to always start off the song. We used to sing - he would start off some song and the whole bus would be singing, all the players. It was just a great atmosphere with those guys." Stephen McPhail said Kelly was not only a regular singer, but a crucial changing room figure. "He always made you smile and made you laugh. He was always a great character around the place … we had a lot of young players coming from the youth team through the ranks at that stage. A lot of us were in our second year, probably third year in [and] around the first team so we had to grow up and they [senior players] just set examples. They were all good players, they were unbelievable. But I think it was the all round togetherness within the group [that] made us go on and never stop believing that we could achieve things."

Leeds had every reason to feel confident ahead of the first leg against Valencia at a sold-out Elland Road after a 13-match unbeaten run in the Premier League, 10 of which were victories, and Radebe remembered after the quarter-final progression that he "still had a chance to play in the next game". Radebe would not be fit enough to feature, though, as Leeds lined up with the same side that scraped through in Spain a fortnight earlier. Jacob Burns, among the substitutes, said he felt a different vibe to the semi-final, as the disrespect showed by the likes of Anderlecht and Deportivo La Coruna faded. "You start really growing even more self-belief and the team's belief when you're getting those results," he said. "Elland Road was just a fortress. I think through that Champions League period, I think teams realised it. The biggest clubs in the world were realising they had to be at their very best to stand a chance, to get a result at our place." Matteo remembered Elland Road producing its "best atmosphere" for Valencia's visit, but Leeds, who started brightly, needed Nigel Martyn to keep out John Carew's overhead kick before Gaizka Mendieta headed against the crossbar. Alan Smith should have scored before half time, but he headed wide from close range as things remained level at the break.

Another great chance came to Matteo after the interval and with a free header at the back post, the Scotland international thought he had scored. "Geez, honestly, that save by [Santiago] Canizares - it was an incredible save," he said. "I thought I'd scored, to be honest." Dacourt knew it would be a big moment. "The goalkeeper made a save, a crazy save … I said, 'Fucking hell'. It was crazy." Canizares almost went from hero to zero after he charged off his line but Lee Bowyer could only head onto the bar and Valencia could have pinched an away win in stoppage time, only for Rio Ferdinand to clear a Vicente Rodriguez effort off the line. "It was tough. We just couldn't score … it was frustrating," Bowyer said. "It was one of those games where nothing would go in for us." Matteo's thoughts soon turned to the final, to be held in Milan. "I probably didn't think about the final until we'd played the first leg and it was 0-0," he said. "I remember thinking, 'I would love to have gotten, just to get one goal', … but they had a couple of chances as well, big Carew had a couple and Mendieta was always a threat and people like that. I actually spoke to Mendieta last year [2018] about the game and he said it was one of the incredible atmospheres … I think sometimes, those top players, they remember something like Elland Road more than Old Trafford because it's a bit more unusual to play at … I didn't think it was the worst result in the world because we could always score on the road. I thought, 'If we get one, they need two', sort of thing. The first leg, it was a bit disappointing not to win but at the end of the day, it wasn't the worst result because of the away goal scenario. They needed to score. But I knew they were a good side."

Others leaned on United's previous road triumphs for confidence. "0-0, it's a good result at home because if you score there, 1-1, you go through. We knew that we could score some goals [in Spain]," said Dacourt, while McPhail was also optimistic. "There was not much in the game," he said. "We obviously knew they had Mendieta and players like that that could really turn the game at any moment, so we were quite cautious … we definitely felt going away that we had a chance." In a show of togetherness, United's players - except Ian Harte - shaved their heads ahead of the second leg. "We thought that was going to be the dealbreaker [and get us victory]," Viduka said with a huge laugh. "Ian Harte was getting married so he couldn't do it." Bridges added that Harte "did not suit a skinhead" but that everyone else's participation was another positive sign. "The camaraderie - it was one in, all in. And senior players like [David] Batty and Martyn doing it - that just speaks volumes of what we were all about. I was a fan [due to injury], I was just riding on the crest of a wave when I saw the boys on the training ground. I had my own goals and targets then. I'd really got my head back screwed on and [was] training all hours with [physio] Dave Hancock but seeing the lads, the banter, the camaraderie - it was just a great vibe … the lads were playing so well and embracing and enjoying it. The training ground was just a great place to be around."

Leeds were hit with a major blow before the second leg when UEFA, using video evidence, gave Bowyer a suspension for stamping on Juan Sanchez in the first leg at Elland Road. "We were training on their pitch [in Spain] when the manager told me, 'Look, you've been banned'. And I thought that a ban was harsh and for it [the ban] to happen that quick - it just seemed like they didn't want us to go any further. That's the way I felt at the time. I was gutted I had to watch it from the stands." United were given no real right of reply, with any appeal to be held after the Mestalla fixture. Not only would O'Leary be robbed of Bowyer's energy, he would also be missing a midfielder who had scored six goals in the campaign. "He had a lot of stuff going on off the field with the trial … and Lee played the best football of his career," Bridges said. "The mental strength of that man is absolutely phenomenal … he'd absorb information on a football level brilliantly. He'd absorb information but he'd just go and work. I loved playing with Lee because as a striker you want to hold the ball up and if you're going to hold the ball up, you need people that are going to be willing to run off you … he just had this engine that was incredible." Dacourt knew Bowyer would be a major loss in the semi-final because of his ability to "score at any time". "Lee was a very good guy, very nice guy," Dacourt said. "When I used to say, 'Lee is a fisherman', nobody wanted to believe he is a fisherman.

Nobody! It was crazy … he scored a lot of goals in the Champions League this year."

Eirik Bakke came in for Bowyer on matchday and Matteo recalled a lengthy trip just to get to the stadium as thousands of fans arrived from England. "I remember getting there a couple of days before the game, all the Leeds fans on the beach in Valencia because the stadium was pretty close to the beach as they are sometimes in that part of Spain. The atmosphere was building, building, building, incredible atmosphere everywhere we went. We went for a walk, fans were in town, I think the chairman was out with the fans in the town the night before. It was just building. Even though we were only two minutes from the ground, it took us about an hour to get there because it was just fans in the street. It was hectic and I had a lot of friends and family over there." Perhaps it was the presence of family and friends of the players, perhaps it was the magnitude of the match, but Matteo sensed something different before the game. "I must say it was the only game where I felt maybe there was some nerves. The dressing room was vast. Some of these stadiums have huge dressing rooms … I just felt there just wasn't quite that buzz about the dressing room. I think we knew they were a good side and we'd have to play well but it was the semi-final of the Champions League, second leg, you should know that anyway. But I just think we got caught out a little bit."

Valencia would take a controversial lead, Sanchez appearing to use his hand to turn in a cross for the goal that broke the deadlock. "Rio still says that it was a handball for their first goal," Matteo said. "I do think that goals change games and maybe if we'd got the decision [to] go our way - but we didn't get the decision to go our way." Viduka recalled Valencia offering Leeds the toughest challenge they had faced in their European run. "We came there, we weren't scared of anybody," he said. "Even when we went to the Bernabeu with [Real] Madrid, we weren't scared of them at all, we went out and played. To be honest, sometimes it's easier to play against the bigger teams than it is the smaller teams because they give you space. When they have the ball, they can do damage, but when they don't have the ball, they sometimes give you more space than the other ones do because they want to play. They don't really want to be physical, whereas Valencia was both. They were physical … they were technically very good."

"Even at half time, I feel we were a bit flat," Matteo said. "Even though we were still in the game … I remember thinking to myself, 'Come on, come on, can one of us lift the boys or something?' But it just didn't quite happen … I think the mistake we made is we went chasing the game at 1-0. Even with five minutes [left], just stay in the game, you stay in the game, we [had] got the players to get a goal … that was our inexperience that cost us for me, personally. And it was very difficult out on the field, once you lost that shape and you are chasing it at that level, with the noise levels, to get your unit back together. Because I thought that's one thing we had - a good stable unit with Dacourt and Batty in front of the back four for us … I still think the wide lads, Eirik Bakke who played there with Kewell, and 'Vidukes' [Viduka] and 'Smithy', they could still get a goal for us. But we just didn't stay in the game long enough." Valencia scored just after half time as Sanchez got his second with a long-range effort, and Mendieta also scored from distance to put Valencia in control. Leeds were never coming back from there and Sanchez was denied a hat-trick by the woodwork before Smith was sent off for a late, reckless challenge. United's European dream was over, one match before the final. "On the night, they were just superior to us, to be honest," McPhail said. "They outplayed us. It was one that they fully deserved to win … we didn't have many chances."

"Great atmosphere, I have to say," Bowyer said. "All the Valencia fans … I remember having 70-year-old people sitting next to me and the whole stadium had a scarf and they were all waving them. It was an unbelievable experience and obviously watching it from the side was disappointing but that's the memories I take from that - the disappointment of not playing and thinking, 'Wow, what an atmosphere.'" McPhail, an unused substitute at the Mestalla, then sat drinking with Valencia star Pablo Aimar as the pair were taken away for routine drug testing. "It felt like a couple [of] hours … I just made the bus, to be honest," he said. "[There's] a person that sits with you until you can give a urine sample. I was sat around, funnily enough, with Aimar that night … he was really respectful. He just seemed a lovely lad. Obviously, his English wasn't great … we sat together for probably an hour and a half … [it was] broken English chat … he was very respectful after winning a Champions League semi-final and being in the final. He didn't celebrate, there was no shouting or roaring coming into the room … we ended up having a couple of beers together."

So what was thc mood like afterwards? Was it disappointment? Pride? Or a mixture? "That game haunts me … I'll never forget that game because I'll always think that [I was] one step off playing in a Champions League Final. I wouldn't be a footballer if I didn't think about it. I do think about it regularly … disappointment," Matteo said. "I think any footballer, if you get to that stage, it's a semi-final - I've lost in a Cup Winners' Cup semi-final, I've lost in a Champions League semi-final, an FA Cup semi-final - it's the worst. I'm not saying it'd be any better in the final but at least you get the day, the fans get the chance of winning it. I think the semis are always the worst for me, personally. It was disappointing, I'll be honest. It was disappointing." Viduka added: "It was frustration. Disappointment. Obviously, you're happy that you've gotten this far but you always want to do better, don't you?" Dacourt said just talking about the game brings back feelings of sadness. "I try to forget this night. I never watched this game." Radebe said there were positives to take, too. "We were disappointed that we got that far [and lost] but we knew that we could have got to the final … I think we were proud as a club to become one of the top clubs in the English Premier League," he said. "There was a lot of positives as a club, [more] than negatives, so we always wanted to focus on them."

One positive lurking around the camp was the thought that Leeds would be back in the Champions League soon. "We knew with this team, we will do some things," Dacourt said. "Because we had some quality, we had some good atmosphere … people used to say we will become the next Manchester United, we will win everything … [but] everybody left." United's financial problems and eventual mass exodus meant that Dacourt and many of his teammates were left with a sense of regret. "My time in Leeds, I've got some regrets because we didn't win anything with this team," he said. "We had all the qualities to win things."

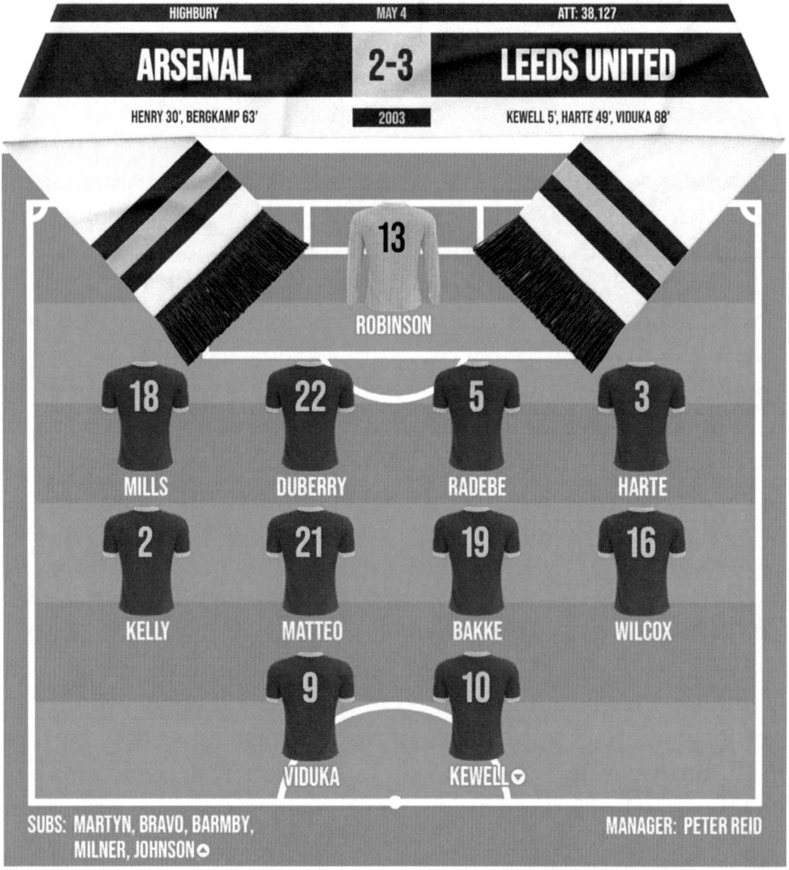

ARSENAL

SEAMAN, TOURE, LUZHNY, KEOWN, COLE, WILTORD, PARLOUR, SILVA, PIRES, BERGKAMP, HENRY

SUBS: TAYLOR, VAN BRONCKHORST, PENNANT, KANU, STEPANOVS

MANAGER: ARSENE WENGER

OUR FORM HEADING IN

LEEDS UTD	2-3	BLACKBURN
LEEDS UTD	2-0	FULHAM
SOUTHAMPTON	3-2	LEEDS UTD

"We finished fourth and that was the killer. That killed it."
- Jonathan Woodgate

Just one point separated Leeds United from a place in the 2001-02 UEFA Champions League, a key moment in the club's swift, dramatic and painful fall from grace. In a lengthy 59-game season that saw United make a famous run in Europe's premier club competition, a 2-1 loss at Arsenal in May - just three days before the second leg of a Champions League semi-final in Valencia - would prove costly. Leeds finished fourth and had to settle for a place in the UEFA Cup, and while the outside world did not know it, all was not as it seemed. Dominic Matteo received an indication when Leeds signed Rio Ferdinand from West Ham United for £18 million in November 2000. "Rio came in which really boosted the team, when you sign a player of that level. Me and Mark Viduka were actually part of the transfer, which was also quite surreal, because we were leased out to a finance company … it was quite bizarre but me and the big man just did it. We cracked on, we're owned by some American finance company." While Matteo's eyebrows were raised, Viduka did not pick up on anything at the time. "I thought, 'I know nothing about running a football club. Maybe that's a normal thing? I don't know. I don't have a clue,'" he said.

Despite missing out on the Champions League cash injection, Leeds, already operating in a peculiar financial manner, gambled on more signings, hoping another big outlay of money would see them make a quick return to the pinnacle of European football. Robbie Keane's loan was made permanent and Robbie Fowler and Seth Johnson also joined a bloated first-team squad, the trio costing United a reported £30 million. For a while at least, the roll of the dice looked like working out, David O'Leary's side losing just two Premier League games before Christmas, and when Viduka scored twice and Fowler also netted in a 3-0 win over West Ham on New Year's Day 2002, Leeds were top of the table. But a shock 2-1 FA Cup loss at Cardiff City just five days later kickstarted a 10-match winless run that saw United's dreams of winning both the title and the UEFA Cup come to an end. Things picked up before the season ended but even with four English sides reaching the 2002-03 UEFA Champions League, Leeds missed out, finishing fifth, five points behind fourth-placed Newcastle United. The gamble had failed and O'Leary was sacked, a move that did not sit well with several players and caught most fans by surprise. Asked when he first felt things were not as they should be, Olivier Dacourt said: "When David O'Leary left, for me. I liked David … I came [to Leeds] for him. I came for the project … when I saw him leave, something was broken for me." Viduka added: "I think it started getting wrong with the sacking of O'Leary … I don't even know why he got the sack … if they were going to do that, they should have thought about who they were going to bring in properly. But the big problem was the finances."

With Barcelona, Tottenham Hotspur, England and Australia on his managerial CV, Terry Venables was appointed as O'Leary's replacement, but player sales were now necessary to plug the financial gaps and while Ferdinand's £30 million move to Manchester United in July 2002 looked like good business from afar, it was not. "I don't think they made any money on the deal, so that's how bad things were," Matteo claimed. "I think that really summed it up for me. That's a lot of interest to pay [on loans], isn't it? Over a couple of years, 12 million quid. So we must have been really struggling and when I heard that, I went, 'Wow.'" Keane was also sold to Tottenham and after winning four of their first six league encounters in the 2002-03 season, Leeds started to slide.

Just one win in 11 Premier League matches and a third-round UEFA Cup exit at the hands of Malaga heaped the pressure on Venables, who was soon flanking chairman Peter Ridsdale at a press conference after the surprise sale of Jonathan Woodgate to Newcastle United for £9 million. "I was assured that if Fowler went, Jonathan Woodgate wouldn't go," an unhappy Venables told reporters, adding he was "clearly thinking" about his future. Woodgate and Fowler, who went to Manchester City, were not the only departures, either, Lee Bowyer joining West Ham and Dacourt moving to Roma on loan in January as Leeds desperately tried to reduce the wage bill. "I was gutted that I was leaving. I'd been there since I was a 14-year-old kid," Woodgate said. "My dad used to bring me, every Tuesday, every Thursday, to training down from Middlesbrough to Leeds. Then I end up moving to Leeds when I was 16 years old - it was the best thing I ever did. From being there, I knew everyone at the club, I loved the club … I just didn't want to leave but obviously the chairman explained, 'Listen, it's one of those things that we have to sell you', … I think Ferdinand was the first one to leave, we all just started leaving."

At the time, Michael Duberry thought the sales made sense. "We just thought [we] didn't qualify for the Champions League, there's big high wage bills so they've got to sell off some players … you don't qualify for that league ... players want to move on because they want Champions League football." But as players kept leaving, standards started slipping. "It was disappointing when you see all these players going," Viduka said. "And then they're bringing in players who are not up to the level … and then you start asking yourself the question, 'What's going on?'" The quality of training is a major gripe among many of United's key figures who were involved until the bitter end of the club's Premier League era and Matteo said he remembered thinking the club had "an issue". "I always thought, personally, once the training - once you lose training, the training ground, the vibe of that goes and there's players bickering and you're not quite sure of who the manager is or who to speak to - I think you've got serious problems. And that's when I generally thought, 'We've got an issue here'. Because the standards dropped in training. I don't know why that was. Not by every player but by some. I thought there was bickering, there was groups forming and we never had that - we were always together. I think if any player was honest, they would say the same. But everyone says different things about it, it's just my opinion. That's how I saw it, that's how I felt and, obviously, I was captain at the time."

Viduka was excluded from first-team training at times, too, and thought it might have been a sign his time at Leeds was up. "Somewhere around that [Christmas] time, I come into training and I get ready for training and all that sort of stuff … I start going out to training and [coach] Brian Kidd goes, 'You know what? 'Dukes', you're not training with us today'. And I go, 'What?' And he goes, 'You're training with the second team'. So he, Terry Venables, puts me into the second team for I don't know how long … couple of weeks or something like that … what he was trying to do, whether he was trying to send me a message … I don't even know … I was very pissed off. Especially because I knew Terry because of before with the [Australia] national team as well. And he had also done it to 'Ollie' as well, Ollie Dacourt. Now I knew that they were trying to get rid of Ollie, get some money in, maybe that's what they're trying to do with me as well at that stage. These are the ins and outs that people don't know about. They don't know about that."

Leeds' results picked up around the festive period as teenager James Milner hit the headlines but form soon tailed off again, six defeats in eight Premier League games ending Venables' tenure, with Peter Reid brought in on a caretaker basis as United were seriously threatened by relegation. Venables did leave a parting gift, at least, in the form of an angry Viduka. "That whole thing with Terry pissed me off pretty bad," he said. "And I said [in my head], which is what I did a lot of the times in my career, I said, 'Fuck you'. I didn't say it to him … I said [in my head] … 'Fuck you. I'm going to show you what I can do.'" Viduka said that while he was a relaxed man, he could also get very fired up. "My problem was, as a player was, I'm too laid back. I'm a very laid back person. But when I get angry - my problem is it takes me a long time to get angry - but once I get angry, you can't stop me from being angry. And that's why even O'Leary used to say [to] the players before [games], 'Punch him a few times before every game,' [laughs]. That was the problem … that's that Croatian part in me." Viduka had a point to prove to the world and after scoring three goals in Venables' last two league games in charge, he netted in Reid's first match as manager, a 3-1 defeat at Liverpool. And his strikes would soon start inspiring victories, the Australian finishing with 14 goals in the last 10 Premier League matches of the season, form that would ultimately ensure Leeds' safety. Viduka's hat-trick in a 6-1 win at Charlton Athletic was followed by a double in a 2-2 home draw against Tottenham and while he failed to score in a 3-2 defeat at Southampton, he then got both goals in a vital 2-0 triumph over Fulham. Leeds then lost 3-2 at home to Blackburn Rovers, setting up a crucial trip to Arsenal in the penultimate match of the season.

Going into the weekend's fixtures, Leeds sat 16th, one point ahead of Bolton Wanderers and three ahead of West Ham, and with a much better goal difference than both of their relegation rivals. But by matchday at Highbury, United were level on points with both Bolton and West Ham after surprise results. Leeds needed an upset of their own to secure safety and also knew if they were to win, it would hand Manchester United the title. "Going into that game, I couldn't sleep the night before," Matteo said. "Eirik Bakke, my roommate, he was like, 'Are you going to get any sleep?' I was like 'No, I can't sleep, I'm too [nervous].' I was thinking about the game, I was thinking, 'Oh my gosh'. You think about the team you have got to play, you're thinking about every scenario. I was thinking, 'I think I'm going to play in holding midfield', ... I was trying to work out my game, because I was moving around in different positions [that season]." Radebe remembered the must-win mentality. "It was an absolutely beautiful warm day ... we needed to win to stay up and to win at Highbury against such a great Arsenal team, with [Thierry] Henry and [Patrick] Vieira."

Players could have been forgiven for being nervous but Matteo recalled how Reid broke the ice. "'I remember me and him going into the referee's room. I think Vieira must have been captain for Arsenal on that day ... [Arsene] Wenger and Vieira go in and me and 'Reidy' go in ... hand our team sheets in and I was thinking, 'Let's have a look at their team, gaffer', sort of thing." Matteo said Reid then went into Leeds' changing room and said: "They're shite, these [players]. We'll batter these." The skipper added that Reid's comment changed the pre-match vibe. "I needed something like that to relax a little bit," he said. "I looked through the team and went, 'Have we read the same team sheets?' And it was the full [Arsenal] team - it couldn't have gotten much better, maybe one or two, but apart from that, it was full strength Arsenal and I feared the worst, to be honest. We went into the dressing room and the whole atmosphere when the gaffer said that changed a little bit."

Woodgate may have left Leeds but he was still invested. "I was watching it at home when they beat Arsenal, [Harry] Kewell and Viduka [scored] and it kept them up. Oh my God ... I thought to myself, 'Come on lads, come on lads, come on lads'." After Gilberto Silva hit the crossbar, Kewell gave Leeds a fifth-minute lead with a tremendous effort from distance. "We had to go in there for a result," Viduka said. "That was do or die for us and we set out the game plan ... I would say that was just sheer resilience. Harry's goal was unbelievable ... I mean that hasn't been talked about much but that was an unbelievable goal. First goal.

That's a big lift when you go to Arsenal and you score a goal like that." Henry levelled for the hosts, who started to dominate, but Leeds made it to the break at 1-1. "[Dennis] Bergkamp's always a handful, strong, tough and [he would] get his elbows up at the same time and he's so skilful," Duberry said. "Thierry Henry, you've got to be near perfect all the game ... a season later, he can score four goals [against us]. You always want to put yourself together against the best ... fortunately for us, we did well."

Ian Harte restored Leeds' lead with a deflected free-kick just four minutes after the break. "He'd pop in with a free-kick and he'd relieve pressure ... and then they scored," Viduka said. "They had a few chances and we were defending for our lives." Bergkamp soon equalised and Henry hit the post, while Arsenal also spurned other opportunities before Jermaine Pennant lost the ball in midfield and Matteo pounced. "I was playing midfield," Matteo said. "I remember getting the ball and thinking, 'I'm just going to try and put this in behind the Arsenal defence and let Mark run to it', ... I just hit one left-footed to Mark and I just followed it which is not like me, usually I'm staying right in that central [area] of the pitch." Viduka could have been offside but was not going to waste any time thinking about it. "I just had one thing in my mind and that was, 'Go for goal'," he said, recalling a moment where he headed the ball down and then cut inside Oleg Luzhny. "In those situations, all these moments depend on split seconds. If you do a little dummy on one side, what has he done? ... It [my touch] opened me up on the inside. If that didn't happen in that split second ... I would have [had] to have gone a different way ... instinct. I was going towards goal so I've got to somehow get myself into a position to shoot and that was that. I just dummied in one way, flicked it in the inside and I thought, 'I've got to go for it'. Left foot, top corner. Hey, I was just as surprised as anyone [laughs]. That could have went anywhere!"

The sheer joy on Viduka's face was evident as he sprinted across the pitch to celebrate his 88th-minute winner with his teammates. Leeds were staying up. "That is one of the happiest moments of my football career, definitely," he said. "That goal at the end of that [season with some troubles], that goal was so satisfying. Not just that goal. Just winning, beating Arsenal at Highbury. Staying up in the Premiership.

Seeing the club [survive]." Duberry said it was a hugely satisfying result. "They were going for, trying to take the title. Defeat hindered them and helped us. The whole analogy of who wants it more, us who are [threatened] by relegation or them with the title and we just outworked them, outfought them and got a great victory. Obviously, celebrating it was like, 'Wow, come on, well done'. You saw by the post-game celebrations how much it meant to us." Duberry's defensive partner on that day sung a similar tune. "It was an absolutely fantastic day … we just managed to hold on to the victory on the day," Radebe said. "It didn't have to depend on the next game for us to stay up, a great victory and one of those games that I remember and will cherish forever, beating Arsenal at their home ground. I don't remember many teams going to Arsenal and to Highbury and getting the full three points so that is one of the games that I will remember."

Victory meant Leeds did not have to worry about a final-day match against Aston Villa - that United won 3-1 - with survival already secured. Matthew Kilgallon, a promising young player who travelled to Arsenal for the experience, recalled the changing room happiness. "It was just mental, really. I can remember the celebrations after. I'm just sitting [in] the corner watching them all go berserk, how much it meant, and [it was] just great to be a part of it. And I'm just thinking, 'I've got to clear all this up', [laughs]." The celebrations continued on the way back to Yorkshire. "The coach journey home on that bus, I think we did play Pop Idol or something - whatever they call it," Matteo said. "The singing contest one with Simon Cowell … we had to go up the back and sing in front of the boys … me and Peter Reid stopped off and got about 10 cases of ale at the off licence, loads of bottles of wine. He [even] came up for a sing-song at the back of the bus!"

When the dust settled, Matteo found reason to be optimistic ahead of the 2003-04 campaign. "The players actually had a go together [at Arsenal], we worked hard ... the pressure was on, we produced the result and then I thought we'd re-build after that … that moment I thought, 'Alright, okay, we're alright here'. Because if you can produce a result like that, I always have belief that you can build upon that and obviously we won the last game of the season … then I thought, 'Right, re-build in the summer and then get back to basics, move up the table'."

FRATTON PARK | NOVEMBER 8 | ATT: 20,122

PORTSMOUTH 6-1 LEEDS UNITED

STEFANOVIC 16', O'NEIL 45+1', 71', FOXE 63', BERGER 75', YAKUBU 86'

2003

SMITH 19'

SUBS: CARSON, HARTE, BRIDGES ▲, SAKHO ▲, CAMARA

MANAGER: PETER REID

PORTSMOUTH

HISLOP, SCHEMMEL, FOXE, STEFANOVIC, DE ZEEUW, STONE ▼, SHERWOOD, O'NEIL, BERGER, SHERINGHAM, YAKUBU

SUBS: WAPENAAR, ZIVKOVIC, TAYLOR ▲, PRIMUS, ROBERTS

MANAGER: HARRY REDKNAPP

OUR FORM HEADING IN

LEEDS UTD	1-4	ARSENAL
LEEDS UTD	2-3	MAN UTD
LIVERPOOL	3-1	LEEDS UTD

"It was a shambles ... it was just falling apart in front of our eyes ... I was very sad."
- Mark Viduka

Only two years earlier, Leeds United's Australian striker was a transfer target for AC Milan. Mark Viduka grew up hooked on Italian football, idolising Marco van Basten, but was not interested in a move because he was convinced success was around the corner. "Milan offered 30 million quid for me or something like that," he said. "I had just moved from Celtic that year ... I really, honestly, didn't want to go ... I loved playing for Leeds, it was a great club to play for ... and I honestly thought that that club was going to go win the Premiership." Just months after Viduka almost single-handedly saved Leeds from Premier League relegation, another chance to play in Milan surfaced, this time with Inter. Frustrated with transfer business that had seen Rio Ferdinand, Robbie Keane, Jonathan Woodgate, Lee Bowyer, Robbie Fowler and Harry Kewell all leave Leeds, Viduka wanted to explore the opportunity and organised a meeting with manager Peter Reid. "I wanted to be up front with him and I didn't want to be behind his back ... looking at the club, I'm thinking, 'Everybody's leaving. There's no more players. I have to leave as well', ... I had a meeting with Peter and I said, 'Look, Inter Milan are in for me. If they make the club an offer ... I have to go. This is falling apart. I have to go'. The players he was bringing in and all that sort of stuff - it wasn't [the] Leeds United that I signed for." Viduka added that Reid told him: "Don't tell anybody. Let's just keep it between me and you."

"The next game we played was a friendly match [against Burnley] ... we lost," Viduka said. "And at half time, he [Reid] gets up in front of everyone and goes, 'If anybody doesn't want to be here, come and see me, just like 'Vidukes' did', ... you can imagine what sort of an atmosphere ... he created ... the thing is he said to me, 'Let's keep it between us', ... a few days later that was, he goes [off] at half time in front of the whole team and I was sitting in the dressing room and the whole team is looking at me saying, 'What the fuck? What's this? It already looks like we're struggling', ... I was pissed off after that game. I went into the team bus and then he calls me to go, that he wants to have a meeting with me, calls me out of the bus ... in the hallway, he starts talking to me. I said, 'Do you know what? You can get fucked. I know what you are. I know what you're about. When you needed me to score fucking 14 goals in 10 games [last season], you were fucking licking my arse'. That's what I said to him. And then I went back into the bus and I said, 'I know exactly what time it is'. It was time to go." Viduka's trust in Reid was completely broken and just a few days later, the manager asked the striker to go in for a meeting after training. "We were all sitting down stretching after a warm-down … and I said, 'No, if you want to talk … talk in front of everybody. Let's all talk in front of everybody', … he had nothing to say." It would not be the last row between Viduka and Reid.

As pre-season continued, Leeds' money problems continued to make a significant impact. "No money. No money whatsoever," Reid's assistant, Kevin Blackwell, said of the club's inability to make signings. "I think even Pete was a little bit astounded by the lack of support, financially. He'd kept the club up the year before and they just sold Harry Kewell to Liverpool. I think one or two others had gone so there was money coming in but it certainly wasn't coming in to go on the team, to work on the team … Peter Reid tried to sign three or four players [but] couldn't sign anybody."

United were restricted to loan signings and free transfers, as Olivier Dacourt completed his move to Roma and Nigel Martyn later joined Everton. Joining Leeds on a temporary basis were five signings from Ligue 1, Marseille trio Lamine Sakho, Salomon Olembe and Cyril Chapuis, PSG's Didier Domi and Lens' Zoumana Camara. Jermaine Pennant, from Arsenal, and AC Milan's Roque Junior also joined on loan, while Jody Morris signed on a free transfer. "Quality players, your Rio Ferdinands, your Kewells [are] leaving and you're getting players like Salomon Olembe and Camara and stuff like that. You're going, 'We're fucked'," Michael Bridges said, while Blackwell recalled the language barrier with most of the club's new arrivals. "Five of the lads didn't speak proper English. I remember having to get English lessons sorted out for them … we had to try and integrate foreign players into a team that struggled the year before and we knew it wasn't going to be easy." Blackwell, who described the French loan signings as something that "looked like a desperation move", was still positive about the club's survival chances. "I always felt there was enough quality within the team to stay up."

Leeds captain Dominic Matteo was unsure, though. "It was a strange move for me … I didn't really think they [foreign loan signings] were going to have much of an impact because of where we were. We needed a different type of player." The initial signs were promising from Sakho, at least, who caught the eye in a 2-2 draw with Newcastle United on the opening day of the season, but Leeds won just two of their first 11 Premier League matches heading into a trip south to face Portsmouth. Training levels had dropped again and United were leaking goals at an alarming rate, 4-0 defeats at Leicester City and Everton particularly concerning. Matteo remembered Viduka taking a proactive role at training to try and ensure standards remained high and the latter acknowledged sometimes things got physical. "I was very disappointed in some of the players, some of the players' attitudes. Very disappointed," Viduka said. "In some instances, it actually got to physical sort of things where people would be coming and mucking around at training. We're in the relegation zone for most of the season and that pissed me off … I tried to [improve things], it's difficult, though. It's a difficult situation to be in where you see what level it should be at."

Viduka may have wanted out in the summer but he was still keen to help Leeds in their survival fight. He would miss the Portsmouth match, though, left out after another issue with Reid. "The results were bad. He [Reid] was looking really, really, really bad," Viduka said. "I had to tape my ankles, I had problems with my ankles all the time, rolling the ankles, so I had to tape them … you go in to the training ground, you get taped up by the physio, Alan Sutton. 'Sutty' would tape us up and then I'd go out. And what happened [was] sometimes he'd put it too tight and it would start hurting … I went out and I started doing the warm-up and it started hurting me so I said to the physio, 'I'm going to go in and get it loosened up a little bit'. And I start walking away towards there and Peter Reid comes to me … it was a simulated thing where in front of everybody ... he wanted to make a conflict intentionally. He goes, 'Where are you going?' And I said, 'I'm going to do my thing [tape]', … and he goes, 'No, go inside'. I go, 'Why?' He goes, 'Nah, go inside, you're not going to the game. You're not coming to Portsmouth', ... he made a conflict because he probably knew the end was near and he needed a scapegoat." Viduka felt like he was an easy target. "Obviously [the] media put pressure on him and all of us and he was looking for a scapegoat. What better scapegoat is [there than] the highest-paid player, a striker and a foreigner? It's always the case ... I was ready to go and play in that [Portsmouth] game. 100 per cent."

Leeds travelled south without their talisman and were in dreadful form, having conceded 10 goals in their last three matches. Australian Hayden Foxe, who scored at Fratton Park for Portsmouth, remembered being surprised at the team news. "To see that he wasn't involved in the line-up was a shock for us ... 'Vidukes' was a very prolific goalscorer and striker in the English Premier League. We knew there was something amiss there." Foxe and Portsmouth, who were newly promoted and would be involved in the relegation fight with Leeds later that season, had been given a major boost.

There was drama at the ground, too, Blackwell remembering how "the floodlights went", forcing a delay. Leeds were caught cold when the match started, Portsmouth making a fast start before they opened the scoring through Dejan Stefanovic. "You're playing against a team, they're all confident, they've just come up, we're on a decline," Michael Duberry said. Alan Smith levelled proceedings for Leeds but Gary O'Neil's 25-yard screamer restored Pompey's lead before the break. And the pressure applied on Leeds was relentless in the second half, Foxe making it 3-1 with an excellent strike from distance. "You looked on their faces [and they said], 'Oh, shit, we're playing away at Portsmouth who are newly promoted and we're finding it very difficult to be in this game'. Then, it's difficult. It's difficult for them to turn that mentality and turn it into a positive," Foxe said. "And what happens then is they get frustrated and then they're thinking about their mistakes before and what happened before and it's very difficult to be able to turn that around. And that was definitely the case in this game."

O'Neil, on his Premier League debut, made it 4-1 and the floodgates were well and truly open, Patrik Berger and Yakubu also scoring before Leeds were put out of their misery. "They smashed [us] ... you try to wipe it out of your memory when shit like that happens ... I really can't remember much apart from the goals just going in and going in and hearing our fans just abusing us," said Bridges, a second-half substitute, who also remembered a tense changing room. "I think that's when the panic alarms really hit home for the boys. There was lots of arguments and fights in the dressing room ... people blaming each other. You look for answers and excuses and things like that but it was just a horrendous atmosphere." Duberry said the feeling was of "professional embarrassment". "It should have never happened, 6-1, you're a defender, it should never happen ... you just feel low - you just know the week's going to be a tough week ... it was a massive shock."

"Don't get me wrong, they had some good players back then. But we shouldn't be getting beaten like that," Matteo said. "I remember thinking, 'This is hard work'. I never felt any time I'd played for Leeds that there was a game that we weren't capable of getting a result in. That day, it was just awful. It was dreadful. Absolutely hated the game, the whole thing about it." Lucas Radebe, battling injury at the time, shared a similar view. "We were at the bottom of the league. It was so sad. It gets to the players mentally and physically ... it was a bad feeling about going down and you could see the quality in the field of play was sad for such a great club that has played in the highest [competition] - the Champions League. Yes, it was disappointing and it was sad for us as players to stoop that low."

A common theme amongst all of United's players was the significance of the Portsmouth loss. This was not just any old defeat. This was the day they realised it would be a major, major battle to avoid relegation. "I always believe that we weren't good enough to take our eye off the ball or foot off the gas. And we did," Matteo said. "It doesn't matter who you are playing, they'll find you out, because every team in the Premier League has got people that can score goals and cause problems. They outworked us and they got the result ... I think that was the start of that slide." Blackwell said "that was the game that confirmed that we were in a desperate struggle", while for Duberry, it "rubber-stamped that there was a massive, massive turnaround [in our fortunes]."

Tony Dorigo, working at Portsmouth on that day as a radio analyst, was similarly worried about United's future. "I didn't see any fight … Leeds fans … if you try and you lose 6-1, fair enough, but, no, there was some stuff out there which wasn't good. There was a lot of stuff that was wrong and you just felt, 'Oh my God, this is going to be really, really tough', … okay, it is only three points, but mentally you can't keep doing that sort of thing … it was just horrific. It was absolutely awful and after a tough season it was, 'Okay, this is bad, how do we recover from this one?'" Reid did not recover and was sacked, but he went down swinging when talking to the press in the aftermath, saying "that second half was the worst 45 minutes of my managerial career". He added: "I won't resign but I'm certainly not happy about the lack of desire."

That lack of fight stuck with Matteo, too. "[I] really struggled after that game for a few weeks. Mentally, I was drained because I'd never lost like that before ever in my life, anywhere, anytime in football. I've never been battered like that before … it was hard to take and I think we all knew it. We all knew things were bad that day. It was a struggle after that to really lift ourselves."

Leeds United were in serious danger of relegation - and the players knew it. Photo: Andrew Varley Picture Agency

REEBOK STADIUM | MAY 2 | ATT: 27,420

BOLTON WANDERERS 4-1 LEEDS UNITED

DJORKAEFF 47', 53', HARTE 55' [OG], NOLAN 78' | 2004 | VIDUKA 26' [PEN]

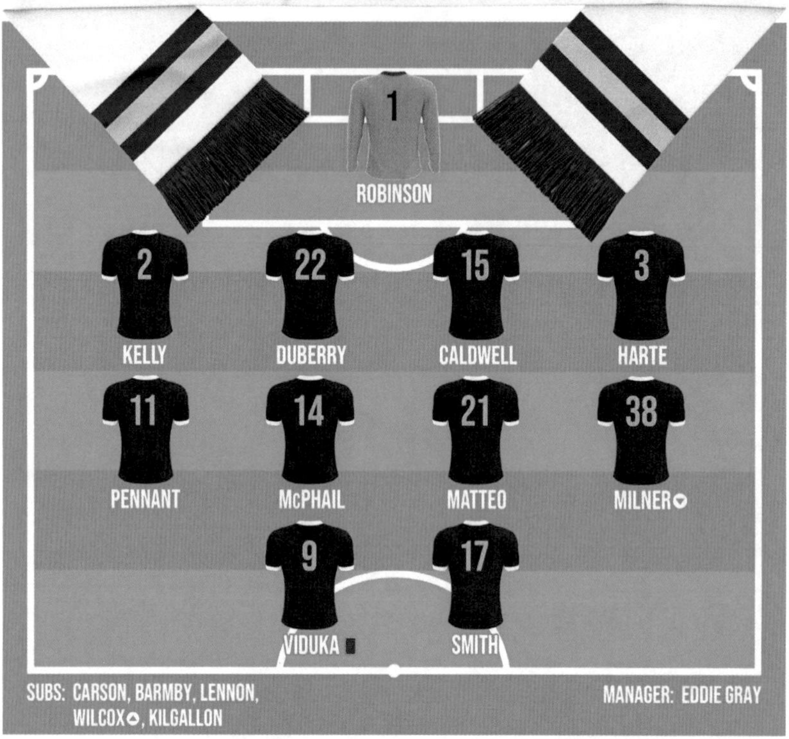

BOLTON WANDERERS

JAASKELAINEN, HUNT, THOME, N'GOTTY, CHARLTON, NOLAN, CAMPO, OKOCHA, DJORKAEFF, PEDERSEN, DAVIES

SUBS: POOLE, BARNESS, FRANDSEN, MORENO, GIANNAKOPOULOS

MANAGER: SAM ALLARDYCE

OUR FORM HEADING IN

LEEDS UTD 1-2 PORTSMOUTH	ARSENAL 5-0 LEEDS UTD	LEEDS UTD 1-1 EVERTON

"The biggest regret I've ever had since I walked through the gates as a 15-year-old was coming back. I shouldn't have come back."
- Eddie Gray

He knew that Leeds United were doomed but Eddie Gray also knew his football club needed him. "Trevor [chief executive Trevor Birch] came and he said to me, 'Eddie, I'd like you to come back in as caretaker [manager]'. I thought about it ... I knew the financial situation of the football club was horrendous. And I took it." Peter Reid's sacking led to Gray's return to Leeds, just six months after the ex-Sunderland manager decided to get rid of him. You could not get rid of a club legend that easily. An outstanding spell of 18 years as a player and then stints as manager, first-team coach and youth-team coach meant Gray knew Leeds United better than anyone. "A Leeds United man through and through," Stephen McPhail said of Gray. "When the chips are down and things are going against the club, Eddie puts his hand up ... what a brave, brave decision from him." Gray inherited a Leeds United side that were bottom of the Premier League and leaking goals, but spirits were raised after his appointment as caretaker manager was confirmed. "He definitely gave everyone a lift with that announcement. I remember the feeling - I was just lifted," McPhail added.

Gray's first game in charge ended in a 2-0 home defeat to Bolton Wanderers but an unbeaten run of five matches, including wins against Charlton Athletic and Fulham and a draw against high-flying Chelsea, raised hopes. "There was a decent run of form ... but it wasn't long before I was back in at the football club [that] I realised it wasn't going to work," Gray said. "The players were coming in to me saying, 'Oh, the club tried to sell me last night', ... there was a lot of it and the people that were running the club at that time, I don't think they realised the extent of the trouble the club were in. I think it was handled badly. That's why I felt for Trevor Birch." United's form nosedived, too, with six successive Premier League defeats coming as the financial issues started to get out of hand. "Instability is the worst thing. Not just for a football club - for any organisation," Mark Viduka said. "A restaurant, cafe, whatever. The worst thing is instability and we were in a situation, that last year [in the Premier League], when the cleaners, the cleaning ladies, who, every day we used to sit and have coffees with them and all that, they didn't know whether they were going to get paid that week. When the club is in that situation, like it or not, it has to affect the results. It has to affect the results. If they've got no money to bring in good players, if they've got no money to pay their workers … that creates instability. And once that creeps in, it's very difficult."

Issues between players were only getting bigger, too, with an initially rejected proposal to defer player wages frustrating captain Dominic Matteo, who wanted his teammates to help the club in a time of need. "I just couldn't understand because the deferral means you're going to get it back," he said. "I was just thinking, 'You've got to be clever about this', because the fans, they want players to do the right thing and that's what I thought we were going to do … the right thing. Some players were at different stages of their career, different wages, I get all that. We've all got families but at the end of the day, for giving up some money for a couple of weeks for me, for any of us at that point of our lives, wouldn't have been the end of the world. We could have done the right thing and made ourselves look a lot better and in the end, we had to do the deferral anyway. Alright, it wasn't quite as much, but does it really matter? None of the boys were earning peanuts. It would have been fine but instead you make yourselves look a little bit greedy, in my opinion, and I didn't agree with that. A few of the players didn't agree with me for that … everyone was earning good money and it wouldn't have mattered for a few weeks to try and help the club out and do the right thing."

"The camp becomes a bit split … it wasn't a happy camp," Gray said of discussions surrounding wage deferrals. Stephen Caldwell, who joined on loan from Newcastle United in January, immediately picked up on the unrest between players. "I could see that there was maybe some issues with a couple of players, a couple of relationships … we were a team that really needed to come together quickly if we were going to get anywhere close to being successful and staying up … we had some guys who were not even on the fringe of the team, they were literally out of the team and I don't think they were great for the harmony of the squad … I can remember thinking there's four or five guys who are getting large salaries, who were big names and [had] great reputations in the game, who were like completely detached from the squad and that didn't help because they obviously didn't care."

Those who were at Leeds in better times, like Matteo, Viduka and Lucas Radebe, were increasingly frustrated with training, too. "It was sad because when things are that bad, that's when you need the players to stand up and be counted and show the commitment to the club," Radebe said. "Some of the players - they looked to go somewhere already [and were looking for a] route out of the club. It was sad to see but most of them, they already gave up. It was hard to motivate some of the guys because of the status that we were in. We were not getting great results."

Caldwell remembered Viduka and Matteo doing their best to raise standards, even if it annoyed others. "Mark was maybe even more vocal than Dom, but [they were] two great leaders and two guys that have been there and done it and [guys] we really respected. He [Mark] was a polarising guy, because he didn't take any shit and he didn't allow standards to drop and it's exactly what you need in any winning team, winning group. You've got to call people out, you've got to be able to look people in the eye and say, 'That's not good enough', and then you've got to accept it from other people as well, because that's part and parcel of it. Mark was very vocal in training and very vocal in half times and full times, but he could also be an incredibly fun guy … when you're losing games, it's hard to be bubbly … Mark had that presence about him and he tried to pick the guys up at the right times, call people out at the right times and be that leader, that vocal character within the squad. I learnt a lot from him."

A 4-1 win over fellow strugglers Wolverhampton Wanderers lifted some of the gloom and successive draws against Manchester United and Liverpool suggested Leeds United might make a late push for survival. And those feelings were intensified when Leeds picked up nine points from a possible 12, Viduka scoring important late goals in wins against Manchester City and Blackburn Rovers, and Alan Smith doing the same against Leicester City. "The win at Blackburn was probably one after the game [where] I thought, 'They could go and we could stay', because we beat them and I think that game was a massive game," Matteo said. "Because we got the result that day I thought, yeah, that was the one." Caldwell, who also scored against Blackburn, remembered "real momentum" behind Leeds, something they carried into another important fixture against Everton. Goalkeeper Nigel Martyn, now playing for the Toffees, produced an outstanding performance against his former club, a 1-1 draw harsh on Leeds, before Thierry Henry scored four times in Arsenal's 5-0 win over Gray's men at Highbury. A vital clash against Portsmouth followed, but Leeds were very poor and lucky to only lose 2-1 at Elland Road, meaning they travelled to Bolton Wanderers' Reebok Stadium knowing defeat would essentially condemn them to relegation.

"You're half hoping the next game would [be the one to turn it around]," Michael Duberry said. "[Bolton], it's a must win, it's pressure. You want to win, we're going here to win, but when it's must win, it adds something different. You're chasing, you're straight away on the front foot, your mindset is that we've got to get this and you've got to be perfect. You can't make mistakes." The first mistake came from Bolton when Emerson Thome brought down Smith in the penalty area, Viduka converting the resultant spot-kick. But the Australian was sent off in the 33rd minute for two bookings in quick succession, his red card the second he had received in less than a month. Viduka's second yellow card came after he raised his elbow in a challenge with Bruno N'Gotty and he said the incident was down to frustration. "I take responsibility. I got sent off, okay. But I probably got sent off out of frustration … I went up and I lifted my elbow up but I didn't go to hit him. I didn't go to hit him. I just lifted it up as you normally do. It was an accumulation, for me, of frustration of this whole season and it's the same thing again [as the 2002-03 campaign]. What has changed? Nothing. We're doing the same thing. And we're hoping what? Luck is going to get us out of it." Viduka, whose goals kept Leeds up a season earlier, suggested that the pressure on him was too much. "It's like everyone's looking for me to save us again. And yeah, I can, to a certain degree. But I'm not Jesus Christ."

Viduka walked off the pitch "very disappointed" and Gray knew then and there, it was game over. "Viduka was a great player. Viduka could play in any team in the world," Gray said. "I think he just lost his discipline that day. Of course, we go [a goal] up and you're thinking,

'Yeah, well, okay. We might have a chance'. When he gets sent away, then the game's finished because he was a big player." Leeds made it to half time still holding on to a 1-0 lead but Youri Djorkaeff's goal just after the break changed the complexion of the match. Leeds conceded three times in eight minutes, Djorkaeff adding another before an unfortunate Ian Harte own goal. "We were all over the place … you shouldn't be like that, especially when you know you need to get a result, you've got to be organised and ready to get a win at all costs but without being sloppy and we were sloppy again," Matteo said. "Obviously, Bolton weren't a bad side back then, they had some players, [Jay Jay] Okocha and those kind of boys who can hurt you."

Okocha was magnificent for Bolton, who toyed with Leeds in the second half, to Matteo's annoyance. "I think they quite enjoyed that, actually, Bolton … I think sometimes teams were thinking, 'We can hurt these [players]', and they quite enjoyed it, which hurt me. That hurt me … Bolton and Portsmouth, teams like that beating Leeds United the way they did - it hurt." Kevin Nolan got Bolton's fourth goal despite loud, proud defiance coming from the away end. "Somehow, you've got to try and focus on getting through the game but you know you're down. You can still hear those fans singing and that's what breaks your heart a little bit as well," Matteo said. "I still think the Leeds fans are the best out there, they are an incredible bunch as we see every season and I don't think they deserved a performance like that. And I think they got too many of them in those couple of years."

"It was a roasting hot day and I remember just thinking, 'I just can't believe this is happening'," McPhail said as the final whistle was blown. "The heartbreak and the tears … it's definitely the worst feeling I've ever had in football … to see the young kids crying [in the stands], yeah, we felt it, especially the players that were there a long, long time, the likes of Alan Smith." On the pitch, Smith could not control his emotions and back in the changing rooms, barely a word was spoken. For Gray, it was "like going back to 1982 all over again", another painful season that ended in relegation, and Duberry remembered feeling "numb". "You can't be angry at anyone because everyone played their role, everyone played their part," the defender said. "It's a whole season. Yes, you're frustrated, you're numb. What can a manager do? A manager can shout but the damage is done … so everyone's just numb. I remember 'Smudge' [Smith] crying … you have this thing as a player, professional, you always think you're great, you're one of the best, you have to have that confidence level - you have to boost yourself. But this has just told you you're not good enough. This is the rubber-stamp saying you aren't good enough as a team, [an] individual. You're not good enough. You don't belong. So it's like, 'Oh my God'. You don't believe you're ever going to be part of that."

Caldwell recalled a vibe "like a funeral" while Matteo could not shake the feeling of guilt. "I did feel responsible and I still do to this day about that. If you're a captain of any club, or any level, you have to have some kind of responsibility." Viduka struggled to process the result, three years to the day since he played against Valencia in the first leg of a UEFA Champions League semi-final. "I hated losing … I was very, very disappointed, very sad … obviously being sent off, yes, as well," he said. "But [the disappointment was] more so of the whole environment in the club, having known what it was before and what it got into … I was just disappointed that it ended the way that it did in terms of with the club, not just in my time, even now … I'm gutted when I see them in the Championship. They should be up in the Premiership. They're a club with a huge tradition … Leeds United grew close to my heart as a club and to my wife and to my kids - they are born there. My kids are Leeds fans now at home and all that. They've got the new tops and we watch them … we met so many beautiful people in Yorkshire and around the club … that would have been a club where I thought if everything was alright, I would have been happy to stay there for the rest of my career, if everything was in order."

Nothing was in order at Leeds, though, and a 3-3 draw with Charlton Athletic was followed by a 1-0 defeat at Chelsea as a tumultuous season finally ended. "Usually you're looking forward to going away with your family and stuff and enjoying your summer," Matteo said. "I didn't enjoy one bit of that summer. It was the lowest point in my footballing career."

Perhaps the worst affected was Gray, with the pain in his voice when talking about relegation immediately obvious. "I still look back on that period disappointed with myself. Although I was wary of taking it [the caretaker manager job], your ego still thinks you can. You still think you can come back and do it … that [relegation] has been the most disappointing thing that's ever happened to me from a club point of view … getting relegated, being in charge, although it's only caretaker, that was disappointing … since that [Bolton] game, I've always been hoping somebody could take the club back into the Premier League so I can at least see them playing [in] the Premier League again. Hopefully it will happen this year."

ST MARY'S STADIUM | NOVEMBER 19 | ATT: 30,173

SOUTHAMPTON 3-4 LEEDS UNITED

PAHARS 27', QUASHIE 35', 45' [PEN] | 2005 | BUTLER 71', BLAKE 77', HEALY 84' [PEN], MILLER 86'

SUBS: BENNETT, HEALY, PUGH, WALTON, DOUGLAS

MANAGER: KEVIN BLACKWELL

SOUTHAMPTON

NIEMI, DELAP, LUNDEKVAM, SVENSSON, HIGGINBOTHAM, OAKLEY, WISE, QUASHIE, PAHARS, WALCOTT, ORMEROD

SUBS: BELMADI, HAJTO, McCANN, FULLER, SMITH

MANAGER: HARRY REDKNAPP

OUR FORM HEADING IN

LEEDS UTD	0-0	PRESTON
CREWE	1-0	LEEDS UTD
READING	1-1	LEEDS UTD

"They couldn't pay the wages. They had no money. I had to pull the staff in ... we had a meeting and [I] just said, 'Look, this could be our last Saturday'."
- Kevin Blackwell

He was not just talking about his job. Kevin Blackwell was talking about the very future of Leeds United. Just 24 hours before a January 2005 trip to Stoke City, Blackwell thought the club was about to be wound up and unable to fulfil their fixtures. The problems were that bad. "We had a meeting ... I didn't want them [staff] to not know what exactly was going on because pressures were coming from around the building and I'm sure they were thinking, 'Why is he here?' And 'What's that going on about?'" Blackwell was also overcome with guilt. "You've got your family, your wife, your kids and you've got to look after them. And knowing that I'm looking at people that I brought to the club and thinking, 'I've brought them here and now I could put them in real trouble'. It was difficult." The manager brought a sports psychologist into the club to work with staff as he feared the worst. "The [Gerald] Krasner consortium had never been involved in football ... they were in desperate trouble because they had no money to pay the wages. That was a fact." Tensions were spilling over in the boardroom, Blackwell recalled. "I said, 'If I bought a house and couldn't pay for the mortgage, I'd lose the house. You've bought this football club, you can't afford it'. I said, 'And now we're going to lose the house. We're going to lose the club'."

Things were going okay on the pitch, at least, Leeds gradually improving after a huge clear-out of players in the summer following relegation from the Premier League. After a raft of free transfers arrived, United used their pulling power to attract the likes of Sean Gregan and David Healy, who signed from West Bromwich Albion and Preston North End respectively. "When I spoke to Kevin, he was open and honest to admit that when I did sign, and it was in October that I signed, that this year was about consolidation, to improve in the summer and sign a few players, which he did, and then [he would] try to take the club forward," Healy said. "So I knew when I signed that it wasn't going to be the initial first season [that we would challenge], but it was going to be the season after."

But Healy, Gregan and the rest of United's squad, still containing the likes of club legends Lucas Radebe and Gary Kelly, would have been looking for new homes if Blackwell's fears were confirmed. A Ken Bates takeover eased those concerns, though, and although the ex-Chelsea owner angered fans by raising ticket prices, more funds were provided to Blackwell to strengthen his squad. Shaun Derry and Rob Hulse, who would become key figures in United's promotion push in the next season, arrived before the close of the 2004-05 campaign, one Leeds finished in 14th. Hulse's loan was made permanent in the summer and Robbie Blake and Richard Cresswell also joined, giving Blackwell plenty of options in the final third. There were other arrivals, too, with Eddie Lewis joining Leeds and Liam Miller and Jonathan Douglas making loan switches from Manchester United and Blackburn Rovers respectively. "I was confident," Blackwell said. "I was going for a top-six finish and that was always the aim. Could we get to [the] top six having consolidated the team in the first year outside the Premier League?"

Derry recalled the competition for places being extremely high. "We had a real gifted group of players, we really did. We had a strong, strong squad. I think, in my opinion, looking back now and even whilst I was at the football club, I thought there were too many players. It's very difficult to keep all the players happy but we had up to about 35 pros. There was a real clamour to try and pull on those 11 shirts and obviously you can only keep 11 guys happy … it was very difficult for the management and the staff there to keep everybody happy but thankfully I was one of those 11 who normally was playing. Obviously, I was absolutely delighted with that. There was a great start [in 2005-06], we were up there, we were bouncing around the right places in the Championship but we just couldn't find that true consistency. We'd probably win back to back [matches] and then we'd drop points."

Leeds were without a win in four league matches when they travelled to Southampton's St Mary's Stadium in November 2005. A quirk of the fixtures meant that last win was against Southampton at Elland Road, Hulse and Blake scoring in a 2-1 triumph also notable for being Theo Walcott's first start in a Southampton shirt, one he marked with a goal. Draws against Sheffield United and Reading - the two sides automatically promoted from the 2005-06 Championship - followed before a loss at Crewe Alexandra and a goalless draw against Preston.

If United were out of confidence, it showed in a wretched first-half performance at Southampton. "We lost the physicality in the first half," Derry said. "I remember Dennis Wise playing for Southampton and Dennis was obviously coming to the end of his career. Personally, whenever I played against Dennis, he'd really hold court in midfield. He was an experienced pro. He could run a football pitch and he ran that football pitch." The hosts came out firing, taking the lead through Marian Pahars' far-post header following a corner. "I didn't have a good first half at all. I was poor … [I] lost my man for one of the set-pieces and they scored from it," Matthew Kilgallon remembered. Kilgallon was then beaten by Walcott for Southampton's second goal, the winger charging from inside his own half and storming past the defender before crossing for Nigel Quashie. "I was fast. A fast centre-half. That was one of my attributes that I had," Kilgallon said. "Theo Walcott … got the ball out wide and I thought to myself, 'Well, go on then. You knock it [past me] and let's have a look'. And he knocked it and I swear to God, before the time I got into two, three strides, he was two, three strides past me. I thought to myself, 'Oh, dear', [laughs]. He's running and I'm not gaining on him and he crossed the ball across and they scored. I thought to myself, 'This kid's going to be a player'." Southampton forward Brett Ormerod echoed Kilgallon's thoughts. "He had so much pace and confidence … there were no worries. He had just come straight out of school. He just ran at people. He did that to a lot of teams in that first year, hence why [Arsenal manager] Arsene Wenger shelled out the money he did for him." There was still time for Southampton to score a third in a one-sided first half, too, Quashie netting a penalty after left-back Dan Harding was penalised for handball.

"Dennis Wise … within the game, we were niggling at each other," Hulse said. "And I remember walking off at half time and Dennis Wise saying, laughing to me and saying, 'I wonder who's going to get sent off first? Me or you?'" Little did Hulse know, but Wise would not return to the pitch. He had a thigh injury and was one of three Southampton players who were injured, Pahars' ankle playing up and Claus Lundekvam suffering a rib problem. All three would be substituted at the break.

In United's changing room, a range of strong views were expressed. "We were second rate all first half," Blackwell said. "We were second to the ball. It was a long trip down but excuses are excuses. Southampton, in the first half, were way better than us. At half time, I basically said to the players, 'Listen, you've got yourselves into this fucking shit, you get yourselves out of it … we can't play like we did in the first half because it will be at 6-0 at full time', … I just said to them, 'Every one of you is way better than what I've just seen there.'" Derry agreed, saying he was ashamed at half time. "To find yourself 3-0 down anywhere is embarrassing. It really is … I'm quite self-critical, in terms of the performances of both myself and the team that I played in. I was embarrassed in that first 30 to 45 minutes. I really was. It was, personally and collectively, an embarrassment … Kevin Blackwell, he let us know in no uncertain terms that we were bordering on a disgrace in that first 45 minutes. And I think when those kind of words are spoken to you at half time, you either sink or swim … I remember Kevin pinpointing his team talk on the amount of fans that had come to watch us. That was never really anything strange to us because we took a fantastic following everywhere. But I remember on that game, particularly, just how many Leeds fans had made that effort [to be there] and they proved to us how disappointed they were going in at half time. That resonated with the players, it really did."

Hulse remembered "lots of arguing and shouting" at the break while Kilgallon knew his spot in the side was in jeopardy. "I lost my man again for another set-piece but they didn't score from it. Kevin … he was massive on, 'If that's your man at set-pieces, he doesn't score. Do what you have to do to stop them getting a header on it', … Sean Gregan was on the bench and he was playing well for Leeds. I thought to myself, 'If I don't produce in this second half, I'll be out of the team.'" The mood in Southampton's changing room was, understandably, a confident one. "You never think you've got anything won … but when you play the first half and you're 3-0 up, you're thinking, 'Just keep it tight, keep a clean sheet, you've won the game … Leeds are going to have to come onto you, they're going to leave space at the back to exploit and you can go and get four or five,'" Ormerod said.

And as Leeds walked out for the second half, an incorrect assumption about Southampton's injured trio gave Kilgallon and his teammates an extra source of motivation. "They were all showered in the tunnel," Kilgallon said. "And I thought to myself, 'They think this is over here. They think they've won. They were resting the older players for the next game', ... all of the lads saw that." Ormerod acknowledged the changes "disorganised us" but recalled Southampton starting brightly in the second half. "We missed a couple of chances early doors," he said. A save from Neil Sullivan kept the margin at three and, strangely, was the moment that gave Hulse some hope. "He was an amazing goalkeeper ... he made a save and I just remember thinking, 'We've got a chance here. I fancy us here, if we get one'," he said. Derry also felt Leeds were working their way back into the game. "Dennis came off in the game and it gave us a lift. It gave us a lift as a group of midfielders, to really get that nitty, gritty side of it [going], jumping on the second balls ... there were some big challenges going in ... when you're 3-0 down, that's what the Leeds fans want to see."

Leeds needed a goal to have any chance of putting pressure on Southampton, though, and after 67 minutes, Blackwell introduced Healy off the bench. "I'd been sitting on the bench and frustrated ... I think the players were slightly embarrassed by the situation we found ourselves in," Healy said. "We were way off the mark ... as the minutes go on you think ... 'We might get a consolation [goal] back'. I was hoping to get on the pitch." That goal came in the 71st minute, Leeds captain Paul Butler heading in a corner, and Healy was immediately buoyed. "Once we got the first goal back, Southampton started to get an edge about them. They started getting edgy, they looked nervous." Leeds quickly got a second, too, Healy setting up Blake. "Dave Healy slid the ball to me ... I hit it first time in the bottom corner," Blake said. "I think the keeper got a hand to it but obviously it was too close to him to get down to it. And then I actually felt that we were going to get something from the game when were 3-2 down. I could just see that all momentum switched."

Attacking the same end 3,500 Leeds fans were housed in, United's players and fans were now full of belief. "The second goal really changed [it] and you could see a nervousness in the Southampton players.

They were really affected by that second goal," said Derry, while Healy remembered being urged on by the travelling thousands. "I certainly thought we were well in with a shout of certainly nicking a point at the time. We were shooting into the away end … I always remember that the Leeds fans were absolutely incredible that day, considering the start we had in the game. We were coming back … it was basically wave after wave after wave [of attacks], we were having. It probably only seemed a matter of time before we were going to get the equaliser."

Healy, causing all manner of problems, gave Leeds the chance to level proceedings, winning a penalty that Southampton's Danny Higginbotham still contests. "It was a handball," Healy said. "I went on to play with Danny at Sunderland after that. I knew Danny, I grew up with Danny playing at Manchester United … Danny always proclaims he was innocent, it was never handball. And in this day and age, it probably wouldn't have been given. But we were given a penalty." Healy, who less than three months earlier hit the headlines after scoring the winning goal in Northern Ireland's shock win over England in a 2006 FIFA World Cup qualifier, stepped up to take the spot-kick. "Antti Niemi was the goalkeeper in the match, somebody I knew who had played for Rangers," he said. "I grew up supporting Rangers and I always wanted to score against the Rangers goalkeeper. People say, 'Do you get nervous when you're stepping up to take the penalty?' I wasn't because I knew the game was basically gone at half time. It was gone when I got on the pitch. I'm sort of thinking, 'Well, you have nothing really to lose. We have got ourselves back into it'. You're hoping to score."

"If anyone told me that David Healy was going to be on the penalty, I'd be pretty happy and very confident that he will score … 'Heals' was a fantastic footballer, great finisher, a natural finisher," Blake said. And Healy made no mistake from the spot as Leeds equalised with six minutes to play. "When I did score, the noise in the stadium from the Leeds away end was incredible," he said. "That certainly helps. We probably thought on the pitch, 'Wow, we've come back, we've got a point from nothing here.'" Ormerod instinctively knew that if there was to be a winner, there was only one team who would be getting it. "By then, all the momentum is with them. You're trying to kickstart yourself again but it's only ever going one way when it gets to that stage, and it did for Leeds."

Leeds made the most of that momentum, too, scoring a dramatic winner. Miller - who tragically passed away in 2018 due to pancreatic cancer at the age of just 36 - found Hulse out wide before continuing his run into the penalty area. And when the striker's cross fell invitingly for the Republic of Ireland international, he instinctively threw his left foot at the ball. Miller's quick thinking caught Niemi out as Leeds, stunningly, took the lead with four minutes remaining. "The late, great Liam Miller ... is somebody I loved, I drove to training with. I lived in Manchester, along with Liam," Healy said. "That day, when talked about, when mentioned to me, first and foremost my mind just goes back to Liam Miller ... I don't think it was a clean hit of a finish ... we were obviously jumping in and around where the Leeds supporters were [after the goal]. There were barriers kicked over ... I still remember looking at the bench and everybody was running down the touchline." Kilgallon added: "When Miller scored that last goal, the fourth goal, it was mental scenes. It was over by the fans. It was just berserk."

Douglas, an unused substitute, spoke glowingly of Miller's contribution to the Leeds team that season. "We went on trial at Celtic when we were very, very young together. We were in the underage Irish teams as well together so I knew him for quite a long time. Great lad ... a great player as well who went on to have a fantastic career ... when he came to Leeds, he did really well for us." Leeds still had a job to do, but saw out the final stages in perhaps the most remarkable comeback of the club's rich history. "The celebrations at the end, when everybody went over to the away fans - that's what you play football for, to share moments like that together," Derry said. "The Leeds fans have had dramatic highs and incredible lows over the past 20 years and you could just sense that it was a big game for them. And it was great to share it with them. It really was ... I can't overuse the word embarrassment too often. It was a real poor, poor performance in that first 45 minutes and I'm glad we were able to reverse it."

"I can still remember celebrating ... and then sitting in the dressing room afterwards and going, 'Wow, what happened there?,'" Blake said, while Blackwell had a simple message for his players in the aftermath. "We all got together in a huddle and I said to them, 'Listen, lads, if that doesn't tell you you're a fucking good side, nothing will. Let's go for it.'" Some of Leeds' Manchester-based contingent flew home while others settled in for a long bus trip back to Yorkshire. "We celebrated with a couple of beers and it [our comeback] made the five or six-hour journey back up north all worthwhile, to be honest," Blake remembered. The mood could not have been more different in the Southampton camp. "It was just one of them games … magical if you're a Leeds fan and absolutely disastrous if you're a Saints fan. It just ruins your weekend," Ormerod said.

Liam Miller celebrates his goal that sealed an incredible comeback victory.
Photo: Andrew Varley Picture Agency

DEEPDALE | MAY 8 | ATT: 20,383

PRESTON NORTH END 0-2 LEEDS UNITED

2006 | HULSE 56', RICHARDSON 61'

PRESTON NORTH END

NASH, MEARS, DAVIS, MAWENE, ALEXANDER, ORMEROD, O'NEIL, McKENNA, STEWART, NUGENT, DICHIO

SUBS: WARD, SEDGWICK, AGYEMANG, WILSON, WHALEY

MANAGER: BILLY DAVIES

OUR FORM HEADING IN

LEEDS UTD 1-1 PRESTON

PRESTON 2-0 LEEDS UTD

LEEDS UTD 1-0 CREWE

"He [Billy Davies] had said a comment and I used it against him. I put it above every player's peg, all around the dressing room. 'Job done, job done'."
- Kevin Blackwell

Leeds United's manager did not need to motivate his players for the second leg of a 2006 Championship play-off semi-final at Deepdale. Preston North End boss Billy Davies had done it for him. Speaking after Preston had earned a 1-1 draw in the first leg at Elland Road, Davies was feeling confident and rightly so. His side had lost just one of their past 21 home fixtures, a run that included a 2-0 win against a much-changed Leeds on the final day of the league season. That result saw Preston finish fourth, two points above United, and an impressive performance in West Yorkshire meant Davies' men were heading home with the tie in their favour. "The first leg, it was pretty intense. Preston got the lead and then, obviously, we didn't really play particularly well," Robbie Blake remembered. After Matthew Kilgallon hit the post, Preston took control of the match, David Nugent scoring a brilliant solo goal that the visitors deserved, but Eddie Lewis levelled proceedings with an excellent free-kick. "We were just looking for a little bit of magic," Blake added. "To be fair, Eddie produced those bits of magic. He had a brilliant left foot. My lasting recollection of that game was when Eddie did score, just how noisy Elland Road was. I was like, 'Wow'. I'd never heard Elland Road like that before. It was an incredible atmosphere of celebration when he scored - it was so loud."

It was not just the Leeds players impacted by the atmosphere, as Brett Ormerod, who had moved from Southampton to Preston in January, recalled. "It was ridiculously loud. I remember Billy Davies trying to shout something to me and I went over and they were telling me [to] pass the message onto David Nugent. I went on the field and I was shouting in 'Nugey's ear from two yards away … we still couldn't hear each other because the atmosphere was that electric. It was frightening." Preston got their draw, though, after 90 tense minutes in front of more than 35,000 fans. "It was quite angsty. I know they didn't like us, we didn't get on with them," Rob Hulse said. Perhaps Preston's feelings for Leeds could be traced back to the fact Lewis, David Healy and Richard Cresswell all made the switch from Deepdale to Elland

Road as Blackwell's men chased promotion.

But even without that trio, Davies was confident after the first leg, as a post-match article in The Times revealed. "It's a tremendous result for us. We can ask for no more. We've come here, done the job and it now swings towards us," he said. When Kevin Blackwell read the comments, he knew he could use them. "I used that in my team talk in the second leg ... I went to each and every one of them. I said, 'Gary Kelly, Irish international, Premier League player, you're better than him', ... 'Neil Sullivan, you're better than him', and went through [the team]." Blackwell's team talk had the desired impact, with the squad in unison on how they felt. "It motivated us all," Kilgallon said. "Kevin Blackwell - he was a very proud man ... [he was] saying, 'He [Davies] is taking the 'mick' out of us here. He thinks they've won it. He's saying we can't beat them at their ground. What do you all think of that?' And we're all just saying, 'He's joking, isn't he? Of course we can'. We had a good mix of experience and youth in our team at Leeds and the older lads had brought it up to say to us that, 'We can't stand for this'."

"We did have the articles pinned up on our dressing room wall. 'Job done' was around, it was right on the back of the door as we went out to the corridor for the pitch," Shaun Derry said. "Sometimes you can put articles up and they don't really mean a lot. I think that hurt us all that night. It hurt us all. It was disrespectful. It was a comment that was put there [in the press] from a manager who, quite rightly, believed in his team. But it gave us an edge. It gave us an edge [that] perhaps Billy Davies didn't need to give us."

United's players were confident in their ability, too, and were hoping that Preston's play-off record - North End had not been promoted in six previous play-off attempts - would continue. "We always fancied, with the leadership we had, and the experience, that we could go to Preston and do a job on them," Blake said. Blake and Healy would sit on the bench for the duration of the second leg as Blackwell opted for a more defensive looking line-up in an ultimately successful quest for a clean sheet. Frazer Richardson replaced Healy, while Jonathan Douglas came in for Eirik Bakke, with Blackwell acknowledging Preston carried "a real threat going forward". "As a player, you always get an inkling, an idea that maybe the manager might change it up … it was Rob Hulse through the middle, along with Eddie Lewis on the left and Frazer Richardson on the right, which proved to be a big call at the time," Healy said. "It proved to be the right call. I was on the bench."

The first half was unsurprisingly feisty, with Ormerod leaving the field on a stretcher in the early stages after a challenge from Douglas. "His knee just caught my leg and it was just one of those freak things," said Ormerod, who was sent to hospital, with Douglas left "gutted that happened to a fellow professional". And the Republic of Ireland international was given even more time to contemplate that incident when a floodlight failure at half time sent the ground into darkness and a lengthy delay followed. "We thought there was a real possibility that it could be postponed," Derry said. "There were mixed messages coming into the dressing room but we were there, we didn't want it to end and, as players, you just keep yourselves ready, mentally and physically. We were delighted when the lights came on and the lights came on for us as a group of players in the second half as well."

Leeds felt Preston were vulnerable from set-pieces, so much so Blackwell was even working with his players "in the dining room at the hotel" on how they could exploit their opponents. And, once light returned to Deepdale, Hulse sent the travelling thousands crazy when he nodded in Kelly's corner. "Kevin Blackwell was very big on set-pieces, defending them and attacking, so he had three or four set-pieces that we'd worked on through the week," Kilgallon said. "It was one where it was a two and a two. It was me and Rob Hulse as a two … and 'Greegs' [Gregan] and someone else. We'd walk away from the ball and then run back at it and try get a block on someone. It was a perfect ball in and we'd worked it well … I remember just turning round over my shoulder, because it went way over my head, the ball. And I'm thinking, 'That's a great area. Hopefully 'Hulsey' has lost his man'. I turned around and he was there and nods it in … he runs past me and I'm trying to catch him and Leeds fans are trying to get on the pitch! You could see it in the celebrations - we weren't going to lose the game." For Hulse, the goal is a memory he will never forget. "We did a lot of stuff for that [particular move] … just a great feeling. [It is] always a great feeling to score but obviously on nights like that and, particularly, for Leeds. We were right in front of the fans as well and it was just something that lives with you forever."

"It really put us in a massive advantage by getting the first goal," Blackwell said. "It meant that we could really absorb something and we were, defensively, very good anyway. We could hit them on the counter and that was exactly what we were able to do … they had to change their game." That change did not work well for Preston, with United doubling their lead just five minutes later, Richardson scoring at the far post after excellent build-up work from Hulse. "He tried his best to miss it, didn't he?" Kilgallon said with a laugh. "I don't know if he was trying to see if the keeper was warm or not, but he hits it at him, but the keeper sort of fumbles it into the net and that was it. I can remember 'Greegs' looking at me and he shouted to me, 'I'll race you over to the celebrations'. I think he turned up about 30 seconds later, but it was [a] great celebration and that was the game done then. It was over."

"Frazer, cracking lad, massive, amazing engine, so fit. He didn't score that often, to be fair … [I] just really remember it just being that we're clear. There was no coming back at that point, at that stage. You could almost see them deflated," said Hulse, while Ormerod, sitting in hospital, was waiting for updates. "I just remember the nurse coming and being like, 'Leeds has scored', and then, 'Leeds just scored again'." Preston pushed for a goal and they did put the ball in the back of the net, only for a Tyrone Mears effort to be disallowed after it was judged that a corner had momentarily gone out of play. And although it was United's night, they finished with nine men after Stephen Crainey and Cresswell were both given two yellow cards. Both dismissals would cause problems for Leeds in the play-off final, with Cresswell's red card particularly frustrating after his second caution came for kicking the ball away.

For now at least, Leeds United were in celebration mode, with the final whistle being met with roars of approval from the away end. "When you really need the Leeds fans … they carry you through some difficult moments and they carried us through on that night. They were brilliant," Derry said. "I was so pleased the goals were in front of the Leeds fans as well … the noise we made on that night, the fans made on the night, I think it frightened a lot of Preston players. In fact, I know it did, because further down the line when you play or you come up against some of the opposition, they recognised just what an intimidating atmosphere was caused that night at Deepdale … as a group of players, we were equally brilliant."

As Leeds headed for Yorkshire, a discovery was made at Preston, Ormerod revealing "job done" was "all over the change rooms". "I remember getting back to Deepdale … [my teammate] Paul McKenna was at the ground and he was just like, 'Yeah, they've obviously used it to motivate them', … whatever Billy did and what he said didn't really help us in any way but you know, it's one of them. It's history now, it's gone."

Kilgallon did not want the night to end and when he returned home, he did what so many of his fellow Leeds fans will have done. He watched the replay. "It was mental. It couldn't have gone any better, the end we scored in and the timing and the celebrations. I remember watching the game when I got home and the cameras were zooming into the Leeds fans and you've got lads with tattoos hugging each other and kissing each other on the head and people welling up. It was just great to be involved in."

MILLENNIUM STADIUM | MAY 21 | ATT: 64,736

WATFORD 3-0 LEEDS UNITED

DeMERIT 25', SULLIVAN 57' [OG], HENDERSON 84' [PEN] | 2006

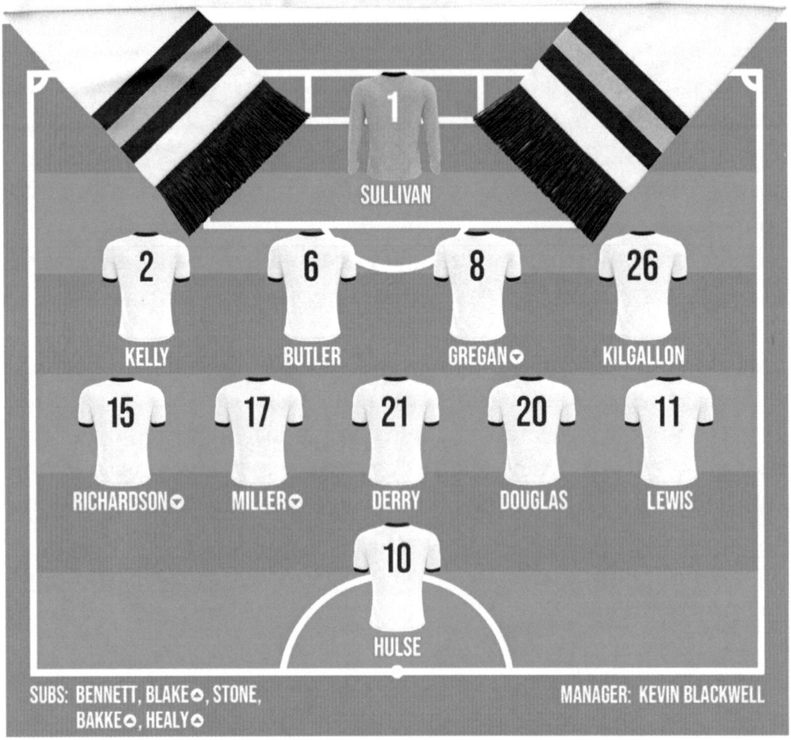

WATFORD

FOSTER, DOYLEY, MACKAY, DeMERIT, STEWART, CHAMBERS, MAHON, SPRING, YOUNG, KING, HENDERSON

SUBS: CHAMBERLAIN, EAGLES, BOUAZZA, BANGURA, MARIAPPA

MANAGER: AIDY BOOTHROYD

OUR FORM HEADING IN

PRESTON	0-2	LEEDS UTD
LEEDS UTD	1-1	PRESTON
PRESTON	2-0	LEEDS UTD

"This is what my dreams were made of. They really were ... to hopefully be one of the players to help us get back into the Premier League was everything that I wanted."
- Shaun Derry

After just two seasons in the Championship, Leeds United were on the cusp of returning to the big time. Leeds had only one more match to win, a play-off final against Watford at Cardiff's Millennium Stadium. "I couldn't wait for the game. Couldn't wait," Shaun Derry said. "I loved the build-up, loved the intensity of the build-up, loved the magnitude of what the game is all about. I'd played in a play-off final before and won it at the Millennium so I knew what it felt like to win there. I was just looking forward to it ... I lived in Harrogate ... the intrigue of the game was [on] every single corner you turned, walking down the street, having a coffee, taking the kids for a walk in the pushers when they were young, even being stopped in supermarkets, it was all about the game. For a player who wasn't playing in the Premier League, I felt like a real big-time player because I was playing for a big-time football club and we were 90 minutes away from the biggest league in the world."

Kevin Blackwell was excited, too, as he pondered how to solve selection issues forced by the suspensions of Stephen Crainey and Richard Cresswell. "I'd seen how we had taken the club from nowhere in 18 months to, financially, the biggest game in the world. [I was] proud of the players for doing that," he said. Cresswell could be covered by Blackwell's many forward options, but Crainey's absence created a real problem, given a dearth of trusted left-backs and the fact Matthew Kilgallon and Sean Gregan played so well together in the centre of defence in United's play-off semi-final win over Preston North End. Kilgallon could deputise at left-back but that would create another selection problem at centre-back, given club captain Paul Butler had not played in nearly a month due to a calf injury. "It started off as 'Butts' [Butler] and Gregan and I was a young lad and they had experience and they were doing brilliant for Leeds and I couldn't get in," Kilgallon said of the 2005-06 season. "And I think maybe 'Greegs' [Gregan] got a suspension or something, might have been an injury, and I got in and stayed in ... I think I had that good a season that it started off with them two, but almost ended up near the end there, who is going to play with me, sort of thing."

"Paul Butler - he had had a calf injury," Derry said. "We had no idea at all, none whatsoever as a group of players, that he was even going to be close to fit for the play-off final until a couple of days before where Paul arrived back on the training field … those two games [against Preston] gave us a lot of hope and there was a massive, massive desire from the players to go and get promoted. But we just knew two days before the game that Kevin Blackwell had got this option in his head of Paul coming back into the group. Without being personal towards Paul, because that's not the case at all, we knew that Watford carried their major threat at centre-forward with Darius Henderson and Marlon King. We knew that Ben Foster, the [Watford] goalkeeper, bypassed the midfield and put a lot of pressure on the opponent's back four so we knew that we needed durable, capable, athletic players who were fit going into that final. And, unfortunately, Paul wasn't one of them, purely down to his history of fitness over the past three or four weeks with his calf." Blackwell was happy to bring Butler back in, though, and said he was passed fit to play. "I had to play Kilgallon at left-back because we had no left-back … obviously it then left us short at centre-half. Paul Butler, I mean he was the captain, he was the leader. My fitness physios had said he was fit and therefore I made that decision based on his leadership skills and also on a needs must situation, having Kilgallon out at left-back."

"I was getting a massage all ready to go … buzzing and that, when he [Blackwell] told me. I will be honest, I was disappointed," Kilgallon said. "I was playing so well, I was very comfortable at centre-half and Watford had pace there as well with Marlon King up top … I can remember him telling me I was gonna play there [left-back] and he was just saying, 'We've got no one to play there. Butts is fit again', … Butts was a hard man … but to come into a final of a Championship [play-off] without playing, you just can't do it. It doesn't matter how good you are, you can't just come into a game like that." Kilgallon also sympathised with Blackwell, who he said "wasn't sure on Dan Harding" and acknowledged "it's hard because I don't know who else he was going to put there at left-back". "It's a massive game and I think

Butts had played in play-off finals before. I think he [Blackwell] went for experience," Kilgallon added.

That was not the only selection issue that was bubbling away, with David Healy and Robbie Blake both frustrated with a starting 11 that contained only one forward in Rob Hulse. "Being left out of the second leg [at Preston], I understood the reasons why the manager wanted to play the players that he did and the formation that he wanted to play. I understood that," Healy said. "In the build-up to the play-off final, I had in the back of my head, maybe the manager might go back ... I was thinking, 'I have a right chance of playing', ... [but] two or three days before, you start getting an inkling that, 'I'm not going to start here', ... I was hugely disappointed. I was gutted. No matter how many highs and lows I've had in football, I always go back to when that team was named for the play-off final, how gutted I felt. How annoyed I felt. How frustrated I felt. I gave basically everything I had to play out of position at the time, so when he named the team, I was hugely disappointed and frustrated. In the back of mind, I'm also saying, 'I desperately want to play in the Premier League. I desperately want us to win as a football club, to get back to the Premier League, where the club deserved [to be]'." Yet as he sat on the bus going to the stadium, Healy could not help but be angry. "That was the one big opportunity. I felt this was the reason I signed for the football club, to play in this type of game, to play in the Premier League."

Blake, also left out, was questioning selection in the hours before kick-off as well. "The build-up was one of frustration, disappointment ... certainly with the personnel that was left on the bench for that game. And the formation and stuff we played, in my opinion, I felt it was just a little bit wrong. But that is the [job of the] manager, he picks the team and, to be fair, he picked a lot of the teams that got us to the play-off final." Players left out for finals are usually disappointed, though, and some of those involved from the start remembered being in a confident, positive mood. "We were feeling great ... we knew we had lads that had been there before and we were very confident going into it," said Jonathan Douglas, while Hulse remembered a real sense of excitement. "I just remember the bus driving up and feeling really excited, seeing all the fans. I remember seeing the fans with Sean

Gregan masks on which made us all laugh on the bus. I was excited. I thought we had enough quality in the team to win the game."

"We were going into the game with confidence," Blackwell said. "I just asked the players, the senior players, [I said], 'This is your game. You've been here before. This is for you now, to carry on forward and really, to keep doing what you've been doing. We haven't got here because you haven't done something right. You've been doing a lot of things right all season. Carry on and do it and treat this game like any other game. Don't play the occasion, play the game.'" Blackwell almost watched his side take an early lead. "'Dezza' [Derry] had a shot kicked off the line by Ashley Young," he added. "He [Young] turned his back and it hit the back of his ankle and went out … the first goal was crucial … if we'd have got the first goal, I think it could have been different."

Leeds were to concede the opener, though, Watford's Jay DeMerit nodding in from a corner. "Their first goal, if I'm being completely honest, I still think of it today," Hulse said. "Up to that point, I'd had a really good season. I'd played some good football. Every corner, I would always go back because I was one of the bigger guys, better in the air. I would mark and be issued with a player to mark or go back. All year, I'd not lost a header against my man. I know in that final, my man scores the first goal and that still haunts me to this day. I still think of that. He ran off the back of me and then scored … still gutted, really … you can't describe how bad you feel."

"The lads knew how hard we worked on set plays and they knew defensively what their job was and for some reason, Rob switched off. But Rob had played with a hip injury for quite a while … I would never blame Rob. It's just sometimes that's how life is. Sometimes you've got to accept that people make mistakes and hope you can get away with it. We didn't get away with it," Blackwell remembered, while Douglas immediately felt it would be tough for Leeds from that point. "Watford, a team who were very strong, very defensive, to go 1-0 down to them - that's the worst possible thing that can happen because then they'll just sit in and play to their strengths. I think if we went 1-0 up, they'd have to come out and attack us, then we could have been like, two, three nil to us. But to go one goal down against a team like that who are defensively very strong, play for set-pieces, long throws, stuff like that, it meant that we had to probably take chances where we wouldn't really have had to do if we'd have been 1-0 up."

Leeds were well and truly second best in the first half but got to the break trailing by just one goal. "We knew, again, that we hadn't turned up," Derry said. "We knew once again it was a disappointment. I wouldn't say it was typical of Leeds but we'd seen it before. We'd seen big players not turn up on the day. We'd seen disappointment take hold of us … [it was] still only the one goal but we knew Watford were capable." Blackwell recalled a "flat" changing room at the interval. "It was flat at half time, if I remember rightly. There were maybe four or five players who were off the pace. It was difficult to get them [up]. It's 1-0, we're always in the game, you weren't out of the game. But what it meant then [was] we had to chase the game a bit more."

Blake was introduced for Frazer Richardson at half time to give Leeds more of a threat in attack but a wicked stroke of luck brought them undone as James Chambers' effort deflected off Eddie Lewis, hit the post and then went in off goalkeeper Neil Sullivan's body. "It's a freak goal … I remember that happening and just thinking, 'This just isn't our day,'" said Douglas, while Blake concurred. "You just think, 'Oh, this is not meant to be', when things like that go against you, freak goals." Derry was equally as perplexed. "You'd never see a goal like that again at any cup final. You probably see them at League Two, you see them in the non-league, you wouldn't see them at a major event like that. Neil couldn't believe it … [it] obviously gave them the 2-0 advantage and then we were chasing. We had to chase, we had to leave big gaps, we had to change the formation that we played in, left spaces in between our back four and midfield."

It was time for Healy. "I'm thinking, 'We're still in the game because we'd had the previous experience at Southampton, where we'd been 3-0 down'. I'm thinking, 'Well, we've been in a worse situation'. I still had firm belief in myself that if I was given the opportunity, a golden chance, I might have scored. I also knew that Robbie Blake was on the pitch, Rob Hulse was on the pitch, that given the opportunities, we could have got ourselves back into the game … I wanted to get us back into the game. More importantly for me at that time, whether it's right or wrong, I wanted to prove Kevin Blackwell wrong, that he got it wrong by, first and foremost, leaving me out of the starting 11 that day. That was my first goal when I was coming on the pitch, 'I'm going to show you.'" Derry was again denied in front of goal but Leeds struggled to put on constant pressure and it was the midfielder, storming back in a desperate effort to clear a Watford counter-attack, who gave away a blatant penalty, that Henderson scored. "They caught us on a counter-attack," Derry said. "I've gone sprinting about 60 or 70 yards to try and make the tackle. I think it was a lunge that was full of aggression, anger, disappointment - everything that I felt at that moment of the game and it was game over, 3-0."

The final whistle soon followed, with United's players left gutted. "It hurts everyone, it really does. But what hurt me more was that we could have gone down in history there as a player that got Leeds back into the Premier League," Kilgallon said. "What an opportunity to get such a big club back into the Premier League [that] was missed by 90 minutes of bad football … that's what hurts the most." Blake's thoughts turned to the fans. "Pure frustration, really, and sheer disappointment. We felt that as a club with a fanbase, the support, we let everybody down." And Blackwell was internally torn between pride in his players for getting there and the fact it had turned so sour. "It was the flattest day I have ever known in football, personally, and I know the lads cared about the club so much as well … I felt that season was a possible top six [finish], that's what I was aiming for. We went way beyond that and just came up short at the end. But the players had done terrific to get there … to end up in the final and to lead Leeds United out in the final … is one of the finest things I have ever achieved in my career. And I'm so proud of that fact."

From the outside at least, Blackwell appeared disconsolate and he acknowledged himself that "nothing could be said" in the aftermath, something Hulse is quick to mention. "I remember going over to Kevin Blackwell. He was sat with his head in his hands in the corner in the changing room, obviously gutted and was inconsolable. I tried to have a word with him and say, 'Come on, gaffer', … but he was just absolutely, I mean, seriously devastated … there was just nothing coming from him. He just had his head in his hands. I don't remember him saying anything after the game." The trip back to Leeds left plenty of time for reflection. "It was a major, major low and we ended up being embarrassed on the day," Derry said. "We had something like 50,000 Leeds fans there. We had Leeds fans [who] couldn't get into the ground. We had Leeds fans back home in Yorkshire all willing us on and wishing us on. That bus afterwards was one of the worst buses I think I've ever been on."

And typical of United's day, even the bus trip did not go to plan. "I think some stayed down [in Cardiff], some went home. I just remember being on the coach on the way home … the bus is deadly quiet. Everyone's gutted and nobody's saying anything," Hulse recalled. "And one of the players' wives, for some reason, is on the coach. Because some people stayed down, there was room on the coach to come back … whether she'd had a drink or not, I don't know, but she was shouting down the bus to the bus driver to put Big Brother and Coronation Street on. And I just remember thinking, 'Just fuck off'. I mean, it almost broke out into a fight on the bus on the way home … that will stay with me forever, that moment going home on the bus. [I remember] just being flabbergasted at that."

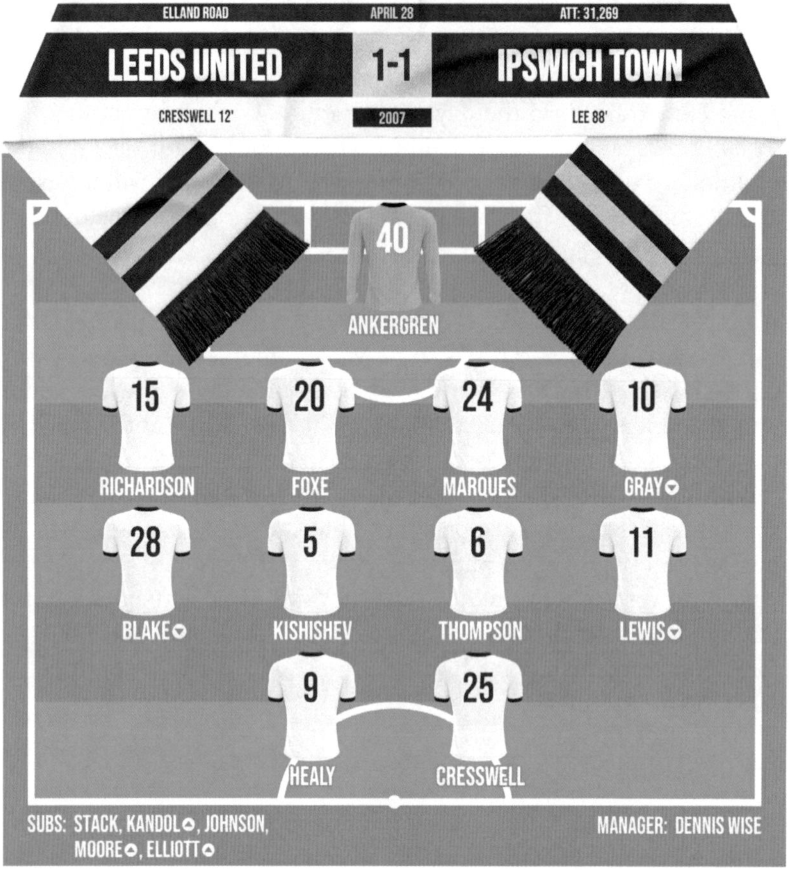

IPSWICH TOWN

SUPPLE, WRIGHT, BRUCE, WILNIS, HARDING, PETERS, GARVAN, WILLIAMS, ROBERTS, JEFFERS, LEE

SUBS: PRICE, CLARKE, RICHARDS, O'CALLAGHAN, WALTERS

MANAGER: JIM MAGILTON

OUR FORM HEADING IN

SOUTHAMPTON	1-0	LEEDS UTD
LEEDS UTD	1-0	BURNLEY
COLCHESTER	2-1	LEEDS UTD

"It was a bit of a letdown in the [play-off] final. We probably took our eye off the ball."
- David Healy

Leeds United's players had an inkling. An inkling things were going to get much tougher after losing to Watford in Cardiff. Externally, Leeds looked a team ready for another major tilt at winning promotion from the Championship but there was a very different feeling building inside the club. "We went into pre-season still very much on a low from the [Watford] game," Shaun Derry said. "And we never, ever recovered from that … there was a bitterness around the football club. We knew there were financial problems around the corner … we just weren't ready. When you go into a play-off final like that, you have an extra two, two-and-a-half-week season, so the impact of a nine-month season - you need time for your bodies and your heads just to relax, get ready for the next stage. I think we were back on the training field within three [to] four weeks. It felt like the [Watford] game was only played yesterday."

Kevin Blackwell, who would be sacked in September, said he felt it was always unlikely United would burst out of the blocks. "You just go back to the annals of history ... the losing side in the Championship play-off final tends to have a spell where they [struggle] to get them going again … everybody knows about the kickback after losing a play-off final." A slow start was not the only thing going against Blackwell. "There were rumours that they [club] needed money again and they were looking to get rid of players off the wage bill," Matthew Kilgallon, sold in January of the 2006-07 season to Sheffield United, said. The Blades might have waited to sign the defender but they lured Rob Hulse and Ian Bennett to Sheffield in the summer, while Simon Walton was sold to Charlton Athletic and Danny Pugh moved to Preston North End. Liam Miller's loan was not renewed, either, while Dan Harding went to Ipswich Town and Eirik Bakke was allowed to walk on a free transfer. It was a mass exodus. Of particular annoyance to Blackwell was a lack of money for new signings. "Four or five players [were] sold, raising five or six million pounds - I was told I could use that money to bring players in and then never had a penny … not a penny of that was given to me when it was promised," he said.

One signing who did cost United money, David Livermore, was bizarrely sold to Hull City less than two weeks after joining from Millwall. The arrival of Kevin Nicholls from Luton Town had reduced Livermore's chances of featuring, Leeds said, but Nicholls injured his knee shortly after arriving and made just 15 appearances in the 2006-07 campaign. It was that sort of season. Blackwell eventually brought in some new players, Jonathan Douglas returning to the club on a permanent deal from Blackburn Rovers, while Tony Warner and Geoff Horsfield arrived on loan and Hayden Foxe joined on a free transfer. "It was the worst possible build-up I could have had and that played its part. I knew we'd need a little bit of time to bed them [new signings] in, get my other [injured] players back," Blackwell said. "To be honest, I never looked to be doing anything until about September, October time, when I thought we could get going … obviously at Leeds, you can't afford to have a bad start. I thought I'd earned the right and people knew I could handle the pressure and they knew I could handle problems at the club. And everybody could see the problems that we'd had … but unfortunately the results weren't good enough."

After an opening-day triumph against Norwich City, Leeds won just one of their next seven league games, with the concession of late goals becoming a frustrating theme. And three defeats in the space of six September days, highlighted by a one-sided 3-0 home loss to Roy Keane's Sunderland, led to Blackwell's departure with United sitting 23rd in the table. John Carver stepped up as caretaker manager but after a 3-2 win over Birmingham City, watched his side lose four games on the trot, conceding 15 goals in the process.

Change was clearly needed and Leeds chairman Ken Bates went for Dennis Wise and Gus Poyet, bringing in the ex-Chelsea pair from Swindon Town, with Wise appointed manager. "We started working together, we started very well at Swindon," assistant manager Poyet said. "At that moment in time, Leeds had started doing badly, with Ken Bates as the owner and chairman … there were many ex-Chelsea people working at Leeds, [technical director] Gwyn Williams … [it was] unexpected, obviously, because Swindon was our first job, but very welcome because we knew the potential of Leeds." The pair were unveiled at a League Cup fixture against Southend United at Elland

Road that Leeds lost. "I remember him [Wise] and Gus from the far side of the ground, walking around to the dugout … the supporters were shouting, 'Shoot that Chelsea scum', [a line in a song sung by Leeds fans] or something like that," Robbie Blake remembered. "I thought to myself … 'Whatever this guy does, he might be on a hiding to nothing', … I just felt that was a really bad omen for Dennis, to be honest."

The new regime immediately set their sights on improving player fitness levels, something Poyet insisted was not a criticism of the previous management group, but necessary for the style of football they wanted to play. "Maybe we were a little bit too aggressive in terms of how we wanted to do it but we thought it was necessary to put things right from the beginning. We couldn't just wait because it was in the middle of the season," he said. Wise also stripped Paul Butler of the captaincy, replacing him with Nicholls, and Poyet quickly remembered the eye-watering wage bill. "We were a team that was in very, very big difficulties financially, but we were still paying incredible amounts of money to players that they were not playing for us, but they were in another team … we couldn't afford these wages … we had players away from the club … they were earning more money weekly than most of the players that were playing for us weekly, which is scary."

Matt Heath, a Wise signing, quickly realised his new boss seemed to be on "a mission". "Obviously, the club were going through financial difficulties. I just feel like it was a time when he [Wise] probably had a bit of a mission and he had been told to try and cut the wage bill, get rid of players … that obviously creates a little bit of a negative atmosphere around the club." Rui Marques was asked if he would move on. "The first week [of Dennis and Gus] … they offered me a deal to finish my contract … even they said to me, 'Look, Rui, we [have] got orders to make you train apart or by yourself'," the Angola international claimed. Kilgallon, who still had significant transfer value, was under no illusions that he would be going in the January transfer window. "Dennis Wise came in … he didn't like me. He wanted me gone. He didn't like anybody," Kilgallon claimed. Brutal, honest feedback was also delivered on a regular basis. "You knew where you stood with Dennis," Foxe said. "He'd tell you exactly how he felt, if you were good, if you were shit, what you needed to improve on … when you're players and you're getting told in front of the group that, 'You're shit', some players don't like that … some players can handle it, some players don't like to be embarrassed in front of the group, some players cop it on the chin and they move on."

The uneasy feeling around the club was enhanced by the treatment of Leeds legend Gary Kelly, something Blake said was "very unfortunate, very unnecessary". "A player [of] that quality and that calibre and that servant to the football club - he got treated pretty badly and it was just affecting people, it was affecting the dressing room, it was affecting morale around the place," he added. Kilgallon was even stronger in his criticism, insistent the way Wise spoke to Kelly made him want to leave the club. "I couldn't wait to go then and that was something that I'd never thought I'd say," he said. Douglas said that the off-field drama was not helping things on the pitch. "I think he [Wise] came in with orders from above to try and rattle a few people … it didn't go to plan and a lot of the seniors, the senior pros and stuff like that were getting treated unfairly," he said. "I was still a relatively young professional coming through. I didn't like to see that. I respected Gary Kelly and people like that. To see the way they were getting treated by some of the staff wasn't very nice and I think that added to problems probably on the field as well."

When these concerns were put to Poyet, he felt that some players would "try to defend him [Kelly] because they were friends and they were not looking at him as a professional leader who was one of the main guys in the dressing room". The Uruguayan added: "I know that the decisions of Dennis sometimes had an impact on him [Kelly], a negative impact, obviously." Kelly barely played during Wise's tenure as he also battled injuries, while Butler and Sean Gregan were allowed to leave. Derry was injured, too, meaning that with all the off-season departures, Leeds were a very different side to the one that made the play-off final. "He [Wise] wanted to move some players on and bring some players in, which all managers will do. And then that didn't work - so he got frustrated. The players got frustrated," Foxe said.

Leeds won just three times in 17 league matches from late November to March and were staring relegation in the face, with even one of those victories marred when Wise sensationally claimed an unnamed player had leaked information about his team to their opponents, Crystal Palace. Heath, who scored that day, recalled sitting in United's changing rooms in shock. "He [Wise] came in after the game and he said something along the lines of, 'One of you in here is a snake, one of you, I've just been told by their manager that they knew our team'. They knew, maybe, our set-piece tactics … he had no idea who did it and to be honest, to this day, I've got no idea who would have done it, whether even it was true or if it was just another way to cause a little bit of friction … the writing is on the wall if that's happening." Goalkeeper Casper Ankergren, making his debut that day, said he remembered Wise addressing the players flanked by someone who looked like "a bodyguard". "He just lost it. I remember him just screaming that somebody's been leaking the team," Ankergren said.

Derry emphatically denied he was 'the mole', the midfielder a rumoured culprit at the time. "Everybody put two and two together and came out with five because I had obviously played at Crystal Palace before and obviously I was a player who was presently not in the side. People thought it automatically was me … I was so disappointed with that accusation." Derry left Leeds in 2008 and did not speak to Wise again until they ran into each other at an Under-23's fixture in London in 2019. "I saw him at a game and we sat down together and I said to him, 'Dennis, why did you let me be the one to take the blame for that?' And he actually apologised … he apologised to me and I said, 'What a horrible moment that was for me, to leave Leeds United under a cloud', … to leave under that cloud, that doesn't sit well with me at all. It never did when I left the club. It still doesn't now even though I've spoken to Dennis … that particular situation will forever hurt me, definitely."

Leeds failed to win in five after that Palace triumph as the threat of relegation and potential administration loomed large. "It was obviously nerves," Poyet said. "It was too many things going around the club. And the situation of going into administration was getting stronger and stronger … so many people [were] nervous." A 1-0 win at home to Luton Town sparked a five-match unbeaten run that included three victories, though, and Leeds were briefly out of the relegation zone as they prepared for an April trip to Colchester United. Leeds were ahead

1-0 with eight minutes to go but would lose 2-1 at Layer Road, a big blow in their survival fight. Douglas, sent off after the final whistle, was fearing the worst. "You go into the dressing room thinking that, 'We are in serious trouble.'"

Leeds bounced back to beat Burnley but lost at Southampton, setting up a vital home fixture against Ipswich Town on the penultimate weekend of the season. Michael Gray, who arrived for a second loan stint at Leeds in March and felt "relegation was on the cards" because "there was no communication between the manager and the players", recalled a high-pressure build-up to the Ipswich match. "There was probably too much pressure on the players. In the build-up to the game, we all knew the ramifications ... we needed to go and win that football match ... I just felt a weight of pressure on every single player. I could sense fear as I was walking out of the dressing room door, that it was just too hard - it was too much to take for the players." Blake was not one of them. "We knew it was a must win. It does add that little bit of pressure but certainly, speaking for myself, you want to be in those pressure games. Of course, you don't want a pressure game where you're relying on it to win for [saving yourself from] relegation."

Leeds' position was helped by the fact Ipswich had "nothing to play for", David Healy believed. Ipswich striker Alan Lee disagreed. "We were safe, which is also a nice way to play football ... you're playing with a bit more freedom. I think that's the way we entered the game. It was quite a big story at the time that the mighty Leeds United could be getting relegated ... there was a feeling driving in as well ... I didn't get a nice feeling before the game from the other fans, from just driving in, walking from the bus into the stadium. There was a feeling things had gone badly wrong here ... it's like you can smell a bit of danger."

Leeds took a 12th-minute lead, giving the likes of Healy some hope. "Richard Cresswell put us one up that day," Healy said. "It was piping hot, huge crowd ... we were at least going to give ourselves an opportunity still of staying up." But that joy was tempered by news that Hull City - the side Leeds were fighting with for survival - had taken a second-half lead at Cardiff City. If both sides won, Hull would remain one point and a big chunk of goal difference ahead of Leeds going into the final day. United sat deeper and deeper against Ipswich, though, inviting pressure. "When you're negative like that ... you're asking for trouble. I remember that," Foxe said. "We were under a lot of pressure for a lot of the game since that 12th-minute mark ... eventually something's going to give. The anxiousness of all of the players and the nervousness of them, of all of us, to try and get another result took over. It totally took over, mentally." Gray, playing at left-back, agreed. "We should have been able to have the experience of being able to sit back and soak up the pressure from Ipswich but unfortunately it wasn't to be ... the atmosphere at the game, I think, going into the last 10 or 15 minutes, you could sense it in the crowd, you could sense it in the players and unfortunately we weren't good enough to hang on to that lead."

Lee provided Ipswich's goal, scored in the 88th minute to knock the stuffing out of a nervy, tense crowd. "It was a corner and I started my run at the back post," Lee said. "I remember throwing myself at it and I remember thinking, 'I'm going to get clattered here', ... I just managed to get the back of my head to it ... it was quite lucky that it went in." The Ipswich man then ran to the away fans to celebrate. "Scoring an important goal in football as a striker, or a goal that counts, is the ultimate feeling ... you're certainly not thinking, 'Yes! We've got Leeds down!' ... When you're walking back, you start to realise, 'Oh, shit. Right, this ... it could go off here.'" Lee could sense the danger as Poyet, on the bench, quickly realised "score a goal again [or] we are down". The mood of disbelief quickly turned into anger and frustration and Leeds fans soon stormed the pitch, forcing a lengthy delay to proceedings. "I understood their frustrations," Healy said. "They were hugely disappointed in the way the club was going at the time."

"The Leeds fans there were behind the team on the day," Lee said. "But really, they were disillusioned with their club because they could see it being mis-run for how many years ... the Leeds fans, fair play, they turned up that day to support their team and they were going to be positive as much as they could. But the second it looked like it was going the other way, it was like all that five, 10 years of this club being mismanaged all came out at once. The atmosphere really, really changed. It became really sour ... it wasn't aimed at us for celebrating the goal, it wasn't aimed at Ipswich, certainly initially. It was just a general horrible feeling … the fans start running on … I run near the tunnel, I watch what's happening and a few of our players had longer to run so we're looking out, a bit worried here, but to be fair, the Leeds fans caught up with the Ipswich players but nothing happened." Lee said an encounter between a Leeds fan and Ipswich's George O'Callaghan summed up the invasion. "He was surrounded by Leeds fans and he was laughing. He was laughing when he came in [to the changing room]. I said, 'Well, what was going on?' He said, 'A Leeds fan ran up to me and said, 'Oh, hi, George. We don't want to touch you. You're fine. We're not after the Ipswich players. We just hate the club for the way it'd been run.'"

Players from both sides ran down the tunnel with time in the match still remaining and waited more than 20 minutes for the pitch to be cleared. Leeds still had a corner to take, giving them a small chance of scoring an incredible last-gasp goal that would have seen them win and keep their hopes of survival alive. Wise and Poyet got to work on a corner routine, the latter admitting he was surprised the game was not just called off. "The referee, for an incredible, incredible decision, is convinced that we need to come out because we've got a corner and we've probably got five seconds to go … I was in the dressing rooms, thinking, 'I want to go in. I want to attack that corner … give me that chance, you know? Please, put the ball up in the air and give it to me. I'm going to head it. I'm going to score the goal that [will] win it,'" Poyet said. "I was desperate to be able to go into the action and I'm pretty sure that many of the players that were in that situation were not even thinking like me. They were thinking, 'We're down. We've got no chance.'" Gray remembered Wise giving "another team talk" but the corner amounted to nothing, the final whistle essentially sealing Leeds' relegation, given Hull held on in Wales and were now three points ahead of United, with a vastly superior goal difference.

"I was hugely, hugely embarrassed … I look back now and I think [of] the great players who captained Leeds United to success and better glories. It still hurts me to the day that I wore the armband that day we were relegated to League One," Healy said. Douglas, who watched on from the stands due to suspension, said he was in disbelief. "You're frustrated. You can't believe it actually happened. You're gutted, you're devastated." Blake added: "I just felt so sorry for the supporters because they've been through a lot of rubbish."

For Poyet, it was "probably one of the worst, if not the worst moment of my career", while Foxe was thinking of many of the club staff. "They've got mortgages to pay and they've been at the club for so many years and they were forced to leave the club … it was a disaster. It was embarrassing. As a player, I felt embarrassed with the performances, 100 per cent, and the way that we got relegated … it ended up being a disaster of a season for everyone involved … we didn't play well at all, personally, and as a team, we didn't do well at all and it reflected. You can blame certain people, players would have wanted to blame Dennis Wise, I know that, for sure. They would have blamed him but everybody's got to have a look in the mirror."

Leeds' fate was rubber-stamped when they announced they had entered administration, triggering a 10-point penalty in the build-up to a season-ending clash at Derby County. And a truly miserable campaign ended with a 2-0 defeat, as Wise's side were finally put out of their misery.

PRENTON PARK | AUGUST 11 | ATT: 11,008

TRANMERE ROVERS 1-2 LEEDS UNITED

GREENACRE 22' | 2007 | HEATH 55', KANDOL 89'

SUBS: FLO ▲, CAROLE, ELLIOTT, HOWSON ▲, PARKER

MANAGER: DENNIS WISE

TRANMERE ROVERS

COYNE, STOCKDALE, CANSDELL-SHERRIFF, CHORLEY, GOODISON, McLAREN, JENNINGS, SHUKER ▼, ZOLA, GREENACRE ▼, DAVIES

SUBS: ACHTERBERG, TAYLOR ▲, KAY, CURRAN ▲, TREMARCO

MANAGER: RONNIE MOORE

OUR FORM HEADING IN

LEEDS UTD	1-2	WIGAN
DARLINGTON	0-1	LEEDS UTD
BURNLEY	2-0	LEEDS UTD

"Going through my mind [is], 'How am I going to afford my mortgage? How am I going to afford my bills? What club am I going to play for?'"
- Ben Parker

Leeds United's decision to enter administration during the 2006-07 Championship campaign triggered a chaotic, drama-filled off-season. With relegation to League One essentially confirmed, Leeds took the 10-point penalty that came with administration but there was another deduction just around the corner. The very future of Leeds United was in doubt, too, with players asked to agree to a major wage deferral. "The PFA [Professional Footballers' Association] were involved, ringing players," Ben Parker said. "Richard Jobson [from the PFA] ... got a phone call from him ... asking me to defer my wages for a period of time. They couldn't tell me how long [for] or if I'd ever get them back with how bad the situation was at Leeds. He said, 'We need a high percentage, around the 90 per cent mark, of players to defer their wages or there's going to be no Leeds United,'" Parker said.

Even that could not prepare United's players, staff and fans for what was to come next, though. Leeds, already under a transfer embargo, were told just eight days before the start of the League One season that they would be given a 15-point deduction. A Football League statement said Leeds were "unable to comply with the terms of the League's well-established insolvency policy" but would be permitted to play in League One through the transfer of the club's Football League share to the newly formed Leeds United 2007 Ltd. However, the transfer was "subject" to the points deduction. Before a ball had been kicked, United's chances of winning promotion were seemingly dashed. "It was a mental summer. I joined the day they actually got minus 15," Andy Hughes recalled. "People questioned my decision but at the time I was at Norwich City and I felt that when Leeds United come calling, I think it was an opportunity that I didn't want to miss. And even with the minus 15 points, I still spoke to Dennis Wise and [technical director] Gwyn Williams and I was adamant I was going to join the club. They explained to me what was going on ... being from the north [of England] I knew what an unbelievable, big club it was, with the fanbase." A host of other signings had already been preparing for the season with Leeds, 'on trial' until the embargo was lifted. "There were so many players there on trial," Parker said. "One that stood out for me most was David Prutton. Obviously, he had a good career up until then … it [the embargo] kind of galvanised everyone, to be fair, because everybody there at the time, you knew wanted to be there. They weren't there just to pick up the money or whatever. They actually wanted to be there to play for Leeds."

While some players took the points deduction in their stride, others were worried. "When we found out about the minus 15 points we were like, 'Wow, this is going to be difficult', … things were, in the beginning, difficult to believe that we could do something good. We were thinking, 'Okay, this is going to be difficult, we're going to fight against relegation'," Rui Marques remembered. Wise and Gus Poyet were angry, the latter particularly furious at how Leeds' appeal against the 15-point deduction was voted against by other Football League clubs. "It was a very strange one and a very difficult one [decision] … as a worker of Leeds United, for the club, the disappointment with so many clubs, voting against Leeds United, to keep those minus 15 points, just for a matter that it suits them to have Leeds down in League One, because they're going to have a home crowd when we play against Leeds United. Only thinking about themselves, financially, and not thinking about what is right or what is wrong … we were very, very unhappy with many of the clubs … they wanted Leeds United in League One for two years, minimum. That gave us an extra bit of motivation, without any doubt."

Wise and Poyet channelled that annoyance, creating a unity and a mentality that would inspire Leeds. "The message coming from Dennis Wise and Gus Poyet at the time [was] it was us v them," Parker said. "That was the mentality we had … it made you fight for something. I know that everyone [has a] dislike towards Leeds, but it was even more at the time. People were having a good laugh at us, pointing the finger at us, almost happy that it was happening to us. But that galvanises [you]. We wanted to try and prove a point." Matt Heath and Marques both said the mood was very different to the previous season. "Us against everyone else … that just created more of a togetherness … there were no fallouts," Heath said. "Even their [Wise and Poyet's] personalities and their vibe changed so much." Marques added: "Gus and Dennis, they were brilliant … they gave us confidence."

A key part of Wise's plan was the strike partnership of Jermaine Beckford and Tresor Kandol, who had a combined tally of one Leeds United goal before the season started. "We had Jermaine Beckford up front, who I didn't know much about at all," Prutton said. "But Dennis vouched for the fact that he knew he'd score goals. He did exactly that. Him and Tresor Kandol up front were a powerful, pacey combination." While Leeds were unsuccessfully trying to stave off relegation just a few months prior, Beckford was enjoying a fruitful loan spell in League One with Scunthorpe United, scoring eight goals in 18 matches. Scunthorpe were interested in making Beckford's switch permanent but Wise told the forward he was a major part of his plans. "I'd spoken to Dennis Wise … he said to me, 'Look, you and Tres are my number ones'. That's all I needed," Beckford said.

Wise was also desperate to bring Casper Ankergren back after the Danish goalkeeper impressed in the Championship. "I had the conversation with Dennis Wise before I left, saying that he really wants me to stay and he believed we could get out of the league," Ankergren said. "He really believed in me and I think that was really important to me at the time … I made it really clear to Brondby, who I'd spent seven, eight years with at the time. I said I wanted to leave. They didn't want to sell me. The offer from Leeds, they didn't feel it was good enough. They had better offers from, I think it was Norway. I said, 'No, it's fine. I'll just wait 'til next transfer window, because I want to go back to Leeds and I want to play in England again'. And then, finally, after having the conversation again with the director of sport at Brondby, they let me go, which was good. I was really pleased." The jigsaw was slowly coming together.

Ankergren missed out on much of a brutal pre-season training program but walked out on the opening day for a Leeds side captained by Alan Thompson. "He [Thompson] was a real good character as well, looking after all the younger, less experienced lads [in pre-season]," Heath said. Leeds were on the back foot, though, against a Tranmere side who had been preparing for months and featured Chris Greenacre, a passionate Leeds fan who stood on the Kop as a teenager and was a product of

United's school of excellence. "It was quite exciting for us, because it brought about quite a bit of publicity," Greenacre said. "All the hype and the points deduction heightened that … it was very, very difficult for those players because every week would have been a cup final for all the other teams. There hadn't been a team like that in that league before … it was the first fixture I looked for … although you're a fan, you can't let your heart rule your head. Once the game started, it's work time." And work Tranmere did, dominating Leeds in a one-sided first half. "We had chance after chance and we should have put it to bed," said Greenacre, who eventually opened the scoring with a simple tap-in at the far post before giving the Leeds salute to the travelling fans. "I had real mixed emotions. [I was] delighted to score and get off the mark on the opening day of the season … and then also it was at the Leeds end as well and you've got all their fans and it's going deadly silent. You obviously get a bit of abuse from them which is part and parcel of the job. I think the way of the Leeds salute was more to say, 'Sorry about that. I'm still a Leeds fan at heart and I'm one of you guys but unfortunately this is my job', … that was probably the thought process behind it. It was just instinct, really."

Leeds were, in truth, lucky to go in at half time behind by just one goal. "We obviously knew Tranmere weren't a bad team. We probably underestimated what other teams' ability could be … I can remember definitely at half time thinking … 'We're in a pickle, here. I know we've still got good players but these [players] are battering us,'" Heath said. "I remember Dennis Wise giving us a proper bollocking. He lost it a little bit in the dressing room at half time," Ankergren recalled. Tensions were spilling over in the stands, too, as frustrated Leeds fans, on the evidence of their side's first-half performance, pondered what it might be like to experience another relegation.

Early in the second half, Tranmere had a goal disallowed for offside, and Leeds soon levelled proceedings with something straight from the training ground as Heath, who ran out of the wall at the last minute, nodded in a Thompson free-kick at the back post. "He was really, really meticulous [about] set-piece preparation, Dennis," Heath said. "He always found that set-pieces were massive, massive chances to score goals … we practiced them on the Friday quite methodically so that free-kick, that set-piece that we scored off, it wasn't just a fluke … it was Alan Thompson who crossed it and put it on a six pence and it's just there for you to nod in … [scoring] in front of all the Leeds fans - it is probably one of the moments that I look back [on fondly] in my career."

"That is a set play that we trained 50 times during the pre-season," Poyet remembered. "We try to convince the players to do it. The players were doing it sometimes right or wrong. When it gets to the action, we are desperate for them to do it. The players are looking and say, 'Okay, okay. We're going to do it', … then when they are doing it and you score from that set play, that is the moment it changed … I always say this to everybody, 'You can train many, many things, but until those things happen on the pitch and you win, the players don't get fully convinced', … the faces of the players [were] looking at the bench, so delighted that that training action worked, it's like a kid enjoying the moment, saying, 'Yeah, we've done it! While we've been training in a boring way for 50 times, now you come out to give us three points'. That creates a relationship."

More joy was to come, too, Kandol bundling in a Hughes cross from close range in the 89th minute to spark wild celebrations in the away end that continued through injury time and after the final whistle. "It was just pure relief," said Beckford, who was yelling "12 points baby" on the pitch once victory had been confirmed. "Maybe we were fortunate to get that goal and maybe Tranmere were unlucky not get a draw but you take it … having strikers on the pitch that could score at any moment is obviously an asset … the feelings of jubilation as players probably matched how the fans felt," Heath said. An impromptu huddle was then orchestrated by Wise, as United's players got in a circle on the pitch. "That wasn't planned or anything, that was kind of spontaneous," Parker said. "Dennis Wise was the leader of that, we just got into this huddle and it became a thing, almost like a bond. We were just united … every game since then, it's almost like we wanted to win to have that huddle because it was such a good feeling, obviously linking arms, you're looking around at everybody, it's such a good buzz. That became a massive highlight of the start of that year." Hughes added: "The feeling after the game was something very special. We all got together on the pitch and from then on, for that season, it just carried on."

Greenacre could only look on in envious fashion. "[We were] mentally and physically drained knowing that we had had chances and we had opportunities to take the game out of their hands and we didn't … I was clapping the fans and what have you and then I looked around and I remember seeing them all together, with their arms around each other. Dennis Wise … I imagine that's what he was saying, 'Look, we've done this, that was a massive, massive win for us and that's a big fuck you to the rest of the country, the Football League, everybody else, everybody who's against us, look, we're back and we're on our way back.'" If United's players were sending a message to the country, so were the fans, with a loud rendition of 'Marching on Together' ringing in Greenacre's ears as he left the pitch. "The significance of that song on that day and afterwards, hearing that, it was pretty significant … for what they needed to do and needed to achieve."

"There's nothing like winning games of football but when the whole country are against you, the lift that it gives you as players that were in that dressing room is something that you can't describe," Hughes said. And the importance of that August day at Tranmere was underlined by what happened in the following weeks, as Leeds went on a 13-match unbeaten run in the league, winning 11 of those fixtures. It could have all been so different, though. "It was probably a season where if that hadn't have happened and we didn't turn it around in that first game, it could have been a different story. It really could have been a different story," Heath said. "Momentum and getting on a roll is massive in football. It's massive in sport, confidence, momentum, it's huge. I dread to think how it would have gone if we hadn't have got that first win in that first game." Poyet looks back on those last few minutes at Prenton Park as defining. "Even if we were in a lower division, even if we were a little bit ashamed of ourselves, I think it started a new era, that moment. I think that circle on the pitch and the end of the Tranmere game is the start of the recovery of Leeds United."

Jermaine Beckford scored 85 goals for Leeds United in 152 appearances between 2006 and 2010. Photo: Alex Knight Photography

United: The 15-point deduction brought everybody at Leeds United together. Photo: Andrew Varley Picture Agency

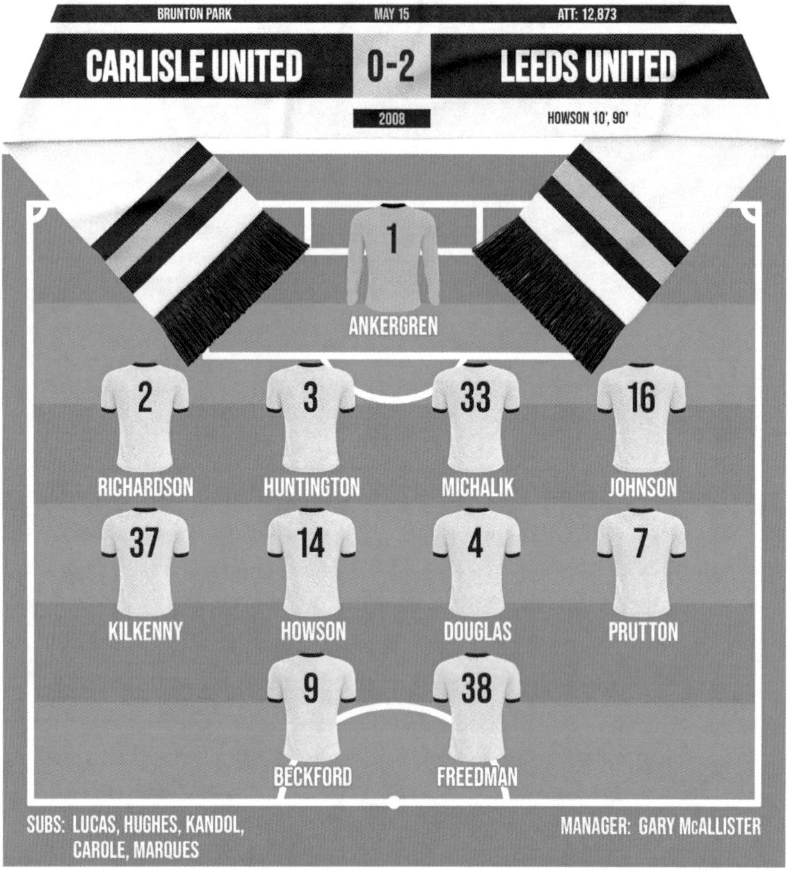

CARLISLE UNITED

WESTWOOD, RAVEN, LIVESEY, MURPHY, HORWOOD, DOBIE, LUMSDON, SMITH, BRIDGE-WILKINSON, HACKNEY, GRAHAM

SUBS: HOWARTH, THIRLWELL, ARNISON, TAYLOR, MADINE

MANAGER: JOHN WARD

OUR FORM HEADING IN

LEEDS UTD	1-2	CARLISLE
LEEDS UTD	2-1	GILLINGHAM
YEOVIL	0-1	LEEDS UTD

"Minus 15 points ... it had just never been seen before. And the way that the players and the staff and the club dealt with it, [it] was the way, probably, northern people deal with things. Roll your sleeves up, get on with it and just go for it ... that was the feeling throughout the squad, throughout the club. Everyone was fighting tooth and nail for everything."
- Andy Hughes

For a few months in the 2007-08 season, Leeds United were unstoppable and mentality had everything to do with it. Buoyed by their opening-day triumph at Tranmere Rovers, Leeds would win their first seven League One matches, amazingly wiping off the 15-point deduction at the first possible opportunity. "It was incredible," then-assistant manager Gus Poyet said. "The end goal at [Nottingham] Forest [Jermaine Beckford scored a 90th-minute winner], oh my God ... to be able to win it at the end, again, in the last minute ... you score the winning goal, you celebrate it like it's the World Cup Final ... we needed to create the mentality, that winning mentality, that strong mentality ... 'We are Leeds and we're going to beat everybody.'" A 1-1 draw with Gillingham - a match in which Leeds finished with nine men - ended an exciting winning run but it did not derail things, the undefeated United making it 11 wins from 13 league fixtures with a 4-2 victory over Millwall on October 27. Promotion was not just a far-fetched dream. It was now a possibility.

"Some fans still say to me now that the minus 15 days were the best days they've ever had because they felt like the whole country was against Leeds and, at times, it felt like that," said Andy Hughes, as the novelty of new grounds to visit, the siege mentality created and a series of late winners delighted Leeds fans. "The goals we were scoring, the way we were playing ... we were almost invincible at that point. And that's what it felt like from within. It was amazing. Absolutely amazing," said Beckford, who was thriving in a new-look strike partnership with Tresor Kandol. "We spent so much time [together] off the pitch, outside of football, and that can only benefit any football team ... you build up an understanding of character and mentality. 'Tres' and I, we understood each other's strengths, each other's weaknesses, and we just bonded really well." Rui Marques said the "really good atmosphere in the changing room" helped Leeds. "These kind of things make the difference," he added.

Poyet would leave Leeds in the aftermath of the Millwall win, though, taking up a job as Tottenham's assistant coach. And while the Uruguayan was replaced by Dave Bassett, the dynamics had changed. "They [Dennis Wise and Poyet] were a great double act," Beckford said. "Between the two of them, they had literally everything. They had the wealth of knowledge in terms of what they had achieved, their experience. But they also had the 'good cop, bad cop'. It wasn't always Dennis the bad cop and that's what people think - Dennis was the bad guy. He wasn't. The gaffer was the good guy a lot of the time as well." David Prutton shared a similar reflection. "I think the chemistry between them [Wise and Poyet] was perfectly balanced. I thought [Gus was] the Yin to Dennis' Yang, [that] was exactly how we reflected on how they led the side."

In the same week that Poyet left Leeds, they were beaten for the first time in League One, Carlisle United recording a 3-1 victory. United responded by winning four of their next five league games but form tailed off from there, before Wise also left the club, to take up a role as Executive Director [Football] at Newcastle United. Prutton recalled the build-up to a mid-week fixture at Southend United being a chaotic one. "We stayed in a place just off the M25 [after playing Luton Town on the Saturday]," Prutton said. "Dennis left over the course of the weekend ... Monday, we'd gone for a training session and by the end of that training session, another couple of members of staff had left ... Dave Bassett ... he was like, 'It's been a pleasure, fellas, but moving on and see you later'. The other coach, John Gannon, came on [to the bus] and did exactly the same thing [laughs] ... we're looking around as if to say, 'Well, who on earth is going to take us for the game?' Gwyn Williams, who was director of football, made his way down from Thorp Arch and took us for the game. It was a surreal game ... you're wondering, 'Who's going to come in? Where are we going to go? Is this going to derail us for the rest of the season? Does this mean we're going to end with a bit of a whimper after such a great start?'"

Leeds were beaten at Southend but a phone call to a club legend quickly solved their managerial problem. "The timing of it - it might not have been ideal. But the facts are that when Leeds come calling, I wanted to give something back … I couldn't say no," Gary McAllister said. "I knew there was good players there or certainly good players for Division Three, effectively … it was quite bizarre travelling to Yeovil and Hartlepool with Leeds United. I didn't really have a great knowledge of that division or that level of football. But we managed … we got to the play-offs."

It took McAllister more than a month to register his first victory, a four-match winless run tempering hopes of a play-off finish. The Scotsman said that if he was able to have his time again, he would have done things differently. "Maybe there was too much change, too much emphasis on trying to get the ball down and playing," he said. "Not that the group of players were direct, but maybe in hindsight, [I] could've left things as they were and maybe not tried to put too much emphasis on keeping possession, which was obviously something that I had tried to coach and preach." Beckford admitted that he had some initial doubts about the mid-season change in style. "He [McAllister] tried to change it too much too soon, rather than do it over the course of a couple of months. I think he wanted to do it and cram it all in within the space of a fortnight, give or take, which is great when you're at an elite level, because it's much easier to take onboard and it's much easier to implement those changes straight away. But I think where we were and the success we had prior to that moment, it was difficult to differentiate, [thinking], 'Well, why should we stop doing what we know works and jump straight into this, which is … it's a nice way of playing football, don't get me wrong, but it's not necessarily getting the results in this league', … but the results picked up."

Kandol gave McAllister his first victory with the only goal in a 1-0 triumph at Swindon Town but it was the arrival of another striker, Dougie Freedman, that inspired a strong finish to the season that saw United win nine of their last 13 matches and book a play-off spot. "I was at Crystal Palace in the Championship," Freedman remembered. "I was coming to the end of my long time there, 10 years it had been. Neil Warnock [Palace manager] mentioned to me that Leeds United were interested … I wasn't really looking to go anywhere but as soon as he said Leeds United, I thought, 'Wow. That's a huge club. Although it's a division down, it's a huge club'. And I knew Gary McAllister from the Scotland squad, so, just straight away, I just felt at ease with it." He netted six times in a 14-appearance stint at United but his influence went far beyond his goalscoring impact, Freedman's assists, nous and experience also proving crucial. "Dougie was somebody who could come and light [up] the team. He had a bit of personality and charisma to cope with the crowd," McAllister said.

Another appeal to wipe United's 15-point deduction was unsuccessful but Leeds could still win promotion, via the play-offs. And Freedman's importance to the club was highlighted by his 96th-minute goal in a 2-1 defeat to Carlisle United in a tense play-off semi-final first leg. Continually thwarted by Carlisle's outstanding goalkeeper, Kieren Westwood, Leeds were also poor at the back on a frustrating night at Elland Road. "I had a very bad game," Lubo Michalik said with trademark honesty. "I think if we lost 2-0, that would be very, very difficult." Freedman popped up in the right place at the right time, though, prodding home from close range. "A tap-in, which delights me more than any goal," said Freedman, who was not lacking motivation. "When I stepped out … that won't ever leave me, that three or four minutes before the evening game … the atmosphere, the excitement. It's very difficult for me to describe but it's certainly up there in the handful of memories that I [will] take with me." His goal gave Leeds belief, something Prutton remembers McAllister making the most of. "He [McAllister] was fucking pumped. He was pumped … he was like, 'You've given yourself a lifeline lads, we're still in it … don't worry because everything's going to be fine!'"

As Leeds prepared to travel to Carlisle for the second leg, Michalik was not the only player desperate to make amends for a sub-par performance. "It was probably the first time that sticks in my mind that I've been really disappointed with my own performance," Jonny Howson said. "This is arguably the biggest game I've played in [to date], the first leg of the play-offs, [I was] really disappointed … after the game, I'd been quite a bit down due to the situation … but we had a chance to put it right." And in the minutes before Leeds walked out at Brunton Park, McAllister urged his side to write their name in the history books. "I looked at that group of players and said, 'Wow, you've done amazing, to get to the second leg of a play-off [semi-final] starting the season 15 points behind. You guys, you can instantly become heroes. You're a couple of games away. Beat Carlisle and then go and win in the final.'"

Howson's first opportunity to put things right came in the 10th minute and he did not need a second invitation, chesting down a Freedman cross before levelling the tie with a smart finish to send the travelling fans wild. "I liked playing with Dougie Freedman because even on the pitch, you could tell that he'd been at a higher level," Howson said. "For me, playing in midfield and liking to get forward, I knew he could pick you out. When he had the ball … the majority of the time he'll see the runs or look for you and can find you. That was the case. I remember him going down [the left] and it was a case of getting in the box. [He] pulled it back nice. You couldn't really miss, I suppose, from there!"

A much-improved performance from Leeds had the tie in the balance, still at 2-2 on aggregate when an announcement over the PA system said just one minute of injury time would be played. "They'd just announced it [injury time] and I suppose you should say, 'Why are you hearing things like this when the game is going on?' But [I was] just thinking that, 'It's probably going to go to extra time, penalties,'" Howson said. Leeds were on the attack, though, and Freedman again found Howson in space, this time on the edge of the penalty area. "I knew 'Becks' [Beckford] was to the left of me, very possibly was on, I'd had a touch and it wasn't on [anymore]. [I was] just thinking, 'Have a shot', … it couldn't have gone in any better. I didn't hit it clean … it's not the best shot … but I think it's probably one of the few places that I could have put it for it to go in. It just goes over the defender's leg and keeper can't get it … it's moments like that that I'll look back [on] probably [for] the rest of my life. It's something I'm extremely proud of." The euphoria on Howson's face as he ran away to celebrate was unforgettable. The teenager, a Leeds United fan still living in Morley, had just sent his club to Wembley.

"He was just a boy. He'd made [his] debut before I got there, but you could obviously see his ability," McAllister said. "But more than that, you could see the fact that he was Leeds born and bred, and that affinity. I played with two young lads at Leeds, [David] Batty and [Gary] Speed. [They] came up through the ranks, came up through the academy. David's a Leeds boy. I know Gary's from Wales but they came through the academy and when you've got players in the team who have that affinity with the crowd, it's very special … he [Jonny] played with an intensity … he's a fantastic finisher. He's a good striker of the ball off both feet, hits it nice and early. Goalkeepers find it hard to get set because he takes it nice and quick." Ben Parker said it was no surprise to see his childhood friend deliver in the big moment. "I was so proud for him … what he's achieved - it is all down to hard work … me and Jonny played on the same team since we were eight years old … growing up, he'd play as a striker and he'd get us 50 goals a season, Jonny … he'd always have that knack of finding space at the right time."

"Leeds United is Jonny Howson. Just seeing the elation on his face and how excited and happy he was when we went back in the change rooms afterwards, after the game - words can't express how much it meant to him," Beckford added, while Freedman praised the match-winner's attitude and professionalism. "We really upped our game. We played fantastically well and if anything, we just should have scored more goals. The young players came of age that night, I felt, in a big game for a big club … Jonny Howson was a fantastic young player, great energy, great desire … I did see a very raw talent but it was attitude to work hard and really have that great desire that made him a fantastic player. It wasn't just his talent."

As the elation subsided in the aftermath of the Carlisle victory, Howson allowed himself a moment of quiet reflection. "I was still living at home then with my mum and dad. I remember [the] next morning, I can still picture it now. I used to lay down in the living room and my dad had brought the papers in. I've still got the paper at home - it was on the back page and 'How was that?' used to be a headline a few times if I'd scored. And that was the main thing on the back of the newspaper … I was obviously chuffed to bits. I think some of the local papers were wanting to speak to my mum and dad and things like that. It was just a bit surreal. I didn't really know how to deal with it, just carry on, I guess, and try and focus on the final against Doncaster."

Jonny Howson had a night to remember in Carlisle. Photo: Andrew Varley Picture Agency

WEMBLEY STADIUM | MAY 25 | ATT: 75,132

DONCASTER ROVERS 1-0 LEEDS UNITED

HAYTER 48'

2008

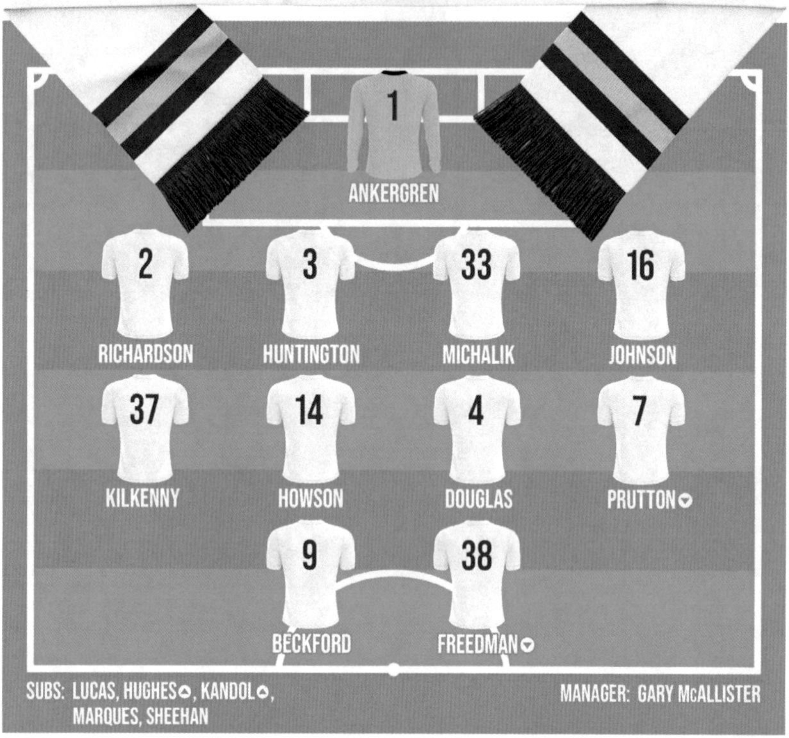

DONCASTER ROVERS

SULLIVAN, O'CONNOR, MILLS, HIRD, ROBERTS, GREEN, STOCK, WELLENS, COPPINGER, PRICE, HAYTER

SUBS: SMITH, McCAMMON, TAYLOR, LOCKWOOD, GUY

MANAGER: SEAN O'DRISCOLL

OUR FORM HEADING IN

CARLISLE	0-2	LEEDS UTD
LEEDS UTD	1-2	CARLISLE
LEEDS UTD	2-1	GILLINGHAM

"We started the pre-season in a tough way and, in the run up to the first game, the points had been deducted. And then, it was almost like, 'Fucking hell, we're actually in the final. We're actually a game away from getting the club back into the Championship', ... it's that feeling of elation, thinking, 'You're almost there'."
- David Prutton

Winning promotion at Wembley would have been the perfect way to end a tumultuous and challenging season. Doncaster Rovers were not going to make it easy for Leeds United in the 2007-08 League One play-off final, though, something Gary McAllister was very aware of. Just 10 days before he took the job at Leeds, Doncaster won impressively at Elland Road and McAllister made watching the match one of his first tasks as United boss. "I didn't know the division," he said. "One of the first games [I watched] when I arrived was that game ... literally in the first few days of being there ... one of the scouts and one of the recruitment [staff] showed me the game. I wanted to see the levels of who was the best team and everybody had always said, 'Doncaster are the best team', ... they battered Leeds at Elland Road and gave them a real footballing lesson. I know [Doncaster manager] Sean O'Driscoll and I know how his teams set up. They were different to most teams in the division ... the game at Elland Road, they [Leeds] actually were passed off the pitch."

McAllister had a chance to act on his learnings in April when he took Leeds to the Keepmoat Stadium and United won 1-0 thanks to an Alan Sheehan free-kick, but it was far from convincing. With 10 days between the Carlisle United triumph and the play-off final, players and staff were left with plenty of time to ponder and for Jermaine Beckford, working as an RAC windscreen fitter just two years earlier, the chance to play at Wembley represented the achievement of a lifetime goal. "It was a dream come true," he said. "My family are born and raised within a seven, eight-mile radius of Wembley Stadium. So we know Wembley inside out. We'd been to Wembley Stadium, never played there. And for me to say to my friends, my family, everybody close to me, school teachers, 'I'm playing at Wembley Stadium', it was incredible."

Leeds supporters queued overnight at Elland Road to get tickets and if they missed out, local fans made other plans as anticipation for the final continued to build. "I knew that all the Leeds fans were going to Doncaster and trying to get [their] tickets and there was a big uproar about that," Neil Kilkenny said. "Really, they should have just given Leeds a bit more of an allocation and try and sell Wembley out. It was a big build-up ... it was fantastic. '15 points, who gives a fuck, we're super Leeds and we're going up', it was a fantastic song, I remember that well."

As the match drew closer, McAllister took his men out of Leeds. "We tried to do it in the right way. We went away and spent a few days [together], tried to make it special. And the preparation with training went well. We were full strength going into the game," he said. But there were differing views on United's preparation. "We went down a couple of days before to a nice hotel," goalkeeper Casper Ankergren recalled. "There were some treatments ... we just tried to prepare really well. I just remember our suits, we had these suits that we got from the club and I remember having photos taken outside the hotel before the game." While Ankergren was pleased, United's loan star, Dougie Freedman, was growing increasingly concerned. "I think looking back, we could have done things a little bit better," he said. "I think we all realised that after the final. I felt there was a certain overconfidence in the squad and in the coaching staff that we were the better team because ... we beat Doncaster six weeks ago and we should win this game. And I felt that hampered our preparations slightly, and our focus."

"We didn't really start focusing in to the game until maybe 48 hours before the game," Freedman continued. "[I wanted] to say, 'I think we should be doing something a little bit more', but I didn't say anything, do anything ... it's [something I've] carried with me, my whole coaching career as well, that you can never over prepare. And I feel that we did under prepare. And our focus wasn't truly there ... it's something I've carried a long, long time with me in my coaching career, my management career ... there was a couple of weeks leading up to it and I felt the couple of weeks leading up to it, we could have prepared a little bit better, in terms of focus and what if we'd done that, or we could have done that, if we'd [had] a Plan B ... it's not just the coaching staff because the players have got to take responsibility as well. I just don't think the focus was as much as it was to get to the final as it was in the final."

Rain fell steadily on matchday but it did not dampen the spirits of a huge United following, as the players walked out onto the pitch, one victory away from promotion in a truly unforgettable season. "To play and captain a club the size of Leeds United, doesn't matter if it's League One or the Championship or the Premier League, it's still Leeds United. To play for them, to walk out of Wembley as captain was great," said Jonathan Douglas, who had the pain of last season's relegation in his mind as he walked down the tunnel. "I was just thinking about the relegation and going into League One and the opportunity to get back to the Championship."

"I remember walking on the pitch feeling quite emotional, just because of the size of the stadium, the people, the noise," Ankergren said. "I remember the big fires [flames] coming up from the side. You could feel the heat from them … I had an idea of what I was going into but it was on a bigger stage. [I] didn't start speculating too much. If you start thinking about how important the game is then I think your thoughts can start going away from what's important, which is just to go and try and perform … to win a game of football. So I just tried to focus on what I had to do, really, and I was called into action quite early in the game. I had to make saves." Leeds started poorly, Ankergren required to make two important saves in the first 15 minutes. Doncaster had other chances, too, in a one-sided start that filled United's supporters with dread. "We got really caught out. I thought we did not perform at all to the level that was expected of us … we could have been two or three nil down quite early on," the goalkeeper said, while David Prutton shared similar thoughts. "I remember it being quite a sluggish start and I think Casper made a save quite early on which almost shakes you into action thinking, 'Fucking hell, we're in a game here.'"

At the other end of the pitch, Freedman was finding it difficult to have his usual impact. "I was paid extra attention but that's not an excuse … I was man-marked and they played three at the back … maybe it's what I analysed myself, in that [less than ideal] preparation … if I was man-marked or they went for a man-marking game, what would we have done? We didn't really prepare for all eventualities and one of the eventualities was [for Doncaster] to play a very deep-lying back three, so Jermaine Beckford couldn't run in behind and one [defender] was man-marking myself. The result was our attacking play - maybe 60 per cent of that attacking play was taken away from us."

"Their main objective was to stop Dougie Freedman from playing and they knew [if they were] to stop him from playing, then they'd have a good chance of winning the game," Douglas said. "I think they've done that because Dougie, that season, was so experienced and just so intelligent … they just came with a game plan and stopped us from getting Dougie Freedman on the ball and I don't think we really had a Plan B after that." Despite a poor first half, Leeds managed to get to the break unscathed, prompting some contemplation. Asked about his team talk, McAllister said: "It was probably along the lines that, 'We've not played well here. We've got to get hold of the ball and make some play', because that was the emphasis. On a big pitch and in the big games like that, you can't be chasing the ball the whole game."

"I just went into my shell [at half time], just to try and re-evaluate and refocus and see what I'm not doing right and what's going wrong and why we're not really coming together," said Beckford, while Ankergren was hopeful for a quieter second half. "I was pleased with what I've done in the first half and all I was just focusing on … was trying to perform and be ready. I always try to say to myself, 'They will always have two or three chances every half', and I had to be ready when called upon. I think it's important as a keeper that you try and stay calm when the team is maybe not playing as well as they probably could." Teams often need some luck to win finals and Prutton was hopeful his side had not used up all of theirs. "To come in at 0-0 was a great time to sit down and work out what we were doing wrong … I think he [McAllister] was just trying to get the point across that, 'Yes, we're in the game, there's still 45 minutes left and beyond, that almost like we got away with the first half in a way because Casper had been busy and kept us in it'. And then, going out into the second half … we were confident. I don't think there was any air of trepidation."

If Leeds were going to win, they needed Freedman and Beckford to have more of an impact. "They denied us space in behind … I was trying to get the ball a bit deeper and I was trying to get them to move the ball a bit quicker when we were moving it," Freedman said of the discussions at the break. But for all the talk, it took just three second-half minutes for Doncaster to score what was ultimately the match-winning goal, James Hayter, inexplicably left free from a corner, heading in from close range. "Any kind of goal that goes [in] from a set-piece, there's always that communal look around of first off, 'Shit, who's man is that. Fuck, who is meant to be marking him?' … Of all the people, he was quite a prolific footballer and he was in the right place at the right time," Prutton said. "There was a striker who was alone. Nobody marked him so that was a little bit [of] a lack of concentration," said Lubo Michalik, while Beckford was in disbelief. "I just remember hearing the fans cheering and thinking to myself, 'No way, no way have these lot scored against us, no way. This shouldn't be happening to us. Not to us. No'. It was just deflation."

On came Tresor Kandol and Andy Hughes as Leeds battled for an equaliser, Beckford going closest when he shot at former Leeds goalkeeper Neil Sullivan, while Jonny Howson had a go from distance. But for all their possession, Leeds never really looked likely to level proceedings. "I remember wave after wave of attack … just nothing was falling into place. Nothing was working," Beckford said. And nothing did work, Andy D'Urso eventually blowing for full time after five minutes of agonising injury time.

"The feeling for me [after the final whistle] would be the amount of people that were there. Obviously, I was manager of the football club and I've let down a lot of people," McAllister said. "That would be my immediate feeling, the fact that these people have spent a big part of their salaries to support their club in the hope of getting back towards where they should be playing … it all falls on the manager. So it was just taking all the disappointment of the people that were there to support us … it's probably one of the worst moments as part of Leeds United, to not get them into what would be the Championship." Douglas was gutted. "[I was] just devastated just coming off Wembley … all my family [were] over from Ireland and [I remember] just being totally gutted that we just came up short again. We had a chance to bring

Leeds back to the Championship, especially after getting relegated [the season before]."

"I remember being really, really disappointed after the game … I found a quiet space and just sat on my own, really, just to try and gather my thoughts … [I] did not really want to speak to anybody," said Ankergren, while Prutton looked around a shattered changing room and pondered. "There was a real, quite obviously, dead atmosphere because of what this group of people had been through together … I've been in good dressing rooms and I've been in bad dressing rooms. That was a very, very good dressing room where you felt that everyone cared about each other, people understood how big the sense of occasion was, but unfortunately it just couldn't come together on what would have been a glorious day … there is that thing where if you sit and think about it, you think, 'Can you fucking imagine what it would have been like if we'd actually gone from there [points deduction], got to the final, won in the final, got promoted?' It would have been almost too perfect an underdog story wouldn't it? It would have been on [television] and you'd have watched it and there would have been an element of, you'd have gone, 'No, it's a bit far fetched, I'm not having that.'"

So why did Leeds lose? "A bit of stage fright, including myself," Freedman said. "We deservedly lost the final and there's no hiding [from] that … sometimes you've got to hand it to the opponents and say that they were the better team than us, the better individuals on the day … we froze on the day because we felt we got to the final and that was all we had to do." Hughes shared a similar view. "We weren't good enough. Doncaster deserved to win. [It was] really, really disappointing with the expectation of the club to go up but Doncaster were a better team, full stop … it was a 1-0 battering … Doncaster were better. None of our players turned up. Sometimes you just have to hold your hands up and say the better team won on the day. They did."

Perhaps it was just one game too many in a marathon season. "There's so many things that had gone on throughout the season," Howson said. "The minus points, changing manager, different runs that we'd had throughout the season, the way that we won it in the semi-final and then to lose at the final hurdle. It was hard to take." Ben Parker, watching the final in the stands with his mates, said the lengthy campaign felt like it had gone on for years. "It seemed like almost like it was two, three seasons rolled into one, with the amount of stuff that went on. I just think everything caught up with us. Too much had gone on in one season and unfortunately when we needed to be at our best in the most important game, we probably just ran into a brick wall."

Difficult reminders of the defeat kept popping up on the way home as the Leeds coach passed thousands of the club's supporters on the motorway. "We were in the bus on the way back to Leeds. A supporter bus drove past us and if you look at the signs they gave us, it wasn't positive … they were disappointed and we were disappointed. They were just obviously upset that we didn't really turn up on that day," said Ankergren, while Michalik remembered a near-silent trip back to Yorkshire. "It's very difficult to even think about it … the bus was very, very quiet. Nobody was talking, just looking outside the window from the bus and seeing disappointed Leeds fans, because they went the same way. That was even more frustrating … in England, we say Wembley is the best place to win a game but the worst place to lose a game."

On a dreadful day, there was one "saving grace" for Beckford. "We made it to the play-off final which was, at the beginning of the season, for the outside world, it's unthinkable. Nobody expected us to get there and we did it, against all odds. But then to have lost and then the reality kicked in, [thinking], 'Wow, we're going to have to do this again'. That was brutal. However, we had to do it again on level points with everybody. And that in itself was almost the saving grace. It was almost, 'Well, cool, so we managed to do what we did from so far behind. Everybody else had a five-game head start on us. Let's see what we can do now, starting on a level playing field'."

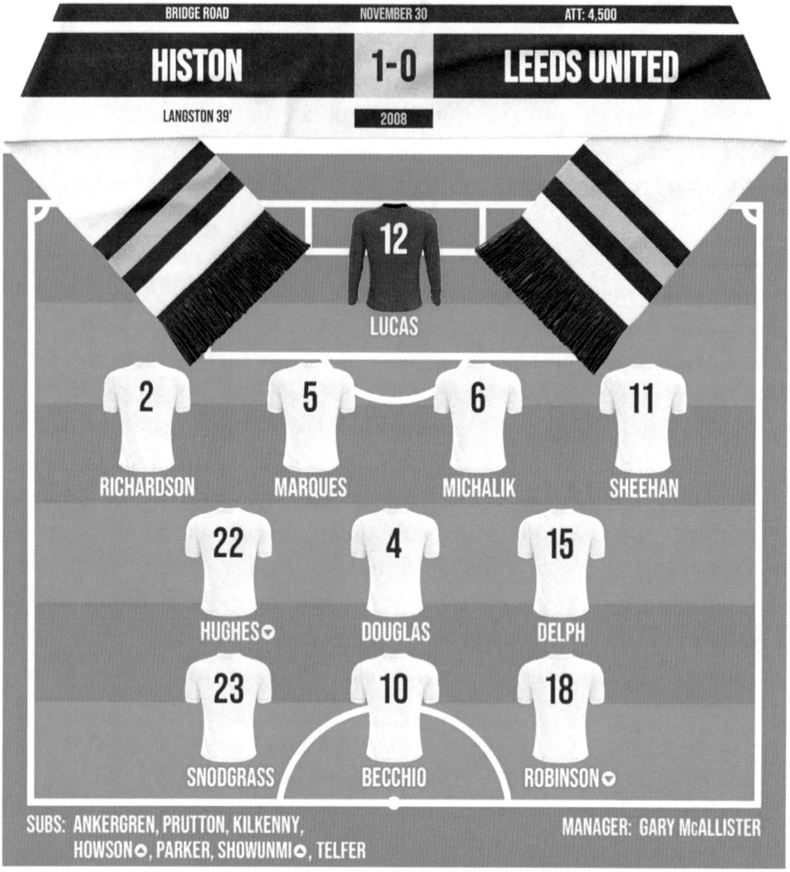

HISTON

NAISBITT, OYEBANJO, LANGSTON, ADA, GWILLIM, BARKER, MITCHELL-KING, SIMPSON, KNIGHT-PERCIVAL, WRIGHT, MIDSON

SUBS: WELCH, POPE, OKAY, KENNEDY, ANDREWS, REEVES, MURRAY

MANAGER: STEVE FALLON

OUR FORM HEADING IN

NORTHAMPTON	2-1	LEEDS UTD
LEEDS UTD	4-1	HARTLEPOOL
NORTHAMPTON	2-5	LEEDS UTD

"The game shouldn't have been played. The pitch was ... the ball didn't move a yard but, obviously, that instantly becomes an excuse. The cameras were there, so it had to go ahead - but it should never have been played."
- Gary McAllister

One of the most embarrassing matches in Leeds United's history almost never happened. Gary McAllister's Leeds were sent to non-league Histon for a second-round FA Cup tie and were confronted by a surface so bad the game could have been called off. There was only one problem. ITV's television cameras were there. "Oh my God," David Prutton said. "We turned up at the ground and I've heard since if it had been scheduled for a normal fixture within the kind of barrage of fixtures for that round, like a 3pm kick-off, or whatever it was, and it wasn't on TV, that game would have been called off because that pitch was absolutely horrendous. Because it was on TV, they moved heaven and earth to get it on. It's funny having done games now from a TV point of view and seen what goes into it I can understand ... there's a lot of money that goes into getting a crew there and the trucks and all the hardware set up. They were like, 'Right, this game's going on.'" Casper Ankergren who, like Prutton, shivered on the bench throughout the match, echoed those sentiments. "The pitch was horrific. There was water everywhere, it was waterlogged, but it was on telly, so they were desperate to play the game."

While United's players were cursing at the conditions, the mood among their opposition was sky high. "We were delighted the game was on, obviously. Every little bit of help, including the pitch and weather conditions, it all helped our cause, really," Histon's goalscoring hero, Matt Langston, said. "It was the tie of the round, sort of thing. There was a big build-up to it so, fortunately, the ref said, 'Yes', [the game is on], and then it's up to 11 men on each side to go head to head ... Jermaine Beckford was doing really well for Leeds at the time ... he got injured ... maybe the Gods were looking down on us? Jermaine, he was their main talisman at the time up front, he was scoring lots of goals ... we had a little bit of luck in our favour, I think."

Beckford's absence was just one of many reasons Langston and his teammates were quietly optimistic. "We were confident," Langston added. "At the time, we were on a great run of form as a team in the Conference as it was. In that stretch, I think we went 10, 12 games unbeaten, beating some big teams in there, Oxford [United] and teams like that. Everyone was full of confidence, [we] had quite a fully fit squad … we were on a really good run of form … we played some good attacking football, we got the ball in wide areas, we had two willing running centre-forwards and everyone worked tirelessly hard … we beat Swindon [Town] at home in the previous round [of the FA Cup], so that was a massive coup for us. They were [in] League One as well, so in the same division as Leeds … Leeds was obviously the main tie [in the second round], the main draw, the main club, because of all their history and everything else. It was the biggest tie on offer and we managed to get that at home as well, so everyone was really excited at the club and looking forward to it."

Leeds arrived at Histon having lost three of their last five matches, with a midweek defeat at Northampton Town, in which Beckford limped off, forcing McAllister to shuffle his pack. In came Robert Snodgrass and three defensive reinforcements in Frazer Richardson, Rui Marques and Alan Sheehan, with Paul Telfer, Ben Parker, Prutton and Beckford making way. "Me and Paul Telfer - Gary 'Mac' [McAllister] had called us into a meeting on the morning of the game. He said that he was changing the team and me and Telfer weren't playing," Prutton recalled. "He was a very good friend of mine, 'Telfs'. He's a very mature fella. I was a bit hot-headed. [I was thinking], 'I got dropped for that', all that type of shite and then slowly but surely as the game unfolded, we sat there thinking, 'Thank fuck for that', [laughs]."

McAllister acknowledged the game was "always a potential banana skin" and as kick-off approached, some of his players started to fear the worst. "I believe that day was in our mind," Marques said. "Perhaps everybody was thinking, 'Okay, we don't need to give our 100 per cent'. I'm not saying that this is my kind of thought but sometimes you feel that when the team is really focused or when the team is not focused. Sometimes, you start the game not taking it 100 per cent serious and after you get yourself in a big problem, because then you try to perform and nothing comes." The weather continued to play on Ankergren's mind. “It was a really bitterly cold day and you were slightly worried about what was going to happen. It was just one of them. I had a bad feeling about it, [I] really, really did. You looked at it and I thought, ‘This doesn’t look good.’”

The match kicked off in awful conditions and the weather only got worse as both sides traded chances before Langston scored in the 39th minute, the centre-back - then working as a postman - nodding in a corner. “The nerves had sort of gone out of the legs a little bit and you were in the game,” Langston said. “We got a set-piece. I think we might’ve had one corner beforehand and I didn’t really get anywhere near it … it was a great delivery in the conditions from Gareth Gwillim … he put it on the money for me, really. I just managed to get across my man, Lubo Michalik, and just tried to direct it towards goal. Fortunately it found the bottom corner … I was right in front of the Leeds fans, so I didn’t really know where to run. I didn’t want to get their back up too much, but obviously I ran away, wheeling away a bit, Alan Shearer type, I suppose. Then suddenly got mobbed by the rest of my teammates … [I was] just running back towards the halfway line looking for my family. It was a great moment for me.”

As Histon celebrated, the giant-killing was well and truly on. “All the things that you watched as a kid on Match of the Day on FA Cup weekend, of the giant-killing et cetera, then you’re suddenly sat in the middle of it and you go, ‘Oh shit, this is what it feels like to be one of those teams’, … you sat there at half time and go, ‘Geez’,” Prutton said. As the Leeds brains trust pondered what was necessary to get back in the game, Histon decided sitting back was not the right option. “We were always positive and trying to not to sit in as much, try and get the second goal if we could. We had a couple of opportunities early in the second half, but then Leeds made a few changes,” Langston recalled, as Jonny Howson and Enoch Showunmi were introduced. “He [Showunmi] posed a different threat, probably better in the conditions. So it was backs to the wall in the second half, I must admit. That wasn’t in the planning and I just think, gradually, we became a bit tired. Leeds became a bit more desperate and it was just the pattern of the game, really.”

Two of United's best chances fell to an unlikely source in Michalik, who initially thrashed an effort against the post after a free-kick was not cleared, before the Slovakian thought he had spared his side's blushes in a separate incident. But in a moment that summed up Leeds' day, Michalik's 82nd-minute strike was somehow cleared off the line by the head of Histon's Antonio Murray. "I had two very big chances … it was a little bit unlucky but against Histon, this is not an excuse," he said. "You have to win three or four nil and go home." There were other opportunities, too, but Luciano Becchio and Fabian Delph could not hit the target as Histon held on for a famous victory.

The home fans and players were ecstatic after the final whistle, but the visitors were embarrassed. "To lose to a team like this is very, very embarrassing. They were over the moon after the game …[it is] difficult to think about games like this," Michalik added. "Obviously, it was embarrassing for us, to get beaten [for] the first time [by a non-league side]. It's not nice," Marques said. Hughes had a similar view, insistent it was "incredibly sad" to be involved as Leeds lost to a non-league team for the first time in FA Cup history. "It was just one of them days in football that unfortunately you experience as a player," he added. "It wasn't through lack of trying … certain players made certain mistakes in that game and switched off and Histon probably got what they deserved. They went through … it wasn't good … we weren't in the best of form leading into that game, and sometimes that happens when you're not in good form and you go to a place that you're not used to the environment - you get found out."

Despite the second-half chances, Howson felt Leeds deserved to lose. "Games like that - if you are, let's be honest, the better side - if you're not 100 per cent at it, things like this can happen. It happens most seasons. As they say, 'The magic of the cup', … [we were] going through a bit of a bad time in the league then as well, so confidence is low, and let's make no excuses, we weren't good enough. If you're not up to the challenge in any game of football, things like that can happen, and it certainly did that day. Fair play to Histon, but it's one that I don't look back on." Langston, understandably, tried to soak up every second. "It was a really famous day. I mean Histon is only a tiny little village outside Cambridge. We'd had great success in previous years, going up through the non-league pyramid. It was just great emotion, the manager, the chairman, the coach, everyone, all the players. Everyone was on the pitch. I remember doing a couple of TV interviews, a couple of radio interviews. I got man of the match, a bottle of champagne, so it was so surreal, really, for the level we normally play at … at the time, I was a postman full time. Got up early in the mornings and then finish early afternoon. I'd come back home, have a little kip and then go out [to train]. We'd have training two or three times a week for Histon and it was full on. I remember we'd have away games at Barrow or Wrexham mid-week and travelling back, getting in at 3am or 3.30am and then being up at work for half five, 6am the next day. So it was tough times but really, really enjoyable."

McAllister, who would lose his job just three matches later, was trying to make sense of the defeat in the Leeds changing room. "They were top of the Conference and were flying. To try and work out why or how they managed to get a result - upsets do happen … if Histon had beaten Leeds United in the Premier League … but the effect is still the same. Because when I say Leeds United, whenever I talk about Leeds United, I think of the Premier League. I don't think of times when they were in the lower divisions. I just think it's a Premier League club, it's a Premier League city. It was not a good day in the history of the football club. To be part of that is not good … there's no hiding place for that. There's no other way to put it." He still found time to acknowledge Histon's triumph, though. "He [McAllister] came in the dressing room afterwards. He said, 'Well done lads, fully deserved it,'" Langston recalled. "Obviously, it had been a tough day. Conditions were up against him and his team … they wouldn't play on a pitch like that normally in League One, not every week anyway. He showed dignity and class in what he did and he was probably the one that probably got the wrath from the Leeds fans after the performance and everything else."

"I just remember being in the proper kind of Sunday league dressing rooms," Prutton said. "At the end it's like, 'Let's get the fuck out of here. Let's try and forget this day as quickly as possible.'"

ELLAND ROAD | MAY 14 | ATT: 37,036

LEEDS UNITED 1-1 MILLWALL

BECCHIO 53' | 2009 | ABDOU 74'

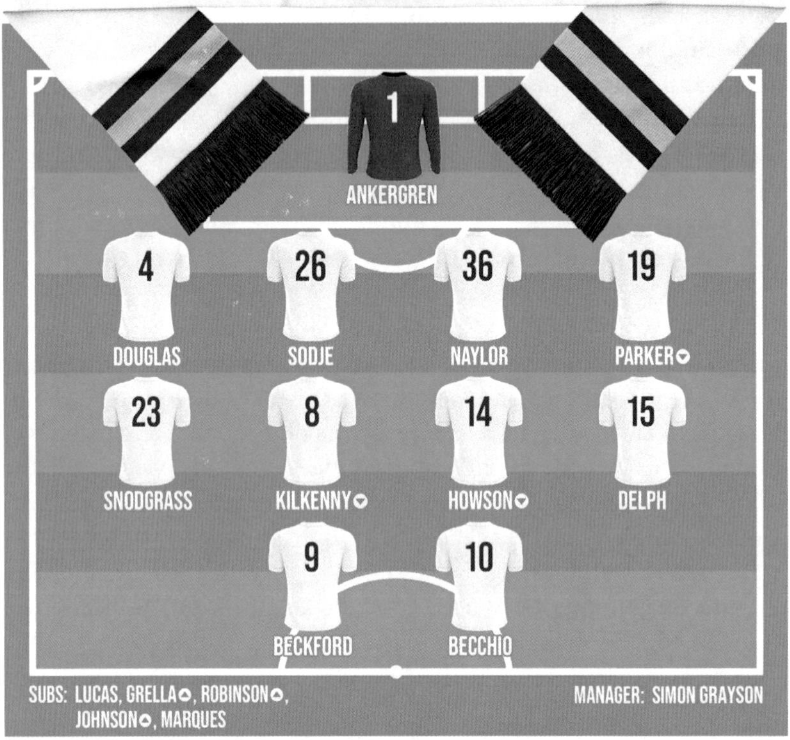

MILLWALL

FORDE, DUNNE, WHITBREAD, CRAIG, FRAMPTON, HENRY, ABDOU, BOLDER, MARTIN, ALEXANDER, HARRIS

SUBS: PIDGELEY, ROBINSON, BARRON, GRABBAN, LAIRD

MANAGER: KENNY JACKETT

OUR FORM HEADING IN

MILLWALL	1-0	LEEDS UTD
LEEDS UTD	3-0	NORTHAMPTON
HARTLEPOOL	0-1	LEEDS UTD

"It was an awful night ... we didn't perform ... I remember the fans shouting, 'You're not fit to wear the shirt', ... to be fair, they were right."
- Glynn Snodin

Simon Grayson had been Leeds United's manager for less than two months but the fans were not in a forgiving mood during a 2-0 defeat at League One strugglers Hereford United. Leeds, out of the play-off places, were staring down the barrel of a third successive season in the third tier of English football, with awful away form particularly concerning. The Hereford defeat was Leeds' 12th in 16 away matches in all competitions and Grayson and assistant manager Glynn Snodin decided enough was enough on a frustrating February night at Edgar Street. "A few home truths had to come out that night about what it means to wear this shirt for this club," Snodin said. "Simon and myself, yeah, we both had a say because we know about the club. We know what it means to the supporters ... anywhere in the world, they'll go. They'll want to see the team win or at least perform and give everything. We had to put it to them that day with some honest words."

Like Snodin, Grayson was a boyhood Leeds United fan who played for the club. It meant that he did not think twice about leaving Blackpool - then playing in the Championship - for the Elland Road top job. "Leeds United is one of the biggest clubs around so when the offer came to manage them ... it was a no-brainer," Grayson said. "It was just too good an opportunity and a dream come true in a way, to be able to complete the trio of supporting, playing the odd game and then managing the club." Grayson, who replaced Gary McAllister and took charge of his first match on Boxing Day 2008, acted quickly to sign defender Richard Naylor. "I was 31 and I thought the chance [to play for Leeds] had gone so to join my hometown club, the club I supported, it was great," Naylor said. "Simon Grayson had just taken over and I joined on a month's loan. Simon wanted to make it permanent after just a couple of weeks, though. He made me captain when I was on loan which was quite unusual, but I was very happy." Naylor had not been at Leeds for long but quickly noticed things needed to change. "When I came to the club, it was a very fractured dressing room. I think I helped galvanise it and play a role there. Ken Bates wouldn't pay appearance money in a contract ... but that took away the incentive of playing. For some lads, football is about money so as soon as some players went out of the team or had a bit of an argument with the manager, they wouldn't be too bothered about getting back in the team. Some of the lads weren't that arsed whether they were in the team or not. To me, it just didn't feel right. Young players needed more guidance, too."

"I think 'Nayls' [Naylor] was a massive part of the resurgence," Jermaine Beckford recalled. "He was no nonsense and that's something that we had - but we didn't have to his extent. We didn't have his experience, we didn't have his communication. I think his signing changed a lot around the place, it made it a lot more professional as well. There was not as much messing around, not as many pranks and all that sort of stuff ... he also had a very, very funny side to him as well. He made sure that everybody knew when the right time to mess around was and when the right time to be serious [was]." Grayson's arrival also lifted Beckford. "He's been my favourite manager to work with because he gives me freedom and he lets me express myself in the way that I feel the most confident ... he's always built a team around me and my strike partner, which has always worked out for us."

That Hereford defeat proved a real turning point for United, who won 11 of their last 15 matches to finish fourth in the table and set up a play-off semi-final with Millwall. "They had a sell-out but it's not a big stadium. People talk about Millwall being an intimidating place to go but it's not really at all compared to Elland Road and other proper stadiums," Naylor said. "First leg [of] play-offs, they're always a cagey affair. It had 0-0 written all over it, did that game," Ben Parker remembered. Millwall were to win it, though, substitute Neil Harris scoring a 71st-minute goal at The New Den.

Leeds had every reason to feel confident heading into the second leg, on a run of 11 successive home victories. "I was fairly confident we would turn them over at Elland Road ... there wasn't much between the two sides [in the first leg] but I thought we were a bit better," Naylor said. Grayson agreed. "Any sort of result where you're still giving yourself [a chance] of being competitive in the second leg was going to be a positive for us going back to Elland Road, I felt. In all the play-off semi-finals that I've been involved in, managed in, you always want to make sure that you give yourself an opportunity in the second leg to go and win it and, obviously, a full Elland Road, going back there - we thought a 1-0 deficit wasn't a bad result, really." A sell-out crowd piled into Elland Road for the second leg, the bulk of fans sharing Grayson and Naylor's confidence. Beckford remembered walking out of the tunnel and being hit with goosebumps. "It's so surreal, being able to speak about it from my own perspective and not just an assumption of what I think it should be," he said. "I knew what was coming but even though you know what's coming, you can't prepare yourself for that [noise]. To know what's on the line as well, and to know where we were the year before [losing at Wembley], it felt like we'd prepared for it much more. I just felt ready. I think we were all ready."

The home fans turned back the clock, providing an unforgettable atmosphere as every Millwall touch was booed, hissed and jeered in the early stages. "Thinking about it, it's making the hairs on the back of my neck stand up," Parker said. "It was one of those nights where words don't do the atmosphere justice ... it's almost a night where you had to be there, just to feel the atmosphere." Naylor added: "That was a night where people were two or three metres away and you just couldn't hear them. It was real loud and real positive from the start." Leeds controlled the first half but failed to score, with midfielder Neil Kilkenny forced off after just 35 minutes. "The atmosphere was rocking and I was absolutely gutted to come off with an ankle injury," he said. "It was massively disappointing."

The chance Leeds had been waiting for came just after the break, referee Mark Halsey pointing to the penalty spot after Millwall's Andy Frampton grabbed Sam Sodje's shirt. Up stepped Beckford, scorer of 34 goals in another brilliant season, but something was playing on his mind. In the days before the second leg, the striker, who regularly struck his penalties to the goalkeeper's left, was practising spot-kicks as Snodin watched on. "The keeper knew where they were going in training, but he [Beckford] would still put it in, because he had that much pace and height and perfection ... I bet he put nine out of 10 in one place," Snodin said. Beckford's other penalty went to the goalkeeper's right, though, and he could not forget it as he prepared to take his spot-kick at Elland Road. "That kind of ruined my mindset because I'm thinking to myself, 'Well, he knows where I'm going to go, because I go that way every time. I'm going to mix it up a little bit, see if I can outsmart him.'" But Beckford only outsmarted himself, David Forde guessing correctly as the tame penalty, hit to the Millwall man's right, was saved. "It was pure frustration," he said. "I thought to myself, 'What are you doing? You've scored these ones all day, every day, after training every single day. You put it in this exact same spot. Why are you changing it now?' These are the questions that I'm asking myself. I was pissed. I couldn't believe what I was doing. I couldn't believe that I allowed myself to talk myself out of doing something that I know works. Yeah, I beat myself up." Grayson, watching on from the sidelines, admitted he was never certain when Beckford stepped up to take a spot-kick. "I don't think he ever felt too comfortable taking penalties in his career, really. I think he wanted to take them because, obviously, it led to him getting more goals, but he was big enough to want to stand up and take the penalty. You never knew with Jermaine's record whether he'd score."

While Parker confessed to thinking "here we go again" as the penalty was saved, he was largely responsible for Leeds levelling the tie in the 53rd minute. "It's a moment where I can remember every part of it, every second," he said. "I remember the ball going to the keeper and I had a bit of space so I started running out so he could roll the ball out to me. First thought, I was like, 'I need to leg it here as quick as possible because their right winger ... he was quick', … that was the first thing, get the ball going as quick as possible. I managed to get up to the halfway line and then Jermaine was out on the left wing. I don't know what he was doing out there! I think he was having a breather so I just managed to flick [it with] the outside of my boot towards him and because I was running up to a high speed by then, I thought, 'I may as well just carry it forward'. So I go out to Jermaine, he's worked it to 'Robbo', Andy Robinson, and as soon as I've seen him have the ball there, it's like their full-back is attracted to him, so it created a bit of space in and behind. Robbo is one of these players where if you do an overlapping run, sometimes, probably most of the time, you're not going to get the ball off him because he'll dip inside, try and get a shot away himself or try and put a cross in. But for some reason that night, he managed to spot my run and play me in … it was kind of an easy cross, to be fair, because there was already a gap between the centre-half and the keeper and it was more concentration. It was a wet night, the pitch was slick, so you just have to put it in a decent area and the ball on the surface would skid through. Thankfully, the big Argentine [Luciano Becchio] was there to stick it in the back of the net."

As Parker surged down the left, the home fans started to stir, and Becchio's finish was met with what can only be described as an eruption of noise as Elland Road roared at its loudest. "It was like the whole roof lifted off Elland Road. It was unbelievable," Grayson said. Jonathan Douglas said the 30 seconds after the goal will live with him forever. "I was playing right-back and just thinking, 'Well, this is too far to go and celebrate with them'. I just remember standing there, hands in the air, just looking around and the whole place was just incredible … I've hung my boots up now … if I think about certain games, certain atmospheres, that's definitely number one in my playing career." For Parker, the moment was extra special. "It was unbelievable. It seemed to go on for ages, the roar. Usually you hear a big cheer, then it simmers down. But it just seemed to go on and on and on and get louder and louder," he said. "People say they haven't heard an atmosphere like that for a very long time … I've grown up being a Leeds fan and I've known Elland Road to be like that, through the Premier League days, the Champions League days, so for me, I've always wanted to play in atmospheres like that in a Leeds shirt. To get to do that was just great … and then we got the goal and you think, 'Right, we're going to get the second, we're going to get the third and run away with it'." Beckford agreed. "I'm going to be forever thankful to 'Luci' [Becchio] for that … he did me a favour. It was relief … at last, finally, we've cracked it. We've cracked the deadlock, this is it now. Everybody was like, 'Well, we're going to do it now, this is it'."

But United's momentum came to a halt as Millwall defender Zak Whitbread required lengthy treatment for a head injury. It was, in hindsight, a game-changing moment. "Everything was going for us. Their centre-back went down … that killed it a little bit, I think. Just settled it down, probably, from their point of view. Sometimes, little things like that can knock you off your rhythm," Jonny Howson said. "It worked in their favour because it just took the wind out of our sails,"

Grayson added. With Leeds' rhythm gone, Millwall then levelled on the night - and took a 2-1 aggregate lead - when Jimmy Abdou scored from close range after Lewis Grabban's cutback with just 16 minutes remaining. "The lad who scored, he was a real box-to-box midfielder, had a real engine on him. It was a scrappy goal. It bobbled into his path and he toe-poked it in. It was not a great goal and was a real dagger in the heart to concede," Naylor recalled. For Kilkenny, now with a set of crutches, it was particularly tough to take. "I would have been marking him … it was disappointing … I was gutted I couldn't contribute." Bradley Johnson and Mike Grella were introduced as substitutes but Leeds ran out of time in a bid to send the tie to extra time, the final whistle marking the end of another failed play-off campaign and setting up another season in the third tier of English football. "Again, we were favourites … and we didn't really perform when it came down to it," Ankergren said. "It was brutal," Beckford said. "There are no words to explain the pain that we all felt again, having to do it [League One] again after we had done so well and after we come so far … the fans didn't deserve that … they didn't ask to be put in this position. They've given everything they could do over the last couple of years to help us, to get us out of that shit situation. It's unfair for them to have to go through it again."

After thanking the fans on a lap of Elland Road, United's players returned to a shattered changing room. "We were sat there in the changing room and you could hear a pin drop ... it was almost disbelief," Parker said. Grayson pondered about the message he should give his players. "You're proud of the way your players have given everything, proud of the way the club was supported," he said. It was not the time for harsh words and instead, Grayson issued a rallying cry. "We did say with the players in the dressing room that, 'We've got to make sure we use this disappointment as motivation for next year ... and make sure we are the ones celebrating', ... they felt like they had failed, really. [I said], 'You've got to go away and have your summer and make sure that we're all doing even more than we've tried to do in the [last] few months ... and leave no stone unturned to try and get promotion the following season.'"

Play-off heartbreak was becoming frustratingly common. Photo: Andrew Varley Picture Agency

MANCHESTER UNITED

KUSZCZAK, NEVILLE, BROWN, EVANS, FABIO, WELBECK, GIBSON, ANDERSON, OBERTAN, BERBATOV, ROONEY

SUBS: AMOS, OWEN, GIGGS, TOSIC, CARRICK, RAFAEL, VALENCIA

MANAGER: ALEX FERGUSON

OUR FORM HEADING IN

STOCKPORT	2-4	LEEDS UTD	LEEDS UTD	3-1	HARTLEPOOL	LEEDS UTD	1-0	SOUTHAMPTON

"After I did it, I went home and I was in tears. It [leaving Leeds United] was the last thing I wanted to happen."
- Jermaine Beckford

Leeds United's biggest match in years was on the horizon but Jermaine Beckford, who felt backed into a corner, handed in a transfer request. The club's repeated failure to win promotion from League One meant the striker, out of contract at the end of the 2009-10 season, was hot property. Benfica, Braga and Celtic were all interested and could offer him the chance to play European football and a likely substantial wage rise. Beckford initially wanted to stay put, though. "I spoke with my wife ... I said, 'Look, these clubs are floating around, what do you think?' And she was like, 'I want you to be happy. Are you happy now?' I said, 'Yeah, more than ever', and she said, 'Well, that's your answer'. It was as easy as that." That happiness meant Beckford was keen on signing a new contract at Elland Road. "I'm assuming that I'm going to be at Leeds forever. This is me - I love this place, I love the city, I love the team, I love the fans ... my contract was running out in the summer and I wanted to extend and I wanted to stay there. I wanted to sign a three or four-year deal. I wasn't asking for massive money. I wasn't asking to be the highest-paid player or anything like that, I just wanted to extend my current deal. The response I got was not one that I'd anticipated getting ... it felt like it was almost a disrespectful offer just for the sake of saying, 'We've offered him a contract'. And it was non-negotiable."

The goals continued to flow for fan favourite Beckford despite the fact he was in contract limbo, as Leeds won 17 of their first 23 League One matches in that 2009-10 season, with the striker contributing 16 goals in that period. But even though promotion seemed a near certainty, a new Leeds deal was off the table, leading to a December 30 transfer request, which was announced by Leeds exactly one week later. "I didn't want to leave Leeds like this. It was heart-wrenching," Beckford said. "But at the same time, I didn't understand why it hurt me so much, but it wasn't hurting the powers that be." Multiple conversations with Simon Grayson followed and the manager kept faith with the forward for a much-anticipated FA Cup trip to Manchester United, even if Beckford's future was up in the air.

After all, having Beckford on the pitch would only help Grayson's cause. The striker scored a 78th-minute equaliser in a 1-1 draw at Kettering Town in a second-round FA Cup tie, a match that was followed by the third-round draw. "You're thinking, 'Wow. We've got Man United at Old Trafford, the winners of this [tie]'," Grayson recalled. "I don't think you could have asked for a better draw." Leeds still had to beat Kettering in a second-round replay and needed four extra-time goals to win 5-1. It was a nervy evening but it was also mission accomplished. Leeds were weeks away from facing their biggest rivals. "They [Kettering] made it very difficult for us," Grayson said, and Aidan White agreed, insisting Leeds "did make a meal of it".

A trip across the Pennines to play the Premier League champions produced contrasting emotions for the players. For White, it was "every lad's dream" but captain Richard Naylor said "it was a once-in-a-lifetime opportunity" that came with "a sense of trepidation". "People are going to remember that match. You want them to remember it for the right reasons. I remember when I first got down to Ipswich [Town] and they lost to Man United 9-0," Naylor added. Another boyhood Leeds fan, Ben Parker, put off a necessary hip operation after the draw was announced. "I sat down with the physio manager [and said], 'There's not a chance I'm having this operation because I don't want to miss out trying to be involved. Even if I've got one per cent chance of trying to be involved, I'm not having this operation'. They were fine with that."

Parker also took it upon himself to educate Leeds' foreign players. "You'd say stuff around the training ground like, 'We hate Man U, they're scum', having a laugh and a joke," he said. "It doesn't take too much for them to click on ... they might be out in the street, they might have a bit of red on their top. If a Leeds fan comes up to them and said, 'Don't wear red, we hate Man U', they get to know pretty [much] straight away." Slovakian defender Lubo Michalik said he "knew they hate each other", while it was car trips with a Leeds United employee that helped the penny drop for Australian defender Paddy Kisnorbo. "We started talking about Leeds and Man United and you find out ... you realise, 'Wow, this is a very big game for us, but more for the people of Leeds'." The determination was growing.

As the build-up continued, Beckford could not stop thinking about his father. "My dad is a diehard Man United fan … I was thinking to myself, 'Oh, this is amazing. I'm going to be able to play against Man United, my dad's team … he can watch his son play against Man United. It's a dream come true.'" It was a thought that would return to Beckford many times on matchday. A chance encounter then saw Grayson run into Brian Flynn at Liverpool Airport while waiting for his son, Joe, to return from a trip. Flynn was, at that point, the last Leeds player to score in a win at Old Trafford, his 1981 strike securing a famous 1-0 victory. "He said, 'You won't remember who scored the last goal [in a Leeds win at Old Trafford]', and I didn't, to be fair. He obviously reeled off the date and everything," Grayson said. Flynn's "fantastic insight" on winning at the venue only increased Grayson's desire to be the man to lead Leeds to a famous victory.

There was no shortage of late drama for the manager to contend with, though. "The day before, [Robert] Snodgrass got injured in training. I think he hurt his hamstring … he was supposed to be playing," Neil Kilkenny said. Snodgrass dropped to the bench as a result, replaced by Bradley Johnson, while goalkeeper Casper Ankergren remained in doubt. "I had problems with my shoulder," he said. "I couldn't train properly the day before the game." Injections in Ankergren's shoulder were necessary and ultimately vital, as the Danish shot-stopper played an important role in victory.

Excellent league form had Kilkenny confident on matchday. "We were playing really well at the time. We were on a good run," Kilkenny said. "We knew that we had ability and we knew that we could push them. Manchester United were the best team in England at the time … a lot of people obviously wrote us off because we were in League One but we were Leeds United. Leeds United weren't a League One club." Kisnorbo added: "With our group, we had belief." Beckford admitted he did not initially share the same optimism and said that on the bus heading to Old Trafford that he was "bricking it". "I was thinking, 'Mate, we're going to get turned over here'. And then I walked into the changing rooms. We sat down, we had a laugh … who's going to smash who and that sort of thing." The warm-ups followed. "There was a buzz," Jonny Howson said. "It was a bit surreal in a way. I'd never played there and just used to see it on the TV … I remember going out for the warm-up and a lot of the Leeds fans were in … there was an atmosphere there … the hairs stand up on the back of your neck." Beckford's memory is similar. "As you walk out, it just opens up … you think to yourself, 'Wow, this is some place'. And then in the far corner, you just hear a mighty rumble … you see a crowd of white and that's all you can hear. You can't hear anything else around the place and you say to yourself, 'I'm comfortable here. This is us. This is what we're about'. So we go back inside after the warm-up and we just said to each other, 'Listen, we're here for these guys [the fans]. Let's do it for this lot'."

Naylor told The Telegraph in the lead-up to the match that he had been receiving plenty of texts from his Leeds-supporting mates asking him to "smash Gary Neville". And while he played down that talk in the national press, he thought about those comments again on matchday. "The two captains meet in the referee's room before the game," Naylor said. "I don't know if he [Neville] saw it [in the press] but he did not even look me in the eye at any stage. It was a bit awkward." Naylor soon returned to the Leeds changing room and Grayson gave his players one simple message. "In all the big games I've ever been involved in as manager … I've always said to the players, 'Make sure that you can have no regrets when you come off the pitch. If you go out there and do everything that you could have done and you wake up in the morning, look yourself in the mirror and you think, 'Right, I did everything', then you've got no worries if you win, lose or draw', … that was something I said in the last few words before the players went out at Old Trafford."

Leeds had clearly come to play and it took just 19 minutes for the visitors to take a shock lead. "I've played a lot of years and a lot of time with Jermaine and his strength was running in behind," said Howson, who set up the goal with a sensational diagonal ball to Beckford. "He [Beckford] had terrific pace … the pitch seemed massive there. [I remember] just looking up and just seeing him pulling away and that was his strength and something I looked for a lot of the time." Beckford, with a laugh, said: "I thought it [my first touch] was shit. I was thinking, 'No! No! My opportunity', but then, as the ball went past me, I'm focusing on the ball and I could feel Wes [Brown], and I'm getting away from Wes and I can feel [Tomasz] Kuszczak coming out and I thought to myself, 'I've got the pace here. I can get here. I can get here before both of them'. And I just got there, I just got there with my left foot just as Wes was sliding in, just as Tomasz was coming out as well, and it was just perfect. As I made connection with it, I knew Wes wasn't going to get it, but I thought the keeper might have stopped it, maybe with his foot or something, but when it went past him I started watching it, and as I'm watching it I'm thinking, 'This is getting closer and closer here. I think it's going to go in', … it creeps into the far corner and I think to myself, 'Oh my God, where's my dad?' I can't imagine what he must have been thinking … Old Trafford had been stunned. The football world had been stunned and the Leeds United fans in the corner were just going mental. Absolutely mental. I felt like I was back at Elland Road. The sound of it, the roar was just incredible. Absolutely incredible."

"As Jermaine does, he made a bad touch into a goal and if he actually took a good touch, it wouldn't have been a goal," Kisnorbo said. Andy Hughes was always confident Beckford would score. "As soon as 'Becks' went through, I'm like, 'He's scoring here', … Becks was just a natural finisher," he said. Naylor said it was a celebration he could not miss out on. "It was a long old way away and sometimes I tried not to go and celebrate to save my legs a bit but I had to get over there! It was unbelievable but I was also thinking, 'We might have pissed these [guys] off, here'." Parker, in the matchday squad but not named as a substitute, could not control himself in celebration before having the same thought. "I was right up and down. I was surrounded by Man United fans, they're all looking at you. You're just like, 'Shut up, have a bit of that!' I was buzzing. But then I heard Grayson say, 'We probably scored too early', … you look at the clock and you think, 'Oh, shit. There's still a long way to go here'. Grayson only briefly allowed himself to celebrate, given the stage of the game, and Leeds were soon on the back foot as Jason Crowe cleared a Wayne Rooney effort off the line.

Half time offered the chance for some reflection and planning, though. "We've just said … 'If we're going to get beat, we're going to get beat. But we've got to play our way, how we want to play … it's no good us sitting in, because we didn't have the players to sit in'," Glynn Snodin said. Manchester United came out in the second half desperate for a goal, ramping up the pressure on Naylor, Kisnorbo and Ankergren. "I want players to run themselves into the ground, put blocks in and you know that Kisnorbo and Richard Naylor – they would certainly be making sure to do everything … to make sure that we came up with the shock of the round," Grayson said. The two central defenders were immense and on a rare occasion they were beaten, Naylor booted Rooney up in the air. "I had to take one for the team there. I've seen that photo a few times. I played for 17 years and all people remember me for is kicking someone!" he joked. "The key that day was concentration. They [Rooney and Dimitar Berbatov] weren't chasing and putting pressure on you like a League One player might but you know if you switched off for one second, they had the quality."

Leeds nearly doubled their lead on two occasions, Snodgrass hitting the bar from a free-kick and Beckford screwing a shot just wide, before the inevitable late onslaught. Michalik and White, thrown on as defensive reinforcements, felt the pinch. "If I said I was shitting myself, I'd be close [laughs]," White said, while Michalik added that coming on so late - he was introduced in the 88th minute - was "a very difficult situation for centre-halves". "It felt like I was on the pitch maybe 15, 20 minutes," he said. "There was so many attacks from Rooney, from these top, top players."

Yet Leeds held firm, Ankergren in top form, before the final whistle was eventually blown, sparking jubilant scenes among the 9,000 travelling fans. "I was just very, very relieved when I heard the final whistle," Ankergren said. "As soon as the whistle went, I looked over and I saw the gaffer's face," Beckford remembered. "He was shouting, I looked at 'Snods' [Snodin] … he was jumping up and down and that's when it hit me, what we've just done. That's a David and Goliath moment." For Hughes and Naylor, their immediate thoughts turned to the long-suffering Leeds supporters. "It was maybe a little bit giving back [to] the fans what they missed out on [in] previous years and previous big games we've lost. It was something to give them," Hughes said. Naylor added: "Obviously in Cup games you can take a massive following and we had so many fans behind the goal. Those fans had a terrible few years so I was really pleased for them."

Like Beckford, Kisnorbo had a parent on his mind. “It’s a surreal moment. You’ve got a kid from the western suburbs [of Melbourne] who has just played on Old Trafford and beaten them … I was actually emotional in terms of all the things my mum had given up for me … hopefully that [day] repaid her in that way. Everyone was watching back home. I actually thought of my mum, in terms of this was something that hopefully made her happy and proud of her son … your mum brings you to training every night, buys you soccer boots, gives up her weekends for you … the hours and hours that she spent driving me everywhere and helping me. That one moment, it’s all for her … kids from Australia - it’s so hard to make it. So when you do, you don’t just do it for yourself. You do it for the people that have helped you on your journey, whoever it may be. And one of them who was pivotal was my mum.”

Grayson enjoyed the celebrations but also had the presence of mind to soak it up, too. “I went out to do my press and I always remember Paul Dews [Leeds United’s head of media] walking with me down the tunnel. He was walking really fast and I did say to him, ‘Let’s slow down a little bit. Let’s just drink in all the 9,000 Leeds fans singing … this might not happen again’. ‘Dewsy’ was a big Leeds fan as well. Then you go and face the world’s media … and go in the office with [Manchester United boss] Sir Alex [Ferguson] … across the room, he said, ‘Do you want a glass of white or red wine?’ I just said, tongue in cheek, ‘I don’t do anything red, Sir Alex. I’ll have a glass of white wine’.”

For some players, it took days to sink in. For Howson, it was much sooner. “I remember sitting on the bus after, outside the stadium, waiting for the lads to get on, just sitting there thinking, ‘I can’t believe we’ve just beaten *them*’.”

ELLAND ROAD | MAY 8 | ATT: 38,234

LEEDS UNITED 2-1 BRISTOL ROVERS

HOWSON 59', BECKFORD 63' | 2010 | DUFFY 48'

SUBS: ANKERGREN, GRELLA, HOWSON, MICHALIK, McSHEFFREY, SNODGRASS, WATT

MANAGER: SIMON GRAYSON

BRISTOL ROVERS

ANDERSEN, REGAN, COLES, ANTHONY, JONES, REECE, LINES, CAMPBELL, HUGHES, DUFFY, KUFFOUR

SUBS: EVANS, WRIGHT, WILLIAMS, BLIZZARD, CLOUGH, SWALLOW, RICHARDS

MANAGER: PAUL TROLLOPE

OUR FORM HEADING IN

CHARLTON	1-0	LEEDS UTD
LEEDS UTD	4-1	MK DONS
GILLINGHAM	3-2	LEEDS UTD

"He [Simon Grayson] said, 'I was walking my dog and I was just thinking about things ... I'm going to make him [Jermaine Beckford] captain'."
- Glynn Snodin

A pre-match stroll with his dog gave Leeds United's manager a moment of clarity. Simon Grayson had been stewing over who would captain his side on the final day of the 2009-10 League One season, knowing victory against Bristol Rovers at Elland Road would finally secure Leeds promotion. He settled on Jermaine Beckford, assistant manager Glynn Snodin saying Grayson told him: "It's his last game. He'll come to the fore." Snodin was surprised. Beckford was many things to Leeds United - a prolific goalscorer, a constant threat and a man for the big occasion. But a natural leader? "Even Jermaine was amazed," Snodin said.

The problem was Leeds United were running short of natural leaders as a now-famous season was threatening to fizzle out. Richard Naylor tore his hamstring in the club's penultimate match of the campaign, a 1-0 defeat at Charlton Athletic. Grayson's men would have been promoted if they won at The Valley, given Millwall lost at Tranmere Rovers, but that would have been too straight-forward for Leeds United. Other recognised leaders in the Leeds squad were on the sidelines as well, Paddy Kisnorbo with an Achilles injury while Jonny Howson had fallen out of the first team. But Beckford had been on the bench, too, as Grayson desperately tried to revive United's flagging fortunes. "[We] had a bit of a hangover from the FA Cup," he said. "As much as it was good, it distracted us a little bit. And we didn't have a good run and started falling away ... Newcastle had come in for him [Jermaine] in that January window ... we obviously turned it down because we felt Jermaine would be so significant in trying to help us out. We said to him, myself and Ken Bates, that if he'd stay then, 'You [can] walk away in the summer on a free transfer'."

Beckford's form dipped, though, forcing Grayson's hand at selection. "I dropped him for a few games ... because I just didn't feel it was working," he said. Leeds, who had lost just one league game until January 16, lost seven in less than three months as they stuttered towards promotion. Howson, who had been part of successive failed play-off campaigns, summed up the mood. "Please don't let it be the play-offs," he remembered thinking. Instead of Beckford, Grayson preferred to use Max Gradel as Luciano Becchio's strike partner for the four matches leading into the Bristol Rovers clash but results were mixed, with two wins and two defeats. That left Grayson with something to ponder as he took his dog for a morning walk just hours before what he hoped was the club's last League One match. "[I was] thinking that, 'He [Jermaine] is a big player. He scores big goals at big, crucial times in big matches … give him the responsibility of a big game because he's a big-game player … the extra responsibility [of captaincy] might just bring the best out of him.'" Howson also found some matchday clarity. "I knew I wasn't starting … in the week, I was obviously gutted … these big games you want to play in because that's where memories are made … I felt really relaxed and calm [on matchday] … I'd got over the thing of, 'You're not playing,'" he said. "From a selfish point of view, I was disappointed, I wanted to play, but at the same time I'd have taken not even coming on and still winning that game because I didn't want the play-offs again."

Beckford, just happy to be back in the starting side after a "horrible" patch, thought Grayson was "taking the piss" when he offered him the captain's armband after arriving at Elland Road. "I thought he was messing around with me," he said. "We walked in next door, talking to the referees … I'm looking at the managers, I'm looking at the referees and everybody's cool and calm and inside I'm shaking … we got out of there and I'm thinking, 'My heart is banging through my chest.'" Asked how he felt walking out of the tunnel, Beckford said: "Super proud. That was my greatest moment, I think, in football. Just having the armband, because that shows the respect … that shows that you're trusted to be the leader." Grayson's decision was having the desired effect. Beckford, United's key man, was raring to go. Andy Hughes was pumped up, too, Grayson's words ringing in his ears as he walked onto the pitch. "Simon just sat us [down] in the dressing room and was like, 'Right, if I gave you a choice at the start of the season to win your last game of the season against Bristol [Rovers] to go to the Championship, you'd bite your hand off', and we were all like, 'He's right.'"

That optimism quickly faded, though, when after a Beckford goal was disallowed for offside, Gradel was sent off for an off-the-ball incident with left-back Daniel Jones. "He [Gradel] was one that we had kind of pinpointed before the game as one of the Leeds players that was one of their best players and biggest threats, but also that you could get into his head," Bristol Rovers forward Darryl Duffy recalled. "You could wind him up and that would put him off his game … I didn't imagine for one second he would turn around and try and headbutt one of our players. He has just lost the plot." Bristol's plan had worked and as Gradel initially refused to leave the pitch, Howson feared the worst. "I'll be honest. That's the time when I thought, 'Oh, we're going to the play-offs,'" he said. Kisnorbo, godfather to one of Gradel's children and the man who recommended the winger to Grayson, rushed down from the West Stand to try and console the Ivorian - an unsuccessful attempt to bring calm to the changing room. "He started crying but I didn't want the players to see that," Kisnorbo said.

"Gradel was under the bench crying his eyes out," Neil Kilkenny remembered of the drama at the break, while the injured Ben Parker said "there was every emotion going possible" and on-loan defender Shane Lowry recalled "shouting and screaming" inside a "quite tense" changing room. "The players had felt that Max had let the team down and we were so close to letting a lot of supporters down," Grayson said. The Leeds manager was fresh off a conversation with Bristol's Jones in the tunnel, too. "I just said to him, 'Second half, you're going to be playing left-back in the North East corner and if we don't win this match, all the best getting off this pitch.'" It was a comment that would stick with Jones for the rest of the match. Back with his players, Grayson did his best to inspire them. "As a coach [now], these speeches very rarely have an impact. But that day, I think he spoke very well and he definitely gave us that belief that we could go out and do it," another on-loan defender, Neill Collins, said.

Grayson can laugh now, but his fired-up players conceded almost immediately, Duffy silencing Elland Road with a 48th-minute goal. "We had an obligation to other teams in the league to go there [and play]," Duffy said. "You've always got your own professional pride to play for as well … Leeds' left-back and Leeds' centre-half, they kind of switched off … Jo [Kuffour] managed to hook the ball back across and then I've took a touch with my back to goal and managed to kind of spin and hook it in ... it was bizarre. In the same way, the noise that makes your hair on the back of your neck stand up when you come out [of the tunnel] - the silence sort of had the same effect after I've scored." Lowry admitted he "was probably at fault" for the goal, while Collins said to concede "such a poor goal was infuriating". Asked for his thoughts after the goal, Grayson simply said: "Fucking hell, right, we are up against it here now."

With the benefit of hindsight, Duffy said scoring was "like poking a tiger", as Grayson reacted by replacing Lowry with Howson. "I knew I was playing shit. It was disappointing," Lowry said. On came a man with a point to prove. "I don't like [being] sat on the bench," Howson said. "To be honest, I hate it ... I always think, 'Get me on, get me on, I want to get on', ... I just couldn't wait to get on ... you just want to try and do something, try and give the lads a lift. The life had been sucked out of them ... you just want to try and give them something, a bit of encouragement to gee them up and the crowd as well." He needed only five minutes to do just that, curling a magnificent 20-yard effort into the back of the net. "That's one of my favourite shots, that. I like to hit that," he said.

"The whole place just erupted," Grayson said. "It was like we were playing with 14 men and they were playing with eight." Nearly 10 years on, Snodin was hit by "goosebumps" when asked about the equaliser and the noise it generated. "You felt like crying, laughing, everything ... the emotion and everything just went through you," he said, while United's captain for the day spotted another reason to have a spring in his step. "If you saw the faces around their whole team ... just seeing the deflation in every single one of their faces, that gave me and the rest of the boys that extra little air of invincibility."

"We'll win this now," Kilkenny remembered thinking. "When I was younger, you say, 'How can a home crowd make such a difference?' But when you're actually playing on the pitch ... and you have 35, 38,000 people screaming at you, pushing you forward, it is unbelievable - that extra five, 10 yards you get as an individual and as a team. As soon as that goal went in when Jonny scored, I knew that we would score again," he added, comments that were echoed by just about every single Leeds player.

And just four minutes after Leeds had levelled, Beckford made his mark. "The crowd and the atmosphere must have got to the goalkeeper. We've just had an attack and for whatever reason he decided to throw it out quickly. It wasn't something that the goalkeeper needed to do," Grayson said. "The ball's broken to him [Bradley Johnson] … he has a shot and I'm square to him and instead of him cutting it back to me for an open goal he's gone for glory, unbelievably," Beckford said with a laugh. Johnson's shot was blocked, but fell straight into the striker's path. "I believe everything happens for a reason," Beckford added. "The way that the ball's bounced, it's bounced literally right in front of me in my path. I've not even had to break stride. I know goalkeepers come out and they spread themselves … nobody blocks the floor. They always block mid-air in case you volley it straight so I'm thinking to myself, 'There's only one way to score here. Hit it into the ground', … because this is something that you practice literally on a daily basis for years and years and years, it's instinct. You don't have to think about it anymore, so it becomes second nature. It bounces underneath the goalkeeper, I get taken out, so I went down, hit the floor [and I] heard the roar and the rumble around Elland Road."

"It landed at the feet of the one person you probably wanted it to land to and that was Jermaine," Grayson said. "It's one of the most incredible atmospheres that I've known." Elland Road went crazy, with United's players and coaches celebrating all over the ground. There was Kisnorbo, Naylor, Parker, Aidan White and others in the West Stand, the mob that swarmed to Beckford, substitute Casper Ankergren watching on a television in the groundsman's office because he was so nervous and Snodin so delighted he "wanted to go on" the pitch. Surveying the carnage was Duffy. "I remember at the time thinking, 'Jesus Christ, it was just meant to be'. I think it was a comedy of errors for us … a terrible throw from our goalie."

Leigh Bromby hit the post as Leeds chased a third goal, but doubts began to creep in. "It went back to being kind of tense again," Duffy said. "I'll always remember … Bradley Johnson … there was about five minutes to go and he was standing beside me at a goal kick or a set-piece … he turned around and he said to me, he went, 'Please, please stop trying, please stop trying, just let us win. Please let us win', … that kind of summed up the mood in the whole stadium." Duffy rejected Johnson's request but this was far from the only conversation going on between the two sets of players. "Andy Hughes was doing a great job, getting into the Bristol Rovers players, telling them, 'They're not going to get out alive if they score or if they do anything'," Collins remembered. "They melted a little bit and we just smelt that as the players," Hughes said.

Bristol, with Jones now shifted to the right wing for a quick departure from the pitch after the final whistle, did not come close to a late equaliser. "We got a message passed onto us as players and it was basically, 'As soon as that final whistle goes, get your arses off the pitch because there's going to be a pitch invasion and there's going to be nothing that anybody can do to stop it, so for your own safety, basically get [off]'," Duffy remembered. The message was correct, as confirmation that United's agonising three-year stay in League One was over prompted thousands of fans to invade the Elland Road pitch.

Promotion meant different things to different people. "At last," was Beckford's first thought. "It's just a massive relief," Howson said. "We'd had three attempts at doing it, went ever so close twice, within a game or two both times … you just can't believe it." For Hughes and Naylor, the main feeling was vindication. "[I was] the first player to join when we had minus 15 … I just thought if we ever win or ever do anything, I'm just going to run and go mental and for some reason I just ran to the Kop," Hughes said. "All the fans were on the pitch and I was running through fans to the Kop. Next thing, someone's ripped my shirt off and I was being lifted [up]. I can't tell you the sense of relief and achievement, because it felt like we'd done it with the fans." Naylor added: "I went there with a real goal. To help the club get out of League One … to come back and play for your club, your hometown club, in front of all my mates, my family, you want to do so well. There's so much pressure … it was just relief."

Jermaine Beckford's Leeds United career ended on a high. Photo: Andrew Varley Picture Agency

HILLSBOROUGH | JANUARY 11 | ATT: 21,224

SHEFFIELD WEDNESDAY 6-0 LEEDS UNITED

JOHNSON 20', NUHIU 45', WICKHAM 50', MAGUIRE 67', LAVERY 80', 90+4'

2014

SUBS: CAIRNS, VARNEY, WARNOCK, BROWN, SMITH, BYRAM, POLEON

MANAGER: BRIAN McDERMOTT

SHEFFIELD WEDNESDAY

KIRKLAND, PALMER, LLERA, LOOVENS, JOHNSON, MAGUIRE, SEMEDO, LEE, MAGHOMA, WICKHAM, NUHIU

SUBS: MARTINEZ, MATTOCK, JOHNSON, HELAN, LAVERY, McCABE, McPHAIL

MANAGER: STUART GRAY

OUR FORM HEADING IN

ROCHDALE	2-0	LEEDS UTD
LEEDS UTD	1-2	BLACKBURN
NOTT FOREST	2-1	LEEDS UTD

"We were on a bit of a bad run and I wanted to wait until the summer [before I took charge] ... but they wanted me to come in because they were having a poor run of results and were getting a bit too close to the bottom."
- Brian McDermott

Leeds United were in trouble, four successive defeats leaving them just five points above the Championship's relegation zone. The 2012-13 season had not gone to plan and Brian McDermott was needed. "I turned up there, literally on the Thursday," the manager said. "[Caretaker manager] Neil [Redfearn] took the training on the Friday and on the Saturday we took the game against Sheffield Wednesday. I was on the line and we won 2-1." McDermott's arrival resulted in three wins from five and a 13th-placed finish, giving the manager something to build on in the summer ahead of Leeds' fourth successive Championship campaign.

After leading Leeds out of League One, Simon Grayson's side finished seventh in 2010-11, missing out on the play-offs by three points. United were second at Christmas in that season, but tailed off and Grayson did not see out the following season, replaced by Neil Warnock, who found his side mired in mid-table mediocrity for much of his time in charge. It was Warnock that McDermott replaced and the latter's assistant, Nigel Gibbs, knew major work was needed on the squad as Luke Murphy, Matt Smith, Scott Wootton and Noel Hunt all arrived in the build-up to the 2013-14 season. "Once we got there, we knew there was going to be difficulties but didn't realise the depth of the difficulties," Gibbs said. "We had a good pre-season, tried to bring in some players, but that was quickly stopped. We weren't able to bring in as many players as we would have liked and it made it difficult ... we needed to improve the group. There were areas that we would have liked to improve. We signed Luke Murphy as a midfield player and we signed a couple of other players, but after that it was a case of having to get players out before we could bring anyone in. We were short of wingers, probably needed to improve that area, but as a manager and a coach, you're always trying to improve your team, and that became difficult to do."

Yet despite the squad's limitations, McDermott's first full season in charge of Leeds United was going better than anyone expected, with one of the manager's new signings getting things off to a good start in the season-opener against Brighton and Hove Albion at Elland Road. "Luke Murphy scored with about a minute to go and there was a real feel of optimism around the place," McDermott said. "He [Ross McCormack] was fantastic for me. He made loads of goals, he scored loads of goals. I made him captain. He was fabulous, absolutely terrific, that lad … we didn't get defeated in that first [month] and September was okay, and I just had the sense of, 'We've got a chance here'. It was brilliant. I have to say that in that period of time, between June, July, August, September, October, going into December, there was a real feel-good factor around the club. I could sense it. I've been around football long enough to know and there was a real good feel-good factor at that time, on the pitch." McDermott's work in uniting the club was not going unnoticed, either. "Brian had come in and he was quite a popular figure and obviously he'd done really well at Reading," defender Jason Pearce said. "He was really liked by everyone around the club, from the bottom to top … he was a real good person. All the staff and everyone liked him and the players liked him and you just wanted to do well for him." Left-back Stephen Warnock shared a similar view. "We had a good start. We had a good pre-season. Things seemed to be going well."

The regular goals of the outstanding McCormack had Leeds fifth in the table at Christmas and they entered the January transfer window in seventh, just goal difference outside of the play-offs. The grind of a Championship season was just starting to catch up with Leeds, though, and successive league defeats against Nottingham Forest and Blackburn Rovers gave United something to prove at fourth-tier Rochdale in the FA Cup. "Obviously, like any season within the Championship, it just becomes tougher and tougher. You lose players. Injuries kick in and form naturally dips as well," Stephen Warnock said. Leeds' performance at Rochdale was embarrassing, though, United outplayed and, crucially, outfought. The 2-0 scoreline was very kind on Leeds, who had goalkeeper Paddy Kenny to thank for it not being a rout. Those at Spotland on a frustrating January afternoon are unlikely to forget the reception dished out by the travelling fans after the final whistle, something Pearce remembered well. "My experience of the Leeds fans is they're obviously very passionate fans," he said. "When things are going well, they really get behind you, but when a performance isn't acceptable then, obviously, they let you know about it … as a Leeds player, you've got to be strong enough to be able to take the criticism and if you don't, if you're not strong enough, then, obviously, you're not going to last long there … losing to a team that's in a lower league - that's not acceptable." McDermott felt the anger was justified. "We had a great following there that day. We didn't turn up. We didn't perform. We got well beat … I remember walking towards the Leeds fans and it's a long walk across the pitch. I always acknowledge the fans, win, lose or draw. I wanted to walk across and, oh, it wasn't a nice feeling. I was getting absolutely slaughtered by the fans as I walked across and fair enough. The team didn't perform on the day. That was tough. That was really tough, the walk across. But I owed it to those people to give them the respect of walking across there that day, as I would have done win, lose or draw, just to show how much we appreciated their support … that was a tough, tough, horrible day … you have to do it. I wanted to make sure the staff and the players and myself showed up. We had to take that on the chin and rightly so."

McDermott told the press afterwards that the defeat "felt worse" than losing a play-off final and that he "would probably say that is my worst moment in football". A local derby was around the corner, giving United the chance to make amends, and two wingers, Jimmy Kebe and Cameron Stewart, arrived in the build-up. "We needed pace in that team. We didn't have enough pace," McDermott said. "We signed two wingers that we'd been crying out for for the season," Gibbs added. "Obviously, we didn't have a lot of time to work with them. We needed to do something to change the players' mentality and give them a little bit of help as well … players coming in brings a little bit of freshness to the group and the training and, obviously, you're building up to a big game." Pearce was similarly hopeful. "Kebe and Cameron Stewart hopefully were going to inject a bit of pace into the side, which was needed." The new-found width saw McDermott roll the dice, but it was a gamble that backfired. "We changed the formation," the manager said. "We worked on the training pitch on the Friday before the game … we changed a few things … I've done 460-odd games as a manager, non-league and league, Premiership, Championship, Conference, and one of my biggest nightmares before a game is when you're sitting in there on your own and you're thinking, 'We're live on the TV'. One of my biggest nightmares is to be publicly humiliated and get beat 6-0. I've actually had that thought in my mind and that day it happened. It became a reality. It had never happened to me before and it was horrible. It was a horrible, horrible day."

"It is a local derby and it is bragging rights," Pearce said. "You want to make sure that the fans go home happy ... we changed to three at the back. [Marius] Zaliukas played in the middle and it was just that we hadn't played together ... it wasn't the best, if I'm honest." Leeds were all over the shop at the back in the first half and Reda Johnson and Atdhe Nuhiu scored goals under little to no pressure. Desperate to get his side back into the game, McDermott made a change, replacing Tom Lees with his biggest striker. "I made a change to put Matt Smith up front at half time to try and get something back and go a little bit more direct. He got sent off straight away." Smith lasted less than a minute, sent off for an aerial challenge on Johnson. Out of form, out of confidence and down to 10 men, Leeds simply capitulated. "'Smithy' - he's a good mate of mine," Pearce said. "[For him to get] sent off straight away obviously didn't help matters ... it went from bad to worse ... it's quite a hostile place and it's difficult when ... you're losing a game there. But when it's your rivals, it is even worse."

Stephen Warnock, stuck on the bench as an unused substitute, said his non-involvement made things even more frustrating. "It's just one of them days where everything seemed to go wrong. Everything that they hit went in and you do have them days in football. It's difficult because when you're not on the pitch, you can't have a part to play in it. You can't try and correct things." Gibbs added: "The second half became a real hard slog. We were 2-0 down, chasing the game and obviously, eventually concede late goals and the game by a big scoreline which is never easy, particularly after the Rochdale result. It wasn't a great week for us. Very disappointing." After strikes from Connor Wickham and Chris Maguire, a pair of poor Zaliukas errors saw Wednesday finish with six goals. The Lithuanian made just three more appearances in his Leeds career, but McDermott refused to single out the centre-back on a day to forget. "I would never point out individuals on that day. Everyone in that dressing room that day - staff, players - it was a shocking day." A moment that perhaps summed up United's day was the sight of Pearce running around with a price tag hanging out of his shirt. "I just put it on, didn't realise, and then obviously it [tag] come out in the game," he said.

Less than a week on from the Rochdale debacle, United's players faced another angry reception from their fans after the final whistle before making their way into a desperately disappointed changing room. "Emotions were very high ... the players were very, very disappointed," Gibbs said. "They knew they hadn't performed ... we'd just lost a big game, but the players were fully aware of the [importance of the] game, as we were as staff. It hurt us all, you know. It's never good to lose a derby game, particularly by that score. That's football but it was a tough time." Pearce added: "I was hugely disappointed at the final whistle. You never want to be on the bad side of a result like that. It's probably been the worst result I've ever had, I think. A club the stature of Leeds United, you don't expect to be on that side of a result ... you come off and go into the dressing room and everyone's on the floor, so disappointed and obviously, the fans made it known how they felt about the result and rightly so. Obviously, I'm a defender and conceding that many goals isn't acceptable ... it was a hugely disappointing day."

For McDermott, the defeat was one he will live with forever. "You do not want that to happen. And to sit there afterwards and have to sit with that feeling and then five years later, we're still talking about that defeat, that just tells you. Defeats live with you and that defeat - there's always a part of you that lives with a defeat like that. You've got your memories of your great wins and then you've got your memories of your really horrible defeats and that was one of mine. That was my worst defeat ever as a manager, by a mile. It was horrible. It was a horrible feeling. The players will remember that and fans remember that day. I'm sure Sheffield Wednesday fans will remember that day. But that's part of football. You have to be strong and live with that sort of stuff ... it was a horrible day, especially being a derby."

ELLAND ROAD | FEBRUARY 1 | ATT: 31,103

LEEDS UNITED 5-1 HUDDERSFIELD TOWN

McCORMACK 45+3', 62', 73', KEBE 50', MOWATT 82' | 2014 | WARD 25'

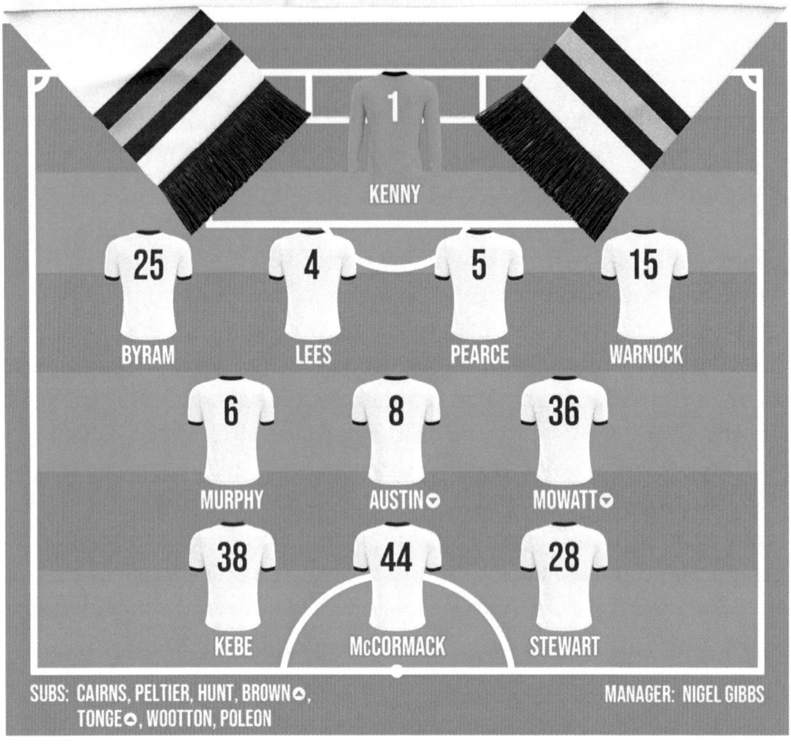

HUDDERSFIELD TOWN

SMITHIES, SMITH, GERRARD, WALLACE, WOODS, CLAYTON, NORWOOD, GOBERN ▼, DIXON ▼, WELLS ▼, WARD

SUBS: BENNETT, CLARKE, SCANNELL ▲, SOUTHERN, PATERSON ▲, LOLLEY ▲, HOLMES

MANAGER: MARK ROBINS

OUR FORM HEADING IN

LEEDS UTD	1-1	IPSWICH
LEEDS UTD	0-1	LEICESTER
SHEFF WED	6-0	LEEDS UTD

"I said, 'No'. It was simple. For me, that just couldn't happen. I didn't even know him."
- Brian McDermott

Asked if Gianluca Festa could sit in the dugout for a Championship fixture against Ipswich Town, Brian McDermott's response was emphatic. Massimo Cellino had not even bought Leeds United yet and he was already causing drama. One of the craziest weeks in the club's history started with ex-Middlesbrough defender Festa's appearances at Leeds' training ground, Thorp Arch. Cellino, in talks with then-owners GFH Capital about buying the club, was reportedly keen on Festa becoming the club's new manager. "It was tough, because you had people around the place that you don't know and if you're a manager, you need to know who is around that training ground," McDermott said. "That's really important. Everything's got to be open and up front ... it was difficult. The ownership hadn't been sorted out and everyone was waiting. There was an air of just waiting for something to happen, for the club to be taken over or not, whatever the case may be."

When quizzed if he and McDermott felt undermined following the Festa request, assistant manager Nigel Gibbs said: "100 per cent. That's how we felt ... sitting in the dugout, I mean, that's just not the done thing. I've never known that before. You're just wondering, 'What is going on?' Obviously that request was turned down." Stephen Warnock was one of many stunned players. "It's not professional at all ... I think it was disappointing because he [Cellino] was only interested in buying the club at that moment in time. I think he was sort of doing the due diligence ... asking [for someone] to sit in the dugout was just unbelievable. How can you even ask to do that? It just became a bit of a shambles, if I'm being honest."

Shambles would be putting it mildly, given what was to come on a mad Friday, less than 24 hours ahead of a home fixture against Huddersfield Town. "I got a phone call at about 5pm by a guy called Chris Farnell ... he was working with Massimo," McDermott said. "He just said that, 'It's Chris Farnell', and I said, 'Who's that?' He said, 'I'm working with Leeds', and I said, 'Okay'. And he said, 'I just want to let you know that your contract has been terminated', ... it was a very difficult conversation … it was bizarre, because at the time, Massimo didn't own the club … [I was thinking], 'I don't get this, this guy doesn't even own the club, what is going on?' I didn't know the guy who rung me. It was bizarre to say the least … I rung Nigel [Gibbs] to tell him that I'd gone but they hadn't phoned Nigel. I think Neil [Redfearn] was going to take the game, I'm not sure." Gibbs was similarly stunned. "The Friday, the manager prepared the team, we picked the team, we picked the squad and picked the training group for the next morning who weren't going to be involved [in the match]," he said. "The Friday night, sitting at home, and I get a phone call from Brian saying that he had been sacked. [I was] obviously shocked at that … then it broke on Sky Sports News that Brian had been sacked, so I had a couple of calls from some players." Defender Jason Pearce, watching the channel on transfer deadline day with some of his teammates, was one who reached for his phone. "I was sat with Ross [McCormack], Noel Hunt, Matt Smith, we were all sat together," he said. "We couldn't believe what was going on."

Warnock's phone kept buzzing. "Texts come through. You're all in a group chat within the team and the lads are sort of wondering, 'What the hell is going on?' … You're thinking, 'How can he [Cellino] sack him when he's not in charge?' … It was just like, 'What the hell is going on at this football club?'" Despite the transfer moves, Leeds United had become the main story on deadline day, with Ross McCormack speaking over the phone with Sky Sports News about McDermott's departure and his playing future. "I'm absolutely gutted," the Scotsman said, adding that if he had "known earlier on that this was going to happen" that he would have had "a decision to make". With 19 goals to his name already in the 2013-14 season, McCormack was a man in demand and clubs were circling. "I think Ross was close to going," Pearce said. "I was with him, obviously, and there were all sorts of rumours going on … we're sitting there … your manager's gone, your top scorer and one of your best players is potentially going, you're thinking, 'What's going on here?'"

As speculation raged over McCormack's future, Gibbs' phone kept ringing. "I had a couple of calls from some players … they told me that they'd had a phone call from Neil Redfearn to say that some of the players who had been training [on the Saturday, so not in the matchday squad] were now in the squad and some of the squad who were selected for the game would now train," Gibbs said. "So I phoned Neil Redfearn and he'd been summoned to the ground and was told to assist Gianluca Festa with the game on the next day and he had to phone around the players and told them the squad. At this time, I hadn't been called from anyone from the football club."

A bizarre night ended with McCormack still a Leeds player, but the Redfearn-Festa partnership never did eventuate. "I was on my way to the stadium [on the Saturday] and I get a phone call from [GFH Capital's] David Haigh," Gibbs said. "[David was] saying that, 'Would I take the team? Because Brian was obviously told he wasn't in charge anymore but we're looking into that situation … Neil will assist you and we will speak when you get to the stadium'. I said, 'Yeah, of course', so I drive to the stadium, speak to Neil, speak to the staff and say, 'Listen, I've been asked to take the team. I know you'll give me your full support. We'll have the meeting with the players at 1.15pm, I'm going to go with the team that Brian worked with yesterday, go with the same subs. I'll speak to the players that are obviously not involved and obviously the most important thing is be professional and we go out and do our best and try to win the game'."

"It was just very strange," Michael Brown recalled. "I'd never seen anything like that before where you can actually have one manager with one team, and other people thinking you're playing in another team when they get to the ground, and then right at the last minute, 'Gibbo' [Gibbs] comes in and actually puts the team back from the day before. So it was a very, very surreal [moment] … Nigel Gibbs is a great football man and he dealt with it in high esteem." Warnock, who said it felt like the situation "was changing every single minute", remembered the club's leaders taking the players aside. "A few of the senior players just said, 'Right, we need to sort this out', [we] sat down with the players in the change room and said, 'We can't influence anything that's going on from the boardroom … that's nothing to do with us, so all we can do is try and get the right result today', … we didn't want to go out and embarrass ourselves in a game. You've got to be very proud of wearing the Leeds badge, if you like, and playing in front of the fans at Elland Road. We knew it was still a big occasion, especially with it being another local derby as well." Gibbs had a similar message for the players. "I spoke to the players at 1.15pm, told them the situation … [I said] '[I] apologise if you've had mixed messages', but [I] named the team, named the subs, and [I said] the most important thing is, 'You're playing for the football club and we go out there and put on a performance.'"

As Gibbs and the players were preparing for the match, McDermott received a phone call. "I was instructed by one of the directors from GFH to stay home, to stay there at the time, that it was going to get sorted out." Very few people were privy to that, though, and United's players weren't even on the pitch and they were fielding questions about the chaos. "We were just going out for the game, standing in the tunnel … even their players were like, 'What is going on at your football club?' … [They were saying], 'We're watching Sky Sports News and we're seeing all this and we're wondering who is going to turn up today?'" Warnock recalled.

Leeds, without a win in eight, were on the back foot early, Oliver Norwood hitting the post before Danny Ward gave Huddersfield the lead. "I remember going 1-0 down and thinking, 'Oh no, here we go [in] another local derby,'" Pearce said. The Terriers had several chances to double their lead, too, before Jimmy Kebe set up McCormack's equaliser on the stroke of half time. "He [Jimmy] was causing them problems, I remember, [in] that game … it was just obviously a big relief [to score]," Pearce added. McDermott, listening intently to match coverage, must have felt a sense of vindication when Kebe, a man he also managed at Reading, gave Leeds the lead. A pair of McCormack strikes then put Leeds in control and gave the forward his hat-trick. "Ross is a top player," Warnock said. "Technically, probably one of the best players at Leeds at the time and a goalscorer. A natural goalscorer. He thrived under Brian McDermott … he took a huge liking to him and he got the best out of Ross. I think Ross had a bit of an affiliation with the fans, as well. He got them and they got him. They appreciated what he was like. He loved playing for the club and I think his form at Leeds was superb."

There was even time for Alex Mowatt to score his first Leeds goal, a delightful chip capping a second half to remember at Elland Road. "Second half, we put in a great performance and won the game," Gibbs said. "The fans were obviously singing Brian's name throughout the game, getting behind the team, which they did throughout. I've got to say the fans at Leeds are unbelievable. Their support for the team is second to none. It's fantastic … it was a great win for us and after everything that went on, it was a big relief … I was pleased for the players, pleased for the supporters and it was a good victory."

Another major curve-ball was coming as shortly after the final whistle, Leeds United released a statement. "The club would like to make it clear that Brian McDermott remains our first-team manager. He has not been dismissed from his post as has been suggested. We look forward to him continuing in his role with us in taking Leeds forward," the statement read. "I heard it on the radio on the way home and I just started laughing," Warnock said. "[I was] thinking like, again, 'Only at Leeds, at this moment in time, could that happen.'" It was a day for statements, with GFH Capital announcing they had agreed to sell a majority stake in the club to a company owned by the Cellino family, but it was the McDermott backflip that puzzled the football world, particularly why the manager would willingly walk back into a situation that seemed certain to end in his departure when Cellino took full control.

"I spoke to Nigel afterwards," McDermott said. "I said, 'Well done, great win, fabulous, really pleased'. I got a phone call … to say to come back on the Monday … I loved it [at Leeds]. I loved it there. Even though there was so much stuff going on and had been in the last month or so, and the results were poor, I wanted to make it work. And I hadn't been there long. In my eyes, I hadn't been there long. And I had massive personal things going on with my mum at the time. My mum was dying at the time. She was at home and she was like 400 miles away. I had that going on as well with my mother so it was a tough time for me, personally. I honestly thought that we could do something and I just wanted to prove that we could do something. And who is going to walk out on Leeds? It certainly wasn't going to be me. I wasn't going to walk out on Leeds. No chance." He returned to Thorp Arch on the Monday to a jovial atmosphere. "When we came in on the Monday morning, I think there was a lot of laughing and joking about it," Warnock said. "I think you have to laugh and joke about it. And I think, as well, at the back of his mind, the manager knew he was a dead man walking in a way … they'd already sacked him before they even got control of it [the club], so once they got control, he was going to be out and I think he knew that."

Gibbs remembered McDermott being so determined that he could not walk away. "We wanted to be successful there and take the club forward … was it going to be difficult? Yes, it was. It was going to be very difficult when the owner who is going to be taking over … put his cards on the table straight away, sacking Brian … it was very, very difficult because it was always hanging over [us] - that Massimo Cellino had already sacked Brian."

A match at Yeovil Town followed, Warnock scoring a free-kick in a 2-1 win. "That was the only game I felt really nervous in," McDermott said. And while he was treated to an outstanding reception from the travelling supporters on a freezing Huish Park day, McDermott watched his side win just one of their next 12 matches as a once-promising season fizzled out in dramatic fashion. That run coincided with Cellino's successful appeal against a Football League decision to block his takeover, meaning the writing was on the wall for the popular McDermott. "It's a ticking time bomb if you're not winning, full stop, in management these days," he said. "February and March, results were poor. They weren't good, it was difficult times and we weren't winning enough games. There was lots of stuff going on … I think there was five games to go and we won three, drew one and lost one. But I kind of knew he wanted to go his own way. I kind of knew it … he wanted to do what he wanted to do and that's his prerogative. He was the owner and I knew it was coming. It was pretty obvious."

Yet McDermott's departure was not handled in a straight-forward manner. With the season over, the manager went to visit his mother, only for Cellino to go on ITV and ask: "Who's managing this club? Brian. Where's Brian? I send a letter to Brian - help us. He's on holiday to get some rest." They were comments that hurt McDermott. "That was the most painful thing for me, because I was by mum's bedside," McDermott said. "I needed to get home. I needed to get back to her. And she died at the end of June. There wasn't much time … I was certainly not on holiday." Contact between Cellino and McDermott's advisor, Pat Dolan, was ongoing, the manager claimed. "Pat was always speaking to Massimo … I tried to ring Massimo at the club. I actually tried to ring. I spoke to Debra Ware, who was his secretary, when I was back with my mum. I tried to ring and he wasn't there. He was at York races or something. I couldn't get hold of him. My priority at that point had to be my family, my mum, and it was. And obviously that would be the same for everyone."

McDermott does not hold a grudge and even thanked Cellino for sending him a card when his mother passed away. But Gibbs was infuriated, dubbing the public commentary as "pathetic". And it was no surprise when, later in May, Leeds announced that McDermott had stepped down by mutual consent, the first managerial departure of a chaotic period that saw the club develop a stigma within the football world.

LEEDS UNITED'S UPS AND DOWNS ARE TO BE CONTINUED …

ACKNOWLEDGEMENTS

Writing this book would not have been possible without the involvement of so many footballers and coaches.

Brian McDermott was the first to put his hand up and his kindness and depth of memory set the ball rolling for more than 80 extensive interviews.

It has been a journey, covering more ground than initially expected, from Australian training grounds and hotels to Croatian restaurants and British houses, cafes and train stations. The end result is one I am very proud of.

With that in mind, I would like to express my gratitude to the following: Brian McDermott, Neil Kilkenny, Shane Lowry, Nigel Gibbs, Lucas Radebe, Paddy Kisnorbo, Simon Grayson, Michael Gray, Matt Heath, Lubo Michalik, Michael Bridges, Hayden Foxe, Chris Greenacre, Shaun Derry, Darryl Duffy, Stephen Warnock, David Wetherall, Stephen Caldwell, Keith Edwards, Robbie Blake, Ben Parker, Michael Duberry, Casper Ankergren, Jonathan Douglas, Jacob Burns, Andy Hughes, Aidan White, Matthew Kilgallon, Matthew Langston, Neill Collins, Danny Hay, Chris Kamara, Jason Pearce, Alan Lee, Andy Ritchie, David Prutton, Stephen McPhail, Micky Adams, Markus Babbel, Gus Poyet, Rui Marques, Michael Brown, David Harvey, Paul Hart, John Pearson, Jon Newsome, Tony Dorigo, Mel Sterland, Richard Naylor, Trevor Cherry, Howard Wilkinson, Dougie Freedman, Eddie Gray, Jonny Howson, Jonathan Woodgate, Dominic Matteo, Glynn Snodin, John Helm, Norman Hunter, Allan Clarke, Brett Ormerod, Peter Haddock, Rob Hulse, Olivier Dacourt, Alan Sutton, Mick Jones, Johnny Giles, Peter Shirtliff, Kevin Blackwell, Frank Gray, Andy Gray, John Sheridan, Gary McAllister, Richard Jobson, Jermaine Beckford, Mick Bates, David Healy, Mark Viduka, George Graham, Alan Maybury and Lee Bowyer.

Special thanks to Norman Hunter for kindly writing the foreword.

In addition to all those interviewed, a host of others have also played a role in getting this book to print. Dave McCabe has been instrumental from day dot, designing the excellent covers, graphics and layout. Dave, a big Leeds fan himself, has also proved a great sounding board through the project and it simply would not have been possible without him.

Thanks to Russell Greaves, a colleague who helped inspire this project in its infancy, and Daniel Dorizzi and Linnéa Brisling for regularly nudging me to turn an idea into reality. Several kind souls edited and proofread the book, so to Matthew Scott, Richard Howe, Greig Johnston, Mark Bowering, Mike Bruce and Chris Kenner, thank you so much. I really appreciate your help and advice.

Thanks to Andrew Varley, Alex Knight, Steve Riding and Dubravko Lenert for the great photos in the book, and Ryan Francis from CLOC Ltd and Paula Charles from York Publishing Services for their help in getting this project over the line.

A significant amount of research was necessary to write this book and many websites were a great resource, including Tony Hill's OzWhite database and Marc Bracha's Sheridan Dictates page. Leeds fans - both are well worth a visit.

I can't write this without thanking the many people who have made Leeds feel like a second home for me over so many years. To Scotty, Tommy, Katie, Bowlesy, Emma, Rich, Michelle, Gatt, Trimbo, Keely, Alex, Sophie, MB, Thommo, Tingle and many others - thank you. What a group of people you are.

My long-time mate Ed Mitros deserves a mention here, too. Ed is the reason I support Leeds United and life would have been very different if I didn't follow him on that one. Thanks also to Matt Ronaldson for taking two impressionable kids to watch Leeds United play Colo Colo in Melbourne in 2002.

Finally, a massive thank you to my family, especially my parents, Kirsten and Adrian. They always encouraged me to act on my passion for journalism from a young age and have provided endless support and guidance over the years. I will never forget visiting Leeds for the first time with my father in 2005 and I am very lucky to have such a great family.

I hope you have enjoyed the read.

James Willoughby

ABOUT THE AUTHOR

James Willoughby was born and raised in Melbourne, Australia, and has been a sports journalist for more than a decade. He has followed Leeds United since Mark Viduka was an Elland Road star and has spent several extended periods living and working in Leeds. James has worked for news wires, media organisations and sporting bodies and has reported from events like the FIFA World Cup, Commonwealth Games, grand slam tennis tournaments and Formula One races. You can follow James on Twitter @jwilloughby26. This is his first book.